JAMES ORR, POET AND IRISH RADICAL

Poetry and Song in the Age of Revolution

Series Editors: Michael Brown
Katherine Campbell
John Kirk
Andrew Noble

Titles in this Series

1 United Islands? The Languages of Resistance
John Kirk, Andrew Noble and Michael Brown (eds)

2 Literacy and Orality in Eighteenth-Century Irish Song
Julie Henigan

3 Cultures of Radicalism in Britain and Ireland
John Kirk, Michael Brown and Andrew Noble (eds)

4 The Politics of Song in the Age of Revolution
Kate Horgan

Forthcoming Titles

Reading Robert Burns: Texts, Contexts, Transformations
Carol McGuirk

www.pickeringchatto.com/poetryandsong

JAMES ORR, POET AND IRISH RADICAL

BY

Carol Baraniuk

PICKERING & CHATTO
2014

Published by Pickering & Chatto (Publishers) Limited
21 Bloomsbury Way, London WC1A 2TH

2252 Ridge Road, Brookfield, Vermont 05036-9704, USA

www.pickeringchatto.com

All rights reserved.
No part of this publication may be reproduced,
stored in a retrieval system, or transmitted in any form or by any means,
electronic, mechanical, photocopying, recording, or otherwise
without prior permission of the publisher.

© Pickering & Chatto (Publishers) Ltd 2014
© Carol Baraniuk 2014

To the best of the Publisher's knowledge every effort has been made to contact
relevant copyright holders and to clear any relevant copyright issues.
Any omissions that come to their attention will be remedied in future editions.

BRITISH LIBRARY CATALOGUING IN PUBLICATION DATA

Baraniuk, Carol, author.
James Orr, poet and Irish radical. – (Poetry and song in the age of revolution)
1. Orr, James, 1770–1816 – Criticism and interpretation. 2. Orr, James, 1770–
1816 – Political and social views.
I. Title II. Series
821.7-dc23

ISBN-13: 9781848935136
e: 9781781444887
ePUB: 9781781444894

This publication is printed on acid-free paper that conforms to the American
National Standard for the Permanence of Paper for Printed Library Materials.

Typeset by Pickering & Chatto (Publishers) Limited
Printed and bound in the United Kingdom by CPI Books

CONTENTS

Acknowledgements · vii
List of Figures · xi

Introduction · 1
1 Critical Reception and Canonicity · 7
2 Raising a Radical: Orr, Ballycarry and '98: James Orr (1770–98) · 25
3 The Construction of the Bard of Ballycarry: James Orr (1798–1804) · 43
4 Bard in Residence: James Orr (1804–16) · 61
5 Rude Scotch Rhymer? Scottish Enlightenment Influences on James Orr · 81
6 Men of Independent Mind: Ulster Scots Poets and the Scottish Tradition · 101
7 The Rebel Experience · 123
8 The Robert Burns of Ulster? · 143
9 Enlightened Romantic · 165
Conclusion · 187

Notes · 193
Works Cited · 219
Index · 229

ACKNOWLEDGEMENTS

My thanks are offered to the editors of *Poetry and Song in the Age of Revolution* who accepted this work for publication in the series. I am grateful to Andrew Noble who read the original manuscript for his many helpful, thought-provoking suggestions. Special thanks go to John Kirk who proofread the completed manuscript and provided invaluable advice on copy-editing and other matters. I am indebted also to Mark Pollard of Pickering & Chatto who dealt with my many queries concerning presentation and about the submission process in general.

This study has its basis in my doctoral thesis and I wish to express the warmest possible appreciation of Gerard Carruthers, who while I was his student at the University of Glasgow, proved himself the kindest, most generous and inspiring of supervisors, and continues to be a wise friend and guide.

Sincere thanks also to Kirsteen McHue for much good advice, always offered with sensitivity and good humour, and to Rhona Brown for her wise counsel, fine example and, above all, for her friendship.

I wish to record my gratitude to my former colleagues at Stranmillis University College, Belfast, in particular Hilary Avery, whose support and backing were crucial as I embarked on academic research and who offered much excellent advice on early conference papers. Warm thanks also go to Linda Hagan, a great conference partner and a great friend.

John Erskine of the Ministerial Advisory Group – Ulster-Scots Academy and Frank Ferguson, co-director of the Centre for Irish and Scottish Studies at the University of Ulster, have generously and graciously assisted the development of this study over the years. I have time and again benefited from their guidance, enthusiasm and learning. I remain indebted to them for many stimulating and informative conversations, and I continue to be inspired by their example; as scholars and as friends they set the bar extremely high.

The greatest debts, of course, are personal. My husband Kris has offered constant, loving, practical encouragement and endless patience throughout the process which has brought this study to publication. The book is dedicated to him with my gratitude for all his selfless support. My children Christopher and Marianne grew to adulthood as I researched and then wrote the text that appears here; their love and understanding even when I was very busy contributed massively to enabling its completion. My mother Mirion Shields has been unfailing in her encouragement, providing a listening ear and an astute perspective on everything. Warmest thanks go to her, and to the memory of William Shields, my father, whose pride in anything I achieved motivates me still. It has been a great delight to be able to share my enthusiasm for research with my niece Jennifer Orr. I wish to thank her for her many insights and for discoveries generously communicated. My friend Sheelagh Sleath has for many years encouraged my writing in all aspects. My thanks go to her for her wisdom and calm, unstinting support.

I wish to thank the staffs of the many libraries and archives where I carried out research for this study. These include Glasgow University Library; the Mitchell Library, Glasgow; the Belfast Central Library Newspaper Archive; the Linen Hall Library, Belfast; the Special Collections Department of the McClay Library, Queen's University Belfast; Stranmillis University College Library; the Centre for Irish Migration Studies, Omagh; the British Library Newspaper Collection; the Public Records Office of Northern Ireland (PRONI); the Manuscript Room, Trinity College Dublin; the National Archives of Ireland, Dublin; the John Hewitt Collection, University of Ulster and the collection of the former Ulster-Scots Academy Implementation Group.

Parts of this work first appeared, in different form, in the following publications: 'James Orr: Ulster-Scot and Poet of the 1798 Rebellion', *Scottish Studies Review*, 6:1 (2005), pp. 22–32; 'An Antidote to the Burns Idyll: James Orr's "The Irish Cottier's Death and Burial"', *Burns Chronicle* (Spring 2006), pp. 6–11; 'Disagreeably Scottish'?, *Drouth: Dialect*, 19 (Spring 2006), pp. 13–17; 'Setting His Own Standard: James Orr's Employment of a Traditional Stanza Form', *Journal of Irish and Scottish Studies*, 1:1 (2007), pp. 73–86; 'Ulster's Burns? James Orr, the Bard of Ballycarry', *Review of Scottish Culture*, 19 (2007), pp. 54–62; 'Christ's Kirk on the Green Isle: Tragedy Commemorated in Comic Form', in M.-C. Considère-Charon, P. Laplace and M. Savaric (eds), *The Irish Celebrating: Festive and Tragic Overtones* (Newcastle: Cambridge Scholars Publishing, 2008), pp. 118–32; 'The Leid, the Pratoe and the Buik: Northern Cultural Markers in the Works of James Orr', in J. P. Byrne, P. Kirwan and M. O'Sullivan (eds), *Affecting Irishness: Negotiating Cultural Identity within and beyond the Nation* (Oxford: Peter Lang, 2009), pp. 103–20; 'No Bardolatry Here: The Independence of the Ulster-Scots Poetic Tradition', in F. Ferguson and A. Holmes (eds), *Revising Robert Burns and Ulster: Literature, Religion and Politics c. 1770–1920* (Dublin: Four Courts Press, 2009), pp. 64–82; 'James Orr, Napoleon and Lord Nelson', *Ullans: The Magazine for Ulster-Scots*, 11 (2010), pp. 107–8. I am grateful to the respective editors for permission to reproduce material.

The Scots poems discussed include glosses which are in many cases context-dependent. John Kirk's expertise was invaluable in checking my glosses, as were the following resources:

Dictionary of the Scots Language (*DSL*) http://www.dsl.ac.uk/

C. I. Macafee (ed.), *A Concise Ulster Dictionary* (Oxford: Oxford University Press, 1996).

J. Fenton, *The Hamely Tongue: A Personal Record of Ulster-Scots in County Antrim* (Belfast: Ullans Press, 2000).

Finally, James Orr's two original volumes of poetry, now digitized, may be viewed on this University of Ulster website: http://www.arts.ulster.ac.uk/ulster-scotspoetry/.

LIST OF FIGURES

Figure I.1: James Orr's monument, Templecorran Cemetery, Ballycarry   4
Figure 2.1: James Orr's Ulster   28
Figure 2.2: James Orr's cottage (privately owned)   29

For Kris

INTRODUCTION

James Orr (1770–1816), a native of the Presbyterian, Scots-speaking village of Ballycarry in east Antrim, was virtually forgotten by the public for most of the last century, but in his own lifetime and for a period afterwards he was admired and respected as a leading Irish writer, particularly within the province of Ulster. During the turbulent 1790s Orr, who was a weaver by trade, first achieved fame, or notoriety, as a contributor to the United Irishmen's newspaper, the *Northern Star*, printed in Belfast. Politically radical, he was angry about the injustices he observed within Ireland, such as rural poverty, inequalities suffered by the Dissenting population among whom he had grown up, and humiliations endured by Catholics as a result of the Penal Laws. Committed to the Enlightenment ideals of liberty and democracy, he is known to have participated in the Rebellion of 1798 in the neighbourhood of Antrim as a supporter of Henry Joy McCracken.

After a period on the run in Ireland, for a time in the company of McCracken and James (Jemmy) Hope, Orr fled to America, probably to the neighbourhood of Philadelphia, for an interval of a few months. There a newspaper editor printed a sample of his verse, prefacing it with the first recorded, approving comment on his work: 'We understand the present production is by James Orr, an humble weaver from the North of Ireland. We could wish that his writings were better known.'[1] That wish was fulfilled when Orr availed himself of an amnesty extended to rebels and returned home.

In 1804 Orr published a volume of verse, *Poems on Various Subjects*,[2] and was a regular contributor to the poetry columns of Ulster newspapers and periodicals well into the 1800s.[3] The courtesy title Bard of Ballycarry, by which he is still known, demonstrates the esteem for his talents that prevailed among his neighbours in the Broadisland district of east Antrim.[4]

Following the poet's death in 1816 Alexander (Sandy) McDowell, Orr's friend and brother Freemason, gathered a selection of his poems for a posthumous publication which was issued in 1817.[5] McDowell contributed both a verse elegy and a biographical sketch of James Orr to this second volume. He was circumspect and restrained in his praise, commending his friend's works on the grounds that they would not impair the morals or offend delicacy. He seems to have been attempting an honest evaluation of Orr's powers, not wishing to claim for him the genius of a Pope or a Milton, yet recognizing that at times his poetry soared far above the merely commonplace:

> there are passages in his works, which would not have disgraced almost any author to have written. In the pictures which he draws of country manners in the lower ranks of life, he is always accurate, and his descriptions are often not only just, but beautiful.[6]

McDowell's hesitant commendation suggests he believed that Orr was at his best when he kept to subjects that arose from his own station in life. He proved less restrained, however, when liberated by the muse of poesy. In his 'Elegiac Stanzas on the Death of the Author', Orr is permitted to cut a romantic figure, identified with the linked tropes of Ireland and freedom:

> While truth and right bless Erin's plains,
> Or freedom's sons her standard rear,
> Or while they spurn at slav'ry's chains,
> The name of ORR they shall revere.[7] (ll. 21–4)

The selection of poetry which McDowell made for the 1817 volume, *The Posthumous Works of James Orr of Ballycarry*, is now manifestly incomplete. His purpose, at Orr's request in 1816, was to gather the dying poet's remaining works and to sell the new volume for the benefit of the poor of the Broadisland district, but he omitted no fewer than twenty-nine texts which were to lie undiscovered in newspapers until the historians Donald Harman Akenson and William H. Crawford located them for their study of 1977.[8]

It is intriguing to speculate on the possible existence of an unofficial canon of Orr's works, a selection which McDowell may have deemed too indelicate for publication, particularly since Orr is known to have complained that his audience was often a somewhat uncouth company whose preference was for ribaldry.[9] If such a body of crowd-pleasing poems ever existed it appears to have been most thoroughly suppressed and in all likelihood destroyed. McDowell's role in some respects may parallel that of Dr Currie's with regard to the selection and publication of the works of Burns, and at the time must have appeared both decent and sensitive. He may even have been acting in accordance with Orr's own wishes. Currently, Orr's extant vernacular texts comprise between twelve and thirteen percent of his *oeuvre* as a whole.[10]

Ample evidence remains that Orr enjoyed the respect of other Ulster writers from the labouring and middle classes during his life and following his death. The County Antrim bards, John Dickey of Donegore and James Campbell, the Bard of Ballynure, responded to Orr's death with respectful elegies. Campbell's talent was for the composition of rollicking broadsides, but here we may observe him making a valiant effort to produce a dignified and decorous tribute:

> His soul possessed that quality,
> He loved the truth that made him free; (ll. 7–8)
> ...
> You on inspection this may find,
> He had a clear capacious mind;[11] (ll. 11–12)

It was the poet James Russell English, however, who more than a decade after Orr's death called attention to the need for an appropriately imposing monument to mark Orr's final resting place. In a note to his poem 'The Late James Orr', English deplored the fact that 'So lightly has Irish genius been estimated, that James Orr, though styled by contemporary writers the "Burns of Ulster" has reposed in a nameless grave in the Churchyard of Templecorran, for fourteen years'. Both the poem and the note underlined Orr's close identification with Ireland, showing his contemporaries considered him to be a national poet, or wished to promote him as such. Indeed, English expressed the expectation that 'every genuine lover of their country' would be supportive of the plan for a monument.[12] Figure I.1 shows the impressive memorial which was raised in Orr's honour following English's appeal. While English's portrait appears romanticized, it is in perfect accord with the ideals which may be inferred from Orr's *oeuvre* and from the few details of his life that are known. It is in part the purpose of this study to demonstrate that throughout his life Orr remained true to the United Irish ideal of establishing a nation where the common name of Irishman would replace the terms that divided the population on the basis of creed, and where the social justice favoured by Henry Joy McCracken's and Jemmy Hope's wing of the movement might be achieved.

English identified Orr as a 'man of independent mind' but made the Burns reference still more explicit with his claim that Orr had been regarded as 'the Burns of Ulster' by contemporary poets.[13] The reference to Burns was a potent one and should be read as a calculated stratagem; English was recognizing Orr's exceptional talent and urging his claim to be honoured as a national bard. He may also have been implying particular appreciation of Orr's vernacular works, but certainly not that Orr was no more than a gifted imitator of the Scots genius. A generation after Orr's death, Robert Huddleston of County Down, himself a prolific vernacular poet, began to focus public attention specifically on Orr's vernacular poems, asserting that these testified to his untapped potential. 'Is there nothing that is worthy in Orr of Ballycarry?', he demands, going on to insist that had Orr received the patronage that was offered to the Scots poets Hogg and MacNeill he might have achieved still more and been remembered for longer.[14] This, of course, raises the question of why patronage was offered and to whom. MacNeill was a conservative figure, while Orr was an anti-establishment radical and in his youth an active United Irishman, therefore less likely to attract wealthy supporters. Orr certainly warned his former mentor Samuel Thomson against accepting the patronage of the rich, presumably because it might lead to the loss of his independent poetic voice.[15]

Figure I.1: James Orr's monument, Templecorran Cemetery, Ballycarry.
Photograph by the author.

In the late twentieth century some of Orr's best work was republished and he began to be openly recognized and promoted by scholars and enthusiasts as the greatest of the writers represented within an Ulster Scots poetic tradition. While the present study argues that Orr, a patriotic citizen of Ireland in an era long before partition was ever imagined, should be acknowledged as an Irish writer of exceptional talent, it also demonstrates that his Scots cultural heritage is securely nested within this identity. Thus his poetic output represents a northern tradition, or school, within the literature of Ireland but may also be read as Scots diasporic literature, which vigorously transforms and extends the range of the Scottish poetic tradition in an Irish setting.

For many students of Orr his life and character have proved as fascinating as his verse, particularly his experiences of rebellion and exile, and his autodidacticism. Throughout the nineteenth and early twentieth centuries, while knowledge of the breadth of his poetic output declined, Orr's memory was kept alive by local historians, men of letters and newspaper editors. Articles about Orr tended to focus on his United Irish involvement, his honest character, his concern for the poor, his personal attractiveness, and the regrettable descent into alcoholism which may have brought about his premature death. Often the same sketchy details, anecdotes and traditions were repeated, or embellished with no reference to sources.

The first chapter of this study reviews how Orr has fared in the estimation of scholars, critics and canon formers, both Irish and Scottish, from the nineteenth century until the present. It demonstrates how Orr's vernacular compositions suffered a creeping exclusion from the canon of Irish literature and argues that an increasingly monist view of Irish identity, related to the forces of cultural and political nationalism, has ignored both the Lowland Scots heritage of parts of Ulster, and the northern school of Ulster Dissenter writers to which Orr belongs.

The increased interest in Ulster Scots poets, particularly Orr, recently expressed by some Scottish academics is considered and welcomed. It is evident, however, that while Orr's considerable abilities as a poet are noted, he is too often evaluated in relation to Robert Burns. This study argues that Orr must not be interpreted as Burns-dependent, but should be understood and appreciated in his own right and within his own cultural context. The trend among academics from disciplines such as history or linguistics to mine Orr's *oeuvre* for data is also discussed, and it will be demonstrated that little true scholarly appreciation of the literary merit of his work has ever been attempted. In particular his standard English work has rarely been subjected to serious scrutiny. This has allowed many facile generalizations and prejudices concerning its alleged dullness or stiffness to remain unchallenged.

Three chapters of the present study are devoted to unravelling and reimagining more thoroughly than has been attempted in any previous enquiry the details and circumstances of Orr's life, and to cross-referencing accounts gathered from local tradition with contextual information, archival material, uncollected works and what appear to be biographical details in the poems. The present writer contends that Orr was, almost certainly, closely linked with the northern United Irish leaders Hope and McCracken, and that he was the main United Irish contact in Ballycarry.

A further four chapters demonstrate Orr's originality and independence as a poet through a detailed exploration of the relationship of his work to Scottish Enlightenment thought, and to the language and poetic genres of the Scottish tradition. Orr's major vernacular works are evaluated and the extent to which the eighteenth-century Scots vernacular masters, particularly Burns, may have intrigued, stimulated or provoked him is discussed. Orr's effectiveness in transforming and developing key aspects of the Scottish poetic tradition in order to reflect his Irish cultural context is thereby established. This study argues additionally that Orr's choice of the standard English register in which to compose most of his verse was quite deliberate, and was grounded in his desire to speak to the whole nation of Ireland in a bardic-prophetic persona.

Orr has conventionally been regarded as a post-Augustan writer. In the final chapter a range of his verse is subjected to critical close reading; this process elucidates his success as an innovator who engaged dynamically with Romantic nationalism and with Romanticism more generally as it developed in the wake of the publication of *Lyrical Ballads*. Thus, this study reveals that Orr embraced innovation and engaged dynamically with contemporary trends. Its major purpose is to confirm the substantial nature of Orr's achievement and to argue for the restoration of this neglected poet and patriot to his proper place within the literary canon of Ireland, the 'lov'd lost country' to which he dedicated his life.[16]

1 CRITICAL RECEPTION AND CANONICITY

It was only with John Hewitt's research into the rural bards of Ulster during the middle decades of the twentieth century that any serious retrospective assessment of James Orr's poetry began to be undertaken. A few articles about him appeared in journals during the nineteenth century and allusions to his experiences were made in local histories; these will be considered in later chapters which reconstruct Orr's life. While it is clear that Orr the poet was affectionately remembered, even venerated, for some time after his death, one must ask if there is any evidence that his reputation extended beyond Belfast and its heavily Scots-settled hinterland where he had acquired his audience. Apparently this was indeed the case. Research for the present study has uncovered an article that dates from 1829, two years before his monument was raised at Ballycarry. The *Irish Shield and Monthly Milesian*, an American journal aimed at Irish migrants and their descendants, presented to its readers an apocryphal account of his life along with a selection of his poetry.

In Ireland, Orr was sufficiently well-regarded to merit a place in several important Irish anthologies, including *The Literary Remains of the United Irishmen* (1887), compiled by R. R. Madden (1798–1886) and *The Cabinet of Irish Literature* (1879–80), the great compendium edited by Charles Read (1841–78).[1] Madden included Orr's 'Donegore Hill' (1804), which offers a compelling account of the experience of the rebel army in the vicinity of Antrim on 7 June 1798.[2] Significantly, this poem, which will be discussed in detail within the context of Orr's engagement with the Scottish vernacular tradition, is expressed in dense Ulster Scots, which Madden accepts without any apparent need for explanation into an anthology designed to honour those who had committed themselves to liberty in Ireland.

Charles Read's four volume anthology subtitled 'Selections from the Works of the Chief Poets, Orators and Prose Writers of Ireland', had the stated aims of producing a work 'thoroughly National in character' and of reclaiming writers assumed to belong to English literature who had actually been born on Irish soil. T. P. O'Connor (1848–1929), who contributed the Preface to the edition of 1884 and, following Read's death in 1878 edited the fourth volume, recognized the anthology's potential to buttress the Irish people's confidence and sense of nationhood. Its purpose was also to challenge the Anglo-centric attitudes of the British literary establishment which privileged 'London writers of comparatively small importance' over 'some Irish writers of genius'.[3]

Since the *Cabinet* project was evidently intended to establish an Irish literary canon and to promote this in the United States through the American edition, it is surely significant that the editors chose to include a small selection of Orr's pieces. The list of contents incorporates many very illustrious names: writers from a broad range of confessional and political allegiances, including Sheridan, Tone, Grattan, Abernethy, Edgeworth, Moore and O'Connell. Of the Orr poems selected, 'The Irishman' (1805), 'Song, Composed on the Banks of Newfoundland' (1804) and an extract from 'Ode to Danger' (1817) are in standard register, while 'The Irish Cottier's Death and Burial' (1817) is in the vernacular. Of these, 'Song, Composed on the Banks of Newfoundland', which describes Orr's traumatic voyage to America following the Rebellion, makes an important contribution to the Irish emigrant literary tradition, while both 'The Irishman' and 'The Irish Cottier's Death and Burial' articulate Orr's intense patriotism. The latter work, often regarded as his finest, begins in English but modulates into fairly dense Ulster Scots and, while expressing his deep commitment to the nation, also voices his fears for the survival of his community in Ireland. The editor prefaces the poem with a note that appears designed to be merely explanatory, but actually confirms an othering within Ireland of the Scots-descended inhabitants of the north, based on their accent, language and perceived racial differences: 'They were ... considered by the native Irish of the other provinces an alien race'.[4] There is a palpable contrast here with Madden who seamlessly incorporates Scots vernacular poems into the literary heritage left by the United Irishmen.

Towards the end of the nineteenth century apparently scholarly, but in reality shallow, judgements dismissed Ulster vernacular verse as an interesting if somewhat derivative curiosity. D. J. O'Donoghue (1866–1917) provides an example that reveals either his complete ignorance of a vernacular Scots tradition with characteristic genres, or at least his failure to notice with what originality and sophistication these forms had been employed by the best Ulster poets. In a discussion of 'the dialect poets', including James Orr and Hugh Porter, he commends but patronizes: 'Some of these are excellent and simply because they are so homely and natural'. Then comes the most damning generalization, all the more reprehensible because it is indiscriminately applied: 'It must be admitted, though, that the dialect poets too often slavishly imitated Burns'.[5]

In the twentieth century a continuation of this regrettable process of 'writing out' or discounting Scots vernacular poetry produced in Ulster continued, even though Orr's was of high quality, focused on the condition of Ireland, emanated from the pen of a committed patriot, and endorsed the inclusive values espoused by Wolfe Tone himself. Following partition, a major debate concerning the perceived Irishness of Anglo-Irish literature developed, with Daniel Corkery (1878–1964) expounding an essentialist view of what Irish literature should comprise. For him there were 'three great forces' working in 'the Irish national being', which he believed Irish literature deserving of the name should reflect. These were: '1. The Religious Consciousness of the people; 2. Irish Nationalism; and 3. The Land'. Anglo-Irish literature, such as Edgeworth's novels, he interpreted as Colonial, 'all written for their motherland, England, by spiritual exiles', while the contribution to cultural nationalism of those Ulster poets who wrote in Scots went unacknowledged.[6]

It is disappointing to find this state of affairs perpetuated in *The Field Day Anthology of Irish Writing* (1991–2002) which, despite its apparent breadth and inclusivity, finds space only for Orr's 'The Irishman' and 'Song, Composed on the Banks of Newfoundland'.[7] While Orr has not been excluded from *Field Day* his vernacular works do not feature. If this is accidental, and not, as some have inferred, a late twentieth-century nationalist conspiracy, one can only say that the general editor Seamus Deane, a respected cultural analyst and a Derry man, really should have been better informed. The north-west of Ireland has been particularly affected by migrations from Scotland to Ulster (and vice versa), including and pre-dating those of the Plantations period. Indeed John MacCloskey, in his statistical reports on six parishes in the county of Londonderry in 1821, noted of local speech that 'the dialect abounds in Scotticisms'.[8]

The Ulster Scots poets have been afforded space in some recent collections, though it is rare to find them appropriately or sensitively categorized. Andrew Carpenter, in *Verse in English from Eighteenth-Century Ireland* (1998), anthologizes several fairly dense Ulster Scots poems by Samuel Thomson and compares Thomson's delight in language and the 'sprightly force' of his work to that of Burns.[9] One has to ask if he would have considered placing Burns's work in an anthology purporting to showcase 'verse in English'. In his prefatory note to the selection from Thomson's work, however, Carpenter does acknowledge that Thomson wrote in Ulster Scots.

It is encouraging to discover that the recent anthology *Irish Literature 1750–1900* includes a fresh selection of Orr's poems in both vernacular and standard registers.[10] The pieces are prefaced with a brief commentary on Orr's life and references to some of the influences on his work; the selection also incorporates a brief list of articles for further reading, including some recent essays. The influence of Burns on Orr is a little overstressed in the commentary and is related to his use of 'the Scots dialect that Burns had so innovatively used himself'.[11] This is despite the fact that the writer cites the works of critics and researchers who have emphasized that Scots was as indigenous to parts of Ulster as it was to Ayrshire in the eighteenth and early nineteenth centuries. However, the selection effectively draws attention to vernacularity in Orr's work and to the influence of Presbyterianism on his thinking. Works selected include the vernacular 'The Passengers' and the 'Elegy, on the Death of Mr Robert Burns, the Ayrshire Poet'.

The main body of Orr's poems remained largely unavailable to the public until 1935 when a group of determined individuals from Ballycarry, many of them local historians and creative writers, achieved the republication of his two volumes of verse in a single edition.[12] Their purpose was to stimulate local pride in Orr's achievements by stressing he had acquired some status as a national poet having, as William Calwell makes clear in his foreword, 'long been classed with the Irish immortals'.[13] Presumably those nineteenth-century anthologies that included Orr's work were in Calwell's mind.

That the poetry of James Orr and his contemporaries began to excite serious interest among scholars and from the public is in large measure due to the efforts of the twentieth-century poet, critic and cultural commentator, John Hewitt (1907–87).[14] In the 1940s, while researching his MA thesis, *Ulster Poets 1800–70*,[15] Hewitt brought to light what he described as 'a period of surprising poetic activity on many levels, including peasants and craftsmen'.[16] He rediscovered early editions of poetry by James Orr of Ballycarry, Samuel Thomson of Carngranny, James Campbell of Ballynure and many more, mainly published through subscriptions gathered from their neighbours, and nearly all resident in the Scots-speaking heartlands within Antrim and Down. He was particularly delighted to discover poetry that recorded and dignified community life in the people's own Braid Scotch.

Culturally committed to regionalism, it was clearly with a sense of mission that Hewitt set about publicizing these works of locally produced verse through radio talks, magazine articles and correspondence which communicated his excitement at his discoveries to academics and literary enthusiasts throughout Ireland and Scotland. Their responses reveal the extent of the work of rescue and recovery that he was undertaking. The historian J. C. Beckett wrote, 'James Orr and David Herbison were familiar as names, but Herbison is the only one whose works I have ever gone through'.[17] Another correspondent commended Hewitt but added a pertinent warning: 'I'm greatly interested in these poets and I've often wished somebody would compile an anthology such as you mention, but unless it's done within a few years, I'm afraid a glossary will be necessary for Ulster readers!'.[18]

Hewitt's research into the Ulster vernacular bards was eventually published with an anthology and accompanying glossary as *Rhyming Weavers and Other Country Poets of Antrim and Down* (1974).[19] It remains a worthy introduction to the subject, but a thorough, detailed updating of its conclusions is long overdue. Although Hewitt's study was genuinely groundbreaking, it betrayed particular blind spots from which appreciation of these writers is only beginning to emerge. He established and discussed several of the contexts from which the verse of his Ulster poets arose and which their poetry reflects. These include their linguistic and literary kinship with the Scottish lowlands; local traditions and customs; rural life and the linen industry; Presbyterianism; radical politics; Freemasonry and self-education. He acknowledged the importance of the rural reading societies, to which many of the poets belonged, and he also recognized that these book clubs were suspected by the government of promoting radicalism and sedition, but he chose to present and commend the poets primarily as recorders of rural community life and customs, failing to ascribe sufficient weight to their national and supranational perspectives and to their intellectual breadth. This is most noticeably the case with his treatment of Orr, whom Hewitt in effect deradicalizes.

Though he cited some poems which seem based on Orr's direct involvement with the events of 1798 he appears to have regarded these mainly as vivid evocations of Orr's unhappy personal experience. Thus, although he commended the vernacular 'Donegore Hill', about the Battle of Antrim, and 'The Passengers', which deals with emigration, he regarded them as of 'limited aim' and anthologized neither.[20] Today it would be legitimate to interpret these pieces as intense and vivid entries in a representative narrative of northern-based Irish radicalism. Furthermore, Hewitt included only severely truncated versions of 'The Irish Cottier's Death and Burial', 'Song, Written in Winter' (1804) and 'To the Potatoe' (1804).[21] In the case of the latter he chose only the stanzas that sensuously recreate the wholesome potato-based dishes enjoyed by the peasant community. Incredibly, for a *soi-disant* man of the left, he chose to omit the more radical stanzas. Thus the reader is denied the daring power of Orr's comparison of England to a bird of prey whose wings might easily be clipped if his compatriots resisted oppression by withdrawing their labour from the fields and from the armed forces. In explanation, Ivan Herbison argues that Hewitt's presentation of the 'rhyming weavers', including Orr, was designed 'to bolster his promotion of regionalism as a literary movement'. He shows that 'While this approach literally grounds the poets in particular localities, it makes it more difficult to assess their work in the context of larger social, political and cultural concerns'.[22]

With regard to the Ulster poets' relationship to Scotland's vernacular tradition, Hewitt was determined to rebut the 'Burns imitators' charge, pointing out that the Ulster Scots poets, in their choices of language and verse forms, were no more imitators of Burns than Burns himself was of earlier Scottish masters. He acknowledged that the three great stanza forms, standard habbie, the *Cherrie and the Slae* stanza, and the *Christis Kirk* stanza appear repeatedly within the works of the Ulster bards but, crucially, he believed 'it would be fair to suggest that the Ulster vernacular bards were in much the same relationship to Burns as he had been to his predecessors, and were working free-handedly within the same tradition'.[23] As Andrew Noble has commented, 'Creative influence, after all, is present in varying degrees in all poetry and is a primary force, unlike secondary imitation'.[24]

Hewitt rated Orr as a master craftsman in the utilization of Scots verse forms and in the composition of vernacular verse. However, Hewitt acknowledged that he had not made the selection for his anthology on 'rigorous literary grounds'. The writers in general he characterized as 'companionable men' but 'clumsy old poets'. Unfortunately, such language has contributed to their relegation to the status of interesting curiosities, fascinating for their revelation of folk life, its customs and its concerns, irredeemably average as writers. Such unfortunate generalizations undercut Hewitt's genuine admiration of Orr and did a disservice to many other writers, notably Samuel Thomson of Carngranny (1766–1816).[25]

Hewitt's concept of regionalism was too limited to incorporate what is now understood as hybridity. As a man and a poet Orr's concerns were of necessity local, but also national and global. In choosing sides in the Rebellion, in coming to terms with its failure and with the Act of Union, he embraced and grappled with the question of his cultural and national identity. While he chose to describe himself as an Irishman, linguistically he had the options of Ulster Scots or standard English in which to express himself. These choices and conflicts contributed an important dynamic element to Orr's poetic persona, as did his lifelong commitment to the social radicalism that had motivated many of the United Irishmen. In an earlier work Hewitt dismissed the decade of the 1790s thus: 'Late in the eighteenth century ... the educated northerners were wasting their intellectual substance in theological disputation and abortive political gestures'.[26] More surprising still, the cataclysmic effects of the Rebellion and its aftermath Hewitt passed over in a mere subordinate clause: '*When 1798 saw the sun set on the republican dream* [my italics] the educated Ulsterman found himself caught up in the rapid progress of the new machine age'.[27]

Hewitt's favouring of regionality predisposed him to privilege vernacular verse and he recognized Orr's expertise as a vernacular writer, but while he emphasized that Orr was working within the Scottish poetic tradition, he attempted no assessment of the importance of Orr's contribution to that tradition. Furthermore, with regard to the greater part of Orr's *oeuvre*, that which is expressed in standard English, for many years Hewitt's opinion that Orr's English verses were 'competent, but seldom more than that' has been the received estimate.[28] At the very least this ignores some innovative and sophisticated pieces in the standard register, including soliloquy-style monologues and 'The Assizes' (1817), a long, thought-provoking and exceptionally well-crafted meditation on the contemporary system of justice.[29]

By its very nature *Rhyming Weavers*, which was designed to give an overview of the works of a wide range of poets, may now be viewed as limited both by its breadth and its brevity. The author discussed several generations of vernacular poets. He explored only their collections of poetry, little books published mainly by subscription, but did not research newspaper publications. Nor had he space to subject any of the included poems to the close readings which many deserve. After the publication of *Rhyming Weavers* the relevance to Irish and to Scottish studies of the Ulster bards, and particularly the significance of James Orr, still remained to be thoroughly evaluated, though several details in Hewitt's commentary were to provide crucial leads for a later generation of researchers. These included his observation of the 'clustering' of the Antrim bards,[30] which now may be more clearly understood as a writers' network, and his recognition of the essentially original, rather than imitative, spirit of Ulster vernacular verse.

Hewitt's regionalism was perpetuated, not countered, when the historians Donald Harman Akenson and William H. Crawford mined Orr's *oeuvre* for social history in their study of 1977, *Local Poets and Social History: James Orr, Bard of Ballycarry*.[31] Akenson and Crawford provided some invaluable and thorough research, for example they located twenty-nine of Orr's unpublished pieces by exploring contemporary newspapers and journals.[32] In addition, they established the publication dates of many of the texts in Orr's posthumous volume. Unfortunately, and to the detriment of their work, the dismissive tone they adopted when offering evaluative comments frequently strikes a jarring note. Repeatedly in their discussion we find Orr designated 'local' and 'minor', in effect labelled and patronized. Their stated purpose was threefold:

> to illustrate how the work of a minor poet can be used as data for the social historian ... Second [we wish] to indicate that literary data of the sort provided by Orr's poems are best treated by relating them to contemporary documents of the sort available in public archives ... Our third intention is to suggest that scholars seeking to understand any Irish literary figure of significance should look to archives and contemporary documentation as well as first editions and letters.[33]

There is much in the above with which any contemporary historicist critic is likely to concur. However, the first and second points make clear the authors' intention to employ literature as the servant of history: to provide 'data'. Their approach was, in effect, history-centric.

In addition, the authors seem to have been heavily influenced by Leavisite notions of canonicity. They asserted that Orr was 'scarcely the calibre of poet who would merit scholarly study solely on the basis of his literary achievements'.[34] As a whole, their work is characterized by a failure to interrogate such initial assumptions.

While Hewitt had referred to Ulster's 'rural bards', only occasionally employing the term 'folk poet', the latter was the term Akenson and Crawford preferred, but such a designation does not do justice to the sophistication of Orr's work. They shared Hewitt's prejudice against his English poems, which they regarded as 'derivative' and as 'awkward imitations', while the vernacular tradition was 'indigenous'.[35] English poetic genres, however, and the works of writers such as Thomas Gray, the Anglo-Scot James Thomson and the Irish poet and playwright Oliver Goldsmith were part of a four nations literary heritage in which Irish and Scots poets participated, and those poets often adopted an eclectic approach to language, adding English 'to their repertoire, as the *lingua franca* of the ... British state'.[36]

When discussing the relationship of the poet to his own community they characterized it as 'a splendidly self-policing intellectual system' in which 'the poet was supported and given status only so long as his work met the elementary tests of being pleasing or amusing and of being accurate'. Quite why the authors considered such a system 'splendid', if this was indeed how it operated, is beyond imagination since they appear to have ascribed no value to the poet as an interrogative voice, or as a guide to public opinion and taste. Instead they cheerfully reflected that this

> implicit critical structure embedded within the poet-village relationship means that the social historian can employ the poems of the Ulster bards as social documents with the confidence that they represent not the keenings of an alienated versifier, but the observations of a central local figure, validated by the villagers themselves.

Clearly they failed to appreciate the literary persona of lonely, even alienated, 'versifier', which Orr frequently adopted, in the tradition of Gray and of many Romantic poets.[37]

In fairness it must be acknowledged that the study does possess several exceptionally positive and serviceable aspects. In setting out an account of Orr's life, Akenson and Crawford very carefully referenced almost all the extant sources of information and tradition which exist in addition to McDowell's biographical 'Sketch'. This has proved of inestimable value, though they made little attempt to piece together and cross-reference the available information, or to link its hints and details to Orr's own writing on autobiographical subjects.

While Hewitt had shown little interest in Orr's politics, Akenson and Crawford did usefully refocus attention on what they identified as Orr's, and his community's, attitude to 'Irish nationalism':

> James Orr's attitudes to Irish nationalism are representative of those of the Scots-descended Presbyterian community of County Antrim in three ways: first, in his participation in the rising, second in his subsequent disillusionment with violence; and third, in his continuing attachment to an attenuated form of nationalism.[38]

The catch-all term 'Irish nationalism' is problematic for the revisionist reader. In plain terms it now appears old-fashioned and unfit for purpose, for it fails to distinguish between the politically radical Enlightenment republicanism of the United Irishmen with which Orr certainly identified, the Romantic nationalism with which he very actively engaged in the post-Union era, the later militant Gaelic republicanism of Pearse, or the various forms of nationalism that surfaced during the Ulster 'Troubles' era, against the background of which Akenson and

Crawford were writing. At one point they reduced Orr's post-Union politics to the level of a slogan: 'Nationalism through moralism'. However, their commentary recovered as they observed his open, courageous 'affirmative references to Catholic Emancipation' and the influence of Lockean philosophy on his moral outlook.[39]

The study was one of the first to bring out the richness, breadth and humour of Orr's poetry in its brief treatment of local food and drink, rural entertainment, Methodist revivalism, education, reading societies, poor relief and the emigration experience. Akenson and Crawford also meticulously sourced the origins of the airs which Orr assigned to many of his poems, confirming that many were of Scottish origin.[40] Finally, they confirmed Hewitt's literary research, noting, 'Everything that is viewed as being characteristically Burns's actually is derived from pre-existent poetic and linguistic patterns which prevailed in both lowland Scotland and in Ulster'.[41]

Undoubtedly, the most valuable aspects of Akenson and Crawford's work are to be found in its second and third sections. The second sets poems side by side with contemporary documents which confirm the historical accuracy of much of Orr's writing. Thus Orr's caustic 'Lines Written Under the Portrait of Newell the Notorious Informer' (1804) is followed by facsimiles of several letters from Edward John Newell to Edward Cooke, Under Secretary in Dublin Castle, which confirm Orr's accusations of treachery.[42] In the final section, 'Bibliographical Material', Akenson and Crawford performed a great service for later researchers of Orr's literary output. Following a minute and painstaking search of contemporary newspapers and periodicals, they were able to construct a rough chronological outline of much of the work in Orr's 1817 posthumous volume and also, crucially, of many uncollected works. In this respect they took the study of Orr significantly further forward. They even succeeded in locating a holograph copy of Orr's poem 'Unanimity', undated but initialled 'J. O.', among the Rebellion Papers in the National Archives of Ireland, Dublin.[43] The discovery of the poem in that archive, which includes papers seized by the state from suspects, lends weight to local tradition which reports that Orr's brief exile in America in 1798 or 1799 resulted from investigation and pursuit by the authorities in the wake of the Rebellion.

In conclusion, Akenson and Crawford failed to appreciate much of the breadth and power of Orr's writing. They made only passing reference to the wider historical context within which he wielded his pen, as they were limited by the terms of their own study: a search for 'social history' within Orr's verse. The project contributed nothing directly of value to the literary appreciation of James Orr, though it identified much documentary material that has proved invaluable to the preparation of this study.

Of those scholars who have written about James Orr, Linde Lunney is one of the closest to him in background, since she has many connections within Ulster

Scots-speaking areas of County Antrim.[44] For this reason, perhaps, her discussion of Orr demonstrates sensitivity and respect. In 1981 Lunney, then Rosalind Connolly, successfully submitted her thesis entitled 'An Analysis of Some Linguistic Information Obtained from Eighteenth and Nineteenth-Century Ulster Poetry'.[45] In a sense she was contributing to a growing tradition of 'mining' Ulster vernacular poetry for information of one kind or another, rather than examining it primarily as literature, but in several learned articles Lunney has revealed herself as a distinctly unpatronizing reader whose aim is to elucidate and pay tribute to the complex, cultured personality she detects behind Orr's written text.

Lunney's 1985 essay 'Attitudes to Life and Death in the Poetry of James Orr, an Eighteenth-Century Ulster Weaver' was intended as 'an exploration of one man's outlook and value system'.[46] In the article she examined how Orr stood in relation to his community on spiritual matters and based it on her interpretation of internal evidence from the poems. By community she meant the Ballycarry-Broadisland district itself, and more generally the Scots-colonized areas of east Ulster. Thus she developed the intensely localized view of Orr presented by Akenson and Crawford, but demonstrated far greater subtlety and deference.

While Akenson and Crawford had devoted little space to the often puzzling landscape of Presbyterianism in Ulster, Lunney helpfully raised the issue of the tensions between New Light believers who were sympathetic to the views of Francis Hutcheson and John Abernethy, and the more orthodox, Calvinistic groupings. Orr she placed firmly in the New Light camp, believing him to have been 'influenced by deist or Unitarian thought'. She argued that Orr's poetry showed he believed that 'all could live so as to earn salvation', and that he did not accept Calvinism's 'emphasis on the salvation of only a predetermined few'.[47] It is greatly to Lunney's credit that she was first to look seriously at areas in which Orr's Presbyterianism may have diverged from the mainstream, revealing him at the centre of a debate that certainly raged within his own community and which had persisted within Ulster since earlier in the eighteenth century.[48] She was also first to explore the more general beliefs, attitudes and superstitions of Orr's community, and to assess the position he took in relation to these. Once again her information was mainly collected from his poems, and her exploration of them was significant in that it began to dispel the view that his most interesting work resides in his vernacular output. In a further genuine 'first', she recovered Orr the essayist, bringing to light a piece 'On Accidents' which he had written for the *Belfast Monthly Magazine*, and which had been all but forgotten.[49]

Lunney's stated purpose was to elicit the poet's ideas and feelings from his poems, however that in itself begs the question of whether it can ever be appropriate to search poetic texts apart from their literary context. Many of the works she cited are expressed in the voice of a persona adopted for the duration of the poem but often Lunney appears to assume that Orr was projecting his own views onto the speakers when in reality the correlation may be less simple. In addition, many pieces really require to be assessed with reference to their forms and genres. A poem such as 'The Wanderer' (1817) can only fully be appreciated when explored as a contribution to the mini-genre of wanderer and vagrant poetry ubiquitous in the magazines and journals of the period, and also in the light of the fascination such figures exercised over the Romantic imagination.[50]

'The Irish Cottier's Death and Burial', Lunney regarded as Orr's 'finest poem', rightly remarking that it 'deserves to be much better known'.[51] While it is satisfying to find the work foregrounded through extensive analysis and quotation, it must be stressed that it was impossible for Lunney to do justice to its stylistic and thematic complexity given the constraints of her stated intentions and taking into account the publication of her article in *Ulster Folklife*, a journal aimed at academics primarily concerned with the folk customs of Ulster rather than with its literary heritage. Particularly interesting to such an audience would have been the details Orr supplied concerning the rituals and customs associated with Presbyterian deathbeds, wakes and funerals. Ultimately Lunney's reading shows exceptional sympathy with the custom, ritual and community aspects of the work but, paradoxically, appears somewhat prosaic due to its failure adequately to address mood and narrative voice. While Lunney's study was of a non-literary nature, however, it still appears astute and original in drawing attention to the subtlety of Orr's work. Quite deliberately, however, Lunney presented Orr as a writer primarily rooted in his own community, even if he at times diverged from its prevailing orthodoxies. While not denying his United Irish connections, she made little of their significance, referring to his involvement in the 1798 Rebellion in a manner that relegated it to a merely temporary disturbance that was quickly over and done with:

> The only event which disturbed his life was the United Irishmen's rebellion of 1798. Orr, like many other Ulstermen was influenced by the new political ideas of his time, and took part in an armed rising against the government's policies. The inspiration came in part from the American and French Revolutions, but the Irish revolt was unsuccessful.[52]

The theme of the Ulster Scots community and its distinctiveness was raised again by Lunney in a paper of 1996. In a lengthy section devoted to Orr, she discussed language, Freemasonry, Presbyterianism and United Irish ideals, presenting these as bonds which connected him to his community. She argued that 'the perception of rootedness, of connectedness' in Orr is 'almost mystic'. While she recognized that language, religion and other factors also connected the Ulster Scots communities to Robert Burns and to south-west Scotland, the impression this piece leaves is that the primary purpose of the Ulster poets was to write for their own communities, to 'involve as strongly as possible, people from their own background'. Lunney contended that Orr's 'poems attempt to recreate the network of acquaintances, the shared experiences, and the communal judgements of a small area of east Antrim at one point in its history'. While this judgement is not inaccurate, it is hardly the whole story. The impression created by this section of Lunney's article borders on clannish. In it, she presented Orr as a community 'insider' writing about and for his own folk, a grouping with which Lunney herself clearly feels identified. From her analysis of the markers of belief, language, shared history and custom which helped bond Orr's community together, perhaps the reader is meant to infer that such bonds are also boundaries which can never be fully or effectively negotiated by non-members.[53]

Lunney gives little emphasis to the global consciousness so evident in Orr's work, both vernacular and formal.[54] Nor does she discuss his persistent return to a condition of Ireland theme, or the sense of alienation that is a marked feature of much of his writing. The extra-village networks which, it will be demonstrated, Orr negotiated indicate that he had aspirations which took him well beyond his locality. If, as Lunney asserted, the community supplied all the emotional and intellectual needs of the Ulster Scots poets, how may we understand Orr's personal melancholy as he meditated on national and supranational politics, or his letter to Thomson confessing his loneliness, or his, possibly, drink-related death at the age of forty-six in 1816?[55]

All Lunney's work is minutely informed by the linguistic scholarship which is her primary area of expertise. It is surely her consciousness of the very distinct nature of Ulster Scots speech which determines the view of the community's cohesive independence that she disseminates. That linguistic emphasis was once again clearly evident in an essay written for a volume produced to commemorate the work of Robert Gregg, the linguist who first mapped the Ulster Scots-speaking areas of the north of Ireland in the early 1960s.[56] Her subject, 'reading and orality in eighteenth-century Ulster poetry', permitted her to discuss Orr's verse epistles, including one to Samuel Thomson which, as she observed, 'adopts the style and tone of colloquial Ulster Scots speech, rather than the more formal register usually adopted for letters'. She pondered Orr's possible reasons for writing in Ulster Scots when his few extant letters reveal him to have been 'perfectly at home' with the contemporary conventions of letter-writing in English and followed this with speculation that Orr may have 'been aware of the novelty value of writing a letter in Ulster-Scots' or that he 'may have been attempting to reclaim genres in which Scots could be written'.[57] Given that Orr's choice of form for his 'Epistle to S. Thomson of Carngranny' (1804) is the difficult but very distinctive *Cherrie and the Slae* stanza, it is surprising that Lunney discusses the letter as if it were a fairly functional written communication, despite the fact that she must be aware of the eighteenth-century vernacular verse epistle tradition with which Orr and his contemporaries, from their knowledge of the works of Burns, Fergusson and Ramsay, would have been very familiar.[58]

The published work of Linde Lunney here discussed supports the regionalist representation of Orr proposed first by Hewitt. Though she appropriately accorded dignity and sophistication to Orr's image, she did not explore his engagement with the great literary and historical movements that inspired him and with which his work merits association.

That selections from the works of James Orr, and indeed of Samuel Thomson and Hugh Porter, have achieved republication in the contemporary period is in large measure due to the efforts of Philip Robinson, a leading figure in the revival of interest in Ulster Scots literature during the 1990s and at present. In partnership with the late J. R. R. Adams, Robinson collected material for the *Folk Poets of Ulster* series, in which *The Country Rhymes of James Orr, the Bard of Ballycarry* was the second volume.[59] The series and volume title foreground yet again Orr's local and regional status, and as a native of east Antrim himself, Robinson may in part be understood as one of a series of 'insiders' who have assumed responsibility for the direction taken in Orr's critical reception. Robinson, however, is an academic historical geographer with wide-ranging interests in the humanities and social sciences; he is also a talented Ulster Scots poet whose work demonstrates strong political and global awareness.[60]

The general introduction which Robinson and Adams provided for the *Folk Poets of Ulster* series gave appropriate emphasis to the relationship between the Ulster vernacular tradition and 'a much broader literary movement focused in Scotland and culminating in the work of Robert Burns', though the editors were careful to follow Hewitt in stressing that this 'virile Ulster tradition ... has its beginnings in the eighteenth century, before the work of Burns'. They stated that the poems had been chosen for their 'themes of local and historical interest', rather than their literary merit, and that the selection 'prefers those written in Ulster-Scots rather than standard English'. Notes and a glossary were not provided because, the editors explained, their purpose was essentially to make the poems 'accessible once more'. While this might be regarded as an opportunity lost, undoubtedly the recovery and republication of Orr's work ensured that his vernacular poetry once more fell into public domain.[61]

Robinson himself provided the introduction to the Orr volume; he caught some of the flavour and breadth of Orr's mind and experience, describing him as 'a radical thinker, a patriot, a United Irishman, a "New Light" Presbyterian, a humanist with a penetrating social concern for the poor ... and a man who until his death in 1816 continued to speak "braid Scotch"'.[62] The rather frustrating lack of detailed, corroborated information about the poet's life with which any commentator has to come to terms is clear from Robinson's often tentative phrasing. Expressions such as 'As far as can be judged', 'probably' and 'it has been suggested that' abound in his references to the theology of Orr's parents, their reasons for keeping him from the village school, or the date of Orr's brief exile in America.

One of the most interesting features of this introductory essay is that Robinson was the first modern commentator to address with real emphasis the importance of Freemasonry in Orr's life. He explained that many of Orr's poems were composed to be performed at festive occasions in Masonic Lodges and clearly showed that Freemasonry, with its emphasis on tolerance and harmony, often went hand in hand with radical politics in Ulster during the 1790s. It should be remembered, however, that some of the most politically radical Presbyterians, for example the Covenanters, were theologically conservative and not renowned for their tolerant attitude to other faiths.

A further contribution made by Robinson to the study of Orr may be found in his brief discussion of Orr's Presbyterianism. He acknowledged that Linde Lunney had 'argued convincingly that Orr himself favoured New Light theology which we would today identify as being acceptable only to Non-Subscribing Presbyterians', but Robinson was scrupulous in painting a broader picture which drew attention to the friendship and support that Orr apparently enjoyed among Presbyterians of varying shades of theology. For example, he found a spread of New Light and Old Light opinions among the five ministers named on the subscription list for Orr's 1804 volume.[63]

In presenting the anthologized selection of Orr's work, Robinson acknowledged that Orr wrote important poems on international issues and historic events, but explained these had been omitted in favour of nearly fifty poems that provide 'some descriptive content of local historic or social interest, along with a few poems that help us understand the man himself better'.[64] The selection was made based, in the main, on the poems' local and dialect interest. As such, it reiterated the undoubted importance of the vernacular poetry to which Hewitt had already drawn attention but Robinson, in common with earlier commentators, chose not to address the intriguing issue of Orr's relatively low vernacular output.

Until fairly recently Scottish literary critics have shown little interest in those Ulster poets of the 'rhyming weaver' tradition whose works, whether vernacular or formal, are often rooted in Scottish literature and culture.[65] It is encouraging, therefore, to find Liam McIlvanney prepared to break with convention in order to explore the relationship between Ulster Scots poets and Robert Burns. In the final chapter of his masterly *Burns the Radical*, McIlvanney commented that 'This neglect of Ulster vernacular poetry [was] unfortunate', noting the paucity of critical work on even the best known of the Ulster poets.[66] His main purpose, however, was to discuss the connection between Burns and certain radical Ulster poets of the 1790s in order to highlight Burns's influence on eighteenth-century bardic nationalism, which, he argued, had largely been forgotten. In McIlvanney's view Burns's success galvanized 'the local Ulster verse tradition ... inspiring a new wave of Ulster poets and prompting them to publish their own volumes'.[67] This is in itself a major claim, but McIlvanney went much further. He represented Burns as part of a 'politicised cultural nationalism' that had 'developed in response to the 1707 Union'.[68] Not only did he contend that Burns galvanized Ulster vernacular poets into publication, he claimed that for those Ulster poets associated with the United Irishmen, and who wrote for the *Northern Star* newspaper, Burns was 'the inspiration and figurehead ... He was, in many respects, the tutelary poet of radical Ulster'.[69]

James Orr is widely regarded as the leading radical poet of his generation in Ulster, both for his United Irish activism and for the quality of his verse. Since the present study is concerned with Orr, it is worth examining McIlvanney's claims regarding Burns's tutelary role in relation to Orr himself. Within the chapter 'On Irish Ground' the reader may note a generalizing tendency that encourages the inference that all the Ulster poets who wrote for the *Northern Star*, or its reformist, but less revolutionary, rival the *Belfast News-letter*, exhibited a common attitude to Burns. He wrote, for example, 'From the perspective of Burns scholars, however, the most conspicuous feature of the Ulster poets is their unrestrained bardolatry'. This evaluation McIlvanney justified, citing Samuel Thomson's verse epistle to Burns which he describes as 'a rapturous fan-letter' and the 'pilgrimage' style visits made by Thomson and his friend Luke Mullan to Burns in Ayrshire or Dumfries.[70]

It must not be overlooked, however, that Thomson himself had a tutelary role towards his Ulster contemporaries, exercised through his regular contributions to the *Northern Star* and by virtue of having established a literary circle at his home, 'Crambo Cave', that included both Mullan and Orr.[71] It also seems fair to say that Thomson and Mullan appear to have been, temporarily at least, dazzled by Burns's celebrity status, but neither remained at the cutting edge of radicalism in Ireland. By the late 1790s Mullan, the brother-in-law of McCracken's comrade, Jemmy Hope, was employed as a purser with the Royal Navy at Spithead.[72] Thomson, unlike Orr, did not take an active role during the Rising of 1798.

That Burns influenced, even tutored, the more active or pugnacious radical spirits is certainly open to dispute. McIlvanney has asserted, for example, that Burns's 'nationalist strategies – such as his celebration of native Scottish fare' were emulated by Orr, 'so that Burns's "To a Haggis" becomes James Orr's "To the Potatoe" and Burns's "Scotch Drink" becomes Orr's "Address to Beer"'.[73] In fact, both the Orr poems were published well into the Union period, not the 1790s, and in both, particularly the latter, Orr, far from transposing Burns's strategies into an Irish context, is consciously opposing what may have seemed to him the Scots bard's bombastic style of literary nationalism and ploughing a more sober radical furrow of his own. Burns's tone is, however, quite understandably different from Orr's since the latter published the 'Address to Beer' some years after experiencing the defeat of his revolutionary hopes.

Furthermore, since Orr did not publish his first volume until 1804 and since no-one has definitively established which of the anonymous or pseudonymous pieces in the *Northern Star* emanated from his pen, the extent of Burns's influence on Orr's writing in the 1790s remains indeterminate and unproven. Despite this, McIlvanney asserted that Burns's 'egalitarian and democratic sentiments, his outspoken pro-Americanism, his anticlericalism and his depiction of the Westminster government as a "System of corruption"' all 'endeared him ... to poets like Orr and Campbell who were to participate in the 1798 Rising'.[74] The employment of Orr's and Campbell's names and the specific reference to their participation in the 1798 Rebellion, here juxtaposed with a list of attitudes to which Burns gave voice on particular occasions, again encourages the reader to infer that these Ulster radicals were explicitly heartened and inspired in their activism by Robert Burns when there is no actual record of this having been the case.

Much of this chapter is taken up with McIlvanney's defence of 'The Dumfries Volunteers'(1795), which he believes to be entirely consistent with Burns's 'real Whig' radical politics since 'The prospect of being "liberated" by foreign arms is not one which anyone imbued with civic humanist principles could relish'.[75] The United Irish movement to which Orr belonged was, beyond question, imbued with such principles. Many of its members, McCracken, Hope and Orr, were citizen soldiers, members of local Volunteer companies.[76] Yet right up to 1798 the hope of the United Irish movement lay in a rising in Ireland that would be supported by troops of the French Republic. Not only was the radicalism of the Irish more practical than that of Burns, it was also, apparently, significantly more international in orientation.[77]

Helpfully, McIlvanney has confirmed from a Scottish viewpoint the similarities between the enlightened intellectual culture of south Ayrshire and east Antrim, which in both areas centred on the Kirk, the reading society and the Masonic Lodge.[78] Although McIlvanney has written the Ulster poets into a subordinate role, he has played a significant part in calling attention to the need for greater critical interest in their works. He commended Orr, Thomson and Porter for their 'intimate understanding not merely of Burns's work but of the whole Scots vernacular tradition', confirming that they 'are fully conversant with its genres and metres'. He noted how Orr's work was enriched both by his immersion in local folk culture and his 'broad knowledge of contemporary Scottish Enlightenment Literature'. However, the following evaluation seems designed to ensure the Ulster poets keep to their place: 'Orr and Thomson, then, are no clumsy poetasters; they are significant, if undoubtedly minor, poets'.[79] While the present writer does not claim that Orr's work, in quantity or in overall quality, is on a par with that of Burns, a number of individual works are most certainly masterpieces and in some cases, it could be argued, are as good or better than comparable pieces Burns produced.

In a more recent essay, McIlvanney returned to the subject of the Ulster Scots poetic tradition, paying tribute to its ability to 'complicate and illuminate our understanding of archipelagic identities in the eighteenth and nineteenth centuries'. He went even further, acknowledging that 'The Ulster-Scots canon provides a corrective to the more glibly totalizing views of Irish and Scottish writing' and remarked, 'It may be that Scots have something to learn about their own culture from that Irish "Scotland" across the North Channel'.[80]

It is refreshing to read a scholar and critic of McIlvanney's stature confirming that previous commentators on Orr have done him a disservice by exploring his work primarily for 'the insight it provides into social and historical conditions'. That this is 'a comparatively barren [approach] to take in the case of a poet like James Orr' is undoubtedly the case.[81] Furthermore, all previous discussions of Orr's work have been rendered unsatisfactory by their brevity, which inevitably has resulted in superficial or insufficiently substantiated evaluations. The present enquiry seeks to remedy the inadequacies in earlier studies and to subject Orr's works, within the context of his life and experiences, to a thorough and detailed analysis. Its purpose is to extend appreciation of Orr's literary excellence and to argue for a proper recognition of his place within archipelagic literary heritages.

2 RAISING A RADICAL: ORR, BALLYCARRY AND '98: JAMES ORR (1770–98)

James Orr's career invites us to interpret him as a Romantic figure who during his life played a series of iconic Irish roles including rebel poet, fugitive patriot, emigrant, returning exile and revered bard. As a radical writer and activist he developed close links to Henry Joy McCracken and James Hope, northern leaders of the United Irish movement; in support of their attempt to establish a more independent, democratic Ireland he led a troop of men from Ballycarry, his own County Antrim village, to the Battle of Antrim during the Rebellion of 1798. Orr's best-known work until relatively recently was the much anthologized 'The Irishman', which was first published at the time of the invasion scare during the Napoleonic conflict and which celebrates the national character in idealized terms. While he identified strongly with his native land and with her distresses, however, Orr's personal heritage was Scottish. His ancestors, and those of the vast majority of his community, had migrated to Ulster from Scotland in the seventeenth century. Undoubtedly it was the liminality of the culture he inhabited which provided the cradling for his radical mindset and propelled him into the series of Romantic roles he executed during one of the most unstable and significant periods in Ireland's long, difficult history.

Ballycarry, or Broadisland, as the district is still known locally, was first settled in 1573 by John Dalway, a cornet in the army of the Earl of Essex, but in 1609 William Edmonstone of Stirlingshire leased an area of about 2,870 acres from Dalway and agreed to plant on it 'forty-eight able men of eighteen years or upwards and of English or Scottish descent'.[1] The Scots then began migrating in large numbers to the area where they would significantly shape and determine its culture and character. A journey of only a few miles would have taken those Scots into an environment where English Ascendancy authority was sited and which had a palpably different ethos. Ballycarry sits in the hills above Carrickfergus, a Norman town that had been established by John de Courcy in 1180. There, on the shores of Belfast Lough the English garrison was housed, the gaol and the courthouse were established, and native Irish insurgents or brigands were tried and executed. At the close of the eighteenth century the condemned included United Irishmen, such as William Orr, the so-called 'Presbyterian martyr'.

The writers of the *Ordnance Survey Memoirs*, commissioned during the 1830s and 1840s, noted the visual link with Scotland which then, as now, signalled a reminder to the inhabitants of their Scots descent:

> The views from the parish, particularly from the higher points along its eastern side, are perhaps the most extensive along the coast of Antrim, embracing the North Channel from the Isle of Man to as far beyond the extremity of Kintyre as the eye can reach. On the east it is bounded by the western coast of Scotland which, even in ordinary weather, exhibits all its bolder features.[2]

But there were factors far more significant than a stunning view or sentimental memory that maintained the 'Scotch' character of Ballycarry. One was the staunch adherence of the inhabitants to the Presbyterian faith. In 1613 an event occurred that significantly strengthened the hold of Presbyterianism in the north of Ireland and certainly reinforced the confidence of Ballycarry's Presbyterian culture. The event was the arrival of Edward Brice, the first Dissenting minister in Ireland. Brice, a staunch Calvinist, enhanced his reputation among Presbyterians as one of those who refused to sign acceptance of the Anglican Thirty-Nine Articles of Religion during Wentworth's period as Lord Deputy in Ireland (1633–40). As a result he was denied permission to preach or to conduct communion services with his congregation.[3] Ballycarry, therefore, has acquired a long history as a place of resistance to the establishment. The fact that it was William Edmonstone who brought Brice, a former Regent of Edinburgh and minister of Drymen, Stirlingshire, to Ballycarry, offers a striking illustration of the unity that then existed between the local tenant population and the master of the 'big house', a situation that was not to last.

Within the Parish lies the ruined Old Church, originally an episcopal foundation but used for worship by the Presbyterians during the so-called 'prescopalian' period, 1611–36, when Presbyterian ministers were permitted to preach in the parish churches, received the tithes and were recognized by the bishops of the dioceses until Bishop Jeremy Taylor put a stop to this in 1661.[4] A Presbyterian meeting house was eventually erected c. 1710, but during the later seventeenth century the ranks of Presbyterians in communities throughout Ulster, including Ballycarry, were swollen by Scots Covenanters fleeing the persecution of 'the killing times' under Charles II. Such memories of persecution in Scotland and of enforced exile contributed powerfully to the Presbyterian mindset in the 1790s and to the willingness of many Presbyterians to support the United Irish challenge to the Protestant (Anglican) Ascendancy. Thus the Ulster Scots lived with a dilemma: while they were often reviled as colonists by a hostile native population, they were far from being natural supporters of the colonial power that had in many instances been the cause of their forced migration. Orr's recognition of this dilemma informs his best and most tragic work.

A further and deeply significant factor in maintaining the Scottish character of Ballycarry was its Braid Scotch tongue. From the *Ordnance Survey Memoirs* we may infer deep-rooted official unease regarding the Scots ethos of the district which remained powerfully present well into the post-Union period. In entry after entry local language, customs, habits and personal characteristics are evaluated, often in a tone of disapproval. The 'othering' of the community is expressed in remarks that are distinctly pejorative in character: their speech is 'disagreeably Scottish' or 'broad and coarse'. In addition, the people's manners are depicted as 'dry and uncommunicative', while their traditional music is denigrated as unsophisticated and derivative: 'They have not any national music: their songs are merely the common ballads of the country and their airs are Scottish'. The taste for theology and theological disputation central to Presbyterian life is disparaged: 'They have much taste for reading ... works on theology and divinity such as might in every respect be deemed beyond their comprehension and as unsuited to their taste'.[5]

While undoubtedly these comments reveal a class-based antipathy towards members of the lower orders who are obstinate rather than docile, literate and disputative rather than rustic and inarticulate, in their clear preference for standardized forms the judgements bear the hallmark of official writing during a period of imperial expansion throughout the globe. A further entry in the memoirs records that all the villagers 'to a man', were 'out' in the 1798 Rebellion, suggesting the writers were very aware of the area's anti-establishment bias, which its unfamiliar language and cultural traditions very graphically underlined.[6] If this was the official attitude in a period of relative tranquillity one can imagine how deeply hostile it must have been when the United Irishmen were active in the 1790s and the country stood on the verge of revolution. In such an atmosphere Orr passed from the impressionable years of adolescence to active young manhood. In Ballycarry the strong local sense of identity was at odds with the infrastructure put in place by the authorities for administration, justice and security. Geographically, Ballycarry's position in the hills set it apart from Carrickfergus, the garrison town and location of the assizes. At some point on the road from Carrickfergus to Ballycarry the traveller would pass an invisible boundary beyond which the territory simply felt alien and to government representatives, whether 'redcoats' or civil servants, 'disagreeably Scottish'.[7] Figure 2.1 shows the location of Ballycarry, County Antrim and the position of other sites associated with Orr or referred to in his works.

Figure 2.1: James Orr's Ulster. Map by Chris J. Baraniuk (not to scale).

Orr was closely identified with this community and its Scots culture. He wrote some of his finest works in the Braid Scotch speech of the area, much of his reading had a Scots focus, and many of his poems were written as song lyrics to familiar Scots airs.[8] He could write fluently, even elegantly, in English when contemporary conventions of decorum demanded it, but in everyday intercourse 'his voice was slow, and he continued to speak in the homely "broad Scotch" of his native district, up to his death'.[9]

The anti-establishment ethos and sense of marginalization pertaining in communities such as Ballycarry were compounded by widespread resentment concerning the abhorred tithe which the Anglican Church raised from Dissenters and Catholics alike. The United Irish movement easily tapped into bitterness concerning this issue in Ballycarry and throughout the north of Ireland, but the evidence, as we shall see, points to Orr's also having understood and shared the aims of the movement's leaders as they aspired to achieve democratic freedoms and independence for all the citizens of Ireland, irrespective of creed. Those leaders, when their calls for reform met with a repressive government response, were prepared to rise in rebellion with the aim of establishing a republic on the American model, inspired by the radicalism of *The Rights of Man* and assisted by revolutionary France.[10] A careful examination of the events and circumstances of Orr's life leads to the conclusion that he not only shared the aims of the northern United Irish leadership but had close connections among that group. It is within this context that we should understand his readiness to turn out in support of armed revolution.

Figure 2.2: James Orr's cottage (privately owned). Photograph by the author.

Orr's long weaver's cottage still rests, though on private land, on a hill to the south-west of Ballycarry village. Figure 2.2 shows Orr's cottage after its original thatched roof was replaced by a slate roof in the early twentieth century. Here James Orr senior, traditionally believed to have been conservative or Old Light in theology, personally undertook his son's education out of a concern for the boy's morals, or so Orr's biographer McDowell claimed. This has been interpreted as a wish to protect him from New Light theology and its associations with radicalism.[11] However, a more likely explanation may be found in Orr's own poetic account of an incident in which the unruly pupils within the village school rose in rebellion against their master, locked him in the schoolroom and appropriated the day as a holiday, during which they roamed unsupervised in the countryside.[12] Orr was, in any case, permitted to attend the church singing school where he reportedly distinguished himself by surpassing his peers in the composition of 'crambo', verse that was employed for practising the singing of psalm tunes since the metrical psalms themselves were considered too sacred to be sung in any context other than that of actual worship. The story provides evidence of an early aptitude for the crafting of language.

Orr appears to have been a natural scholar as a youth, and was soon supplementing his father's education with his own extensive reading. Living a little apart, and keeping the company of adults for most of the day can only have encouraged his capacity for serious reflection, and prepared him to engage in discussion of new, radical political and theological matters when friendships developed with other young men outside his immediate community. Given the breadth of his reading, it is possible that Orr found himself at odds with a conservative father who was in a threefold position of authority over him, being also his schoolmaster and the teacher of his trade. However, Orr wrote tenderly of his father who, unusually for the time, trained him 'without a rod'[13] (l. 78), and it is very likely that his early signs of outstanding intellectual ability were valued and encouraged by his parents, perhaps until they began to fear exactly where the thoughts his reading provoked might lead him.

In Orr's day the economy of Ballycarry throve on the farming of subsistence crops such as oats and potatoes, animal husbandry and on cottage-based spinning and weaving. W. H. Crawford's brief history of the Ulster linen industry presents a concise, vivid account of the life of a weaver and of the character associated with it.[14] These artisans were distinguished by their independence and toughness, and frequently by their love of vicious sports such as unregulated prizefighting or cockfighting. The latter activities were considered to be contrary to the principles of sincere Dissenting religion, and to the standards of the Age of Sensibility. In Orr's poem 'The Penitent' (1800) when Christy Brown, a weaver, turns to cockfighting, the poet presents this as evidence of his moral degeneration.[15] If such amusements may be understood to represent the dark side of the tough weaver character, Orr's offering of resistance to government on behalf of the poor and dispossessed may represent a more positive channelling of his weaver's energy. Most weavers were obliged also to be small farmers to supplement their earnings at weaving. They grew oats and potatoes to live on and thus were less dependent for livelihood on the market prices offered for their cloth. His experience of growing the potato in particular may have helped Orr to bond with the poor in his community.

Weavers, intelligent, combative and argumentative as many were, often felt attracted to radical or revolutionary politics. By the end of the eighteenth century, Belfast had textile mills in operation and the treatment of workers in these establishments certainly influenced and helped to politicize the thinking of the radical weaver and United Irishman, James Hope.[16] Orr, in common with many other weavers, also came to channel his weaver's energy into resistance to the government on behalf of the poor and dispossessed in the rural localities. Visits to markets outside Ballycarry in connection with his trade would have given him opportunities to develop contacts with members of secret United Irish cells who, during the 1790s, used busy public venues such as markets or reading clubs to expand their network and pass on information.

That Orr thought about his community and the benefit raised by the state from the efforts of the labouring poor is clear from his poem, 'Ballycarry' in which, with resentment, he reminds 'the great who rule the state' of how much is raised in 'rent, tax, tithe' in Ballycarry by the 'loom and wheel' (ll. 31–2).[17] Within his own district, Orr would also have learned of disputes between landlords and tenants that frequently erupted into violence. One such involved the Hearts of Steel, a secret society of agrarian agitators, which undoubtedly contributed a strand to the growth of support for the United Irishmen in rural communities. During the 1770s landlords, many of them absentees and Anglican, evicted long-term tenants in order to replace them with others who could pay higher rents. The Steelboys, mainly Dissenters in the north, carried out violent reprisals against land agents, tithe collectors and new tenants who had displaced former sitting ones.[18] The Carrickfergus district and in particular Islandmagee, near neighbour to Ballycarry where Orr at the time was an infant, suffered widespread disturbance which he would have heard discussed as he was growing up.[19] The landlord of Islandmagee, Viscount Dungannon, was virtually an absentee, while the landlords at Ballycarry were the Edmonstones of Red Hall, who shared a common Scots ancestry and religion with the inhabitants. That situation changed during Orr's boyhood in the 1770s when the Edmonstones returned to Stirlingshire and sold their land to Richard Gervase Ker whose brother owned an estate across the Belfast Lough on the County Down coast. The Ker family was Anglican in religion and identified with the privileged Ascendancy.

Ker probably quickly developed suspicions regarding the loyalty of his Dissenter tenants. Establishment distrust of Ulster's Presbyterians was openly expressed in two remarks quoted by A. T. Q. Stewart in a discussion of the Presbyterian role in the '98 Rebellion. In 1787 the fourth Duke of Rutland, making his Viceregal tour of Ireland, observed that 'the province of Ulster is filled with Dissenters, who are in general very factious – great levellers and republicans ... The Dissenting ministers are for the most part very seditious, and have great sway over their flocks.' This opinion was endorsed by John Beresford in 1798 who writes, 'Again, the Dissenters are another set of enemies of the British government. They are greatly under the influence of their clergy, and are taught from their cradles to be republicans.'[20]

If these undoubtedly sweeping remarks held any truth we might expect to find that Orr had imbibed revolutionary principles from his minister the Rev. John Bankhead, and that the singing school he attended was in reality a radical seminary.

That Presbyterian theologies were a major influence on Orr's thinking throughout his life is evident from his poetry and extant letters. That local Presbyterian teaching was the major force behind his activities in the 1790s is much less likely.

The Session Book of the Ballycarry Presbyterian Church from 1704–80 reveals developments that point to the nature of Bankhead's ministry. Before his arrival the Book is little more than a dismal account of censures for adultery, fornication and Sabbath-breaking. The following extract is typical: 'August 28 1757. John Robinson apeired [sic] and confessed his sin of fornication with Mary hear [sic] and was exhorted to repent. He appeared before the Congregation and was absolved from the scandal.' Soon after Bankhead's arrival such entries ceased, however. The new minister was of a charitable and prayerful disposition. A lengthy entry in the Session Book for 20 February 1774 detailed the arrangements he established for the relief of different classes of poor within the parish.[21] From Bankhead Orr is unlikely to have received encouragement to rebellion. To understand his commitment, however briefly, to the United Irishmen's plans for violent revolution, we must look further afield, to his relationships with a radical set of young men, writers and United Irish activists, who were associated with the *Northern Star* newspaper.

J. R. R. Adams has documented in detail the network of reading societies that existed in Antrim and Down from the later eighteenth century until well into the nineteenth. Adams traces their popularity to excitement generated by the American and French revolutions, and to 'the general questioning of established values [which] was reinforced by the growing tide of radical nationalism'.[22] These local and global factors stimulated a great desire for information about political issues. Once the Society of United Irishmen had been established in 1791, the leaders capitalized on this desire by launching the *Northern Star* which carried information about the progress of the revolution in France and the successes of revolutionary movements in other parts of Europe.[23] Its influence was disseminated, even among the illiterate, through a well-organized process of reading parties in homes, taverns and at meetings in the popular book clubs where vigorous political debates were carried on.[24] These places were regarded with deep suspicion by the government and in June 1798 one of the oldest and most successful, the Doagh Reading Society, was sacked by the yeomanry. The *Northern Star* building and printing presses were destroyed by the Monaghan Militia on 19 May 1797.

That James Orr was deeply involved with the reading society movement and approving of its practices is clear from his poem 'The Reading Society', which lists several authors to whose works such clubs gave him access, including Hume, Gibbon and Cooke.[25] There is no record of any reading society existing in Ballycarry until after Orr's death.[26] It is clear, therefore, that Orr as a young man in the 1790s had to go beyond Ballycarry in his search for the reading material with which he supplemented his father's early teaching. If so, there were several book clubs in the

Antrim hills to the north-east of Belfast to which the back roads and moorland trails from Ballycarry would have given him access. These included Doagh, Lowtown and Roughfort[27] and possibly Craigarogan and Mallusk.[28] These areas too were populated by Ulster Scots and in them support for the United Irishmen was strong. The company in such places included members of a very radical set with direct links to United Irish activists in Belfast, such as Henry Joy McCracken and Samuel Neilson, editor of the *Northern Star*. McCracken's trusted comrade Jemmy Hope, for example, was a member of the Roughford (Roughfort) Volunteers; his brother-in-law, Luke Mullan, who was a close friend of the poet Samuel Thomson, lived at Craigarogan. Thomson's home on Lyle Hill, Templepatrick was within walking distance of the Mallusk/Craigarogan area.

At some point in his early life and well before the Rebellion, Orr made the transition from avid reader to writer, accomplished and politically committed enough to provide copy on an occasional basis for the *Northern Star*. He is believed to have received encouragement in this from the Templepatrick poet and hedge schoolmaster, Samuel Thomson. Thomson, Orr's senior by a mere four years, gathered around him a coterie of young men who composed verse and who were enthusiastic readers of the works of Robert Burns, perceived by many in 1790s Ulster as a politically radical poet. Orr's name appears as 'James Orr (Jnr.)' on the list of subscribers to Thomson's first volume of poetry which was published in 1793, meaning he must have offered his subscription some time before that date. Henry Joy McCracken's name also appears on that list.[29] Orr may initially have met Thomson at a reading society, or he may have been introduced to him by Hope or Mullan, both of whom were also weavers. Alternatively, hungry for advice and tuition, he may have gone in search of Thomson as a result of the latter's growing reputation.

McDowell, in his 'Sketch' of Orr's life, explicitly states that Orr's 'first appearance before the public was in the *Northern Star*, a newspaper at that time published in Belfast':

> the pieces which he wrote for this paper obtained for him a considerable degree of notice ... They appeared under a fictitious signature, and were mostly of a political nature ... Flattered by the attentions which he received, he continued to publish occasionally down to the unhappy period of 1798.[30]

Encoded within McDowell's rather mealy-mouthed account, which neglects to mention that the *Northern Star* was the organ of the United Irishmen, is the information that Orr acquired a significant reputation as an articulate radical. From it we may legitimately infer that Orr's work was admired by leaders of the movement who read or wrote for the *Northern Star* themselves, and by the population of east Antrim where United Irish support was strong. None of Orr's later published verse is to be found in the *Northern Star* but an essay included on 12 January 1792, just a few editions into the paper's life span, is signed 'O', and may well be his.

The essay, written when Orr can have been no more than twenty-one or twenty-two is perhaps what one would expect of an intelligent, well-read, socially aware and committed young man. The writer begins with a brief discussion on the significance of the printing press but speedily moves to the related and highly pertinent issue of press freedom. In the course of his essay he covers the European and American Revolutions of which he is, of course, approving; the politician Charles James Fox, whom he commends as a champion of press liberty; the plight of Roman Catholics whose situation he describes as 'aliens in their own country'; the injustices suffered by the Presbyterians; and the deplorable nature of the sport of hunting. The essay concludes with an emotive piece of anti-hunting verse, siding with the hare, 'the weak, helpless, timid flying creature'. In short, the writer has supplied a barnstorming, comprehensive performance which would undoubtedly have gained him 'a considerable degree of notice'. In many passages the essay prefigures opinions and vocabulary employed in Orr's mature work. His genuine belief in religious toleration for all denominational groupings, and his anger at 'the fruits of [Presbyterian] industry devoured' by a 'rapacious hierarchy' appear in several later poems.[31] His disapproval of hunting is evident from 'Song, Written in Winter'; his recommendation that people should acquire more civilized habits through 'the study of science, or the polish of literature' is echoed in the concluding stanza of 'The Penitent'.[32]

Orr's work for the *Northern Star* certainly established him as a staunch radical writer while the friendship with Thomson linked him with other literary radicals, but evidence exists from which we may infer his connections with *activists* – the younger northern United Irish leadership, in particular the weaver Jemmy Hope. Hope was of similar age to Thomson and both grew up in the neighbourhood of Templepatrick, a village that lies near to Craigarogan and not far from the county town of Antrim. Both were members of the Presbyterian Seceder congregation there – a particularly pietistic and Calvinistic sect.[33]

In his memoirs Hope remembered the *Northern Star* as a powerful moral force. He also revealed the process by which the Society of United Irishmen developed its network of members: a promising man, often a member of a local Volunteer company, would be approached and invited to join a United Irish Society. Then, as the group grew in size, it would divide into further companies under cover of Volunteer membership.[34] Hope was approached while a member of the Roughford Volunteers and invited to join the Highton Society of United Irishmen. From that group a deputation formed the Molusk [Mallusk] Society.[35] Significantly, Orr too appears to have been a Volunteer. In his 'Elegy Written in Templecorran Churchyard' he remembers the pride in his father's eyes as he watched his son marching with the brave 'in self-raised ranks' (l. 88).[36]

The Volunteer–United Irish–*Northern Star* network with which Orr became involved maintained shadowy links with a highly ambitious radical network that, inspired by the successful revolutions in America and France, had developed throughout the British archipelago. That the Government had monitored and taken alarm at its growth is very evident in the 'Report from the Committee of Secrecy to the House of Commons' made following the Rebellion in 1799. The report found 'the clearest proofs' of a 'systematic design', resting on 'those destructive principles, which originally produced the French Revolution', to overthrow 'every existing establishment, civil or ecclesiastical, both in Great Britain and Ireland; as well as to dissolve the connexion between the two kingdoms'. Within its narrative, with unconcealed horror, the report discussed the dissemination of the works of Paine 'and other seditious and impious publications' throughout the kingdom, and purported to expose the links between The United Irishmen, the London Corresponding Society, and the Friends of the People in Scotland.[37]

The strength of the Scottish connection, and the enthusiasm among the Ulster United Irishmen in particular for developing their movement in the country that was such a short distance from them across the North Channel, and with which they had strong historic and contemporary links, is confirmed by the researches of Elaine McFarland.[38] She notes that

> The Belfast leadership had been making full use of emissaries to boost numbers and to spread their political ideology at home since 1795. McCabe, McCracken and the self-educated James Hope are the best known examples in an extensive network of agents ... in Scotland, peripatetic hawkers of Irish linens and cheap cloth were a familiar sight, as were a swelling complement of Irish beggars and vagrants. This itinerant population could provide a useful cover for United work, much as they did in Ireland, where pedlars and packmen were also employed directly to disseminate radical literature.[39]

The 1790s proved a period of great optimism when many believed that all three kingdoms were progressing towards liberty and democracy on a great global tide. This global perspective, and with it general enthusiasm for tolerant egalitarianism in every sphere, is evident from even the most cursory scanning of the columns of the *Northern Star*: a recent revolution in Poland was commended for 'having caught its spirit from the American', extracts from works such as Wollstonecraft's *A Vindication of the Rights of Woman* (1792) were incorporated, and the poetry column might include anything from samples of the works of Burns to pieces deploring the evils of the Slave Trade.[40] This was the world with which Orr through his literary connections and his friendships with activists now directly engaged.

Hope, in his autobiography, speaks of his own relationship to the United Irish leadership. His respect for McCracken, the son of a prosperous mill owner, and his commitment to their friendship which transcended the class barrier are evident throughout, but crucially he states: 'I received my orders generally from

Russell, Wilson and McCracken, and communicated with several persons I was sworn never to name'.[41] It is highly feasible that Orr, already in a position of trust through his Volunteer membership and his reputation as a rising writer on radical subjects, could have been one of those persons to whom Hope communicated orders from Russell or McCracken. McCracken and Hope were very intimately connected with the production of the *Northern Star*.[42] This provides a further link with Orr and it may be that he was their main contact in the Ballycarry region. The course of events on 7 June 1798 within and beyond Orr's native village also suggests this.

From 1795 government repression drove the United Irishmen underground and convinced many that revolution with the assistance of the French, rather than simply reform, was the only possible way ahead. Dixon Donaldson (1866–1943), who collected the local history of the Larne, Ballycarry and Islandmagee district for a privately printed account of 1927, reports that the original oath taken by northern members of United Societies was as follows:

> 'I — do voluntarily declare that I will persevere and endeavour to form a Brotherhood of affection amongst Irishmen of every religious persuasion. I do further declare that I will persevere and endeavour for a Parliamentary Reform, and for an equal representation of all the people in Ireland. So help me God.'

As the authorities adopted repressive measures towards the United Irishmen they 're-formed as a secret society and the oath [was] considerably modified to suit the intention of those who had now determined, with the aid of France, to set up a republic'.[43]

Events such as the show trial of the Presbyterian William Orr, followed by his powerful and moving pre-execution speech at Carrickfergus and burial at Templepatrick, enraged and grieved Presbyterians throughout the province of Ulster, but must have proved particularly potent for those, including James Orr, Thomson, Hope and their circle, for whom those towns were extremely close to home.[44] Finally, the destruction of the printing presses of the *Northern Star* silenced the voice of public protest, delivering a blow to those such as Orr whose works throughout his life show his preference for mounting a challenge to injustice with reasoned argument.

W. Mayne Knox (d. 1924), a local author, historian and journalist spent a holiday in Ballycarry in the early 1920s. During that time, much closer than today to the date of the Rebellion itself and to Orr's lifetime, he collected information and traditions about him. While the nature of Knox's evidence was anecdotal, he was certainly inclined to ascribe to Orr a leading role in garnering support within Ballycarry for United Irish activity, as he reveals here: 'It is quite likely that the influence of James Orr the Ballycarry poet was the main reason for the adhesion of the villagers to the cause of the United Irishmen'.[45]

To achieve a more lucid impression of the level of Orr's importance to the United Irish movement in the Ballycarry district, it is necessary to consider further evidence regarding the course of events within and beyond Broadisland on 7 June 1798. McDowell, in a characteristic piece of humbuggery, attempted to draw a veil over the extent of his friend's involvement by taking refuge in a convenient but implausible memory lapse: 'Whether he held any official situation in the associations of that period, the writer of this does not remember to have heard'. Yet even McDowell admits that Orr was involved in the Rising.[46]

The most detailed account of events involving Ballycarry men on that date is to be found in the work of the local historian Dixon Donaldson. Of Orr's contributions to the *Northern Star* Donaldson remarks: 'It was perhaps this association with their journal that led him into the confidence of the leaders of the revolutionary party of the period', which suggests that Orr's position in the confidence of the United Irish leadership was an accepted fact.[47] Donaldson cites information from James Burns, also a Ballycarry man and known as 'The Old Croppy', who was an eyewitness of most of the events described and is buried close to Orr in Templecorran churchyard.

Donaldson records how the Islandmagee United men were summoned across Larne Lough to Ballycarry to muster in front of Red Hall, which Richard Ker had quitted earlier, aware that a Rising was imminent and that the men of Ballycarry would be deeply involved. The house was broken into and arms, which Ker had disabled, seized. A letter from Ker to his brother from the period of the Rising reveals that he was actively involved in quelling it, thus indicating the extent of the division in political opinions that existed between him and his tenants. He wrote: 'As to myself I am in Garrison and we yesterday declared for permanent duty, so that I could not be at Red Hall, for any constancy ... We are all in good spirits on this side of the water.'[48]

Donaldson's version confirms several details mentioned by Orr in his vernacular poem 'Donegore Hill', first published in 1804.[49] Donaldson describes how the assembled men were seen off by the women, while not all who had promised to turn out actually did so:

> Amongst the crowd assembled to see the 'boys' off, were women and children, whose entreaties prevailed on several of them to withdraw from the ranks at the last moment; others, from the vigilance and preparations of the previous night, or from an over-indulgence at the adjacent refreshment house, were found to be unfit to march with their comrades.[50]

Similarly, Orr recalls:

> But when the pokes o' provender
>   Were slung on *ilka* shoulder, ['every'
> Hags, wha to henpeck didna spare,

> *Loot* out the yells the louder. – ['let'
> Had they, *whan* blood about their heart ['when'
> *Cauld* fear made cake, an' *crudle*, ['cold', 'curdle'
> *Ta'en twa* rash gills *frae* Herdman's quart,[51] ['taken two', 'from'
> *'Twad* rous'd the calm, slow puddle ['it would have'
> I' their veins that day.[52] (ll. 28–36)

He also remarks contemptuously that some '*hade* like hens in byre-neuks' ['hid'] (l. 13) in order to avoid the muster.

Donaldson mentions a meal of bread and cheese taken during a pause on the march in the neighbourhood of Ballynure, after which some insurgents tried to disappear from the ranks by pretending to urinate or to remove gravel from their boots.[53] In Orr's version we read:

> Some fastin' yet, now strave to eat
>   The piece that butter yellow'd;
> An' some, in flocks, drank out cream crocks,
>   That wives but little valu'd:
> Some *lettin' on their burn to mak'*, ['pretending to urinate'
>   The rear-guard, goadin', hasten'd; (ll. 46–51)

Eventually, a greatly reduced force pushed on to Donegore only to find that the Battle of Antrim was lost and all but concluded, and that insurgents were fleeing all over the country with troops and yeomanry in pursuit. As Orr vividly described:

> The camp's *brak* up. *Owre braes*, an bogs, ['broken', 'over hills'
>   The patriots seek their sections;
> Arms, ammunition, bread-bags, brogues,
>   Lye *skail'd* in a' directions: ['scattered'
> Ane half, alas! *Wad* fear'd to face ['would have'
>   Auld Fogies, *faps*, or women;[54] (ll. 73–8) ['fops'

Given that Orr is undoubtedly drawing on his own memories to describe the march to Donegore and the Broadisland troop's experience there, it is worth also exploring the poem for clues confirming his leadership on 7 June, which is strongly suggested in several passages. The third stanza, for example, is clearly spoken by a commander who is recalling his review of his mustered troop and includes his evaluation of their individual usefulness:

> A brave man firmly *leain'* hame ['leaving'
>   I ay was proud to think on;
> The wife-obeyin' son o' shame
>   Wi' kindling *e'e* I blink on: (ll. 19–22) ['eye'

The same 'son o' shame' is then disclosed promising his wife that he will desert 'before the morn / In spite o' a' our chieftains' (ll. 26–7). Thus Orr, one of the 'chieftains' in question, is taking the opportunity in verse of letting the deserter know that he was overheard. This is one of several instances of 'fingering' by Orr in a mini-narrative running throughout the poem which is composed of episodes directly related to one of his major preoccupations: the exposure and condemnation of treachery. A further such episode involves an individual who mistook colourful weeds in the distance for 'Nugent's redcoats, bright in arms' (l. 70).[55] This caused a panic that sent half the force into flight. As if reliving the incident in flashback, the narrator's voice utters the imperative: 'Come back ye dastards!' followed by a further withering evaluation that has the ring of some military-style authority: 'martial worth you're clear o"(ll. 82, 87).

Orr stops short of naming the person who took fright, but he does send a clear signal that he knows his name by including a series of asterisks in the text that signify a Christian name and a surname of seven and five letters respectively: 'For ******* ***** took ragweed farms ...' (l. 68). A similar code is used later in the poem, in a reference of great significance. It appears towards the conclusion of 'Donegore Hill' as Orr imagines the conversation between one of the deserters and his wife on his return home:

> What joy at hame our entrance gave!
>   'Guid God! is't you? fair fa' ye! –
> 'Twas wise, tho' fools may ca't no' brave,
>   To rin or e'er they saw ye.' –
> 'Aye wife, that's true without dispute,
>   But lest saunts fail in Zion,
> I'll hae to swear *** forced me out;
>   Better he swing than I, on
>   Some hangin' day'. (ll. 109–17)

The asterisks this time indicate a name of three letters: Orr. This surely identifies Orr as a leader who was responsible for ensuring the Ballycary men turned out as they had promised to do – a role which exposed him to resentment and to further treachery as the recalcitrant informed on him to ensure their own safety.[56] It is also worth noting that McDowell's account of Orr's activities states that: 'his conduct will long be remembered in having been actively employed in preventing his companions committing acts of cruelty'.[57] This too suggests that Orr exercised a leadership role and did so to prevent the commission of atrocities.

Orr, in all likelihood because of the position of authority he had held, felt unable to creep back to Ballycarry as many of his troop did. Following the Battle of Antrim, Reverend Bankhead went to Carrickfergus to assure the military authorities that most of the inhabitants had 'returned, very sensible of their folly, and that the Donegore party are quite dispersed'.[58] This resulted in the issue of a pardon to all who immediately reported and handed in their arms. Excluded from this, however, were the leaders. James Burns claimed that Orr's name was on a wanted list of 'fifty pounders' – men considered significant enough to attract a reward of fifty pounds, a very considerable sum, for their capture.[59] Burns also reported that Orr was among those whom Henry Joy McCracken and Jemmy Hope trusted enough to share their period on the run in the area of Slemish, near Ballymena, and later in the district of Glenwherry.[60] Several of Orr's poems published in his 1804 and 1817 volumes make reference to this time as a renegade. These include the fairly well-known 'The Wanderer', an enigmatic song in which a young woman gives shelter to a desperate fugitive.[61] Orr's cousin Thomas Beggs, also a poet, alluded to the same incident:

> Where Slemish lifts his barren head
> Enamoured of the nipping air,
> Beneath the herdsman's hearth-less shed,
> The smile of mercy met him there
> And purple Collin's healthy height
> And Wherry's fairy-haunted glen,
> Have often seen the luckless wight,
> Like felon, seek a secret den.[62]

According to McDowell Orr's decision to go to America was a personal one, taken because 'he did not imagine himself safe in his own country'.[63] The latter is in keeping with Burns's claim that Orr was a 'fifty pounder' and with Orr's brief references to his wanderings as a fugitive in Ireland, made in his little-known work 'To Miss Owenson: the Authoress of *The Wild Irish Girl*'. The poem was published in his posthumous volume, but had appeared in the *Belfast Commercial Chronicle* on 2 May 1807:

> Ne'er shall I, thro' bigot blindness,
>   My compatriot's virtues stain;
> Far from home, I've proved their kindness
>   On my country's wildest plain:
> To their language quite a stranger,
>   Looks of love their soul express'd,
> While they shelter'd me from danger,
> Trimm'd their fire, and shar'd their feast.[64] (ll. 25–32)

This stanza is clearly written in praise of Irish-speaking Catholic peasants who had offered the poet asylum. This work and the earlier 'The Wanderer', set near Slemish, suggest he was familiar with a network of safe houses across the country, and are suggestive of the extent to which he was in the confidence of supporters not only in the United Irish movement but also, perhaps, among the mainly Catholic Defender movement.[65]

A further piece of tradition which supports the argument that Orr was, and had been for several years, on terms of intimacy with Jemmy Hope is to be found in the popular ballad 'McCracken's Ghost'. This appears in R. M. Young's commemorative work on the rebellion issued sometime prior to the centenary year. Young quotes James Burns's claim, that the ballad was 'a song made by James Hope (Belfast) and James Orr (Ballycarry), after his return from America'.[66] The poem portrays an appearance of the ghost of Henry Joy McCracken to an unidentified narrator in the dead of night. If it is indeed a joint composition by Hope and Orr it demonstrates that they were fully in each other's confidence and further links Orr to McCracken himself.

Hope's memoirs provide another tantalizing hint that he and Orr were of similar minds and that they may have discussed their opinions and experiences at length. In recalling his life as an active radical in the 1790s, Hope stated that when he first heard of the secret, oath-bound Society of United Irishmen his reaction was that 'oaths will never bind rogues'.[67] There is a striking similarity between this opinion and Orr's acerbic remarks about the craven deserters in 'Donegore Hill':

> ... what'er ilk *loun* ['every fellow'
> May swear to never *swithrin'*, ['dithering'
> In ev'ry pinch, he'll basely flinch –
> 'Guidbye to ye, my brethren'.
>   He'll cry that day. (ll. 95–9)

Finally, it should be noted that Richard Gervase Ker of Red Hall was in no doubt that Orr had been a dangerous subversive within his community. When, during the Napoleonic invasion crisis, Orr attempted to join the Ballycarry yeomanry, formed in 1800, Ker, so the local story goes, objected to him, which occasioned James Campbell's poem 'The Rejected Yeoman'.[68] Before this event occurred, however, Orr had briefly experienced life in the American Republic. He would return to an Ireland on the verge of Union with Britain.

3 THE CONSTRUCTION OF THE BARD OF BALLYCARRY: JAMES ORR (1798–1804)

James Orr's first volume of verse did not appear until 1804, by which time he had returned from his brief period of enforced exile in America. Following the Rising, and for a period during the late autumn of 1798 or spring of 1799, he fled, probably to the neighbourhood of Philadelphia, as according to McDowell he did not believe himself 'safe in his own country'.[1] While Orr left virtually nothing as a record of his brief period in enforced exile, the experience was clearly deeply significant and traumatic for him. We must now consider what may be gleaned, or at least inferred, about that experience. What were the effects of the 'sea-change' he suffered? How does he emerge from it as a poet and a patriot?

James 'Balloon' Tytler, an exiled Scots radical, travelled to Philadelphia in 1795, after a period in Belfast. During his voyage he composed an ode in praise of America where, he writes, 'Fair Liberty her Course began' (l. 84).[2] The United Irish leader Wolfe Tone spent a period in Philadelphia in 1795 before going on to France but was far less complimentary. He describes the people of Philadelphia as 'a disgusting race, eaten up with all the vice of commerce and the vilest of all pride, the pride of the purse'. About fellow Irishmen who had migrated to Pennsylvania he says: 'If you meet a confirmed blackguard, you may be sure he is Irish'.[3] So how satisfactory or otherwise was Orr's experience of the 'city of brotherly love'?

Shiploads of emigrants regularly set sail for the new world from the east Antrim port of Larne on the Ulster coast, close to Orr's home village. His poem 'The Passengers' (1804) depicts a voyage to Newcastle on the Delaware near Philadelphia which is so vividly realized that it has the ring of personal experience.[4] It portrays migrants leaving Ballycarry with heavy hearts, boarding a ship and experiencing the confusion and overcrowding of the passenger quarters in the ship's hold. Catholics and Protestants are cooped up together along with distraught parents trying to comfort crying babies. Orr also mentions the presence of 'blacks wha a' before them drave' (l. 111). These are aggressive young men, probably fugitives from the late Rebellion, who are soon left pathetically 'cheepin'' (l. 112) like chickens when a violent storm breaks on the vessel. The term 'blacks' may have been employed as shorthand for 'blackguards', meaning dangerous rascals, or may hint at Presbyterians, who were often known colloquially as 'blackmouths'. It may be intended by Orr humorously to combine the two meanings. Additionally, it may encode a reminder to the reader of the human cargo of black slaves carried to America by many emigrant ships.

Migrant diaries record that the voyage could take as long as eleven or twelve weeks if the weather was severe, putting a great strain on supplies. In addition, passengers were entirely at the mercy of crew and captain. Orr claimed, for example, that the crew threatened to dry shave any male passenger who refused to pay a shilling 'poll-tax' once the ship reached the Banks of Newfoundland. Naturally, with passengers cooped up for so long, disease quickly spread. In his 'Song Composed on the Banks of Newfoundland' (1804),[5] Orr refers to the ship as 'A huge floating lazar-house, far, far at sea' (l. 24), while the following tragic detail is included in a letter from a migrant from Carrickfergus who made the journey in 1773:

> It has pleased God to spare all the principals of our two families, but it was sore on our children; for on the 19th of June, Tommy Jackson died, and the day after the two girls, to our great grief, both died in one hour. This was the greatest trouble I ever felt, to see our two fine girls thrown into the ocean after they had been seven weeks on board.[6]

Storms and disease were not the only dangers that beset the voyagers, however. The *Northern Star* attempted to make political capital from reports confirming the villainy of the British whose naval vessels regularly intercepted emigrant ships and press-ganged the male passengers into service, as the following brief account from 1796 reveals: 'The Susanna, Captain Baird, from hence, arrived at Philadelphia on 17th July – She was boarded on her passage by two British frigates and forty-six of the passengers taken out!!! – Oh! Ireland! Independent Ireland!'[7] Orr's 'The Passengers' (1804) records panic breaking out among the males aboard when a ship was sighted. The cry goes up, 'is she British, wat ye, / Or French, this day?' (ll. 152–3), and he appears to place his hopes in the latter, but in truth vessels were in as much danger from them as from the Royal Navy. The ship turned out to be a brig from Baltimore bound for Larne, so the panic was soon over. Morgan Jellett, in his record of a trip to America from Dublin in 1799, describes how the vessel in which he had travelled was confronted by a French privateer. The emigrant ship's captain effected a daring nautical manoeuvre to foil the would-be attackers, as he was well aware that his cargo of Irish linen represented a valuable prize to the French, and that his crew and passengers would be robbed, then left to rot in a prison in San Domingo.[8]

It is likely that Orr disembarked at Newcastle on the Delaware, as did the passengers in his poem. While Scotch-Irish migrants had been welcomed during the American Revolutionary era the Republic was to prove much less welcoming to Orr's generation of radicals. Already in 1797 Harrison Gray Otis had stated, 'I do not wish to invite hordes of wild Irishmen, nor the turbulent and disorderly of all parts of the world, to come here with a view to disturb our tranquillity'.[9] Orr appears, in any case, to have settled briefly in the neighbourhood of Philadelphia where little work in his own trade of weaving was available, though this thriving, expanding cosmopolitan city port did offer well-paid employment for painters, carpenters and glaziers.[10] McDowell records that he found work with a newspaper, in which a number of his poems were published, prefaced with a commendation from the editor.[11] Perhaps he had hoped to establish himself once again in a literary set, among the thinkers and exiles who had found shelter in the city. There is evidence that other migrants from the Ballycarry district went to Philadelphia in the 1798–9 period and with some of them he may have lodged.[12] In addition, a United Irish society existed in the city, which drew the wrath of William Cobbett who, as America threatened to go to war with the Napoleonic regime, alleged a French–United Irish conspiracy against the American Government.[13]

In many respects the cosmopolitan nature of the city, where the tolerance and liberty to which Orr was committed were everywhere in evidence, would surely have suited him. Burial lists reveal the rich variety of religious denominations among Philadelphia's population, including Episcopalians, Presbyterians, Universalists, Free Quakers, Moravians and many others.[14] Also advertised in the newspapers are meetings of the philosophical societies and Masonic Lodges in which Orr would have had an interest. Above all, he must have been impressed by press reports of free elections.[15] These, along with advertisements for theatrical productions and lists of new works of literature, geography and philosophy recalled the *Northern Star* and its characteristic brand, comprising politics, literature and culture.

A report in the *Philadelphia Gazette* in the late autumn of 1798 makes clear that the British authorities were relentlessly suppressing any potential for further rebellious action in the neighbourhood of Ballycarry. The people were under curfew between 9 pm and 5 am and families were warned that they would be 'visited frequently' and held accountable for any absentees.[16] Nevertheless, Orr still chose after a very brief period in America to return home. The period of his residence was certainly inauspicious for any who held, or might be suspected of holding, French sympathies. France, already at war with Britain, was no longer perceived as a fine example of free republicanism, but as a burgeoning and predatory colonial power. One correspondent of the *Philadelphia Gazette* wrote as follows:

> When we fix our attention upon the scenes which occur on the other side of the Atlantic and take into view the insidious conduct of France towards the neighbouring states – when her avowal of 'respect for the rights of nations' is discredited by every act of her government ...[17]

Undoubtedly Orr, an honest and logical thinker, received in America a wider perspective on French ambition than had been available to him in Ireland. Reports on the aftermath of the Irish Rebellion which appeared intermittently in the Philadelphia papers included an account of the French occupation of Castlebar in the west of Ireland. The report detailed a great amount of food, drink and other supplies requisitioned by the French, and the anti-Gallic tone is clear from the cynical editorial comment appended: 'At this rate of paying themselves, the French must find it no unprofitable trade to deal in revolution'.[18]

The continuing rise of Napoleon only endorsed such fears and Orr, in common with many who had hailed the dawn of the French Revolution as 'blissful', may have begun to recoil from what appeared to be out and out tyranny. However, certain other aspects of life in the United States may also have caused him to wish to return home since the liberty professed did not, as he would have observed, extend equally to all its inhabitants. Apart from newspaper advertisements offering to rent out the time of 'negro servants' which would have been both shocking and offensive to Orr as an opponent of slavery,[19] he found himself in America in the period of the Alien and Sedition Acts which looked likely to curtail precious press freedom and implied suspicion of migrants such as himself who could look forward to a long period of probation before they would be fully accepted. These acts, which in large measure arose as a result of American fears concerning security during the period of preparation for war with France, became law during the Federalist John Adams's presidency in 1798. The acts required immigrants to reside for fourteen years in order to attain citizenship, rather than five as previously. They additionally permitted the imprisonment or deportation of aliens considered 'dangerous to the peace and safety of the United States' and restricted speech critical of the government.[20] As David Wilson explains, 'By 1798, when revolution was crushed in Ireland and the Alien and Sedition Acts were passed in America, it appeared to many United Irishmen ... that the republican experiment had gone off track'.[21]

That United Irish migrants resented the acts and took direct action against them which was in turn resented by the authorities is very clear from the following report from Philadelphia, reprinted in Belfast on 21 April 1799:

> The repose of the city was yesterday (Sunday) disturbed by a more daring and flagitious riot than we remember to have outraged the civil law and the decorum of society for more than 40 years. Four men (two of whom are United Irishmen, and the other two of a similar description of character) had the effrontery to assault the members of the Catholic Church, during divine service, with a most seditious and inflammatory petition against the Alien and Sedition laws.[22]

Clearly the city authorities had no wish to see their prosperous burgh rendered disreputable by displaced Irish radicals.

Orr may have experienced disillusionment with America, with France, or indeed with both, and this may have contributed to his decision to return quickly to Ireland. McDowell said only that in America he 'did not find the kindred home he expected'.[23] Orr himself in a gloomy poem from his 1804 volume refers thus to his experience in exile, without specifying details: 'With upright ends I sought a happier plain; / But was unfortunate where felons thrive' (ll. 25–6).[24] Orr's contemporary, the better-known Irish poet Thomas Moore who visited America in the early nineteenth century, also discovered that life and society there did not live up to his expectations. In a series of verse Epistles he exposed and deplored corruption, hypocrisy and in particular the abuses of slavery:

> Who can, with patience, for a moment see
> The medley mass of pride and misery,
> O whips and charters, manacles and rights,
> Of slaving black and democratic whites ...[25] (ll. 137–40).

So whether from disillusionment or from sheer homesickness Orr returned to his own community during the period immediately prior to the Union of the British and Irish parliaments. An Amnesty Bill had been passed in the British House of Commons in July 1798 with all but the United Irish leaders exempted from its provisions. It was this exception that must have caused Orr to fear for his safety in his own country, for as Charles Teeling recalled, 'To charge a proscribed individual with leadership was to ensure the conviction of the accused ... It was in vain for the accused to plead the general act of amnesty in his favour.'[26] Clearly, by the time of his return Orr judged the risk of arrest to have significantly decreased.

Late twentieth-century research into the experience of migrants has documented the 'myth of return' syndrome, in which the exile comes to terms with the shock of displacement by comforting himself with idealized memories of his homeland and by resolving one day to return to it.[27] For a forced migrant such as Orr, the situation would have been complex, in that the sense of security, familiarity and belonging we associate with home had become broken before he left. Some of his neighbours, as we have seen, had disappointed him by their desertions on Donegore Hill, while he clearly believed that there were others who had actually betrayed him. Undoubtedly his own position and relationships would have required renegotiation on his return, and some of his actions and his publications in the early 1800s should be understood as part of a difficult process of re-rooting.

How then did Orr adapt to the changed circumstances? He found no *Northern Star* ready to accept radical essays or provocative patriotic verse, while those would-be rebels who had escaped the initial punitive Government response to the Rising had adopted a low profile. Samuel Thomson's poem 'To a Hedgehog' captures something of the atmosphere in the Antrim countryside in the aftermath of the Rising:

Now creep awa the way ye came,
And tend your squeakin pups at hame;
Gin Colley should o'erhear the same,
    It might be fatal,
For you, wi' a' the pikes ye claim,
      Wi' him to battle.[28] (ll. 61–6)

The spiky, secretive creature Thomson observes and warns to disappear in the early morning may well function as a symbol of the many farmers and labourers who went out to battle armed with pikes in June 1798, while 'Colley', the sheepdog, represents the ever-menacing authorities.

We may picture Orr's return to Ballycarry, then. What appears certain is his undisguised relief at finding himself once more at his own fireside, while after that the poetry he published in two volumes and in newspapers between 1804 and 1817 reveals that his commitment to his country's well-being and to social justice never wavered.[29] He employed his published 1804 volume in particular to provide an honest record of his experience on 'active service', perhaps in an attempt to achieve what we would now understand as emotional closure.[30] If that was indeed his object, he was rather less than completely successful.

The period of 1799–1800 was a tense one throughout Ireland. In the wake of the Rebellion the British Government was preparing to assimilate Ireland into the United Kingdom. The purpose was, in part at least, to divest the Ascendancy-dominated Dublin Parliament of its powers and to allow a new start in a more liberal atmosphere which would eventually permit Catholic Emancipation. Maintaining national security and consolidating Britain's growing imperial status, however, were also important factors. On Orr's return, the situation in the countryside and fears regarding security made him an object of suspicion to the Establishment. Externally, due to the rising Napoleonic threat, the situation was tense and unsettled, while according to Ian McBride the government continued to experience anxiety over a continuing 'spirit of discontent' in counties Antrim, Down and Londonderry a full year after the Rebellion had been quashed: 'Dublin Castle continued to receive reports of arms raids, pike manufacturing, the assassination of loyalists and the activities of outlaw rebel leaders'.[31] A letter from Richard Gervase Ker of Red Hall, Ballycarry to his brother in London, dated 20 December 1799, reveals the anxieties of Orr's own landlord during the pre-Union period:

> I ought to have been this day at Ballyleidy, but I must stay at home to look after Banditti. Six or seven murders have happened in less than a fortnight in this Country – and a letter from the Commander at Ballimena recd. this day says that several parties of Armed Men have been seen, and nightly patrols are now established ... The Banditti have attacked no place where they expect resistance, and I am determined they shall have it from me. To say the truth, I think we are worse than ever.[32]

Despite Ker's robust declaration, he clearly feels besieged. In such circumstances it is hardly surprising that he refused Orr's application to join the yeomanry following his return. But how may we understand such a request on the part of this formerly radical 'young Turk'?[33]

The circumstances in which the Ballycarry yeomanry became established may supply an answer, for it was formed in response to the Napoleonic threat, so Orr's request may be understood not as a *volte face*, but as entirely consistent with his determination to resist despotism wherever he detected it. On 9 October 1805, on the eve of the Battle of Trafalgar, he published a soliloquy-style monologue in the *Belfast Commercial Chronicle* in which Napoleon, the newly crowned emperor, is portrayed weltering in a morass of guilt and anxiety:

> Can shouts like these allay the widow's pain,
>   Who tells her infant, of its sire bereav'd,
> How many thousands bled, like him, in vain,
>   To free the land that BONAPARTE enslav'd?[34] (ll. 5–8)

While Orr had a home and a trade to return to, his reputation as a radical writer on political subjects potentially made his poetry deeply suspect, given his history. His experience of failure and flight may also have exposed him to ridicule or pity, though no doubt some who had proved less than true to their United Irish oaths on Donegore Hill may have dreaded the tale he might tell of them. Yet by 1804 we find him accepted as a published poet, his volume subscribed to by a large proportion of the population of Ballycarry, including Richard Gervase Ker. Once again Orr achieved a prominent role in village life, not as an activist but as 'The Bard of Ballycarry', respected, affectionate chronicler and observer of village life. How was this reinvention effected? To what extent is it, in fact, a reinvention at all?

Orr appears speedily to have re-established his relationships with respected community figures. One of these was Rev. John Bankhead who became the recipient of the poem 'The Penitent' (1800) very soon after Orr's return; it is a poem which extols the virtuous effects on Christy Blair, a drunken weaver, of his conversion to Methodism and may have been offered as a contribution to a theological debate between Orr and the moderately New Light Presbyterian Bankhead.

Relationships such as that with Bankhead may be understood as Orr's respectable, public face. In addition, however, it is alleged he kept faith with his past, and with the subversive, revolutionary figures he still regarded as heroes; if 'the Old Croppy' James Burns's recollections are accurate, Orr reconnected with Jemmy Hope to write the Romantic ballad 'McCracken's Ghost' in honour of the hanged Northern leader. The following lines, spoken by McCracken's spirit, evince a diehard determination, while invoking dead United Irish comrades and recalling the issues that motivated them:

> 'Fear nothing,' he said, 'though my visage be wan,
> It was I lately fell for the dear rights of man;
> I have witnessed your grief, though the green isle lies low,
> Her wrecks and her robberies, her wants and her woe.
> While Stor[e]y lay martyred, and Dickey lay dead,
> And the hands of oppressors on spires placed their heads,
> Their spirits in glory triumphed to the skies,
> And proclaimed through the air that the Croppies would rise. (ll. 9–16)
>
> ...
>
> 'The time is at hand when the heads of the slaves
> Will be took from the spears to make room for the knaves,
> The wanderers in glory then home shall return,
> The 'tender' shall sink, and the prisons shall burn.
> Your sons shall be eased of their taxes and tithes,
> And our brethren in peace turn their swords into scythes.[35] (ll. 21–6)

Orr became renowned for his gentleness and his abhorrence of violence, as his own poem 'A Prayer, Written on the Eve of the Unfortunate 7th June' indicates,[36] but 'McCracken's Ghost' exposes another side of his character: tough, ardent in his demand for justice and unflinching in his loyalty to those who had already laid their lives on the line. Presumably this explains his actions in marching armed to Donegore, and it was this aspect of his nature that had to be suppressed in the light of the subjugation of the rebels. Such self-stifling, along with his dashed hopes, undoubtedly stimulated the sense of alienation, the melancholy, and the identification with the 'outsider' that can be observed in much of his work.

Deeply significant in Orr's process of reintegration proved the friendships associated with Samuel Thomson's circle. While there is some uncertainty regarding what exactly Thomson may have been doing on 7 June 1798 while Orr was on the road to Donegore Hill, his activities in the immediately pre-Union period are easier to determine. He published a second volume of poetry in 1799,[37] and during 1799–80 he contributed pieces to the *Microscope; or Minute Observer*, a literary journal that ran for those years and provided a focus for many Northerners who had certainly supported reform and emancipation, if not outright revolution, and who now opposed the Union. William Drennan, one of the founders of the United Irishmen, was a contributor and the journal became a forerunner of the *Belfast Monthly Magazine* which Drennan co-edited and developed during the 1800s. Thomson the hedge-schoolmaster who had inspired and provided a sounding board in his cottage circle for, among others, more active revolutionary young men from the working classes, was now at the edge of a more refined, intellectual, 'left-of-centre' milieu. This circle Orr was about to enter.

It appears that for a time a least a coolness existed between the two poets. One speculates that this may, in part at least, have occurred as a result of their different experiences of '98, from which Thomson appears to have emerged unscathed while Orr was driven into exile. In addition, Thomson sought patronage for his writing from the landlord class while Orr rejected any such course. Orr's 'Epistle: To S. Thomson of Carngranny. A Brother Poet' (1804), written in the complex *Cherrie and the Slae* stanza, seems to have been composed in order to re-establish their relationship but includes a warning against imploring 'on supple knee, / The proud folks patronage' (ll. 72–3).[38] The poem reveals much about Orr's state of mind in the Union period, expressing his relief at his return, his regret that he and Thomson have not communicated for some time and underlining his continuing commitment to his country. It demonstrates Orr's desire to reconnect with old friends and mentors, but on his own terms. Thus he warns Thomson that he has no interest in currying favour with the rich, aware that this might too easily deprive him of his independence.

In the *Microscope* there are pieces suggestive of Orr's pen. Undoubtedly, he would have fully endorsed the sentiments expressed in the following verses from a poem titled 'My Native Home' and ascribed to 'A Patriot':

> O'er breezy hill or woodland glade
>   At morning's dawn or closing day,
> In Summer's flaunting pomp array'd,
>   Or pensive moonlight's silver grey,
> The man in sadness still shall roam
>   Who wanders from his Native Home.[39] (ll. 1–8)

In addition to the poetry of local writers, the *Microscope* editors printed works by popular British poets, well-known in metropolitan literary circles. These included Coleridge, represented with an extract from 'Fears in Solitude', and the English labouring-class poet, Robert Bloomfield, author of *The Farmer's Boy*.[40]

A sonnet which Thomson dated 1802 indicates both that he and Orr were again intimate and that Orr was becoming highly regarded as a writer.[41] The poem discusses Thomson's own melancholy which keeps him away from Templepatrick Fair on 1 July 1802. He imagines his neighbours speculating on possible reasons for his absence and reckoning that a visit from 'ingenious Orr' might account for it, to which Thomson appends a note, 'Mr Orr, the poet', clearly expecting his audience to understand the reference. Orr's first authenticated appearance before the public under his own name, however, came in the poetry column of the *Belfast News-letter*, the *Northern Star*'s more gradualist reforming rival during the 1790s. During 1800 and 1801 the *News-letter*'s poetry column had revived interest in the poetry of Burns whose works, admired by so many *Northern Star* readers, had caused him to be associated in the minds of some members of the public with the radicalism of the 1790s.[42] The *News-letter* appears to be reclaiming him for the more general reader. First, the 'interesting life of Burns just published by Dr Currie of Liverpool was welcomed'.[43] Then a series of pieces by Burns was printed at intervals over the following eighteen months, with a reminder that the *News-letter* was 'the first in Ireland to introduce the poetical productions of the celebrated Robert Burns to public notice'. The poem included on this occasion was 'A Vision', or 'As I Stood by yon Roofless Tower', described by Liam McIlvanney as one of Burns's 'most vehemently radical pieces'.[44] It was, however, followed by an explanatory note, to ensure that its appearance would not be interpreted as political incitement:

> The poet is supposed to be musing by night on the banks of the River Cluden and by the ruins of Lincluden Abbey founded in the 12th century, in the reign of Malcolm IV ... Though this poem has a political bias, yet it may be presumed that no reader of taste, whatever his opinions may be, would forgive its being omitted – Ed.[45]

Appreciation of Burns was now, clearly, to be understood as a mark of sophistication and literary judgement, not tainted with the aroma of failed revolution. Particularly interesting was the editor's choice of a melancholy anonymous song, printed in the first days of Ireland's Union with Britain, and sourced in 'Dr Currie's Edition of Burns's Works and printed at Liverpool, though it is not Burns's own composition'. The piece concludes thus:

> 'Nae hame have I,' the minstrel said,
>   'Sad party strife o'erturned my *ha*'; ['hall']
> 'And weeping at the eve of life,
>   'I wander thro' a wreath o' *snaw*.'[46] (ll. 21–4) ['snow']

The inclusion of such words at a time when Ulster, and indeed Ireland, was still internally tormented with unrest traceable to 'sad party strife', reads very much like a veiled plea for resignation to the changed circumstances of the Union.

The *News-letter* was still publishing Burns's poems well into 1802.[47] In the same year Orr's 'Elegy on the Death of Hugh Tynan' was included on 24 September.[48] The occasion had the flavour both of an introduction, and for those 'in the know' of a reinvention, for Orr here offers a respectful homage to the pious and conservative Tynan, a customs officer and schoolmaster, whose verse was published in a posthumous volume in 1803.[49] To write an elegy for such a man must have brought Orr to the attention of a new, 'respectable' audience, at whom the accompanying, deferential editor's note following the verses seems deliberately aimed:

> Our readers will, no doubt, be inclined to pardon any inaccuracies in the above poem, when they are informed, that it is the production of a young tradesman who was never a day at school, nor had he ever the assistance of a tutor of any kind (save what instruction his father was enabled to give him).[50]

This suggests that the *News-letter*'s readers were being 'softened up' to accept Orr as a rising star on the literary scene and it is possible that it was Thomson, another regular contributor, who encouraged and assisted his appearance in this new forum. Perhaps Orr was uneasy with the new image, however, and its suggestion of pared talons, for it would be many years before he published in the *News-letter* again. His appearance there, his *Northern Star* publications during the 1790s and his verses for the American press may surely be understood as part of a recurring behaviour pattern which confirms that Orr had always aspired to engage an audience beyond the village. It is clear, too, that a literary circle composed of men who had enjoyed a more sophisticated education than his own invariably attracted him. While a period of weaving and farming in the relative obscurity of Broadisland followed, Orr utilized it for the composition and compilation of his material. He was setting the stage for Ulster's acknowledgement of Ballycarry's bard.

Orr's first volume of verse is an eclectic work into which he poured what at first appears a motley collection of verse.[51] He was, after all, a labouring-class poet for whom a subscription publication might represent the sole opportunity to achieve a printed volume. No record remains of the process by which subscriptions were raised, but the list of subscribers yields some names of more than passing interest. Richard Gervase Ker took two copies, certainly not an over-generous purchase given that some less wealthy subscribers took between three and six volumes each. Copies were also purchased by members of the Dalway family, whose ancestors had originally settled the Broadisland area, while the many subscribers from the Ballycarry-Islandmagee-Carrickfergus district included Rev. Bankhead and several of his daughters.[52]

The strong representation from Ballycarry and its associated townlands testifies to the pride and confidence with which Orr was regarded by his near neighbours. William Herdman, an innkeeper mentioned in 'Donegore Hill', for example, took a copy. Names from east and south Antrim predominate, although there are a few representatives from parts of County Down, and from Dublin and Dundalk, indicating that Orr's reputation was rising. Samuel Thomson of Carngranny was, of course, a subscriber, as was William Drummond, probably W. H. Drummond (1778–1865), a Presbyterian minister and founder member of the Belfast Literary Society. One particularly generous order for fifty copies was placed at Belfast by Robert Trail, in all likelihood Rev. Robert Trail, rector of Ballintoy Parish (1791–1842) on the North Antrim coast and a notable antiquarian. Undoubtedly the subscription list affords several important glimpses of the various networks with which Orr engaged. His brief 'Preface' is addressed to his subscribers and includes a conventional apology for the imperfections of what is to follow, with a plea for leniency from the reader on the grounds of the 'rusticity of the writer'. Readers are reminded that 'He is but an unschooled mechanic'.[53]

Orr gives an assurance that his work 'will not corrupt the morals', but goes further: 'sorry would I be if [my verses] contained a single line that could foment party spirit, alarm the devout heart, or raise a blush on the angelic cheek of female virtue'. He seems at pains to emphasize that he has no wish to court controversy by challenging accepted social, religious or sexual boundaries. The volume proved, however, to be anything but bland.

It is worthy of note that Orr did not trade on the popularity of Burns, or imply any similarity by choosing a prefatory quotation from the still greatly admired Scots bard. When Samuel Thomson's 'The Simmer Fair' appeared in the *Northern Star* on 1 September 1792 he quite deliberately informed his readers that it was 'in the manner of Burns'. Orr, however, chose lines from the English labouring-class poet Robert Bloomfield, thus acknowledging his debt to the literary heritage of the three kingdoms and confirming that his reading included contemporary works.

Burns's Preface to the 1786 Kilmarnock edition, *Poems, Chiefly in the Scottish Dialect*, also makes an interesting contrast with Orr's. While the diction appears suggestive of humility, in both length and tone it evidences Burns's far greater assurance and confidence in his own exceptional talent, and his determination to promote his vernacular work while insisting that it is part of a national tradition:

> The following trifles are not the productions of the Poet, who, with all the advantages of learned art, and perhaps amid the elegancies and idleness of upper life, looks down for a rural theme ... Unacquainted with the necessary requisites for commencing Poet by rule, he sings the sentiments and manners he felt and saw in himself and his rustic compeers around him, in his and their native language ... but to the genius of a Ramsay, or the glorious dawnings of the poor, unfortunate Fergusson, he, with equal unaffected sincerity, declares, that, even in his highest pulse of vanity, he has not the most distant pretensions. These two justly admired Scotch Poets he has often had in his eye in the following pieces; but rather with a view to kindle at their flame, than for servile imitation.[54]

The idea that Orr was primarily a vernacular writer is one of several myths about him that have gained credence in Ulster during the recent revival of interest in Ulster Scots language and culture, and, as the discussion of canonicity in Chapter 1 has demonstrated, debates have followed about whether he and other Ulster vernacular poets should be understood as Scots or as Irish writers. Leaving the broader issue of cultural identity aside for the present, when we focus on the question of the languages he employed we find that Scots verse comprises just under 13 per cent of Orr's total output, and that the majority of these vernacular rhymes are to be found in the *Poems on Various Subjects* of 1804, which includes a total of sixty-three poems and songs, sixteen of which are in Ulster Scots.

John Hewitt, champion of the regional writer, rightly remarked that Orr seemed unable to go wrong when employing his native idiom, but that and similar commendations have encouraged the view that the Scotch poems represent not only Orr's best work, but are also his most interesting compositions. Nothing could be further from the truth. Orr, contemporaneous with the first major wave of Romanticism, was experimenting with new approaches to the writing of verse in English and in Scots, as the discussion in later chapters will demonstrate. Here, however, a brief review follows of the rich verse collection with which Orr rewarded his supporters in 1804.

Orr employs a variety of the forms and genres common in much Augustan and later verse: elegies, odes, lyrics and pastorals, but he can subvert and exploit traditional formats with an originality that deserves to command more attention from critics. The Scotch poems, written in the stanza forms associated with the eighteenth-century Scots vernacular revivalists, include a series in which is encoded a narrative of Orr's experiences as an active radical during 1798. This was surely a daring move, given that the volume appeared in the year following Emmet and Russell's abortive and fatal attempt to revive rebellion in 1803. The series includes 'A Prayer',[55] in which the first-person narrator, on the eve of the Battle of Antrim, confronts the possibility of having to die for his cause, and 'Donegore Hill', in which Orr castigates the perfidy and cowardice of certain United Irishmen, including some of the Broadisland Corps. Such works belie the blandness of his stated intentions in his Preface, as does the 'Epistle to S. Thomson of Carngranny' which reveals him asserting the people's and the poets' ownership of the 'burns an' bow'rs' of "Airlan"' (ll. 82–3).[56]

Orr's songs frequently take a challenging and individual position that refuses to conform, or to pamper the reader. The 'Song, Written in Winter' is in many respects an anti-pastoral but its descriptive passages in some details echo Orr's reading of *The Seasons* (1726–30) by the Anglo-Scot James Thomson (1700–48). We may consider, for example, some extracts from the great passage in *Winter* that portrays the terrifying ravages of the blizzard and its perils for beasts and travellers:

> The bleating kind
> Eye the bleak heaven, and next the glistening earth,
> With looks of dumb despair; then, sad-dispersed,
> Dig for the withered herb through heaps of snow ...
> In this dire season, oft the whirlwind's wing
> Sweeps up the burden of whole wintry plains
> In one wide waft, and o'er the hapless flocks,
> Hid in the hollow of two neighbouring hills,
> The billowy tempest whelms ...[57] (ll. 261–73)

In covering similar territory Orr does not attempt to imitate Thomson's declamatory high style but, employing his vernacular voice and a lilting rhythm, achieves a lyrical effect that dissolves the distance between the reader and the scenes described:

> How dark the hail show'r mak's yon vale, *aince* sae pleasin'! ['once
> How *laigh* stoops the bush that's owre-burden't wi' drift! ['low'
> The icicles dreep at the *half-thow't house-easin'*, ['half-thawed house eaves'
> Whan blunt the sun beams frae the verge o' the *lift*. (ll. 5–8) ['sky'
> ...
> Perhaps, singin' noo the dirge I tak' pride in,
> She thinks on the last storm, wi' pity an' dread –
> How the *spait* crush't the cots - how Tam brak his leg slidin', ['flood'
> An' herds in the muir *fand* the poor pedlar dead.[58] (ll. 25–8) ['found'

'Written in Winter' functions as a protest lyric that speaks out on behalf of the poor and the dispossessed. It also, unexpectedly but effortlessly, develops into a tender, anxious love lyric. Orr, a lifelong bachelor, wrote few pieces that could be designated love poems, but there is a vein of tenderness towards women, characterized by respect and by sympathy for their marginalized position, that may be traced in his work.[59] This poem and several others refer to the mysterious Sylvia whose conversation and humanitarianism supply a major part of her attraction and differentiate her from the conventional Sylvias and Peggys of pastoral verse.

Poems with a local focus celebrating the landscape in the vicinity of Ballycarry or recording community life are very much in evidence among the *Poems* of 1804. They are written with the affection and intimate detail of an insider who observes, appreciates and, when necessary, reproves. Unquestionably Orr can identify with these people and employs his gift, in Ulster Scots or in English, for describing 'the sensations of ... men, and the objects which interest them'.[60] While he is embedded in this community he also has the poet's gift for standing apart to observe and record in such a manner as to invest the patterns of work, their seasonal rhythms and traditional roles, with a ritualistic dignity.

Pieces such as 'The Banks of Larne', 'Fort Hill' and the 'Song, Composed in Spring', the latter particularly evocative of Ulster in the heyday of the cottage-based linen industry, demonstrate warm affection for the local landscape.[61] Many poems honour local characters, for example the standard habbie verse epistle addressed to 'N—P—, Oldmill'.[62] This work, which praises the skills of a local blind fiddler, testifies to Orr's love of convivial society, even of a party. His songs 'Come Let us Here my Brethren Dear' and 'The Dying Mason' are evidence of how he valued close companionship, provided often in the Masonic Lodge.[63] Certainly many of the ideals associated with Freemasonry may be traced in his references to moral values such as Truth, Right, Love, Charity, Wisdom, and in his respect for all sects and races. In addition the preoccupations of the Age of Sensibility are evident in humane pieces such as 'The Bull-Beat' and 'To a Sparrow' which deplore wanton cruelty toward animals.[64]

Orr's love of reading and learning become quickly evident to any student of his verse. His poems abound with references that demonstrate his wide knowledge of the eighteenth-century masters, including Pope, Gray, Young, James Thomson, Burns, Fergusson and Ramsay. A recurring theme in his work is regret that his education was not more extended and formal, and that this experience is all too frequently the lot of the intelligent working man:

> Driv'n from the Tree of Knowledge with a taste,
> Nature's poor nobles wander ev'ry waste;
> And ev'ry stream beholds, as on it flows,
> Some embryo genius near, whose blossom never blows.[65] (ll. 53–6)

The above lines are from a meditative poem in which Orr skilfully employs rhyming couplets and a dignified concluding alexandrine in every stanza. They provide some evidence of the assurance in technique which often characterizes his English verse, even if he occasionally lapses into awkward phrasing or poetic diction. It is readily demonstrable, however, that the voices he achieves in Scots and in English are distinctive and different, with the Braid Scotch poems frequently exploiting the pithy, reductive quality characteristic of Ulster Scots speech.

The 1804 collection also includes several highly competent essays in the sonnet form, one of which is a philosophical meditation on the operation of the conscience, while another, 'Humanity', expresses Orr's Millenarian hopes. Thus, while utilizing the same complex form on different occasions he demonstrates his capacity for wide variations in subject matter and in tone. The latter piece, with a reference to the evils of the slave trade, reveals once again that while he is deeply committed to his country his concerns are often supranational:

> 'Then savage churls who tortur'd beasts before,
>   'Shall spare the nest from which a *parent* flew:
> 'No conscience shall be cross'd; no Negroes gore
>   'Gush, as if glad to change his faulty hue.
>
> 'I am HUMANITY. My precepts mark,
> 'Happy my friends must be.' She said; and all was dark.[66] (ll. 11–14)

The concluding line discloses the pessimism that increasingly afflicted him, for the vision abruptly dies, leaving the poet blind.

Much of Orr's poetry betrays a sensitive, melancholy turn of mind and a deep, questioning thoughtfulness that may have found little empathy among the peasants and labourers of his home village. His poetry often demonstrates a fascination with outcasts and suicides, and a capacity to identify with their distresses. His upbeat opening poem 'The Glen', which portrays a life of idyllic contentment, is immediately followed by the gloomy 'Gormal – An Elegy', for a suicide who 'has drunk a poison'd bowl, / Because the maid he lov'd disdain'd his flame'(ll. 7–8).[67] Orr deplores the superstition and bigotry that deny Gormal a grave in consecrated ground and asserts his faith in a God 'not critical nor yet severe' who will judge more sympathetically.

Other themes, such as failed or unrequited love, grief and loss are also treated. The reader may often infer a strong biographical element and hinted references to Orr's radical youth, along with deep regret at the failure of United Irish hopes. The 'Elegy on the Death of A. McCracken', prefaced with the quotation 'Basely murdered', has the appearance of a clear reference to the charismatic, hanged Ulster leader.[68] The Christian name initial is wrong, of course, but much of it appears to be closely referenced to Henry Joy McCracken's life and to the first person narrator's close relationship with him. Particularly telling are the lines: 'Rever'd M'Cracken! When with thee, my friend! / I last ey'd Nature from the mountain grand' (ll. 5–6), which may recall the period Orr shared with him on Slemish. Once again we note his daring, evident also in the 'Lines Written under the Portrait of Newell', who was a notorious informer and whom Orr, most uncharacteristically, does not scruple to curse roundly:

> May dire Mischance arrest his odious frame,
> Conscious Remorse his hopeless soul inflame,
> Hunger accelerate the Death he fears,
> And realms reviling shock his SPECTRE'S ears,
> Who dupes the simple – Cruelty commends –
> Betrays his Country – or deceives his Friends![69] (ll. 7–12)

The simply titled 'Elegy' is surely autobiographical, unambiguously drawing on Orr's colourful past. It has never been explored in critical writing, but provides an interesting counterpart to McDowell's account of Orr's life and reveals the torture of regrets and self-doubt to which he seems to have been subject throughout the years following his return to Ballycarry. In this piece an unnamed first-person narrator leaves his home in the dead of night, to 'oft accuse myself, and oft my fate' (l. 12). The description of the physical landscape he traverses with its ruined churchyard strongly suggests Ballycarry. In what may be a reference to his success as a writer for the *Northern Star* he recalls that 'Fame early caught my idolizing eye', but 'fled as I pursu'd'. Here he disparages his own poetic abilities, concluding that his 'rhymes are rude' (ll. 17–20).[70] He engages reader sympathy, recalling past and dead comrades in a nostalgic passage that powerfully evokes the lost, hopeful years of the 1790s:

> Fall'n are the friends who cheer'd my gloomiest hours,
>   My brave, bright friends, whose worth was all their wealth;
> They bask in bliss, 'mid antemundane bow'rs,
>   No more, like me, to want content and health. (ll. 29–32)

Orr returned from America to resume the trade of weaving alongside his father but not long afterwards James Orr Senior died. Two poems express Orr's feelings for his parent and first teacher. One is the 'Epitaph for the Author's Father', a formal tribute to his parent's 'immac'late mind' (l. 5), while the other is more extended and intimate in tone. This latter piece, an 'Elegy Written in the Church-yard of Templecorran', bears the influence of the Graveyard School but shows that Orr's sense of humour is not so repressed by decorum that he misses the irony of the levelling, and harmonizing, effects of death:[71]

> How still their hands! How mute their tongues!
>   Nor hearts embrace, nor heads invent,
> With party toasts, and party songs,
>   These trampled roofs are never rent;
> ...
> In vest of green the breast is pent,
>   Who once the badge of Orange chose.[72] (ll. 33–40)

The poem climaxes in a deeply personal expression of grief for his father, the site of whose burial is his destination. The portrait of the man who trained and taught him 'without a rod' is sincere, dignified and employs an extended retrospective in which Orr calls to mind the living man and the pride and pleasure he took in his son in playful boyhood and in young manhood, perhaps in his days as a Volunteer:

> And let him smile, as when, at eve,
>   I chas'd the shower-succeeding arch;
> And fired his eye to see the brave
>   In self-rais'd ranks beside me march. (ll. 85–8)

Late in 1805 Samuel Thomson wrote to Orr complimenting him on his published volume and enquiring how well he had succeeded. Orr refers to this letter in a reply dated 4 January 1806 and is typically self-effacing about his own powers: 'I think you have over-rated the merits of my effusions'. He also, with the canniness of the Ulster Scot, effortlessly parries Thomson's enquiry about the financial rewards of the venture: 'In reply to your question how I succeeded with my publication – you have read the subscription list, and the printers were not immoderate in their demands'.[73] With the publication of *Poems on Various Subjects* the 'construction' of the Bard of Ballycarry was to all intents and purposes complete. From the above preliminary survey of some of its contents, it should be clear that this is a publication of genuine depth and complexity. It would have been evident to many contemporary readers that he had passed the boundaries expected of a mere local rhymer. Much, however, was still to follow in Orr's development as a man, a poet and a commentator on the Ireland of the 1800s.

4 BARD IN RESIDENCE: JAMES ORR (1804–16)

From two poems in particular that were included by Alexander McDowell in Orr's *Posthumous Works* (1817) the reader may infer much about the poetic persona Orr developed in his established position as the Bard of Ballycarry. His 'Elegy Written in the Ruins of a Country School-House' (1817)[1] is a dignified meditation which echoes 'Elegy Written in a Country Church Yard' (1751) by Thomas Gray (1716–71),[2] and Goldsmith's 'The Deserted Village' (1770) in that it reveals Orr taking a backward glance at lost lives and unfulfilled promise.[3] As he reflects on his youth he recalls the conservatism of so many among the parents of his peers who refused to permit their offspring to learn 'elocution's grace, / Or grammar's art' (l. 13) and who rejected the enlightened system of the Belfast educationist David Manson (1726–92).[4] Instead they wished the children drilled as they themselves had been, only in 'the Catechism, / The Youth's Companion, and the Holy Word' (ll. 17–18). Orr's concern now is for the poor of the rising generation, not only of Ballycarry but of 'Erin', whom he wishes to acquire dignity and enfranchisement through a full and liberal education. While he is the poet of the village, therefore, Orr is also consciously speaking to and on behalf of the nation. Here he positions himself a little apart as an observer. Located in the ruined building, he is aware of cheerful sounds from nearby homes but he does not participate in them.

While he was deeply committed to the well-being of his community, Orr's attention was never exclusively held by the minutiae of village life, and in the years following the publication of his poetry collection in 1804 he became a frequent contributor to two contrasting, Belfast-based publications, the *Belfast News-letter* and the *Belfast Monthly Magazine*. Since the United Irishmen's bid for independence had been thoroughly repressed in 1798, and with Ireland now incorporated into a four nation union, artistic and literary statements that challenged the now dominant Unionist, monarchical culture took on a particular urgency and significance.

In the north, a prime mover in the drive to promote Irish culture was William Drennan, a Presbyterian, constitutional patriot and founder member of the United Irishmen. Drennan's radical portfolio included the 'Irish Address' designed to inspire the Scottish Friends of the People organization in 1792. He was tried for sedition in 1794 but acquitted, and later he composed 'The Wake of William Orr', commemorating the 'Presbyterian martyr' hanged for United Irish activities in 1797. Drennan maintained opposition to the Union by literary and cultural means. He was a chief editor of the *Belfast Monthly Magazine*, first issued in September 1808, to which Orr became a fairly regular contributor of poetry and essays between 1808 and 1810. In the magazine there was to be a strong emphasis on items relating to the nation and its identity within a global context:

> Among the subjects which ought to form a necessary and principal part of a magazine published in Ireland and addressed to Irishmen, whatever relates to our native country should have the first place. Whatever information can be collected concerning the origin, antiquities, history, language, manners, or topography of this country, shall be sedulously collected and laid before the reader ... Here then is a field of speculation not merely to the Irish antiquarian, but to the universal philosopher; not discovering the rise and tracing the progress of a single insulated people, but developing the origin of nations.[5]

Each issue included a lengthy 'Monthly Retrospect of Politics', covering affairs at home and abroad, and maintaining a sceptical attitude to the Union. In an early edition an anecdote was recounted concerning a Yorkshireman who swore never to have heard of 'such an event as an Union between Britain and Ireland'. On this the writer wryly remarked, 'Most of our political economists would cry "Ah happy Yorkshireman!"'[6]

In addition to politics, the magazine gave regular space to pieces on astronomy, science, natural history, literature, developments in farming methods and biographical sketches. Two of the latter illustrate the journal's liberal, intellectual, reformist tenor. The first covered the life of Thomas Clarkson, 'The Inspired Advocate of the Abolition of Negro Slavery',[7] while the second, which discussed the learned accomplishments of Margaret Roper, daughter of Sir Thomas More, provides evidence that the journalists and contributors indeed approved the 'liberal cultivation of the minds of women'.[8] Topographical pieces encouraging appreciation of the local countryside and affording glimpses of its historical associations and contemporary character were contributed on an occasional basis by 'SMS', probably Samuel McSkimin (1775–1843), a local historian and member of the loyalist yeomanry during the Rebellion of 1798. One of the 'SMS' essays, a 'Sketch of a Ramble to Antrim, 10 July 1808' includes a visit to a cottage in the area of Slieve Trewe, a hill in the neighbourhood of Carrickfergus and Ballycarry.[9] The occupant is a local artisan and author who welcomes the writer, allows him to view his unusually large collection of books, and then accompanies him on a long walk through the Antrim countryside, including the area of Donegore.

The location and the collection of books have led Linde Lunney to conclude that the unnamed writer is 'probably Orr himself'.[10] If it is indeed he, the encounter reveals that some reconciliation has been effected between members of opposing sides. Significantly, perhaps, the ramble mentions the importance of the Donegore district as an encampment for 10,000 or 12,000 men in June 1798. There is a recurring trope of 1798 in McSkimin's articles and one must infer that their purpose was to retain the memory of the Rebellion in the minds of the readers, though the tone is unremittingly elegiac. Orr's 'Donegore Hill', written earlier, is more urgent and angry than the recollections of 'SMS', though the latter achieve the sense of a respectful pilgrimage and provide considerable insight into the power of landscape to evoke memory.

Much in the general tenor of the *Belfast Monthly Magazine* would have chimed with Orr's own patriotic and enlightened value system, thus the pieces he produced for it are well matched to the magazine's likely audience and stated purpose. It is interesting to observe how Orr, now a respected writer with a published volume to his credit, was accepted into the circle of contributors, many of whom had experienced classical and university education. While it was not uncommon for a rustic poet to be taken up and encouraged by a wealthy patron, there is no question of Orr's having been included in the *Magazine* on anything but his own terms. We find here no apology for his rusticity or his self-education, while his prose and poetic works at this period exhibit real confidence and authority in addressing an audience that included Belfast's post-Union 'chattering classes'.

'Stanzas on the Death of a Favourite Young Lady' is one of five poems printed in the *Belfast Monthly Magazine* during 1809 and 1810 that are clearly attributed to 'J. O., Ballycarry', or 'O., Ballycarry'. They are of considerable interest since they reveal how comfortably, and more than competently, Orr sat within the circle of the *Magazine*'s contributors and readers. They certainly provide insights into his attitudes concerning issues both public and private. The young lady in this instance is identified simply as 'Anna' and the ensuing tribute is a tender memorial in fitting, sincere, terms. It exhibits fairly conventional, pious sentiments, but the opening stanza strikes a passionate note:

> O my rack'd heart! since Erin green,
> From chaos rose at nature's call,
> What other son of Care has seen,
> So many of his fav'rites fall?
> If wrongs and cares had power to gall
> This heart so sorely, when consol'd;
> How can I live bereft of all
> My firmest friends, in clay now cold?[11] (ll. 1–8)

The focus here is on the poet himself; the desperate questions unashamedly expose his long, lonely grief for many lost comrades, grief which the death he mourns now serves to reignite.

Orr contributed both poetry and essays on moral and philosophical subjects and some of these, along with other pieces included in his *Posthumous Works*, provide insights into his particular brand of Presbyterianism. His poetry sometimes reveals tensions between himself and members of the Ballycarry community who were Old Light, orthodox Calvinists. Such tension had been building within Ulster since the non-subscription controversy of the 1720s when the Glasgow University educated Rev. John Abernethy had argued that no-one should be obliged to accept the Calvinist tenets of the Westminster Confession of Faith (1646) if these conflicted with his private judgement.[12]

A story well-known in Ulster Presbyterian circles is told about Francis Hutcheson, the New Light Professor of Moral Philosophy at Glasgow from 1729 to 1746, who as a younger man scandalized his father's Saintfield, County Down congregation by deviating from orthodoxy in a sermon of 1719. The story, though probably apocryphal, serves to illustrate those aspects of liberal, New Light thinking about the human condition and man's relationship to God that unsettled Calvinists because it challenged their exclusive claim on grace leading to salvation. An elder of Hutcheson Senior's congregation is supposed to have complained:

> Your silly son Frank has fashed a' the congregation for he has been babblin' this hoor about a gude and benevolent God, and that the sauls of the heathen will gang tae heaven if they follow the licht of their ain consciences. Not a word does the daft boy ken, speer, nor say aboot the gude, auld comfortable doctrines of election, reprobation, original sin and faith.[13]

Elaine McFarland has demonstrated how Hutchesonian views on man's innate moral sense, and further, his enlightened views on civil and religious liberty, were communicated to his Glasgow students, many of whom were destined to return to their native Ulster as its ministers and teachers.[14] However, Finlay Holmes (1926–2008), a former Moderator of the General Assembly of the Presbyterian Church in Ireland (1990) shows that the popular acceptance of such opinions was not universal:

> New Light theology was particularly attractive to the emerging *bourgeois intelligentsia* of eastern Ulster, who, like their counterparts elsewhere in western Europe, were susceptible to Enlightenment influences and were critical of what appeared to be archaic influences in business, politics and ideas. A rational form of religion eschewing mysterious and metaphysical dogma, and emphasising duty and responsible behaviour, in other words, 'polite Presbyterianism', was popular among them.[15]

Perhaps it was the powerful social and commercial 'clout' of those Presbyterians who approved New Light thinking that allowed it for a time to hold sway within the formerly orthodox Synod of Ulster, for, as J. M. Barkley explains, 'By the end of the century over two-thirds of the Presbyterians belonging to the Synod of Ulster did not require from licentiates and ministers formal adherence to the Westminster Confession'.[16] After the controversy of the 1720s the Non-Subscribing Presbytery of Antrim was set up by the New Light party, but some New Light adherents clearly remained within the Synod of Ulster.

Andrew Holmes has shown that members of the Non-Subscribing Presbytery deliberately cultivated links with non-subscribers who had remained within the General Synod of Ulster. These contacts 'facilitated the rise to prominence of moderate theological views known as New Light'.[17] Such views, however, did not reflect the opinions of conservative, orthodox Presbyterians or of vociferous, sizeable groupings such as the Covenanters or the Seceders, a pietistic sect who adhered tenaciously to Calvinism, stressing 'human sinfulness' and 'the need for divine grace mediated through the person and work of Christ'.[18] During the 1800s an evangelical movement rose to prominence within many of the Presbyterian sects. Spearheaded by the Rev. Henry Cooke, the movement was doctrinally orthodox in its theology but also emphasized vigorous social action. According to Holmes

> the events of 1798 led to a rejection of New Light hegemony as evangelicals portrayed it as a spiritually mortifying and politically dangerous creed, overlooking the fact that half of the ministers implicated in the Rising were Old Light in theology.[19]

This brief outline allows some impression of the complexity of Ulster Presbyterianism and the variety of opinions, theological, social and political, within it. As we have seen, Linde Lunney, who bases her argument on internal evidence from the poems, locates Orr within the New Light grouping, going so far as to claim that he did not assent to the divinity of Christ, and thus making him an Arian or Unitarian. However, John Nelson, a Presbyterian scholar who is currently the non-subscribing minister at Ballycarry, rejects the idea that Abernethy and the eighteenth-century Ulster liberals were anti-Trinitarian:

> If there was any doctrinal position characteristic of the group as a whole it was not concerning the Trinity but rather their abandonment of Calvinistic predestination in favour of an Arminian standpoint. The one common theme of their writing was that mankind had the natural reason and ability to seek the mind and will of God, and that they had the gift of free will either to reject this knowledge or to apply it towards their own salvation.[20]

Orr, though clearly fascinated by theological debate did not set out to write works of theology, but a further survey of some of his poetic and other writings of this period allows us some insight into what his viewpoint both as a Presbyterian Dissenter and an independent thinker may have been. He appears to have been convinced that the evidence of true religious faith lay in moral conduct and concern for one's fellows. This is evident from the two poems he addressed to Presbyterian ministers who belonged to very different theological wings of Presbyterianism. One, the Rev. Henry Cooke (1788–1868), was deeply orthodox. As the nineteenth century progressed Cooke developed the evangelical current within Presbyterianism into a powerful missionary force abroad and at home, laying the foundation in Ulster for the Great Revival of 1859. Orr's 'Ode to Henry Cooke' (1817) commends he 'who saves one worthy man' as greater than 'he who conquers empires vast' (ll. 48–9), but Orr consistently articulates the view that genuine holiness had to be expressed in practical, social action. Thus, in his 'Address to the Reverend William Glendy' (1817), a New Light minister called to Ballycarry to assist Bankhead prior to his retirement, he voices specific expectations:

> A sunday-school shall thee as founder hail,
>   A reading circle's ruler thou shalt be;
> To parts a patron, to diseases pale
>   A rare physician, kind without a fee.[21] (ll. 9–12)

He also affirms his commitment to tolerance and anticipates that Glendy too will practise this virtue: 'All sects shall share thy friendship; all were form'd / By one kind sire, and sav'd by one high Priest' (ll. 15–16).

The reader is struck by the unapologetic assurance with which Orr, the self-taught weaver, here addresses university-educated clergymen, and by the extent and application of the knowledge with which he alludes to Biblical, literary and theological source material as he builds his arguments. The Bard of Ballycarry could clearly perform roles other than the 'folk poet' of Akenson and Crawford's later construction. Here he speaks as the intellectual equal of his addressees, while conscious that his bardic status within the community confers on him the responsibility to speak out in order to maintain the community's reputation as a theological 'centre of excellence':

> And may Broad-Island's fane, in which of old
>   The first Dissenter preach'd on Erin's plain,
> For faithful teachers be through time extoll'd,
>   And congregations free from falsehood's stain! (ll. 71–4)

Poems written for the *Belfast Monthly Magazine* assist further in determining the nature of Orr's religious position which, as the years progressed, appears to have absorbed influences from philosophies broader than the theologies adhered to by denominational groupings. His 'Inscription, Proposed for the Monument of Locke' finds that 'genuine Christian Faith, / with Nature's law completely coincides' (ll. 7–8) and he writes the poem in order to assert his own conviction that if governments would only permit greater democracy and reform then they would not have to fear violent revolution: 'radical Reform shall end the dread / of wild revolt' (ll. 19–20).[22] This was controversial thinking and it is perhaps small wonder that McDowell, anxious to promote Orr's respectability, did not include this poem in Orr's *Posthumous Works*.

Further insights into Orr's personal beliefs and into his readiness to challenge theological opponents are provided in an essay, or series of essays, he contributed to the *Belfast Monthly Magazine*. One of these, 'On the Disasters and Deaths Occasioned by Accidents' is clearly identified as from the pen of 'O. Ballycarry'.[23] Viewed simply as an essay, it is characterized by the elegance of its construction and phrasing, which are appropriate to the relative sophistication of the readership. The writer has evidently been a careful student of the work of respected, able prose essayists but his genuine, even passionate commitment to his subject and his independence as a thinker communicate a strong sense of his individual personality.

Orr begins with an anecdote that vividly describes the shocking and accidental death of a labourer impaled by a branch while he was engaged in felling a tree. He employs the example as a prelude to his exploration of the uncertainty of human life, but his main purpose in the essay is to attack what he perceives as an erroneous Christian fatalism. Thus he opines, 'False principles in religion, or at least unfair conclusions drawn from just premises, have precipitated thousands to their destruction ... through the persuasion that every man must live his appointed time'.[24] We are responsible for ourselves, he argues, and while allowing that Heaven may indeed have decreed a violent death for some individual, he reasonably posits the view that this belief could never be accepted as a justification for the actions of a murderer.

Clearly Orr has the Calvinists in his sights here, for he points out that apparently pious fatalism is actually a misrepresentation of what is meant by predestination. The following remarks contained within his conclusion, however, strongly suggest that something more than the issue overtly under discussion may be in his mind. First he urges, 'The contempt of death is laudable only when safety would be prolonged at the expense of virtue; and hazarding life becomes criminal whenever nothing valuable can be attained by the exploit'. He goes on to urge his view of the reasonable man's response to overwhelming odds: 'if unavoidable casualties overpower him, he endures poverty and pain with a fortitude that was never in alliance with affected courage'.[25] Here we may have Orr's apologia for relinquishing any attempt to achieve freedom and democracy in Ireland by force of arms, and for his resignation in the face of the accomplished fact of the Union.

In addition to his association with the *Belfast Monthly Magazine*, from 1805 to 1811 Orr contributed regularly to the *Belfast Commercial Chronicle*, a popular newspaper that provided domestic and foreign news, and advertising space for the business and mercantile communities. Within this framework it incorporated a poetry column to which original pieces were contributed. The *Chronicle* was certainly a more populist vehicle than the *Magazine* was ever intended to be, and its appearance twice weekly allowed those of its contributors who wished to do so to engage each other in lively debate and to comment with topicality on current affairs. A greater sense of immediacy and vibrancy is communicated in the *Chronicle* than in the measured columns of the *Belfast Monthly Magazine*.

Simon Bainbridge has written eloquently about the role of verse in shaping the British national consciousness during the Napoleonic era. He has argued that poetry 'scripted wartime identities' and in particular endorsed a bellicose, patriotic masculinity.[26] In the Ireland of the 1800s, of course, there were many disaffected citizens, including Catholics whose emancipation was not yet secured, and Dissenters who continued to resent the tithe, and with it their ongoing sense of marginalization. In such a population jingoistic, pro-British verses were hardly music to all ears. But the situation was complex. Orr's own community, in common with many throughout Ulster and indeed all Ireland, sent sons and husbands to the British armed forces, while he himself, as we have seen, responded to the Napoleonic threat as a call to arms.[27] A series of poems he contributed to the *Belfast Commercial Chronicle* clusters in the years 1805–6, prior to and following Nelson's victory at Trafalgar. Several reveal how he negotiated this difficult terrain, remaining true to his belief in the distinctiveness of Irish identity and to his transnational radical politics.

Orr's best-known poem 'The Irishman' dates from this period and is a perfect example of the astuteness with which he employed his gifts.[28] In the cynicism of the late twentieth century the frequent reprinting of the work was dismissed as 'national Narcissism', while Orr himself was suspected of intending it as 'a cruel parody on effusive patriotic verse'.[29] Such judgements pay insufficient attention to the text's literary and historical contexts. Orr is here deliberately commending what he perceives as the essential warmth and decency of the Irish character. In his commendation of Irish faithfulness to 'principle' (l. 10) and 'honour' (l. 25) he may even be tacitly honouring the integrity and steadfastness of the executed United Irish leaders. The hope he expresses is that peace and plenty may be enjoyed by every Irishman, and that any war which must be waged should be viewed as defensive in nature, rather than supported as part of an Imperial project:

> Erin, loved land! From age to age,
>   Be thou more great, more fam'd and free!
> May peace be thine, or, should'st thou wage
>   Defensive war, cheap victory!
> May plenty bloom in every field;
>   Which gentle breezes softly fan,
> And cheerful smiles serenely gild,
>   The home of every Irishman![30] (ll. 33–40)

The piece is both clever and subtle. It commends unreservedly the Irish character, thus observing the self-congratulatory conventions of wartime patriotic verse, but it runs against the grain of the typical bellicose thrust and deliberately foregrounds Irishness rather than Britishness.

In the same series is his 'Soliloquy of Bonaparte', printed in the *Belfast Commercial Chronicle* on 14 October 1805, at a period when 'Boney' often figured in popular imagination as the 'bogey man'. Rather than courting popular appeal with a bombastic denunciation that taps into communal fear and loathing, in this essay in soliloquy or interior monologue, Orr imagines what it is like to *be* the newly crowned Emperor Napoleon. The emphasis is on inner guilt, brought about by the sacrifice of ideals, and on Napoleon's anxiety for the future.

> How does promotion change the patriot's mind!
> He scorns the people whom before he freed: –
> Supreme command has seldom been resign'd
> By prideful chiefs, who private stations dread.[31] (ll. 9–12)

As the speaker's meditations continue, his thoughts turn to the fawning toadies who flatter him with comparisons to Caesar, which only serves to remind him of how Caesar was betrayed. It is proof of Orr's Ulster Scots canniness that at a time when loyal sentiments were *de rigeur* in newspaper verse, he manages to produce a piece that ostensibly satisfies this demand, while at the same time it allows the thoughtful reader to infer his view of the just desserts of anyone, Napoleon or Caesar, who is seduced from enlightened republican values.

This assertion of a specifically Irish patriotism in the face of tyranny, at a time when poets often employed loyalist rhetoric and royalist symbols to rally national spirit, is evident throughout Orr's poetry on the subject of the conflict. In these works two clear strands may be traced: dedication to the cause of liberty throughout the globe and a passionate desire to see Ireland peaceful and secure. 'The Irish Soldier', an early poem in the Napoleonic series for the *Chronicle*, additionally allows Orr the radical to speak up on behalf of the common man.[32] The eponymous soldier is a dying private, wounded during the successful defence of Bhurtpore, India, in 1805. He laments the fact that he will never see his homeland, 'honour'd Erin' (l. 23), or his family again, and the point is made that though he died bravely, he is unlikely to be accorded any special recognition for his courage. Orr does not hesitate to depict the destructive nature of conflict in the lives of individuals and families at a time when many poets felt it politic to downplay such unpleasant truths.

Since Orr's period of writing for the *Chronicle* coincided with the Battle of Trafalgar, it is fascinating to observe how he responded to Nelson's triumph. When news of it filtered through, poets rushed to enshrine the occasion in verse, focusing on Nelson's heroism, his role in the preservation of British freedom, and on the example he had set his countrymen.[33] Until now, it appeared that Orr had been silent on the subject. No poem about Nelson features in his *Collected Poems* or on Akenson and Crawford's previously assumed exhaustive list of his uncollected works. However, 'Lord Nelson's Song of Victory', printed adjacent to an account of the 'Action off Cape Trafalgar', is from Orr's pen. The text, similar to his 'Soliloquy of Bonaparte', with which it functions very appropriately as a companion piece, is a dramatic interior monologue. It is thoughtful and honest in its representation of the brutal nature of military conflict, and effective in its imagining of a naval engagement. Nelson is portrayed comforting himself while dying, by thinking about the success his daring naval action has achieved. The last line of each stanza repeats the refrain that 'Vict'ry consoles me in death', a deliberate play on the name of his vessel. The ugliness of war and the suffering inflicted on both friend and enemy are made very apparent, briefly but graphically:

> Broadside follows broadside, all fatal, how fast
> The French from their masts fall! The masts fall at last –
> In the shrowds [sic] hang the dying, whose limbs lie beneath.[34] (ll. 13–15)

The Admiral follows this with a plea for mercy to be shown to the defeated French: 'Save the suff'rers, kind conq'rors! Nor cruel in wrath, / Stain Vict'ry, that comes to console me in Death!' (ll. 19–20).

Orr's admiration for the British commander at Trafalgar seems rooted in the fact that he stayed at his post, died courageously and acted humanely, but behind the dramatic public events of the battle and its aftermath, Orr's approval may have arisen from an additional source. It may be related to the fact that in 1802 Nelson had appeared as a character witness at the trial for treason of Colonel Edward Marcus Despard. Despard, an Anglo-Irishman, was a member of the radical London Corresponding Society and had links with the Society of United Irishmen which he may even have joined, although the charges at his trial related to other matters. Nelson's intervention was insufficient to save Despard from hanging and decapitation, but as a result of it he was spared the torture of disembowelment.[35]

A further and until now undiscovered poem which Orr contributed to the *Belfast Commercial Chronicle* in 1806 provides evidence of how closely he followed the progress of the Napoleonic conflict. The poem in question relates to an ugly incident which occurred in Germany and involved a Nuremburg bookseller, John P. Palm. Palm had printed, though not authored, a pamphlet, *Germany in its Deep Humiliation*, designed to encourage German resistance to French domination. At Napoleon's instigation, along with five other booksellers he was tried by military tribunal and found guilty of publishing and distributing libellous material. He was executed by firing squad, but before his death on 25 August 1806 sent a courageous and affecting letter to his wife, copies of which were publicly circulated. On 13 October 1806 the *Belfast Commercial Chronicle* reported the affair and printed a translation of Palm's letter. The details clearly stirred both Orr's democratic principles and his compassion.

The monologue, 'The Speech of John P. Palm', clearly attributed to 'J. O. Ballycarry' at a time when he was a regular contributor to the *Chronicle* does not appear on Akenson and Crawford's list of the poems McDowell omitted from Orr's posthumous collection. It has never been reproduced in any published copy of Orr's work or referred to, until now, by any critic or researcher. Orr presents Palm as a type of William Orr, a wronged, sympathetic figure and a family man, unjustly martyred for his principles. Into his mouth he puts a heroic speech, uttered just before his execution and designed to give heart to his fellow accused:

> Why droop your spirits? 'Tis not dread of death
> That loads with stifled sighs your ev'ry breath,
> They for your wives and little ones ascend,
> Left in the world, you fear, without a friend.
> I too was happy in a faithful wife,
> And five sweet children, dearer far than life,
> Yet I've resigned them; ne'er shall they be bought
> With my pure Principles – curse the paltry thought.[36] (ll. 13–20)

As the monologue develops the focus moves to the state of the nation, in which it is tempting to read encoded a daring message regarding Orr's own view of the condition of Ireland within the Union. It says much for the country's preoccupation with the Napoleonic threat, and for the respect in which the rehabilitated Orr was now held, that he brought it off unscathed:

> But who shall shield our country, fraterniz'd
> With the false foe that grasps the rights she priz'd?
> Her fleets and hosts are sent, against her will,
> The mandates of Ambition to fulfil;
> Her Plain is pillag'd; garrison'd the Town
> Profan'd her Pulpit; and her Press nail'd down. (ll. 35–40)

Within this framework Napoleon, originally a man of the people, is presented as the ultimate betrayer: 'Now a Plebeian from a distant plain, / Her free Republic ends, and founds his hated reign' (ll. 43–4). The German bookseller, on the other hand, like William Orr who died 'in the faith of a true Presbyterian', faces death and its awful, visible trappings with a confident assurance that he will soon rest in the presence of his God.

The register and general tenor of Orr's conflict-related poems from this period show him assuming the mindset not of a local rhymer but of a national poet who is addressing the country at large on issues of national consequence.

Such works, and Orr's approach, frequently suggest the influence of two quite distinct traditions. These are the Millennarian-prophetic stream within Presbyterianism, and popular lore associated with the Irish Bardic orders. Interest in the latter was perhaps stimulated by his own courtesy title, 'Bard of Ballycarry'.

The Book of Revelation prophesies the millennial reign of Christ on earth, and all Presbyterian sects would have concurred in the belief that it was the role of the church to prepare the world for this event. This conviction seemed particularly pertinent during the revolutionary decade – the 1790s – when many Ulster Presbyterians believed themselves on the threshold of achieving a more democratic and just society throughout Ireland.[37] There were differing interpretations of Biblical prophecy, however, with regard to the manner by which the Millennium would come about. Some sects, particularly those within the Covenanting tradition which had a history of suffering persecution, believed that first there must be a time of great tribulation, an unleashing of the 'four horsemen of the apocalypse' (war, famine, disease and death) in which the wicked would be judged and the church purified, before Christ's kingdom could come in. The possibility of French invasion revived memories of the Covenanter prophet, Alexander Peden, who had spent some time in Ulster in the seventeenth century. Peden's prophecies had included the following: 'The Lord has letten me see the French marching with their armies through the breadth and length of the land, marching to their bridle-reins in the blood of all ranks, and that for a broken, burnt and buried covenant'.[38] As J. R. R. Adams has shown, the time was 'prophetic', and 'old favourites such as Peden ... were pressed into service', apparently to convince supporters that a French role in the Rebellion was within the will of God, and part of his judgement on a repressive state. At the same time, new 'Peden-like figures appeared in the countryside, such as the Covenanter Gibson', who applied apocalyptic texts from Revelation to the current political situation and prophesied 'the immediate destruction of the British monarchy'.[39]

According to Andrew Holmes, 'the jeremiad tradition remained alive and well within the Covenanters and sections of mainstream orthodox Presbyterianism', while the Presbyterian laity as a whole were 'urged by their ministers to read the signs of the times', in order to discern the will of God from these and from the assiduous study and application of the Scriptures: 'Divine displeasure could be detected in unfavourable weather, diplomatic developments, or in the realm of personal experience'.[40] Naturally, in time of war such beliefs exercise a particular fascination, and in his poetry of the Napoleonic era Orr at intervals drew on this tradition to ensure his message resonated with Biblical authority. In the style of an Old Testament prophet he attempted to call the nation's attention to its spiritual condition and to posit a link between that and its present distress.

In 'The Patriot's Complaint' (1817) Orr prescribes a remedy for the ills and griefs he observes in the nation. This subtle work he describes as a 'free versification of the fifth chapter of the *Lamentations of Jeremiah*.[41] *Lamentations* expresses the prophet Jeremiah's deep sorrow over Judah's occupation by foreign, pagan enemies and the fifth chapter in particular grieves over the nation's experience of famine, lawlessness, violation and enslavement. Orr's free versification is rooted in the Biblical text but suggest parallels between Judah's sufferings and Ireland's in the post-Union era. He records, for example, that 'our youths are fain / To sell their service, bread to gain' in the armies of the Assyrian and Egyptian invaders, which hints at the experience of many young Irishmen who, due to poverty, found themselves obliged to enlist in the British armed forces. Orr's remedy echoes the prophet's; he prescribes a repentant return to God himself and to his 'truths' (l. 54), properly practised, if the people wish to see 'Our ancient eminence restore[d]' (l. 52). He writes correctively, in the spirit of a Biblical prophet and also a national poet, or bard. His conflation of the prophetic and bardic personae is still more evident in his 'Part of the Tenth Chapter of the Apocalypse Versified'. Here he imagines 'bards' rather than 'prophets' declaring the mind and purposes of God:

> What time the last loud trump shall sound through space,
>   Sin, death, and substance, shall no more be spar'd;
> Myst'ry and fate shall be fulfill'd, and cease,
>   As just JEHOVAH by his Bards declar'd.[42] (ll. 29–32)

It is likely that Orr had some knowledge of the key and prophetic role of the ancient Irish bards who rallied the troops of the Irish chieftains and empowered them for battle. He had certainly read Owenson's *The Wild Irish Girl*, which includes an account of a visit to the last of the Order, supposedly living in retirement in Ulster.[43] Owenson's text would have referred Orr to Walker's *Memoirs of the Irish Bards*, with which he was in all probability already familiar. The role of the Filidhe, outlined by Walker, would have had a particular resonance for Orr: 'While the battle raged they stood apart and watched in security ... in order to gain subjects for their lays'. This was precisely what Orr was doing as an observer of the war and a commentator upon it in newspaper verse. Walker adds, 'Some of our Bards were prophets too', confirming for Orr the appropriateness of the direction he was taking in his verse. Finally, Walker summarizes the Filidhe's purpose in terms which balance a requirement for didacticism with an imperative to inspire: 'Applaud the valiant, and the base controul, / Disturb, exalt, enchant the human soul'.[44]

The Napoleonic conflict was, of course, not the sole issue which stimulated Orr's imagination at this period. Another was the growing strength of the Abolitionist Movement. Olaudah Equiano, the freed slave and anti-slavery campaigner, had lodged with Samuel Neilson, editor of the *Northern Star*, during his visit to Belfast in 1791. He sold many copies of his autobiography there, where the United Irishmen had a history of support for abolition. William Drennan, resident in Dublin during Equiano's visit to Belfast, wrote to the United Irishmen of his home town encouraging them to support a boycott of sugar cultivated by slaves in the West Indies.[45] Orr demonstrated his continuing support for Abolition in several works and took a keen interest in contemporary reports on the subject. As the *Chronicle* carried details of Wilberforce's and Fox's activities in Parliament, and of horrors such as the deaths of 740 slaves exposed for sale in South Carolina over a period of fifteen days,[46] Orr quickly took up his pen and contributed 'The Dying African'.[47] The poem voices the thoughts of a dying slave, cruelly separated from his family and homeland. Orr's own experiences as an exile have enabled him to empathize here, but there is no doubt that he attributes the same natural, refined human feelings to members of all other races. He is clear, too, in asserting that all are equally valued by God, the 'Sire of white men and of sable' (l. 41).

Orr's work for the *Chronicle* reveals him taking opportunities to engage dynamically with urgent national and political subjects, but also shows him confidently entering into dialogue with other writers, thus providing insights into what stimulated his imagination. Unsurprisingly, given what we have seen of his adherence to a belief in Ireland's distinctive identity, he endorsed enthusiastically the national tales of Sydney Owenson.[48] His poem 'To Miss Owenson' commends *The Wild Irish Girl* and is particularly noteworthy in that it displays no resentment of Owenson's character Father John, the Irish priest, through whom she articulates a distinctly negative characterization of the northern Ulster Scots community. In Father John's view, 'their manners and modes are Scotch', their language is merely 'Scotch dialect' and among them 'the cead mile failte of Irish cordiality seldom lends its welcome home to the stranger's heart'.[49] Owenson's caricature is, frankly, bigoted, every bit as hostile as that of the Ordnance Surveyors of the 1830s, and it is in marked contrast to her portrayal of Horatio, her receptive young hero whose background is in the Ascendancy.

Rather than taking on directly Owenson's othering of Ireland's Scots, Orr captures the moral high ground, demonstrating both his own tolerance and his personal experience of a parallel tolerance among the Catholic population:

> Ne'er shall I, through bigot blindness,
>   My compatriot's virtues stain;
> Far from home, I've proved their kindness
>   On my country's wildest plain:
> To their language quite a stranger,
>   Looks of love their soul express'd,
> While they shelter'd me from danger,
>   Trimm'd their fire, and shar'd their feast.
>
> In the chapel of devotion,
>   Tho' they knew my diff'rent sect,

> And in scenes of blythe commotion,
>   Me they met with kind respect;
> Whether I with priest or peasant
>   Rang'd the banks of Foyle or Dee,
> Social Love was omnipresent,
>   Friendship, and fraternity. (ll. 25–40)

The works of Ulster writers also aroused Orr's attention. In the 'Address to Master Thomas Romney Robinson', Orr commends Robinson (1792–1882), an unusual member of the literary circle which was led by the Anglican Bishop Percy (1729–1811) at Dromore, County Down. Robinson, a prodigy, published a creditable book of verse when aged only fourteen.[50] As he gathered subscriptions for the volume in 1805, he clearly attracted much public attention, only a year after Orr had published his own collection at the age of thirty-four. Perhaps Orr felt that the youngster's success was taking the shine off his own achievement. Certainly, while he praises 'Sweet Robinson ... / The youngest bard who ever yet / In fame's bright temple found a place', his attitude appears lukewarm, for while he claims to be looking forward to future triumphs for Robinson, he may really be hinting that only time will tell whether the adult man will be able to live up to the achievements of the boy:

> Thy parts, if precious time permit,
>   Will merit this distinction high
> For pow'rful friends arise, when wit
>   With wisdom joins ...[51] (ll. 9–12)

It is rare for Orr to demonstrate anything approaching mean-spiritedness, but something very like it is detectable within the 'Address'. He underlines his labouring-class status, opposing it to Robinson's easier circumstances and in closing appears forgetful that he is addressing a mere boy. Instead, making generalized gloomy references to the hardships he has suffered, with a sour, martyred air he sets his face towards death:

> Deceit around me clos'd her net,
>   Distress full oft my spirit bow'd;
> But life's faint sun shall shortly set,
>   Why should dull care its beams becloud? (ll. 37–40)

Such a conclusion is tasteless, revealing Orr at his most unattractive, gloomy and self-obsessed; this dimension of his character no doubt arose from a natural tendency to melancholy, combined with the trauma of dashed hopes and betrayal suffered by many surviving radicals in the post-Union period. Mercifully for his reputation he appears to have kept it well under control for most of his life, but recognition of it as a facet of his personality allows a more ready understanding of the process of his eventual decline.

Despite his gloomy predictions, in 1805 Orr had five or six very prolific years ahead as a regular contributor to the *Chronicle* and to the *Belfast Monthly Magazine*, years in which he achieved a measure of celebrity status and aroused the approbation of a public far beyond the rustic circle in Ballycarry. Readers of the *Chronicle* corresponded with him and other contributors honoured him in their compositions. 'G.' of Ballytresna, in 'Stanzas Addressed to J. O.' offers a particularly sensitive tribute.[52] The writer, J. Geddis, perceives the gentleness and sincerity that are characteristic of Orr, attributing to him a type of enduring innocence: 'Sweet Poet, Nature's artless child, / As ever wak'd the soothing strain' (ll. 1–2).[53] He presents him as the ideal companion with whom to appreciate the countryside since his poetry is inspired by Ulster's own presiding spirit: 'Ultonia's Genius' (l. 39). Contemporary glimpses of Orr are very few, and it is gratifying to have come upon this previously uncollected example in the *Chronicle*.

Throughout his period of regular publication in newspapers Orr continued to make his living as a weaver and to enjoy the society of his neighbours in reading societies and the Masonic Lodge. The part Freemasonry played in his life was clearly immense, judging from his inclusion of several Masonic poems in both his volumes. According to the present-day Masons at Redhall Masonic Lodge, Ballycarry, Freemasonry officially began in the village in 1809, when Orr's name appeared on a list of forty-two subscribers to a warrant for a lodge. It met initially in a room above what is now Millar's Public House on Main Street. Orr is believed to have been, at different periods, both Master of the Lodge and a Lodge Secretary, the latter suggested by the crossed quill pens on his monument which gives the number of his Lodge as 1014.[54] However, his Lodge membership may date from an earlier period, as suggested by his poem celebrating the Lodge at nearby Ballynure which appeared in his 1804 collection. Repeatedly his Masonic poems extol the inclusivity that had attracted him to the United Irishmen, as we see here:

> The good of ev'ry creed and clime,
>   Calvinian, Cath'lick, Manx, or Moor,
> Shall be accepted, any time,
>   By us, the Lodge of Ballynure.[55] (ll. 13–6)

The expressed willingness to welcome Catholics to the Lodge seems to lend weight to Petri Mirala's view that 'Irish freemasonry as a whole, if not all lodges in all regions, did transcend sectarian divides until the Catholics started leaving in large numbers'. He dates the departure of Catholics from the 1810s, and attributes this to 'the hostility of their own clergy'.[56] Orr's 'Address: Spoken in St Patrick's Lodge, Carrickfergus on St Patrick's Day, 1808' is noteworthy for his expression of faith in Grattan's attempts to secure Catholic Emancipation: 'GRATTAN will befriend FINGAL; / And all an equal right shall gain / T'attend their common country's call' (ll. 33–6).[57] His concern for the poor also found an outlet in the philanthropy which was central to Masonic engagement with the community:

> From Heav'n, men of Ulster! (who bounteously yielding
>   To sympathy's summons, are poor orphans shielding,)
> Shall mercy descend to the mansion you're building,
>   Where want she'll alleviate, and ignorance teach.[58] (ll. 37–40)

His own dignified leadership within the Lodge was commended by James Campbell, the weaver poet of Ballynure in his commemorative 'Dirge'.[59]

Orr's monument in Templecorran Cemetery is adorned with Masonic symbols, including an arch, square and compass. The attendees at the ceremony at which the foundation stone was laid included another poet, James Russell English. It was English who had called for subscriptions for the monument in his poetry volume of 1830, but a letter has recently come to light which expresses delight at the success of English's appeal for funds; it also commends Orr's Masonic connections and poetry, and demonstrates the high regard in which he was held in masonic circles:

> In fact Orr has composed more good Masonic songs than any poet we know ... Very many honest, hard-working sons of the compass and square ... in consideration of their 'Bardie's' poetical labours in their cause as well as in their country's, will be amongst the first in lending their countenance and aid to the present undertaking.
>   An Admirer of Gratitude.[60]

The evidence of the *Belfast Commercial Chronicle* in particular suggests that Orr, in the newspaper's columns and in correspondence, was interacting with a readership composed of people who were attracted to literary and political subjects – the type of company that he had enjoyed at the home of Samuel Thomson during the optimistic 1790s. It is reasonable to ask, then, if at this period of his life the friendship with Thomson continued to develop. Two surviving letters indicate that it did. In one, dated 4 January 1806, Orr expresses appreciation of Thomson's correspondence with him and regrets they do not live nearer to each other, for, he says, 'I am proud to think that there is a congeniality in our tastes'. He suspects that Thomson is lonely and admits that he is equally so. The companions available to him are distinctly uncongenial, with little to offer in conversation but 'ribaldry or scandal'. The letter includes some discussion of their respective publications with Orr revealing that he has recently published in the *Belfast Commercial Chronicle* and offering to send copies to Thomson, if he is 'not a reader of that paper'. It is evidence of the strength of their friendship and the pleasure they take in each other's work that they agree to 'exchange scrawls monthly'. Orr concludes the letter affectionately, signing himself 'your sincere friend and brother poet'.[61]

In a further letter, dated 24 May 1807, Orr makes detailed, confident commendations or criticisms of Thomson's third volume of verse, published in 1806, and arranges a visit to Thomson's home.[62] All the evidence in these letters points to a strong friendship between committed writers who enjoy one another's company, and respect each other. The only surviving letter from Orr among Thomson's collected correspondence shows him perfectly capable of handling the latter's rather prickly temperament. In response to what we may infer is Thomson's offence at Orr's delay in writing to him he adopts a common sense but soothing approach:

> I assure you I am never offended at anyone without a cause; and I believe you are conscious to yourself that you never gave me any ... I design'd to visit you in Crambo Cave as soon as the weather should be favourable ... Be so good then as to excuse this error in me which did not, I solemnly aver proceed from supercilious neglect, but from a kind of off-putting carelessness ... Write soon my worthy sir – after the deserv'd *nettling* you have given me you may believe you'll never find in me a procrastinating correspondent again.[63]

The word 'nettling' is underlined, a knowing reference to Thomson's pseudonym 'Lowrie Nettle' sometimes used in the 1790s,[64] which shows Orr good-humouredly invoking their shared history.

A further link between Orr and Thomson is provided by the Donegore weaver poet, John Dickey, who expressed appreciation of the work of each of them in wry, rambling pieces employing Scots verse forms and vernacular language. Following Thomson's death he wrote to Orr, addressing him familiarly as 'auld neighbour Orr', or 'Jamie lad' (ll. 1, 37).[65] Dickey, a true Ulster Scot, demonstrates that he is not overawed by Orr's status. His tone is jocular in this *Christis Kirk* poem, but there is an underlying sadness as he reflects on the events of 1798 at Donegore Hill, the failure of 'the Union's wondrous plan' (l. 13) and the death of Samuel Thomson.[66] He also provides a compelling glimpse of Orr that could hardly be more different, if it is accurate, from J. Geddis's discussed above:

> My frien' tells me you like a glass,
>   A bard for that, auld brither,
> And likewise adds, a bonny lass,
>   When these come *baith thegither*. (ll. 100–3) ['both together']

McDowell, when writing to excuse Orr's heavy drinking in his later years and the bad company he kept attributed these 'errors' to the fact that he was not steadied and focused by the loving partnership of a married relationship, but in his 'Elegiac Stanzas on the Death of James Orr'[67] he includes the following fascinating cameo:

> His maid, whose breast with love still glows,
>   In solitude's dark shade now grieves;
> Her breast, which knew no ebbs and flows,
>   Is rack'd, and like the wild wave heaves. (ll. 45–8)

Remarkably, there has been no speculation by commentators on the implications of these lines which seem to indicate that at the end of his life Orr may have been in a relationship with a tender and faithful woman to whom the often rather prissy-sounding McDowell here accords considerable dignity and respect.

Orr's decline from enthusiastic young radical, venerated poet and respected social commentator into unhappy, obsessive drunkard has distinctly tragic overtones, and recalls Wordsworth's summation of the lives of poets: 'We Poets in our youth begin in gladness; / But thereof come in the end despondency and madness.'[68] Although he achieved a measure of public success as a writer during the 1800s, the trajectory of his experience illustrates 'the sharp division into a Before and an After' which Kenneth R. Johnston has discussed at length in an essay about the many radical poets of the 1790s whose writing careers were interrupted or cut short 'by their encounters with the massive domestic state machinery of espionage and repression operated by William Pitt the Younger in the 1790s.'[69] In Orr's case that 'After' included illness, depression, loneliness and an enduring sense of loss. His monument celebrates his achievements as 'poet, patriot and philanthropist', but in his last published work he supplies a poignant glimpse of himself towards the end of his life. In 'Ode to a Butterfly on Wing in Winter', with real tenderness he addresses a fragile creature that has miraculously survived the changing seasons. The insect draws his compassion, he explains, because 'since misfortune was my lot, / I mercy can't forget' (ll. 38–9).[70] Undoubtedly he identifies with the butterfly, for he too feels alone and out of kilter with the season. He vows to protect it, then to free it in the spring. As he pictures it flitting 'From grove to glen, from mead to hill, / In peace and freedom' (ll. 46–7) he appears to be wishing he could share the fate he imagines for the butterfly. Powerfully understated, this last published poem movingly conveys his sense of loss as he longs for another spring, while all too aware that time has passed him by.

In 1816 both John Dickey and James Campbell contributed dirges on the death of Orr, demonstrating that he never lost the respect of his fellow labouring-class poets partly, no doubt, because he never became gentrified. Dickey, though, in his commemorative poem, 'On the Death of James Orr, of Ballycarry'[71] is clearly attempting to suggest that there is something momentous and of national import in Orr's passing:

> Hang your heads ye minstrels gay,
>   O'er Hibernia's Island merry –
> Death has laid a Bard in clay,
>   Tuneful Orr o' Ballycarry. (ll. 33– 6)

Orr's reputation has for many years, in essence, been that of a local folk poet, but this and the preceding chapters have called attention to some of the less familiar dimensions of his persona. In volume, variety and quality his poetry and prose for the *Belfast Commercial Chronicle* and the *Belfast Monthly Magazine* reveal him engaging confidently with an urban demographic, with writers and thinkers from the liberally educated professional classes, and supplying an intelligent, individual perspective on national and international affairs.

5 RUDE SCOTCH RHYMER? SCOTTISH ENLIGHTENMENT INFLUENCES ON JAMES ORR

The beauty of Wolfe Tone's attempt to substitute the common name of Irishman for Protestant, Catholic and Dissenter was that it postulated a common national identity around which the three main faith communities might unite and which would enable government to function, while leaving room for a pluralist, rather than an essentialist model of cultural and religious identity.[1] Furthermore, Ian McBride argues that United Irish political thought is 'better described as Enlightenment republicanism than Romantic separatism'. He explains that 'it was not an assertion of self-determination grounded upon ethnic or cultural difference, but an assault on *ancien regime* pillars of monarchy, aristocracy and church in the name of a non-sectarian republic'.[2] Repeatedly in James Orr's work we observe him adhering to such principles, denouncing intolerance and deploring sectarianism.

Supporters of United Irish strategy during the 1790s in Belfast had readily embraced cultural pluralism and employed it as a weapon against the metropolitan-centred outlook of the establishment. Irish cultural traditions in music, poetry and language were enthusiastically adopted and studied in order to underline the Irishmen's sense of difference, but the Presbyterian Dissenters had a further weapon in their cultural armoury, in the shape of their Scots heritage, with which to challenge the Ascendancy. Their 'cultural declaration of independence' was expressed in their renewed enthusiasm for the Ulster vernacular verse tradition, for which the popularity of Burns in contemporary Scotland supplied further endorsement.[3] Scots culture additionally emphasized self-improvement and education, and in the eighteenth century Scots thinkers and literati, such as Blair, Hume and Smith, were at the centre of an Enlightenment that some would say had been 'fathered' by the Ulsterman Francis Hutcheson during his period as Professor of Moral Philosophy at Glasgow. In the later eighteenth century Hutcheson's legacy was still massively influential on philosophers and ministers in both Scotland and Ulster.[4] Here, too, was a heritage which could be tapped, and incorporated into statements of cultural distinctiveness.

Within Tone's inclusive model of Irishness, there is no contradiction in Orr drawing on the Scottish cultural heritage associated with the Presbyterian Dissenters. It does not make him less Irish, except in essentialist constructions of Irishness. What is significant is that since most of his publications appeared after 1800, he persists in adhering to the United Irish 1790s model well into the Union period, embracing both his Irish identity and his Scottish cultural heritage. This chapter will demonstrate how Orr's work is permeated with Scottish Enlightenment thinking, particularly the literary theorizing and religious teachings of Hugh Blair. In addition it will posit an explanation for his decision to publish poetry mainly in English rather than in the vernacular.

Liam McIlvanney rightly draws attention to Orr's 'broad knowledge of contemporary Scottish Enlightenment literature', commenting that 'Although the *persona* of the untutored rustic was a favourite device in vernacular poetry … the poets themselves were no backwoodsmen cut off from the mainstream of Enlightenment thought'.[5] In addition, it should be remembered that there are many references to Locke, Gray, Pope, Shakespeare, Milton, Goldsmith and Bloomfield in Orr's *oeuvre* as well as to Scottish authors and thinkers.

As we have seen, New Light Presbyterianism with its emphasis on the importance of the moral life was the mode of belief espoused by James Orr. It would be very surprising indeed, therefore, if Orr, an avid student of theology and philosophy, had been unaware of Francis Hutcheson's system of moral philosophy.[6] His Braid Scotch poem 'Song, Written in Winter' (1804) contains a hint that he may have been acquainted with Hutcheson's *Inquiry into the Original of our Ideas of Beauty and Virtue* (1726). This work begins as a type of pastoral set in winter, but modulates into a tender love lyric. Few lines express better an insecure lover's combination of admiration and fearfulness than these which portray Sylvia in imagery appropriate to the season, both wintry and exquisite:

> This night wi' the lass that I hope will be *kin'* soon, ['kind'
>   Wi' Sylvia, wha charms me, a wee while I'll *stap*: ['stop'
> Her e'e is as clear as the ice the moon shines on,
>   As gentle her smile as the snaw-flakes that *drap*. (ll. 17–20) ['drop'

Orr is careful to stress that Sylvia's attractions are not limited to her appearance. Indeed, he fears her charitable concern for her fellow creatures is likely to be uppermost in her mind, at the expense of any amorous inclination towards himself. He recognizes that while he writes poetry about deprivation and poverty and feels a sense of pride in his own work, his words stimulate her to more practical concern:

> Perhaps she's now plannin', to pit a restriction
>   Upon my profusion on *niest* new-year's night, ['next'
> To help some poor fam'lie on beds o' affliction,
>   Without food or fuel, attendants or light.

> Perhaps, singin' noo the dirge I tak' pride in,
>   She thinks on the last storm, wi' pity an' dread –
> How the *spait* crush't the cots – how Tam brak his leg slidin', ['flood']
> An' herds in the *muir fand* the poor pedlar dead. (ll. 21–8) ['moor found']

Hutcheson's *Inquiry* had explored the relationship between beauty and goodness, arguing that our moral sense compels us to recognize beauty in the virtuous actions of another, irrespective of our own (selfish) interests.[7] He develops this point thus:

> The quality approved by our moral sense is conceived to reside in the person approved, and to be a perfection and dignity in him ... Virtue is then called amiable or lovely, from its raising good-will or love in spectators toward the agent.[8]

Unquestionably Orr echoes, even endorses, this view in his closing stanza, in which he asserts that a pretty face or lovely body are insufficient in themselves to attract him:

> 'Tis guidness maks beauty. The face ne'er was *lo'esome*, ['lovely'
>   That *weepsna whaur* woe is nor smilesna wi' glee. – ['weeps not where'
> If Sympathy's strange tae the *saft* female bosom, ['soft'
>   Its want's no made up by a bright cheek, or *e'e*. (ll. 29–32) ['eye'

Hutcheson identifies 'sympathy' as one of the 'particular passions' included in the general term benevolence which, he claims, 'denote the internal spring of virtue.'[9]

Orr's insecurity, however, results from his uncertainty over whether Sylvia's 'sympathy' extends as far as tender emotions towards himself. Ironically, he is caught in a dilemma for which Hutcheson offers no comfort or remedy: his moral sense rightly impels him to admire Sylvia's beautifully virtuous actions but this has the effect of making her all the more personally desirable as he observes her. The more unselfish good she does to others, the more attractive she seems. According to Hutcheson, this was a right and proper response:

> the moral beauty of actions, or dispositions, increases according to the number of persons to whom the good effects of them extend ... The moral beauty of characters arises from their actions or sincere intentions of the public good, according to their power.[10]

Orr desires Sylvia's 'sympathy' to include him and to spark a reciprocation of his passion, but had she responded in such a way this would inevitably have made her less available to others. Hutcheson's system is not entirely friendly to personal happiness gained at the expense of the greater good, for as he explains: 'the highest perfection of virtue is an universal calm good-will toward all sensitive natures. Hence it is that we condemn particular attachments, when inconsistent with the interests of great societies.'[11]

It is very likely that Orr had read works by David Hume, since his poem 'The Reading Society' (1817) includes a reference to the Scots philosopher. It is unclear, however, whether or not he had read Hume's dissertation on suicide, in which the author attempts to liberate attitudes to this difficult issue from what he designates 'superstition', by arguing that 'the almighty Creator' governs the world and the natural universe through laws which he has himself established and which his creatures have no power to disturb. Within this system, however, man and all animals 'are entrusted to their own prudence and skill for their conduct in the world, and have full authority, as far as their power extends, to alter all the operations of nature'. Hume points out that every action of man in some way 'innovates upon the general laws of matter and motion'. Clearly man's particular actions, therefore, do not interfere in any way with the general laws that govern the universe. This must mean, he asserts, that everyone has 'the free disposal of his own life'. He then dismisses the view that human life is of such great importance 'that 'tis a presumption to dispose of it'. He claims, rather, that 'the life of a man is of no greater importance to the universe than that of an oyster'.[12]

This decidedly bleak view of the human condition reveals something of a contemporary debate on the subject of suicide, of which Orr would certainly have been aware, and which continued into his day.[13] The orthodox Christian position, held in most denominations, would have been that suicide is self-murder, evidence of the sin of despair and an act of defiance against the Deity who had permitted the circumstances which caused the despair. As an essentially didactic writer, Orr, whether producing essays or composing poetry, consistently adopts a moral position. In this respect, then, his poems which deal with the vexed issue of suicide may be understood as contributions to the contemporary debate. One of these, 'Gormal', a poem about a youth who poisoned himself, clearly rejects conventional beliefs since the narrator unequivocally deplores the view that Gormal, victim of unrequited love, had committed an action too evil to permit his burial in the churchyard.[14] The opening poem of Orr's 1817 volume approaches the issue rather differently. Its title strikes an upbeat note: 'Man was Made to Smile',[15] suggesting it has been composed in deliberate opposition to Burns's 'Man was Made to Mourn, A Dirge' (1784–5). The latter, featuring an encounter between the poet and an elderly 'Sage', reveals Burns in melancholy mode, despondent due to life's hardships and inequalities.[16] Orr's poem purports to be the words of 'a pilgrim' (l. 1) to a young man, 'Error's dupe' (l. 5), who is about to commit suicide and who is 'Repeating oft th'apalling strain, / That man to mourn was made' (ll. 3–4). The suicide attempt itself seems to link the youth in Orr's poem with Burns's conclusion that only death relieves the person who suffers woe and oppression in this life: 'O Death! the poor man's dearest friend, / The kindest and the best!' (ll. 81–2).

Given Orr's own melancholic tendency, his disappointed hopes and the fascination with suicide and madness that can be traced in his work, one can hardly escape the conclusion that here Orr is dramatizing an internal conflict. The young man may represent the poet in his despair, while the pilgrim speaks for reason, faith and conscience. In the end he manages to dissuade the youth from a desperate act. While clearly as liberated from superstition regarding suicide as Hume would have wished, Orr here offers a more positive alternative to the philosopher's reasoned dismissal of religious objections to the act, but he also challenges Burns's profound despair.

The pilgrim's advice, which recommends that a man should face adversity with faith and take comfort from intellectual pleasure, seems to echo Hugh Blair's teaching, rather than Hume's. Blair counsels that 'Religion prepares the mind for encountering with fortitude the most severe shocks of adversity', and also that the educated man's mind 'is a kingdom to him; and he can still enjoy it'.[17] In addition, Blair's guidance on the desirability of a life that is both pious and moral permeates some of Orr's best work. According to Blair

> when beneficence and devotion are united, they pour upon the man in whom they meet, the full pleasures of a good and pure heart. His alms connect him with men; his prayers with God. He looks without dismay on both worlds.[18]

We find an echo of this last phrase in 'The Penitent' in which Christy Blair's family life, reformed following his conversion at a Methodist meeting, displays such Blairite balance: '*They min't baith warls*' ['they took care of both worlds'] (l. 154).

It was not for his sermons alone but for the *Lectures on Rhetoric and Belles Lettres* that Orr considered himself profoundly indebted to Hugh Blair. It is easy to imagine what a joy it must have been for him to discover that in the printed version of Blair's lectures he had in his hands a university course in appreciation and criticism. Denied the technological facilities available to the present-day distance learner, his thirst for improvement meant that he still proved an avid and able student. His 'Elegy on the Death of Hugh Blair, D.D.' (1804) reveals not only how much he would have valued the opportunity to hear his admired teacher in person but also the extent to which he felt indebted to him, both educationally and spiritually.[19] This unusual poem combines the qualities of Romantic vision and mediaeval dream poem on a religious subject, the latter here transposed to a Presbyterian context. It records Orr's, or his poetic persona's, wild grief at the news of Blair's death:

> Dark midnight reigns; but how can gentle sleep
>   (Wildly I cry'd, and wet my couch with tears)
> In kind forgetfulness my senses steep,
>   Since BLAIR is dead, the pride of modern years? (ll. 1–4)

The intense and personal sense of loss expressed are in marked contrast to the genuine but altogether more measured sorrow with which he recorded his feelings on learning of the death of Burns:

> Sad news! He's gane, wha baith amus'd
> The man o' taste, an' taught the rude;
> Whase warks hae been mair read an' *roos'd* ['perused']
> Than *onie*, save the word o' *Gude*:[20] (ll. 9–12) ['any', 'God']

An exploration of the poem confirms Orr's familiarity with Blair's sermons, his literary lectures, and his critical dissertation on Macpherson's *Ossian*. The speaker dreams he is present in Edinburgh as Blair delivers his final sermon and enumerates the precepts, moral, religious and literary, which we are to understand comprise his legacy. This provides a telling insight into Orr's personal reception of Blair's work, and reveals those aspects of it which guided him in his own life and writing.

Undeniably, Blair's approach, whether to literary or religious subjects, is characterized by its moderation. In his *Lectures on Rhetoric and Belles Lettres*, he deplores extremes of poetic diction but supplies copious guidance regarding the effective and proper utilization of literary style. Summarized thus his literary theory may appear somewhat unadventurous and prescriptive, but this is not the case. He recognized that true genius is always innovative: 'No observations or rules can indeed supply the defect of genius, or inspire it where it is wanting'.[21] Equally, while aspects of style such as figurative language may be deliberately employed by writers of genius, they serve only to enhance the expression of genuine imagination and feeling: 'A writer of genius conceives his subject strongly; his imagination is filled and impressed with it; and pours itself forth in that Figurative Language which imagination naturally speaks ... his style will be beautiful because his feelings are lively'.[22]

Blair's discussion of poetry favours and employs examples from the classical masters and from eighteenth-century English writers, such as Pope, Addison and Akenside. In discussing Macpherson's *Ossian* he commends it within the context of his general enthusiasm for ancient poems, remarking that 'They promise some of the highest beauties of poetical writing', since 'those times which we call barbarous, are favourable to the poetical spirit'.[23] Blair's opinion of the Scottish vernacular tradition, however, seems less favourable, as we observe when he comments thus on Ramsay's *The Gentle Shepherd* (1725):

> It is a great disadvantage to this beautiful Poem, that it is written in the old rustic dialect of Scotland, which, in a short time, will probably be entirely obsolete, and not intelligible; and it is a farther disadvantage, that it is so entirely formed on the rural manners of Scotland, that none but a native of that country can thoroughly understand, or relish it.[24]

Liam McIlvanney takes up the issue of Blair's attitude to vernacular poetry in a discussion of Blair's relationship with Burns, in which he challenges the view of Blair, often presented by twentieth-century Scottish critics, as 'the representative of a Scottish critical establishment that was inherently incapable of appreciating Burns's true achievement, and that continually threatened to vitiate his work by encouraging a conformity to polite Anglo-centric norms'.[25] Burns was, decidedly, capable of negotiating both the cultural nationalism inherent in the vernacular project, and the metropolitanizing voices within the Scottish Enlightenment. However, McIlvanney shows that Blair's views on language and primitive poetry which, for example, privilege 'boldness' and 'strength' over correctness and regularity could be read by a vernacular poet as implying encouragement.[26] He argues additionally that Blair would have understood Burns as the very type of original, primitive genius his lectures commend.

McIlvanney's purpose is to challenge what he clearly believes is an overly simplistic view of Blair as an Anglicizing imperialist who is at odds with bardic nationalism. To lend weight to his viewpoint, McIlvanney cites Orr's 'Elegy on the Death of Hugh Blair, D.D.', commenting that 'As a vernacular poet, Orr clearly does not see himself as engaged in a cultural confrontation with "the world of Hugh Blair"'. Orr and Burns, however, composed in very different cultural, political and linguistic contexts. Orr was certainly a vernacular poet, and one of exceptional talent, but unlike Burns he did not write primarily in the vernacular. In his lifetime he was apparently known as 'the Burns of Ulster', a designation that, if it had charmed him, would surely have led him to write far more vernacular pieces than he did. Rather than assuming that Orr's standard register 'Elegy' on Blair provides evidence that the Ulster poet felt Blair's world was not in conflict with his vernacular writing, one should ask why Orr chose to write primarily in a standard register. Was this a result of Blair's influence, or because Blair's opinions confirmed him in his chosen course?

It should be remembered that once transplanted to Ulster, Scots never attained the status of a high literary language that it had originally enjoyed in Scotland. Philip Robinson has found that although it was employed for letters and business by the original Scots colonists of the Plantations era, within a generation or two it had, of necessity, given way to the English tongue of the Ascendancy and was relegated very quickly to the home or the farmyard.[27] In Ulster, Scots did not continue, as it did in Scotland until 1707, within a jurisdiction separate from English authority. Nor was Scots ever a majority language within Ireland as a whole. Orr, though conscious of his Scottish heritage, in his work for the *Belfast Monthly Magazine* and the *Belfast Commercial Chronicle*, appears to have been making a deliberate effort to address the whole of Ireland, maintaining the United Irish vision that was inclusive of all sects. In Ireland, Braid Scotch was the mother tongue only of the inhabitants of rural communities such as Orr's at Broadisland; although they were Scots descended, however, they regarded Ireland as their native country.

In the light of this, and although the reading of Scots literature, including Burns, Ramsay, Montgomerie and others was certainly widespread throughout Ulster in the eighteenth century, it is hardly surprising that Orr, at the dawn of the nineteenth century and facing up to the reality of the Union of 1801, considered carefully the place of vernacular compositions within his published work and accepted that English was the *lingua franca* of the reading public, as well as the idiom of the majority of the writers and scholars he admired. Thus he chose to write primarily in formal English. It is likely that his reading of Blair's lectures confirmed to him that the course he adopted was both practical and tasteful.

Though there is no direct evidence that Burns read the text of Blair's lectures, he too had to grapple with the language issue. As Fiona Stafford points out, in his Kilmarnock Preface Burns, while appearing to confess his lack of a classical education, has the confidence to present himself as an 'authoritative, authentic and continuing' commentator on rural life,[28] but even Burns's verse, she suggests, grew more self-conscious following his exposure to Edinburgh's literary circles where 'critical praise of naturalness, spontaneity and feeling could translate quickly into contempt for ignorance'.[29] Today, of course, Burns is recognized as a giant of international literature. Viewed from Ireland at the turn of the nineteenth century, however, once the initial wild rapture over Burns had settled, the vernacular project may have seemed but one element in a vast array of philosophical, theological, historical and literary composition that was primarily couched in the English tongue. Nigel Leask, for example, reminds us that 'the vernacular poets Ramsay, Fergusson and Burns all published a considerable corpus of English verse which was influenced by Augustan and neo-Augustan models, some of it of high quality'.[30]

Blair's reference to Ramsay's *The Gentle Shepherd*, a text popular in Ulster throughout the eighteenth century, had judged it likely to become obsolete due to its language soon appearing 'unintelligible', and to its 'being so entirely formed on the manners of rural Scotland'. As an aspiring writer, Orr could not afford to risk charges of unintelligibility and he appears to have taken a hard look at the audience with whom his vernacular verse was most popular. In an 'Address to Noah Dalway, of Bella-Hill, Esq.' (1806), a local landowner who had congratulated him on his 1804 volume, he appears dismissive of this section of his *oeuvre* and of its audience: 'My rude Scotch rhymes the tasteful justly slight, / While Scotch-tongued rustics scorn each nobler flight' (ll. 23–4).[31] While this may in part be understood as the conventional, and partly ironic, self-deprecation of the labouring-class poet who is addressing a social superior, it is also clear evidence that Orr did not wish to be known primarily as a writer of vernacular verse. Blair's lectures, with their emphasis on a dynamic, technically superior, but unaffected English style may have confirmed to him the best way forward. For Orr, Blair's guidance had the authority of the printed word, in which the teacher's piety and erudition appeared paramount. In a survey of Blair's works which he imaginatively voices through Blair himself, Orr begins with the sermons, emphasizing the importance of discussion, debate and reason rather than slavish obedience:

> 'I prov'd them – so must you – discuss – decide –
>   'The abus'd apostate whom conviction fires,
> 'Is nobler than the sots who heir untry'd,
>   'Th'implicit faith bequeath'd by senseless sires. (ll. 29–32)

Practical good works are also required as evidence of sound doctrine: 'What is the doctrine worth without the deed?'(l. 36), asks the teacher.

As a reader of John Home's *Douglas*, Orr would have been aware of the controversy concerning the production of a piece of verse drama by a minister and of the conservative forces within the Kirk in Scotland and in Ulster that opposed, or at best merely tolerated, literary prowess.[32] He celebrates Blair's divergence from this anti-literary trend by allowing his 'dream Blair' to summarize his attitude and endeavours thus:

> 'Refinement and religion, long at strife,
>   'I strove to join, and thought the polish'd breast,
> 'More likely to produce a lovely life,
>   'Than the rude soul which no fine art had grac'd. (ll. 37–40)

In fact, the development of 'taste', or the ability to judge and evaluate what is both acceptable and fine in literature, is an issue to which Blair devotes some space, and it is a skill to which Orr aspires, allowing it to occur as a concept in several poems.[33]

Next, Orr draws directly on Blair's comments on *Ossian* and also on his commendation of Pope, made in his lecture on style. Blair could admire what he described as the state in which 'human nature shoots wild and free' because it encouraged 'the high exertions of fancy and passion' which he believed marked good, primitive poetry.[34] However, he placed Pope among the 'first-rate writers of the language' who achieved perfect elegance through being able to inform the understanding of the reader, while employing beauty of expression without 'misplaced finery'.[35] Orr imagines his mentor suggesting that a fusion of the best qualities of both types of writing might be made by a writer of genius in order to achieve the desired sublime effect:

> 'Perhaps my lectures may some genius teach
>   'To judge aright of beauty and defect,
> 'And, steep sublimity! thy summit reach,
>   'Wild, as e'en OSSIAN, though as POPE correct. (ll. 41–4)

Inspired by his reading of Blair, then, Orr clearly aspires to a literary synthesis of these two apparent opposites.

It is in the following verse, most significant of all, that Orr opposes two further extremes, and it is this which may hold the key to the direction his poetry took in his 1804 volume and afterwards:

> 'Perhaps by them,[36] reclaim'd and genuine taste
> 'Alike uncouth rusticity shall scorn,
> 'And affectation, which too long disgrac'd
> 'Th'unwieldy page it labour'd to adorn. (ll. 45–8)

Imaginatively couched in the words of Blair, this may well be Orr's poetic manifesto, as important as the rather coy preface to his 1804 volume. Certainly, throughout his two volumes and his newspaper publications, Orr appears to have striven with varying success for the unaffected style which Blair commends. Most significant of all in this text is his opposing of 'affectation' with 'uncouth rusticity'. This latter quality, which he (and many others) associated with vernacular speech, he sees as an extreme to be avoided; it is as much a distraction from the message as the other extreme of artificial, ultra-poetic diction. Orr remained true to this chosen middle course throughout the rest of his poetic career, reserving the vernacular for works addressed to, recording, or celebrating the life of his own community, or for personal pieces. His sense of decorum did not falter for, as we shall see, in his ethnographic masterwork 'The Irish Cottier's Death and Burial' (1817), which addresses the whole of Ireland, his synthesis of vernacular wildness with correctness of tone and form, enabled him to achieve the sublime at which he aimed, and to speak out powerfully on behalf of his own community. Orr's relationship with vernacularity was complex, and may only be appreciated within the context of the political and linguistic realities of Ireland in the 1800s, and with an awareness of his very particular understanding of literary decorum.

The final stanza of the 'Elegy' hints that Orr regarded himself as indebted to Blair at a very personal level. The concluding words of Blair's shade are:

> 'But if I've forc'd presumption's tears to flow,
> 'Or coax'd young folly into wisdom's yoke,
> Th'unfam'd achievement more consoles me now ...' (ll. 53–5)

Of whom can Orr have been speaking in the reference to 'young folly' encouraged to act more wisely? Surely of himself – the *enfant terrible* of Thomson's circle who thundered from the columns of the *Northern Star* and turned out on 7 June 1798 only to have his democratic hopes dashed and his future suddenly narrowed into enforced and unhappy exile. On his return Blair's balanced, rational piety evidently assisted in restoring his stability, both emotional and spiritual, following the disastrous personal and political trauma he had suffered.

The piece appears in his *Poems* of 1804; Blair died in 1800, which indicates it was written at a time when Orr, recently returned to Ballycarry, was undergoing the process of rehabilitation and recovery. The words of many of Blair's sermons could be cited as likely to have provided guidance and support at such a time, not least his discourse on 'Gentleness'.

In this homily, Blair first distinguishes between different types of wisdom:

> One may often be wise in his own eyes, who is far from being so in the judgement of the world; and to be reputed a very wise man by the world, is no security for being accounted wise by God.

These would have been sobering words to one who had received a great degree of public acclaim for his early work but who had quickly found both his vision and himself rejected. A characteristic of true wisdom, Blair asserts, is the Christian virtue of Gentleness, assuring his audience that this is no 'passive tameness which submits, without struggle, to every encroachment of the violent', but requires 'a manly spirit, and a fixed principle' which 'stands opposed, not to the most determined regard for virtue and truth, but to harshness and severity, to arrogance and overbearing, to violence and oppression'. In addition, however, 'Meekness restrains our angry passions ... Gentleness corrects whatever is offensive in our manners; and, by a constant train of humane attentions, studies to alleviate the burden of common misery ... It is ... temperate in zeal.'[37]

We have here much of the rule of life which Orr followed, and which he sought to promote in his poetry and essays from 1804 onwards. He remained as opposed to oppression as he had always been and employed his verse to speak out on behalf of the underprivileged and marginalized but he was careful to advocate non-violent methods of resistance.[38] His action during his last illness in instructing McDowell to gather his unpublished works for publication and to sell them to relieve the poor of Broadisland certainly demonstrates his humanity and his desire to alleviate suffering. Undoubtedly, after his return from exile, the brashness of his youthful zeal was tempered and his angry passion restrained, though he could still deliver a verbal tongue-lashing when he felt it appropriate. His own horror at violence underlined for him the wisdom of Blair's words. If one is seeking a Scottish root for the stylistic direction of the greater part of Orr's poetry, and for the ideas that informed and comforted his mind, particularly in the 1800–4 period, the influence of Hugh Blair is as much in evidence as that of Robert Burns.

From the same period emanates a remarkable poem, 'occasioned', so Orr himself claims, by his reading of William Robertson's *History of Scotland* (1753–9), and describing an encounter with the ghost of Mary Queen of Scots. 'The Vision – An Elegy'[39] has been several times cited by commentators as providing evidence of the Scottishness of Orr's reading material,[40] but the text itself and its relationship to the work which is its backdrop have not yet been thoroughly explored. It is hoped that the following discussion may function at least as a beginning to that exploration.

The title 'The Vision' in itself has several Scottish resonances, as Orr would have been well aware. It was the title Burns gave the work in which he portrayed his encounter with his Muse, from whom he received his bardic commission.[41] However, it was also the title of Allan Ramsay's intensely nationalist work, included in his *Ever Green* collection nine years after the suppression of the 1715 Rebellion.[42] Ramsay too has a supernatural encounter, in his case with that icon of Scottish independence, William Wallace, whose message includes what could be read as the somewhat dispiriting prophecy that only deterioration in the state of the nation and intensified persecution will perpetuate further revolt. Orr flirts with, echoes and complicates many of the themes, tropes and nuances within the earlier works, tapping into the shared Scots cultural heritage of his community in order to challenge assumed orthodoxies and present a message with global application. Perhaps this is why Orr, unlike Ramsay or Burns in their corresponding works, here chooses to write in the formal register; perhaps he does this also because he is voicing the words of a queen.

In their 'vision' poems Ramsay and Burns present themselves, or their narrators, as Romantic figures, poets wandering and pondering alone. Each experiences a sense of despondency, while Burns is also worn out from the physical effort of farm labour. Both speakers enjoy renewed hope as a result of their encounters with the spirit world. Burns, tempted to give up verse-making altogether, instead accepts that he has a poetic calling. Ramsay, troubled and perplexed while sheltering within a cave located in a wild, classically Scottish landscape, receives encouragement for his Jacobite hopes through his narrator's meeting with the hero Wallace, who is still a vigorous spirit to be reckoned with. Both Burns and Ramsay have been permitted a privileged glimpse of the 'other' world, and as a result of it are in possession of secret knowledge that allows them to face present circumstances with revived hopes.

Orr's 'The Vision' sits very well within this tradition. He provides an epigraph designed to intrigue the reader, which he has taken from Home's popular, controversial and tragic play *Douglas*, referred to above. It is a slightly altered version of a few lines from Douglas's opening speech in Act Five:

> Descending spirits have convers'd with men,
> In such a place as this, at such an hour,
> And told the secrets of the world to come.[43]

The place where his epiphany occurs is a favourite with him for composition – Templecorran Cemetery, with its ruined church. This is a place which links him to his own dead and to the village's historic and prehistoric past. The speaker has chosen to set himself apart from 'the hamlet's train'(l. 1) who are enjoying community dancing in the open air. Instead he peruses the 'tale of Scotia's hapless queen' (l. 4), Mary Queen of Scots, as recounted by Robertson. As night falls he grows conscious of the graves all around which hold 'my peers, the poor plebian dead' (l. 7), reminding the reader of his lowly social status and thereby making the meeting that follows all the more extraordinary, for the speaker experiences a visitation from Mary herself in which she appears both alluring and eerie: 'Her jetty locks the howling night-breeze waved, / And shook the sceptre in her shad'wy hand' (ll. 11–12).

Orr's imagination has clearly been caught and his heart touched by the account of Mary's life and sufferings which transforms Robertson's sober history into a gripping drama. Robertson's purpose was to show how much the Scotland of the Enlightenment, where the Reformation and the Union were established facts, had progressed from the age of uncultivated manners, barbarous conflict, religious controversy and disorder which he depicts. Robertson is no friend to what he designates 'Popery', stereotyping Catholicism as a bastion of superstition and a power base for a self-promoting clergy: 'that form of popery, which prevailed in Scotland, was of the most bigoted and illiberal kind ... The power and wealth of the church kept pace with the progress of superstition'.[44]

The Catholic Queen, while allowing for her youthfulness and the difficult state of affairs in Scotland at the time of her accession, he depicts as inconstant in her dealings with ministers and nobles, tenaciously wedded to her religion, and disastrous in her choices of marriage partners and favourites. However, as befits a true man of feeling his sensibility is moved by her beauty, her beguiling personality and her vulnerability. His presentation of her long captivity, first at Loch Leven and later at the hands of her cousin Elizabeth I who feared she might become the focus for Catholic attempts to overthrow her, is unfailingly compassionate. Elizabeth, on the other hand, he portrays as a cool, ruthless, calculating politician who, once she has Mary at her mercy, fails to relieve the deplorable conditions in which she is held and, ultimately, allows her to be sacrificed for political expediency.

Some of the atmosphere of the Gothic genre, with its trope of a woman in peril in a vast, dreadful, fortified edifice is present when Robertson describes Mary in her incarceration:

> Even that short period of her days which remained, they rendered uncomfortable, by every hardship, and indignity, which it was in their power to inflict ... she was confined to two ruinous chambers, scarce habitable, even in the middle of summer, by reason of cold ... The castle, in which she resided, was converted into a common prison; and a young man suspected of popery, was confined there, and treated under her eye, with such rigour, that he died of the ill usage.[45]

Robertson reports details of the heartless treatment Mary experienced right to the end when the comfort of a Catholic priest was denied her in her preparation for execution, and he allows the heroic courage with which Mary faced death and the moment of execution to speak through an account which loses no detail of drama or poignancy:

> She declared that she hoped for mercy only through the death of Christ, at the foot of whose image she now willingly shed her blood; and lifting up, and kissing the crucifix, she thus addressed, 'As thy arms, O Jesus, were extended on the cross; so with the outstretched arms of thy mercy, receive me, and forgive my sins' ... With calm but undaunted fortitude, she laid her neck on the block; and while one executioner held her hands, the other at the second stroke, cut off her head.[46]

A man must have had a heart of stone not to be moved by Robertson's relation of events, or not to find the Mary he portrays fascinating in herself. Orr was emphatically not such a man, rather one who deplored violence and injustice, abhorred state executions and maintained a deep respect for women throughout his life.[47] When Mary first speaks to the poet she recognizes that his 'bosom smarts' (l. 14) on her behalf. What is interesting, though, is to discover the extent to which 'his' Mary differs from the unhappy, flawed but bewitching creature of Robertson's construction. Robertson himself had moved on significantly from traditional Scottish Protestant representations of Mary, for as R. D. S. Jack points out, the 'bitterness and spite vented against Mary herself and conveyed mainly by comparisons with classical and Biblical villainesses' was 'commonplace in the works of seventeenth century Scottish writers'.[48]

Orr's Ulster Presbyterian community, by his own account, included a vociferous, conservative Calvinist faction. By them Mary was undoubtedly regarded as an icon of Catholicism and a 'scarlet woman'. With typical nerve, Orr challenges their bigotry. In the first place, his encounter with the Queen of Scots occurs on a site recognized as at the very heart of Ulster Presbyterianism: 'Templecorran's ruin'd fane' (l. 3), where to this day is located the grave of Edward Brice, the first Presbyterian divine to accept a call to ministry in Ireland (1613). One can only imagine the reactions to this literary act of sacrilege from those who were, as Orr reveals elsewhere, so ready to 'quote texts again' me' (l. 36).[49] He goes further than Robertson, however, in Mary's rehabilitation, portraying this daughter of the House of Stuart as having developed during her time among 'the illustrious dead' into an enlightened, almost Wollstonecraftian figure who projects a belief in global progress and tolerance.

Just as Burns's Muse commissioned him, Mary reveals what is to be Orr's vocation, employing a series of imperatives which she addresses to him as 'minstrel', an interesting term which Orr perhaps chose both for its courtly associations and for its broader connotation of a wandering 'singer of tales', who functions as a repository of wisdom. Employing a well-known image from Burns she reveals he is to instruct young men 'to stand a steadfast wall' (l. 21)[50] around justice and to avoid 'civil strife'. The ensuing lines seem to locate the poem in the post-Rebellion and Union era when Orr looked with increasing dismay on the rise of Napoleon: 'When knaves intrigue, immac'late patriots fall, / And demagogues grow despots in their turn' (ll. 23–4). His message, she emphasizes, is not only for the people; she commissions him to address the authorities, religious and civil, as well – clear evidence that Orr had aspirations to speak to the whole nation through his verse. The (Anglican) priesthood are to be urged to respect conscience and to avoid the persecution of 'some poor dissenting sect' (l. 28). He is, furthermore, to instruct 'crown'd heads' to respect 'the public will', a reference to the *Northern Star*'s masthead motto which reveals that the 'minstrel' has not, essentially, changed his tune.[51]

Having apprised Orr of his commission Mary pauses to reflect on her own downfall, showing repentance for her errors, or at least those errors Orr has inferred from Robertson's presentation: 'Ah! pride and pleasure hurl'd me from the hill / Of pow'r and glory, to the gulph below'(l. 32). The reflection on her own past, however, leads her to compare her era with Orr's; she advises her minstrel to avoid a judgemental attitude to those who lived in a more 'gloomy' (l. 33) age, the gloom here referring to a period not blessed with the wisdom of the Enlightenment which, she suggests, could have effected some startling transformations and dispelled both harsh religion and superstition:

> Perhaps stern *Knox*, who eloquently rag'd,
>   In later times had been benign as *Blair*; (ll. 37–9)

Knox, doyen of the Calvinists, therefore, is firmly consigned to the past. Still more daring, however, is Orr's putting into the queen's mouth the following lines, which celebrate progress towards tolerance:

> No clouded beam from blest religion sent,
>   Inflames the torch in superstition's hand;
> In thousand shreds that *solemn league* is rent,
>   Which fraterniz'd th'exterminating band. (ll. 45–8)

While the first half of the stanza certainly refers to the burnings of heretics, automatically associated in Protestant minds with the Catholic Mary Tudor, it is an act of deliberate audacity for Orr to permit Mary Queen of Scots to express satisfaction at the dissolution of the Solemn League and Covenant. One wonders what response he received from an audience which included many who had been brought up to revere the Covenanters as heroic martyrs.

Having reviewed the present, Mary moves into prophetic mode, employing a series of powerful, declarative utterances. Improvement and progress will continue; democracy will be inaugurated throughout 'earth's enfranchise'd isles' (l. 51); universal peace will be established; false religion and 'priestcraft' (l. 60), Orr's bane, will cease. The ending is abrupt and reveals the condition of 'universal virtue' (l. 61) which must precede this renewed Golden Age, but she has already given authoritative assurance of its coming: '(I know the time; yet fate forbids to tell)' (l. 50). The line, as every Bible-reading Presbyterian would have been aware, recalls Christ's response to his disciples who ask when the Messianic kingdom will be established: 'It is not for you to know the times or dates the Father has set by his own authority'.[52] By implication, then, Mary is not burning in Hell but is in possession of Heavenly secrets. She sends Orr home declaring her intention to rejoin the 'illustrious dead / Who, in the world of shades, await their final doom' (ll. 63–4). The alexandrine firmly draws the encounter to a close and reinforces the distinctly sober tone, but Orr's prophetic mission has been clearly set forth.

In many respects the poem would not have seemed out of place in the *Northern Star*. Its faith in global progress, and its imagery, echo many of the rhetorical, inspirational pieces that appeared in the paper before the destruction of its printing presses in 1797. The contemporary references noted above, however, suggest the period of Orr's post-1798 experience and the whole piece, certainly, reveals him assuming the role of a writer with a clear sense of calling. But what are we to make of his commissioning by the Queen of Scots? The audacities he has committed have already been noted but before it is too readily assumed that these merely represent Orr's liberalism at work, twitting extremes of Presbyterianism, a closer consideration of the emphasis on millenarian belief within the poem is necessary. Ian McBride has argued that Presbyterian support for the United Irish movement among both New Light and Covenanting Presbyterians was 'predicated upon millenarian hopes for the withering away of "popery" and the final triumph of rational, reformed Christianity'. He has suggested that the delight expressed in Belfast over the French Revolution may to an extent have been motivated by approval within Ulster of the revolutionaries' anti-clericalism and their overthrow of the influence of the Catholic Church in France. McBride has sounded an important cautionary note against counter-revisionist readings of history which, he believes, make an erroneous, 'explicitly present-centred and pro-republican reading of the modern Irish past' and too readily ascribe to all the Presbyterian United Irishmen an inclusivity of outlook and a tolerance of Catholicism which many did not share.[53]

When Orr employed Mary Queen of Scots to express his enlightenment-based vision of progress which, after all, imagines her making an endorsement of the Presbyterian theologian Blair, was he signalling a hope that in the Millennium he envisaged Catholicism would indeed have 'withered away' and been replaced by 'rational, reformed Christianity'? This seems unlikely. Nowhere, throughout the whole of his *oeuvre*, does he display anything other than respect for the beliefs of others, and he reserves overt criticism essentially for those fellow Presbyterians who have personally attacked him. Never does Orr take up and employ the term 'Popery', though Robertson uses it in several places in his history, but his address 'To Miss Owenson' reveals that he has sat with Catholic fellow citizens 'in the chapel of devotion' (l. 33).[54] In reality 'The Vision' challenges extreme orthodoxies on all sides and is expressive of Orr's very particular, genuinely liberal outlook. Thus it presents his 'vision' in a double sense.

As this study has shown, a strong vein of influence flowing from the works of several great figures of the Scottish Enlightenment may be discovered in several of the most significant poems within Orr's non-vernacular *oeuvre*. It was natural for him to draw on the Scots literati for guidance, inspiration and comfort, since their works represented an aspect of the heritage of the Ulster Scots community, and because their intellectual thrust was essentially affirmative of his own rational, tolerant vision. While the teachings of the Presbyterian divine Blair may have underpinned Orr's poetics and provided him with spiritual guidance, another significant Scottish Enlightenment figure may also have impressed him and helped to inform his thinking particularly on the issue of Catholic Emancipation, not only in Ireland but throughout the kingdoms now included within the Union. That figure was the radical Catholic priest, Alexander Geddes.

Recently, Gerard Carruthers has contributed to the retrieval of Alexander Geddes (1737–1802), arguing that he critiqued 'Vested interest and hypocrisy', while also 'castigating the credulous superstition that he sometimes found in his own communion and the narrow phobia that he sometimes sensed in the Protestant mentality'.[55] Geddes in his later years was certainly contemporaneous with James Orr, and published two works in particular which would undoubtedly have interested him. One was his 'Ode to the Honourable Thomas Pelham', in which he chastises this Irish parliamentarian for his opposition to emancipation on the grounds that it was contrary to the Protestant British constitution. Geddes does not mince his words when expressing his distaste for bigotry:

> Yes, there's no heresy so great,
> So ruinous to any State,
>   Or of such hideous features,
> As that which teaches man to make
> Distinctions, for Religion's sake,
>   Among his fellow creatures.[56] (ll. 240–6)

A further, highly developed piece of reasoning was his *Modest Apology for the Roman Catholics of Great Britain*, in which Geddes administers a corrective to Protestant misconstructions of the doctrine of papal infallibility and of the relationship between the Pope and national councils of bishops which represented individual countries. He states: 'In truth, Papal Infallibility is as absurd in itself, as it is pernicious in its consequences'. In support of his view he cites, for example, the Gallican Church which, he says, 'has always taught a contrary doctrine, and asserted the superiority of a General Council; to whose decisions the Pope himself is obliged to bend'.[57] While we may readily infer that Orr as a thinker and an advocate of equality and tolerance for all sects would have responded with enthusiasm to Geddes's well-reasoned arguments and his vigorous style, there is some actual evidence to indicate that he had actually read Geddes's work, followed his career, and openly approved of his ideology.

Orr's essay on 'Accidents' for the *Belfast Monthly Magazine* has already been discussed, but Linde Lunney believes that certain other essays by 'O' and 'Censor', which appeared at intervals in the *Magazine* may additionally have emanated from his pen.[58] Lunney expresses this view but does not state her reasons for holding it. The discussion below is offered as an endorsement of her expressed opinion on the pseudonym 'Censor'.

'Censor' may seem an appropriate choice of pseudonym for Orr, recalling as it does the Roman officials who were guardians of public conduct and morals. It may also be the case that 'Censor' encodes the word 'Sense' conjoined with 'Orr', linking Orr's surname to the commonsense rationality which he sought to promote. Orr may also have appreciated the opportunity provided by the assumption of a pseudonym to develop his persona as an essayist on moral subjects, uncluttered by associations with his more eclectic poetic persona. Two essays by 'Censor' for the *Belfast Monthly Magazine* are worthy of some attention here. The first, which deplores the injustice of the Penal Laws and strongly supports Emancipation, addresses the frequently made accusation that the Catholic population in Ireland could not be trusted to serve the cause of liberty because Catholics owed allegiance to the Pope rather than to the State. 'Censor' suggests that to counteract this claim the Irish Catholic Church alone, independent of Papal influence, should be responsible for the choice of its bishops. He asserts that 'In the eye of sober reason, there exists no sufficient cause why the Irish Catholics should not choose their own Bishop, independent of any extraneous influence, either of the King or the Pope'.[59]

Perhaps irritated by what he may feel is the presumption of a non-Catholic in prescribing such a formula, in the next issue another writer, 'Criticus', accuses 'Censor' of being one of the 'oppressors' and alleges that he really wishes to see the Catholic Church under the authority of the Crown.[60] The reply from 'Censor' further illuminates our understanding of the nature of Orr's tolerant philosophy and of the breadth of his reading:

> I greatly dislike the spirit of controversy, and have seldom found good effects, or the convincement of an opponent, to result from it ... I am a sincere and unequivocal friend to Catholic emancipation ... I wish that my Catholic brethren should enjoy

every political right in its fullest extent: having no inclination to encroach on their right of private judgement, I claim the same right for myself ... Criticus altogether mistakes me if he supposes I desire the King to be invested with any power over the nomination of the Catholic Bishops. I object as well to the interference of the King as of the Pope, and I am pleased to find that Criticus confirms me in the opinion, that there is nothing in the plan I mentioned inconsistent with the ancient strict canonical mode of their church. A numerous body of Catholics in England, at the head of whom was the late Lord Petre, and the late highly respectable and enlightened Dr Geddes, strongly advocated this mode a few years ago, and exposed themselves to much censure from the bigoted party on this very account.[61]

'Censor' is realistic in his assessment of 'controversy', by which he appears to mean not rational debate, which Orr loved, but arguments conducted in passionate heat and a spirit of bigotry, which are destructive and likely to entrench attitudes rather than to bring understanding and mutual respect. He confirms unequivocally his pro-emancipation viewpoint and his appropriation of the 'right of private judgement' for all, thus extending this concept beyond the confines of the various strands of Presbyterianism and making it inclusive of all denominations.[62] Finally, in a reference to the history of the Emancipation movement in Britain he allows a fascinating glimpse of his familiarity with and respect for the work of the radical Scottish priest Alexander Geddes, a poet, thinker and activist, whose patron was indeed the prominent Catholic, Lord Petre. That Geddes's opinions and the course of his career were known and of great interest to north of Ireland intellectuals is clear from a detailed account of his life printed in the *Belfast Monthly Magazine* in 1809.[63]

The genuineness of Orr's commitment to the Enlightenment values of tolerance and equality led him, it seems likely, to recognize a kindred spirit in the 'enlightened Dr Geddes' and also, no doubt, inspired his revisioning of Mary Queen of Scots as a progressive, contemporary figure. At the present time when, as we have seen, some historians are exposing bigotry and sectarianism within the ranks of the United Irishmen, and finding that their Society has been excessively idealized, it is refreshing to discover that Orr, in the original spirit of the movement, extended to all his fellow creatures a genuinely fraternal regard.

6 MEN OF INDEPENDENT MIND: ULSTER SCOTS POETS AND THE SCOTTISH TRADITION

Andrew Hook, writing in the 1980s, pointed out that a tendency to privilege vernacularity has distorted Scottish literary historiography. He noted: 'Use of the vernacular has often been accepted almost as a test of Scottish virility; cultural nationalism has always been happier with the Scottish vernacular than with Scots English.'[1] While this position has undoubtedly begun to change, the perception in Ulster, certainly, is still that Orr's vernacular work is his most significant. He is admired and promoted by Ulster Scots cultural activists and even, tacitly, by some scholars, primarily as a vernacular writer. The result is that until very recently little attention has been granted to the much larger body of work he produced in the standard register. This amounts to a distortion of Orr's poetic persona, for as the discussion in the previous chapter has shown, many of Orr's formal English works make a significant contribution to our understanding of how the literature and philosophy of the Scottish Enlightenment underpin the Irish identity he constructed for himself and assist in securing the platform from which he addressed the nation of Ireland as a whole. Nevertheless, it is likely that Orr's vernacular work will continue to be considered his finest in the purely literary sense.

The purpose of the discussion in this and the two following chapters is to establish clearly the nature of James Orr's relationship to the eighteenth-century Scottish vernacular tradition.[2] These chapters will demonstrate the interventionist approach he adopted in transforming generic Scots verse forms and exercising precise control of language so that new subject matter, and often specifically Irish themes, might be accommodated. In addition two related questions will be considered. First, why should Orr's vernacular work be considered important not only within northern Ulster Scots communities but within Ireland as a whole? Secondly, how effectively did Orr employ the northern Ulster Scots poetic tradition to address the nation of Ireland?

The Ulster Scots vernacular poets represent a significant northern school within the literature of Ireland, but have received very little detailed scholarly attention in their homeland. This is despite the sterling efforts of John Hewitt, who recovered the work of James Orr, Samuel Thomson, Francis Boyle and many others. In Scotland, their ancestral ground, Liam McIlvanney has acknowledged that critics have 'neglected' Ulster vernacular poetry,[3] but has claimed that 'the effect of Burns's success was to galvanize the local Ulster tradition ... inspiring a new wave of Ulster poets'.[4] The present writer acknowledges the importance of Burns's work to his Ulster Scots contemporaries, but in this and subsequent chapters will clearly establish Orr's literary maturity and his rejection of bardolatry, both implicit and explicit.

Travellers in Ulster during or close to the period when the vernacular poets were at their most prolific often noticed and recorded the distinctly Scots character of much of the region. One such was John Gamble (c. 1770–1831), a native of Strabane who had trained as a doctor in Edinburgh and travelled fairly widely in Europe. Gamble published an account of a tour taken in the north of Ireland during 1812, and in it he made many references to the Presbyterians of Ulster, noting, for example, the republicanism of many during the 1798 Rebellion. He also found worthy of comment the very Scottish character of their language, recording that one woman he met told him she sang when spinning, to make the wheel 'gang lightsome', and later directed him to walk up the Hill of Slemish, describing it as a 'wee brae'.[5]

The later twentieth-century researches of J. R. R. Adams make it clear that a tradition of reading Scots literature was retained among the Scots-speaking population in the eighteenth and nineteenth centuries. Adams has shown that before Ramsay, Fergusson and Burns began producing contemporary works in Scots, literary masterpieces from earlier centuries, including Montgomerie's *The Cherrie and the Slae*, were printed in Belfast.[6] This can only have been in response to popular demand. Since Scottish speech and reading habits were common, therefore, it is no surprise to discover that when Scots verse enjoyed a revival in the vernacular poetry of Ramsay, Fergusson and Burns, contemporary Ulster Scots poets employed their native tongue in composition with renewed enthusiasm.[7]

Burns's success may well have inspired many Ulster Scots poets to compose and publish in the vernacular, but some of the earliest surviving Ulster Scots poems appear in *The Ulster Miscellany* which was published in 1753, well before the period of Burns's activity. One of the most striking of these is 'Tit for Tat', a lively, rhythmic, comic dialogue between a Donegal farmer and his wife, who are celebrating the latter's ridicule and successful tricking of the local rector. The dispute concerns the tithe, hatred of which was to provide a spur for many of those Presbyterians who turned out in support of the United Irishmen in 1798. The poem is satirical and subversive, in keeping with the tone of many of the works of Ramsay or Burns. In the stanza quoted below, when responding to criticisms made by the rector's haughty wife concerning the over-fine quality of her dress, the farmer's spouse demonstrates a readiness to cut her opponent down to size, and a striking capacity for well-aimed insult:

> Forbear, proud madam Persian,
> Take back ye'r *ain* aspersion, ['own'
> Wi' tea, ye'r chief diversion,
>   Ye waste ye'r time *awa*: ['away'
> While dressing ye'r and pinning,
> I'll spin, and bleach my linnen,
> And wear my ain hands winning,
>   Ye rector's lazy draw.[8] (ll. 17–24)

The assumed Presbyterian authorship of this piece has recently been questioned and the suggestion has been made that the author was actually Matthew Draffen (*c.* 1703–85), Anglican rector of Gartan Parish, Donegal who was, nevertheless, of Scots descent.[9] Significantly, the poem reveals something of the transformative effect on Scots verse of migration to Ulster, for the speaker is very clearly located in an Irish setting and the poem's theme is rooted in Irish grievances. Orr's contemporary and fellow radical weaver poet, James Campbell of Ballynure, also took up the anti-tithe refrain in a rousing song, probably composed to entertain the company at his local inn. Campbell's work shows little pretension to refinement; his poetry is calculated to address the audience that enjoyed broadsheet ballads and it is not difficult to imagine him raising the roof at noisy pub gatherings where alcohol and conviviality flowed. 'Campbell's Adieu to Tithe', while not a vernacular poem, provides evidence, in typically rollicking style, of the independence of mind that empowered him. Its context was the decision of the local Church of Ireland rector to cancel his tithe debt on the grounds of his extreme poverty. He concludes the song by drinking heartily to the wished-for end to all tithing:

> I'm a poet designed, just from my origin
>   I love drink and music, that's thought my religion,
> Just fill me a bumper, I'll make the house roar,
>   May the church ever flourish, when tithes are no more.[10] (ll. 54–8)

Within his *oeuvre* Campbell may frequently be observed drawing on his Scots heritage. His 'Epicure's Address to Bacon', sits within a long tradition of Scots verse that celebrates regional food as a form of cultural nationalism,[11] but Campbell chooses the emblematically Irish pig. The style and diction are typically Cambellian: coarse, tough, belligerent, irreverent:

> Nae animal in all creation
> Deserves so much my approbation,
> It keeps my tripes in a right station,
>   Without crack or chasm;

> 'Tis of *mair* use to my salvation ['more'
> Than holy chrism. (ll. 37–42)
>
> ...
>
> To eat by instinct on I'm goaded,
> When I want pork I'm discommoded;
> And since great guts were ne'er exploded,
>   Nor thought a sin,
> Mine like a dung cart shall be loaded,
>   Till my lying in.[12] (ll. 61–6)

Though humorous he is even-handed, preferring pork both to the 'holy chrism' of Catholicism, and to the 'grace of God' (l. 68), heavily emphasized in Calvinist teaching on salvation and predestination. Implicitly, therefore, the poem provides insights into some of the tensions in Ulster society, but it also explicitly references Burns and Ramsay. Campbell uncompromisingly rejects Burns's preference for haggis, noting: 'When I do light on't like a bear, / My stomach spoils (ll. 79–84). In an earlier stanza he had rejected Ramsay's favourite tipple, 'good red port' in favour of 'juice o' pork' (ll. 109–14).

The poem illustrates several characteristic aspects of the Ulster vernacular tradition. First, there is the easy familiarity with, and also lack of deference to, the Scots masters. Secondly, he employs a traditional Scots verse form, standard habbie. In choosing to celebrate pork, fried as bacon, Campbell may be signalling his independence, but this choice may have still further significance. In his *Tour in Ireland*, a text certainly known to Ulster readers of the *Northern Star* newspaper,[13] Arthur Young portrays the Irish cottiers he observed welcoming the family pig into their cabin to share a meal of potatoes.[14] While Campbell certainly expresses strong affection for the pig he stresses that this is based on its tastiness rather than on familial regard. Perhaps this is an early example of a northerner rejecting the stereotyped 'pigs in the parlour' image of Ireland that remained fixed in some English imaginations well into the twentieth century.

In common with many writers of the 1790s and 1800s, but in contrast to James Orr, Campbell does not employ a particularly dense vernacular register, though when he was reading his compositions aloud his pronunciation and accent no doubt sounded much more 'Scotch' than they appear on the printed page. It is not difficult to detect failures in Campbell's poetic craftsmanship – several of his lines do not scan smoothly, but this is unlikely to have troubled his preferred audience.

An aspect of Ulster writing in this period that has been in some respects overstated is its association with 1790s radicalism and United Irish hopes for an independent Ireland. Many poets were actually conservative in their theological and political opinions. Hugh Porter, for example, was patronized by Rev. Thomas Tighe, a member of the literary circle of Bishop Percy of Dromore.[15] Even for such as these, vernacular verse functioned as an outlet for their sense of difference, their confidence in their community's own culture and their pride in their Scottish roots. The poems of Francis Boyle (b. *c.* 1730), a weaver (or possibly a blacksmith) of Granshaw in County Down, offer some confirmation of this view. Boyle's sense of his Scots heritage is writ large in his compositions which cover, for example, the melancholy aftermath of the 1745 Rebellion[16] and the exploits of Kenneth MacAlpine.[17] As a poet, however, Boyle is very far from being in thrall to Burns and has no qualms about rounding on him to express disapproval of his indecencies in an extended piece of finger-wagging. His 'Address to Robert Burns', appropriately enough employs standard habbie, the 'Burns stanza', but certainly not to flatter or emulate. Instead Boyle portrays a personified Virtue who rebukes the Bard by roughly castigating his revered Muse Coila as a 'hizzie' (l. 7), who has grown debauched:

> Wrapt up in a religious plaid,
> On *het* debauchery's dung-bed laid, ['hot'
> While rotten passions round her preyed,
>   The Muse peeped forth;
> A bard in Scotia's robes arrayed,
>   All-hailed her birth.
>
> Religion, Virtue, Coila shed
> Some drops of sorrow on her head
> Before pollution quite o'erspread
>   Her nobler views ...[18] (ll. 13–22)

Virtue warns that both glory and 'deathless fame' (l. 30) will ultimately be denied to the 'vicious bard' (l. 29) if he continues in his present manner of life. She concludes with a heartfelt plea: 'O! wad ye tak' a thought, an' *men*" ['reform'] (l. 35). Any Burns enthusiast would, of course, have recognized Burns's own advice to the devil, here used against the poet himself. These few examples reveal the robust character and blunt language of writers within the Ulster Scots tradition. Their familiarity with Burns is evident but rarely, if ever, does their attitude to him take the form of 'unrestrained bardolatry'.

The letters of Luke Mullan, like Orr a member of Samuel Thomson's literary coterie in the 1790s, have occasionally been referred to as evidence of the wildly enthusiastic reception of Burns's works in Ulster.[19] At one time Mullan and Thomson advertised in the *Northern Star* proposing 'for publication by subscription a volume of poems upon different subjects; chiefly in the Scottish Dialect'.[20] The joint project, though it came to nothing, may indeed reveal their admiration of Burns, but it speaks also of a hard-headed, even shameless attempt to cash in on his popularity. Later in the 1790s Mullan visited Ayrshire and recorded in eager, passionate letters to Thomson his excursions to visit the locations of several well-known Burns poems. The following passage is typical:

I visited the Alloway Kirk in Ayrshire – and the bridge that Tam's mare lost the tail crossing – the place is very much surrounded with thick groves as is presented in the poems and the River Doon makes a pleasing and most romantic scene – and murmurs through the long surrounding woods. The banks of Ayr and the river with the Auld and new brigs, Wallace tower, the 'Drowsy Dungeon clock' etc. all very powerfully attracted my enraptur'd fancy. I examin'd them all with the minuteness of an antiquarian, as the favourite scenes of my favourite poet.[21]

It would be a great mistake, however, to judge Mullan a bardolater on the basis of this. He also visited Robert Fergusson's grave in Edinburgh and in another letter to Thomson, this time about a visit to Poets' Corner in Westminster Abbey he refers to Shakespeare as 'our fav'rite' and mentions having admired the busts of Gray, Goldsmith and James Thomson.[22]

James Orr, the best known of the Ulster Scots poets, did not publish his *Poems on Various Subjects*, including sixteen vernacular pieces, until 1804. Whether the delay was deliberate or not, it certainly proved a canny move, for there was now no danger of his own vernacular poetry being lost in the tide of popular enthusiasm for Burns. Orr's and frequently Thomson's compositions stand out from the crowd in adhering to a fairly dense Scots register, thereby indicating that for these writers the vernacular project represented something more weighty than a glancing acknowledgement of Scots ancestry. The following example from 'S. E.' is more typical:

> Up the rough brae, adown the vale,
> Lest sinking cares my heart assail,
> I sing o' needfu' things the *wale*, ['best'
>   In hamely tongue;
> That seed, *whase* fruit keeps firm and hale ['whose'
>   The auld and young.[23] (ll. 1–6)

Thomson's 'To Captain M'Dougall, Castle-Upton, with a copy of the author's poems' is addressed to a wealthy, well-educated admirer and employs Scots idiom very sparingly, but in it he tackles directly the language-related issue of his cultural identity and the importance to him of his Scottishness. Indeed, the poem indicates that Thomson's sense of his connection with Scotland is deeply spiritual; the speaker feels that he is a Scotsman in an Irishman's body, and he experiences the longing for the landscape of his ancestors that is characteristic of the exile:

> Indeed Fate seems to have mistook
>   The spot at first designed for me;
> Which should have been some flow'ry nook
>   In Ayr, or on the banks of Dee.
>
> I love my native land, no doubt,
>   Attach'd to her thro' thick and thin;
> Yet tho' I'm Irish all without,
>   I'm every item Scotch within.[24] (ll. 13–20)

The poem, which should be understood as a defining work for Thomson, was published in his third volume of verse, well into the Union period, as if its author were consciously taking a stand against the homogenizing British spirit of the era. As Frank Ferguson has observed, Thomson is claiming space within the Union for his 'culturally distinct persona'; he is showing that the state has no rights or influence over his 'interiority'.[25] If Thomson explicitly identifies with his Scottish ethnicity and culture, he also certainly acknowledges his Irish *exteriority*. The poem assists in pinpointing an essential difference between Thomson and James Orr. It is his Irish identity which Orr repeatedly foregrounds in both his standard register poetry and his vernacular poems, but without compromising his commitment to the Ulster Scots community or selling his birthright. While Thomson harks back to Ayrshire's flowery nooks, therefore, Orr 'sing[s] the burns an' bow'rs, / O' Airlan', our fair lan'' (ll. 83–4).[26]

That Orr celebrated his community's inherited Scots language, culture, character and beliefs, but viewed them from the perspective of the inclusive, democratic Ireland to which he aspired all his life, may be inferred from many of the poems which comprise his contribution to Ulster vernacular literature. As he employed the genres and metres of the Scots tradition he added variety and value to well-worn, familiar Scottish formats. Nowhere is this more evident than in his handling of the popular standard habbie stanza. Ramsay, Fergusson and Burns had all established personal mastery over the form, yet Orr succeeded in finding expression for his unique voice within this familiar structure and in that respect his work may be understood as representing a further stage in the stanza's evolution.

The general effect of the stanza's pattern is friendly to comic or satiric verse. The initial three rhyming iambic tetrameters permit an idea to be set out and apparently concluded in the dimeter that follows, but lines five and six, which echo the rhyme scheme of three and four, may be utilized for the addition of a satirical rider. Robert Semphill of Beltrees (1590–*c.* 1660) exploited some of the possibilities of the form in his mock elegy 'The Life and Death of Habbie Simson' in which the reiteration of 'Habbie's dead', with minimal variation throughout fourteen stanzas, progressively generates a reductive effect that undercuts the professed grief of the speaker.[27]

While the roots of the form may be traced to troubadours who performed in a courtly setting, Allan Ramsay successfully employed standard habbie to voice the thoughts of tavern and brothel keepers, or of their clients. Furthermore, he sited it firmly within the poetry of the city, revealing a riotous, irreverent, alternative Edinburgh, as the following lines from his 'Elegy on Maggie Johnson' (1712) illustrate:

> Fou closs we us'd to drink and rant,
> Until we did baith *glowre* and *gaunt*, ['stare', 'yawn'
> And pish and spew, and *yesk* and *maunt*, ['belch', 'stammer'
>   Right swash I true;[28] (ll. 31–6)

Despite the apparent subversion of propriety, however, the conclusion of Ramsay's 'Elegy' offers a reminder of a more conventional moral framework. The uncomfortable issue of judgement in the afterlife is raised, while in an echo of 'Habbie Simpson', the speaker grimly stresses the irrevocable finality of death:

> Let a' thy *gossies* yelp and yell, ['cronies'
> And without feed,
> Guess whether ye're in heaven or hell,
> They're sure ye're dead. (ll. 87–90)

Robert Fergusson, in 'The Daft Days' (1772), also chooses to celebrate the tavern culture of the capital, but builds on Ramsay's achievement to produce a work of greater complexity and sophistication.[29] The opening meditation, an atmospheric representation of the countryside in *'mirk* December' ['gloomy'] (l. 1), allows him to incorporate elements of pastoral, but as a prelude to the speaker's rejection of the fields in favour of the vigorous conviviality of city life on dark winter evenings. The poem effectively voices the drawing power which the city exercises, particularly over young people, in every generation. His scenes of 'mirth' and 'social cheer' (l. 55) never attain the level of excess depicted in Ramsay's anarchic cameos, but the stanza's association with insubordination and dissidence is perpetuated in Fergusson's mocking finale. Here, with assumed piety, he supplicates the 'great god of *Aqua Vitae*' (l. 61), for protection from the forces of law and order whom he disrespectfully designates 'that black banditti, / The City-Guard' (l. 64).

Though Ramsay and Fergusson exploited standard habbie with great originality, Burns may be said to have customized it, employing it to portray numerous highly individual characters and as a vehicle for the expression of his own multi-faceted verse persona. His dramatic monologue, 'Holy Willie's Prayer' (1785),[30] is potentially as shocking as Ramsay's 'Lucky Spence's Last Advice' (1718),[31] which details a brothel keeper's guidance to her sex workers, but Burns employs a much more finely-tuned form of satire as he exposes the deception of others and of self that typifies the religious hypocrite. Donald Low has commented that 'It is difficult to over-estimate the significance of "Standart Habbie" in the case of Burns', pointing out that Burns greatly extended the range of its possible applications, for example in 'The Vision' (1785–6) which broadens its scope to 'include the communication of serious ideas'.[32]

Certainly, all the major themes of Burns's *oeuvre* are explored in the standard habbie poems: religion, his poetic calling, Scotland and its symbols, regional identity, natural beauty, friendship, sexual conquest and radical opinions. The richness of this component of his work is in large part due to the variation in the voice he achieves within and between poems. He speaks as Rab the Ranter, Robin Ruisseaux, Robert Burns, as the libertarian, the passionate lover, the predator, the rationalist, the guid billie, the tease, the penetrating satirist, the inspired visionary, the irreverent rhymer. Through this series of skilfully adopted poses, it becomes clear that Burns the poet is determined to resist pigeonholing by remaining elusive, uncommitted and apart.

We may consider first of all those verse epistles in which Burns himself appears to speak through the medium of a first person narrator. Liam McIlvanney argues that these are genuine, intimate letters which

> place the reader in a subordinate position, looking over Burns's shoulder at verses meant principally for the eyes of another ... The epistles shut us out ... The result is a kind of self-regulating community that requires no corroboration, no endorsement from the outside world.[33]

McIlvanney also characterizes the epistles as a kind of 'pub-talk or "blether"', an evaluation borne out by reference to much of the content.[34] Such talk is rarely noteworthy for its sensitivity or diffidence and, certainly, the voice in the 'Epistle to John Rankine' (1784–5) is that of a swaggering sexual predator, 'a rovin wi' the gun' (l. 38).[35] The same poem expresses the speaker's exasperation with the busybodying of the moral guardians from the Kirk, here the 'Poacher-Court', and 'their blethers!' (ll. 47, 72), independent sentiments which most twenty-first-century readers would endorse. It must be acknowledged, however, that the objectifying and belittling of the woman as 'a *Paitrick*' ['partridge'] (l. 39), 'it' (l. 44) and 'a poor, wee thing' (l. 43) achieves a less than timeless resonance. By contrast, 'A Poet's Welcome to his Love-Begotten Daughter' (1785) demonstrates a more responsible treatment of the consequences of sexual adventures, even as it challenges conventional attitudes. Here the impression created is of a man of intense tenderness, courage and natural justice:

> For if thou be, what I wad hae thee,
> And tak the counsel I shall *gie* thee, ['give'
> I'll never rue my trouble wi' thee,
>   The cost nor shame o't,
> But be a loving Father to thee,
>   And brag the name o't.[36] (ll. 43–8)

'Adam Armour's Prayer' (1786) appears to have been written in disgust, to expose bullying which is masquerading as the enforcement of high moral standards.[37] Burns effectively captures a narrative voice of gloating, thuggish bravado and sexual sadism, showing how the process of mob 'justice', carried out against a woman deemed immoral, allows free rein to the worst aspects of human nature: 'we've *stang'd* her through the place ['punished'], / And hurt her spleuchan' (ll. 9–10). As the speaker develops his narrative, lingering with satisfaction over intimate details of the humiliation and of the wounds to the female sexual organs, one suspects that the suffering inflicted has contributed to his own arousal. The poem provides further evidence of Burns's capacity to stand apart from his community, at odds with its judgementalism and its licensed brutality.

While on some occasions Burns seeks to give the impression of carelessness in composition, claiming that his verses come rattling out 'At ither's arses!' (l. 108),[38] in the case of 'The Vision' he is very deliberate in setting a tone and atmosphere that make a prelude to a deeply significant and spiritual experience. In this work of exceptional gravitas he sets forth his poetic calling, demonstrating a sense of his own ability and purpose that sets him far apart even from the bardic fraternity of the epistles. Though initially startled by the appearance of his Muse, typically, when confronted by a female presence, his brashness quickly reasserts itself:

> And such a leg! My bonie JEAN
>   Could only peer it;
> Sae *straught*, sae *taper*, tight and clean, ['straight', 'well-formed']
>   Nane else came near it.[39] (ll. 63–6)

The whole encounter, including the Muse's revelations, her instructions and Burns's implicit acceptance of the commission, make evident his remarkable self-confidence. However, the audacity (as some might have considered it) of his claim to be writing in obedience to Scotland's presiding poetic genii is ingeniously embedded within a rich, rhetorical, sensuous composition that cannily includes very proper allusions to his own rusticity and lowliness:

> 'Then never murmur nor repine;
> 'Strive in thy humble sphere to shine;
> 'And trust me, not Potosi's mine,
>   'Nor King's regard,
> 'Can give a bliss o'ermatching thine,
>   'A rustic Bard. (ll. 259–64)

The dignity and consequence of the *poet's* status and calling are thoroughly enhanced by the encounter.

Undoubtedly, Burns brought unprecedented sophistication and variety to composition in standard habbie, exploiting its flexibility to the full. The temptation must have been to assume that little more could be achieved in this form, that any standard habbie poem must inevitably appear imitative of something Burns had already accomplished. James Orr's handling of standard habbie, which he employed in seven poems, a selection of which will be considered here, is much more than merely competent, and eschews imitation. In these works he effortlessly adopts the stance of a man closely identified with his community. He evokes its life, acts as its spokesman, and, when appropriate, gently satirizes. Linde Lunney has written of Orr's rootedness within his 'intimately structured community where everyone is known'.[40] It is in the vernacular standard habbie poems that this interconnectedness between his life and the lives of his neighbours becomes most apparent.

If the bardic fraternity in Burns's locality was a self-regulating, rather exclusive club, Orr's standard habbie poems show him performing the bardic role with a public, quasi-official status at the heart of village society. Several of these works, written from the viewpoint of an 'insider', celebrate rural village life, which he portrays as sociable and supportive. 'Tea' (1804), a comic monologue, shows the Bard in his persona as local entertainer declaiming a mock eulogy in praise of the popular beverage. With tongue firmly in cheek he deprecates himself as a 'rude' (l. 5) rhymer, but flatters his audience as habituated to 'strains sublime' (l. 3). He proceeds to extol tea's virtues in a series of humorous cameos from which its importance to rural life may be inferred. It has intrinsically soothing properties, and is effective against '*weed*' ['fever'] and 'head-ach' (l. 23), but more importantly, a present of tea can deflect a wife's wrath away from her late-returning, 'sot' (l. 15) of a husband. Then, in a sudden, effortless transition to a vigorous, declamatory mode, Orr denounces the secretive, selfish streak which love of the beverage can breed in a wife:

> But blast the smuggler, *fause an' fell*, ['false and wicked']
> Wha brews't in tinfu's by hersel;
> An', bribes the *sma'-craft* no to tell ['little children']
>   Their drudgin' daddy;
> *Deel* nor he'd *ay* bounce in, pell-mell, ['devil', 'always']
>   Just when 'tis ready.[41] (ll. 25–30)

Orr sketches a minor domestic crisis, exhibiting a wry (bachelor's) cynicism regarding the marital relationship. The alliteration employed in 'fause and fell' augments the melodramatic tone, while the imagery identifies a conspiracy and exposes the wife as the corrupter of her innocent children. The 'echo' lines, five and six, allow the voice to modulate from that of the scandalized narrator to the affronted tones of the wife, while the eagerness of the industrious but hoodwinked husband for a reviving cup is vividly conveyed by the energetic 'bounce in, pell-mell'. As he lampoons the wife's selfish cunning and betrays sympathy for the deluded, overworked male, Orr is clearly confident of amusing an audience whose sense of humour he understands and plays to. As the poem develops, the girls who seek 'The story o' their future match' (l. 50), the gossips who gather over a cup of tea to savage the neighbours, the youth tortured by some flirtatious hussy are presented in turn and affectionately mocked. While irony is undoubtedly present, its purpose is to delight the audience as they recognize themselves and their neighbours. No shock, disgust or offence is intended.

Several of Orr's standard habbie poems adopt the format of verse epistles within which he continues to give prominence to conviviality and friendship in a community context. The verse epistle addressed to 'Thaunie', a talented local blind fiddler, allows him, mindful of his bardic role, to honour individuals who played an important part in village life, in Thaunie's case as an entertainer:

> Frae *ilka neuk* the *spunkies staucher* ['every nook', 'lively young men stagger'
>   To hear your stories;
> The roof re-echoes ev'ry *nicher*, ['laugh'
>   An' every chorus.[42] (ll. 27–30)

The poem is of particular interest in that it provides a clear example of the extraordinary oppositions, the sensitivity and bluntness, that are characteristic of the Ulster Scots psyche. Thus Orr can address, without a hint of patronizing, Thaunie's blindness, praising his fine '*bairn-time*' ['brood of children'] (l. 45) and his canny choice of an exceptionally attractive wife, despite his inability to see. In the next breath, however, he comically deplores the '*jads*, as gruesome as my grannie ['mares'] / *Thraun reestet* deels' ['awkward stubborn'] that are inexplicably courted by many 'seein' *chiels*' ['men'] (ll. 52–4).

Orr frequently employed his verse in protest on behalf of the poor. His 'To a Sparrow' (1804) invites comparison with Burns's 'To a Mouse' (1785) in its tone and diction, particularly in its opening: Wee, wanton, little thought o' birdie! / Pert, keen, an' *crouse, an' unco wordie* ['cheerful and exceptionally chirpy'] (ll. 1–2), which certainly plays on reader familiarity with 'Wee, sleekit, cowran, tim'rous beastie, / O, what a panic's in thy breastie!' (ll. 1–2).[43] Orr's poem arose out of an incident in which he observed some boys robbing a sparrow's nest and he muses on a universal lesson that may be drawn from the experience. His compassion for the creature's helplessness is as tender as is Burns's for the mouse, but the Scots bard also gives way to self-pity and fearfulness. Despite the wider perspective suggested by his acknowledgement of man's breach of 'Nature's social union', Burns throughout this work appears to see his own precarious circumstances mirrored in the mouse's sudden and unexpected experience of homelessness:

> Still, thou art blest, compar'd wi' me!
> The present only toucheth thee:
> But Och! I backward cast my e'e,
>   On prospects drear!
> An' forward, tho' I canna see,
>   I guess an' fear![44] (ll. 43–8)

By contrast, Orr's concern for the oppressed in society and his abhorrence of cruelty are to the fore; his attention is focused on man's inhumanity and its effects rather than on his own experience. First, he compares the sparrow's fate to that of a poor widow suffering eviction,[45] whom 'rich, rude ruffians teaze and taunt' (l. 35), then to a poor man robbed by violent housebreakers of his few possessions scraped up 'wi' *mickle* pains' ['great'] (l. 37). His chief concern is about the devastating effect on the individuals concerned and thus on the security and harmony of community life. His moral sites true courage alongside compassion for the weak.

> Thou needna think this outrage odd,
> For man's to man, like goose an' *tod*; ['fox'
> But still the brave will rapine, blood,
>   An guile *bewaur* o', ['beware'
> An' spare the creature o' their God,
>   Tho' but a Sparrow. (ll. 49–54)

Gerard Carruthers has discussed the anthropomorphism of Burns's 'To a Mouse', its 'projection of human values onto the animal the narrator encounters'. However, Carruthers demonstrates that the poem depicts 'something sinister about mankind as it is nature, paradoxically, that is more truly "social" than humanity', and he concludes that 'The apprehension in the text here looks towards the pessimism inherent in the Romantic attitude in opposition to the progressive optimism of the late eighteenth century'.[46] Orr's narrator too has detected 'something sinister' about the nature of man, whom he presents as involved in 'rapine, blood, / An guile' (ll. 51–2), but he demonstrates in his choice of imagery that all nature, human or animal, is characterized by an opposition between predator and prey: 'man's to man, like goose an' tod' (l. 50). Humans in particular waste their energies in chasing materialistic ambitions: 'sufferin' sair / By *biggin'* castles in the air' ['building'] (ll. 43–4). In the circumstances, Orr's reaction is to identify with the sparrow whose flight path takes it skywards out of the reach of predators, human or animal. Thus he makes the bird a symbol of his own estrangement from the ruthless world of 'getting and spending':

> But we twa will *hae haudins* there ['have holdings / accommodation'
>   *Sae lang's* we've breath; ['so long as'
> An laugh at a' the sons o' care
>   Wha sneak beneath. (ll. 45–8)

There is an interesting movement in Orr's poem, therefore, from radical social concern and late eighteenth-century sensibility towards Romantic alienation.

More usually, however, Orr's standard habbie poems provide a revealing insight into northern rural community life in late eighteenth-century Ireland. They also reveal Orr's adroitness in developing his role as the Bard of Ballycarry who celebrates and participates in village life while reserving for himself some private, meditative space. Of all the vernacular poets discussed here, it is Orr who appears most affirming of the poet–community relationship and of the community itself, an outcome that at least in part arises from his status as village bard. One never doubts, however, that Orr's commitment to his own people, 'warts and all', was genuine and deep-rooted. While never entirely losing the satirical edge frequently associated with vernacular standard habbie poems, Orr's essays in this traditional form frequently represent a welcome, gentle and affectionate modulation of the authorial voice.

Orr's most admired standard habbie poem is unquestionably 'To the Potatoe' (1804), from which Hewitt included an extract in the anthology section of *Rhyming Weavers*. Hewitt's desire to highlight distinctive regional culture led him to choose the initial stanzas that describe the varied, wholesome, local dishes that were created using potatoes.[47] In reality, 'To the Potatoe' [*sic*] is a work of far greater intricacy than Hewitt's anthology suggests. Fergusson and Burns had celebrated Scotland's capacity for self-defence by paying tribute to her distinctive diet of meal, cheese, bread and, famously, haggis. These became symbolic of the nation itself and the poets presented them as essential to the nourishment of national character and virtue. Orr adopts this foodstuff-related motif of the Scottish tradition but effectively adapts it to his context by developing an original Irish national theme.

The potato has long been a powerful symbol of Ireland, most especially associated with the Famine, and thus with tragedy, oppression and victimization. It is intriguing, therefore, to observe how it is accorded iconic status in pre-Famine Ireland by this Ulster Presbyterian. The potato, the food of the poorest class and likely to be despised, he presents as a symbol of Ireland's ability to feed herself and, therefore, of her capacity not simply for self-defence, but for resistance. The opening stanzas celebrate the potato as 'precious' (l. 5) to the poor, an idea which Orr swiftly develops, referring to it as 'my country's stay' (l. 6). He even invests the humble root vegetable with a kind of beauty, rating it above 'the Bean that scents the valley', 'the Pea, that *speels the salie*,' ['climbs the rod'] and the 'blue-bow't lint' (ll. 7–12).[48] These are rich, sensuous phrases that endow the cultivated Ulster landscape with an element of the picturesque.

Orr's eulogy allows him a vehicle for the expression of his radical opinions. These include his sympathy for the cottier families who 'ne'er *tase* butter, beef, or cheese' ['taste'] (l. 21), his resentment of tithes and rack-renting, and his contempt for the 'proud prelatic pack' (l. 13) who sneer at nourishing but unsophisticated potato-based cuisine.[49] In addition, in a series of cameos that evoke community life, he extols the culinary skill of the women who cook mouthwatering 'champ',[50] and the diligence of the men who cultivate and harvest the potato crop in the fields. He explains also that the young women use potatoes in starch-making to smarten their clothes, thus showing the potato to be at the centre of every aspect of village life:

> The *weel-pair't* peasants, *kempin'*, set ye; ['well-matched', 'competing']
> The weak wee boys, *sho'el*, weed, an' pat ye; ['shovel']
> The auld guid men thy *apples* get ay ['seed potatoes']
>   Seedlin's to raise;

> An' on *sow'n-seeves* the lasses grate ye,⁵¹ ['sieved oatmeal husks'
> To starch their claes. (ll. 49–54)

He invests the peasant labourers who devote themselves to the seasonal processes with the status of pastoral archetypes, observed carrying out timeless rituals. The contemporary Irish poet Seamus Heaney employs the trope of sacred rites as he presents labourers at work and at rest in his poem 'At a Potato Digging'.⁵² Here, however, as the speaker dwells on horrific images of the Potato Famine, the workers' movements as they stoop and bend over the soil seem to him unconscious offerings of appeasement to the faithless 'bitch earth' (l. 43) and the voracious 'famine god' (l. 14). For both poets the potato is iconic – inextricably bound up with Ireland and Irishness. The intervention of the Famine in the period that separates Orr and Heaney, however, has brought about a massive divergence in viewpoint and in tone. While Orr is affectionate, celebratory and ultimately defiant, Heaney is shaken with horror, pity and rage.

The climax of 'To the Potatoe' incorporates Orr's most open and challenging expression of radical sentiments. As he reflects with pride on the fact that the soldiers and sailors Ireland sends to the British armed forces have been better nourished than 'hosts, an' crews, / O' fine fed knaves' (ll. 77–8), he poses daring questions. Where would England be without a steady stream of Irishmen entering the army and navy? Or without the Irishmen recruited by the Militia for service in Ireland? Audaciously portraying England as a bird of prey, he suggests that if these 'brow-beat *callens*' ['young men'] (l. 82) withdrew their labour England's wings might easily be clipped and her talons pared. In such a situation, we may infer, he was suggesting that Ireland might be self-sufficient as a result of her cultivation of the potato, for the independent village community he portrayed earlier may be interpreted as representing the nation in microcosm.⁵³

Orr's ideas are truly radical, even revolutionary, here, not least because he is making a clear call for large-scale, non-violent resistance in order to achieve the desired political outcome. This political strand develops until in his final stanza Orr exclaims, 'What pity, folk thou *sairst, sud* tythe ay' ['serves, should']. He deplores the taxation of 'the poor man's *rig*' ['strip of land'], and prays 'May proud oppression ne'er come nigh thee' (ll. 85–90). From his phrasing we may infer a mindset that has dwelt on the revolt of the American colonies against 'taxation without representation', and on the rights to property, security and to resist oppression delineated by Tom Paine in *The Rights of Man*.

Orr employs Scots language and a characteristically Scots stanza form here to express an Irish theme, but the poem is a still more complex structure in that it reflects aspects of another popular genre: the georgic. Juan Christian Pellicer has discussed the burgeoning in the eighteenth century of British georgic verse based on 'Virgil's combination of practical instruction and politically suggestive description'. With reference to examples such as 'Cyder' (1708) by John Philips and 'The Hop-Garden' (1742–3) by Christopher Smart, Pellicer shows that the georgic 'relies on the credibility of an expert speaker and is factual', and that it was progressively absorbed into other poetic forms and genres.[54] On those criteria we may say that the stanzas within 'To the Potatoe' which deal with the preparation of potato dishes and the community's cultivation of the vegetable certainly disclose the influence of georgic poetry.[55]

Pellicer additionally argues, however, that the purpose of such verse after the Union with Scotland in 1707 was often to 'try to demonstrate in emphatically practical "preceptive" (instructive) terms, how the newly unified nation's productive and imperial energies should be regulated and harnessed'. He shows that the 'interplay of maritime and natural worlds precisely defines the georgic' and that the poems move 'from the English and Welsh pastoral valleys to the farthest outposts of Britain's commercial empire'.[56] In those respects, then, Orr may be said to have written an anti-georgic, which subverts some of the imperatives and assumptions of the genre in its earlier phase, since he shows in the wake of the 1801 Act of Union how, in Ireland, the nation's productive energies may be harnessed for resistance. As Orr interplays the naval, military and natural worlds, it appears explicitly his aim to destabilize the loyalty of Ireland's '*soger*[*s*]' ['soldiers'] (l. 74) and '*tar-breeks*' [sailors] (l. 75) within the empire they serve.

'To the Potatoe' provides ample evidence, then, of the creative eclecticism of Orr's style and his power to transform and mould literary influences from throughout the united kingdoms within the traditional Scots frameworks of his vernacular poetry. The poem has been represented as a transposition of Burns's 'nationalist strategies' in 'Address to a Haggis' (1786) into an Irish context, but such an appraisal in no way recognizes the breadth and subtlety of Orr's text.[57] 'To a Haggis', with its mock belligerence and cartoon-style violence is also, of course, a complex master work and a magnificent, humorous piece of popular rhetoric, as the following well-known stanza confirms:

> But mark the Rustic, haggis-fed,
> The trembling earth resounds his tread,
> Clap in his *walie nieve* a blade, ['fine fist'
>   He'll mak it whissle;
> An' legs, an' arms, an' heads will sned,
>   Like *taps o' thrissle*.[58] (ll. 37–42) ['thistle tops'

The sophistication, even cunning, of Orr's composition becomes all the more evident when his language choices are carefully scrutinized. Orr establishes 'To the Potatoe' as a fairly dense vernacular work at the outset and he exploits the diversity of language available to him in his English ruled, Scots settled, Irish homeland, sometimes teasing and prodding his readers to construct and infer meaning from a fine mesh of coded signals and *double entendres*. Undoubtedly, many Scots phrases and lexical items familiar to Burns's readers may be observed. Orr expresses his relish for the potato with: '*leeze me on* the precious Pratoe' ['dear to me is'] (l. 5), just as Burns, in 'Scotch Drink' exclaims 'Leeze me on thee *John Barleycorn*' (l. 17).[59] He curses with the familiar 'Waeworth' (l. 13) the upper classes who sneer at the poor man's 'Point an' Pratoes' (l. 14), while his 'comrades *drouthy*' ['thirsty'] (l. 71) recall Tam O' Shanter's 'drouthy neebours' (l. 2).[60]

Certain differences quickly become apparent, however. In writing vernacular poetry Orr had Scots models to follow but his respelling of certain words, even when the phonology would have been familiar to Scots speakers, can produce variants from Burns's orthographic practice, at least as it appeared in the editions of his work printed in Belfast. Thus the word 'devil' in Orr is rendered 'deel', rather than 'deil', as in: 'What wad poor deels on bogs an' braes, / Whase dear *cot-tacks* nae meal can raise;' ['leased cottages'] (ll. 19–20). Similarly, the frequently found Scots 'claes', meaning 'clothes', appears as 'clais' when Orr is deploring the fact that the Ulster cottiers never taste hearty food or 'pit new clais on' (l. 22), although it is possible that in this instance Orr is adhering to an older spelling which had persisted in Ulster.[61] His work also evinces many examples of Ulster Scots variants from forms found in well-known Scots verse of the period. The busy housewife in 'To the Potato', when making cakes from potato-based dough, sprinkles them with 'mashlin' (l. 32), a mixture of various grains. In Burns's poetry the same mixture appears with a different suffix as 'mashlum', and is used to produce the 'mashlum bonnocks' (l. 116) mentioned in 'The Author's Earnest Cry and Prayer' (1784).[62]

Influences or borrowings from Irish, unsurprisingly, are frequent in Orr's vernacular work, reflecting the proximity of an Irish-speaking population. While his ode is addressed to the 'potatoe' it is the more Irish-sounding 'Pratoe'[63] (l. 5) that he extols as 'precious' within his text. Similarly, the term 'boons', used of those who enter blithely at dinner time for their meal of potatoes, means a band of workers. This may have been influenced by the Ulster (Monaghan) Irish 'bodhan', meaning 'a company'.[64]

Most interesting, however, is Orr's subtle employment of apparently innocent expressions from Ulster Scots or Standard English to create different layers of meaning. In these instances the subtexts are often dissident in character. Employment of a 'secret' language, of course, would have been familiar to Orr, a member of United Irish and Masonic brotherhoods that dealt in code. Two such cases employed in 'To the Potatoe' are worthy of some consideration. The first appears in a stanza which confronts the issue of how people trapped in the most abject poverty manage to survive, and explains what they may be driven to in their desperation:

> They *boost* to forage like the fox   ['must'
>   That nightly plun'ers,
> Or wi' the 'Squires turn out an' box,
>   In hungry hun'ers. (ll. 27–30)

The first image identifies the poor with the fox as night-time foragers; the modal verb '*boost*' ['must'] indicates they feel compelled to adopt a predatory role. 'Plun'ers' too has a predatory ring, especially when, as here, it is related to night-time activity. The image of turning out with the Squires which follows the reference to the fox, suggests a hunting expedition. The verb 'box' means 'to strike a blow'.[65] Perhaps the line is meant to show how the poor are employed by the gentry to assist as beaters during hunting expeditions. The lines could then be translated: 'Or turn out and beat with the squires, / In hungry hundreds.' Alternatively, since 'box' can also mean simply 'to fight' (usually with fists), 'wi' the Squires turn out an' box' may be interpreted as 'turn out and fight with the gentry' in the sense of 'fight against' (i.e. in rebellion). The use of the expression 'turn out' may lend support to this latter interpretation, for the '98 Rebellion was, and sometimes still is, euphemistically referred to among Ulster Presbyterians as the 'Turn Oot'. The expression 'hungry hun'ers' also carries some weight in this context. 'Hun'ers' may simply be intended to convey a large number of people – about a hundred. However, it may, alternatively, suggest something more specific that Orr's community would have recognized: the United Irishmen were grouped in companies of one hundred men. As we have seen, it was probably because he had commanded such a company that Orr felt compelled to flee to America when a price of fifty pounds was put on the heads of men who had held this responsibility.

A further, apparently innocent, stanza employs a blend of Ulster Scots, English and Scots lexical items with remarkable assurance and permits two very different interpretations:

> Sweet to the badger, aft a lander
> At *day-light-gaun*, thou'rt on the *brander*,   ['twilight', 'gridiron'
> Brown skin't, an' *birslet*. Nane are *fander*   ['crusty skinned', 'fonder'
>   To hear thee crisp,
> Ere in some neuk, wi' goose and gander
>   He share the wisp. (ll. 43–8)

'Lander' seems a noun derived from the well-known Ulster verb 'to land in on', meaning to arrive without prior warning. The image suggests charity towards a wild animal – the badger, which appears at evening, is offered some potatoes roasted among the coals of a cottage fire and then proceeds to share scraps with a goose and gander. A charming incident indeed, if one really believes the standard register word 'badger', rather than Scots 'brock', is what Orr would have used for a woodland animal in a vernacular poem.

A different interpretation of 'badger' leaves the visitor's identity more mysterious and undefined, particularly when it is recalled that he arrived unexpectedly and at twilight. The verb to 'badge' can mean to tramp heavily round the countryside, as if under the weight of a heavy load.[66] This hints at a chapman or a packman. Such itinerant workers were known sometimes to have been in the service of the United Irishmen and to have passed messages throughout the radical network.[67] Is Orr here recalling how such clandestine trafficking took place? This seems possible, once the significance of the 'badger' sharing a 'wisp' is considered. The standard meaning of the latter is, of course, a 'scrap' – a crumb of potato – which the visitor keeps and shares with farm animals. In Scots, however, a 'wisp' can figuratively denote 'a piece of suppressed news, a secret, (the possession of) inside knowledge'.[68] If this is the case, the 'badger' may be passing a message to a couple of sympathizers, 'the goose and gander' in a cottage he visits.

Orr employs hints and coded signals in other places throughout his vernacular works, as the further discussion below will confirm. Thomson too, in his apparently innocent 'To a Hedgehog',[69] refers to the creature's spikes as 'pikes', which must be concealed from 'Colley', the sheepdog (ll. 61–6). Here the hedgehog represents the United Irish force (the pike being their key weapon) and 'Colley', the watchful military authorities. Of course it is perfectly possible to read Orr's 'badger' simply as a weary, trudging traveller or tramp who is given scraps of food before he passes on to spend the night sharing the 'neuks' (l. 47) of the farm animals. Much of the text's power lies in its elusiveness.[70] The above examples demonstrate the flexibility with which Orr employed lexical items from the contemporary Scots, English, Irish and Ulster language systems; such language diversity empowered him to articulate a daring, deeply radical *parole*.

The well-known traveller in Ireland, Arthur Young, had commented favourably on the diet of Irish cottiers, deeming it superior to that of English labourers:

> The food of the common Irish, potatoes and milk, have been produced more than once as an instance of the extreme poverty of the country, but this I believe is an opinion embraced with more alacrity than reflection ... When I see the people of a country in spite of political oppression with well-formed, vigorous bodies ... when I see their men athletic and their women beautiful, I know not how to believe them subsisting on an unwholesome food.[71]

It is more than likely that Orr had read Young's *Tour in Ireland*. The passage quoted above may have underlined for him his view of the superiority of the Irish diet and the empowerment he believed the potato could give to the population. Young also mentions 'political oppression', which Orr exclaims against in his final stanza. These details suggest that the poem, or parts of it, may have been composed during the optimistic early 1790s. Certainly its defiant radicalism, its encoded references to United Irish activity and its emphasis on independence would have been appropriate at that time, but these are the very factors that make its appearance in 1804, after the Union, all the more bold. Orr is recommending resistance to incorporation, an idea altogether more challenging to the authorities than Thomson's assertion, discussed above, of his rights over his inner man.

Orr's 'scribbling crony' John Dickey took up the potato theme for the purpose of angrily denouncing the 'ill-bred British sot', William Cobbett (1763–1835), 'Wha rails free gratis' (ll. 75–6) because he had denigrated a potato-based diet. Dickey, writing sometime after Orr published in 1804, adheres to the idea of the potato as a national symbol. As far as he is concerned, contempt for the potato as a food goes hand in hand with contempt for the Irish people, and he mentions several stereotypical images which he believes have been circulated, for example:

> Compare Hibernians to wild hogs,
> That wallow thro' St Patrick's bogs
>   And can but grunt:[72] (ll. 98–100)

Cobbett certainly railed against potatoes more than once. In the following passage he deplores what he sees as an increasing trend of allotting to English labourers a potato patch in part payment of their wages, noting:

> This has a tendency to bring English labourers down to the state of the Irish, whose mode of living, as to food, is but one remove from that of the pig ... For it must be a considerable time before English people can be brought to eat potatoes in the Irish style; that is to say, scratch them out of the earth with their paws, toss them into a pot without washing, and when boiled, turn them out upon a dirty board, and then sit round that board, peel the skin and dirt from one at a time and eat the inside ... I hope we shall, in the words of Doctor Drennen, 'leave Ireland to her lazy root' if she choose still to adhere to it. It is the root, also, of slovenliness, filth, misery, and slavery.[73]

The othering of the Irish, characterized here as dirty, lazy, slovenly and but one step removed from animals (their hands characterized as 'paws') is very evident. Cobbett appears unmoved by the abject state of 'slavery' he depicts but simply wishes to preserve his fellow Englishmen from it. Clearly Dickey has read such a passage among Cobbett's writings and is keen to point out the extent to which England farms Ireland for foodstuffs:

> Deil thank the Englishman to work,
> Wha daily sticks his knife and fork
> In guid fat hams o' Irish pork, –
>   Or wha does *swatter*, ['slobber'
> Wi' beard belubber'd like a Turk,
>   In Irish Butter. (ll. 85–90)

Furthermore, Dickey offers a riposte, characterizing the English as 'barmy cheat[s]' (l. 93) and a 'set o' proud conceited dogs' (l. 97). The deep-seated resentment expressed here would surface again several generations later in literature that referred to the Famine as a 'starvation' and pointed out the extent to which Irish produce continued to support the 'mother country' throughout the period of the disaster.[74] Dickey's readiness to take up Orr's themes provides evidence of the respect with which Orr's work was regarded within the Ulster Scots communities.

The Ulster poets' enthusiasm for Burns is beyond dispute, but should not be overstated. They wrote drawing on their Scots heritage but they confidently addressed Ulster and Irish affairs in their own voices. Those poets, specifically Orr and Thomson, who have been designated 'minor' when placed within the shadow of Burns's massive achievement, in reality produced many individual works of true genius. This study has explored 'To the Potatoe', but several others, such as Orr's vernacular 'The Irish Cottier's Death and Burial', or his formal English 'The Assizes', both to be discussed in later chapters, are certainly major contributions to four nations literary heritage and deserve recognition as such. By the end of the eighteenth century the vernacular poetic tradition in Ulster had developed into a sturdily independent and serviceable plant. Orr's masterly manipulation of Scots language and verse forms, his keen appreciation of national issues, and his affection for the Ulster Scots community, combined to make it flower.

7 THE REBEL EXPERIENCE

The poems considered in the following discussion disclose in intimate detail, moving, comic and shocking by turns, the experiences and emotions of James Orr during and after what his biographer called 'the unhappy period of 1798'.[1] They allow the reader a profound insight into his personal trauma, while they also demonstrate his strength and determination in seeking to rebuild his life and relationships in Ireland following the Act of Union. But, as will be argued, these poems are much more than simply a personal record. Technically excellent, the series comprises some of Orr's most important vernacular pieces, executed with exceptional original flair. They encompass themes such as piety, rebellion, betrayal, exile and renewal that for centuries have recurred within 'the matter of Ireland'. In representing tragedy they eschew sentimentality while often evincing robust humour, but they also express striking compassion and humility. In these works James Orr ably redirected and refocused the Scottish poetic tradition for service in his native land.

In choosing the vernacular for all but one of these poems, Orr acknowledged his own community's intimate connection with the subjects and events he covered. It is possible that that community may have been his initial audience for the informal circulation of these verses. He did, however, include them in a volume subscribed to by individuals resident in parts of Ireland beyond the Broadisland district, and in going to print he must have hoped eventually to access a still wider reading public. The poems quite naturally develop as a narrative, a linked series of episodes reflecting Orr's and the Ulster Scots communities' experiences during and following the United Irishmen's Rebellion of 1798.[2] In Edward Said's words: 'stories become the method colonized people use to assert their own identity and the existence of their own history'.[3] As Dissenters, that is non-Ascendancy Protestants, Orr's community had suffered disadvantage and marginalization throughout the eighteenth century, and continued to be required to pay taxes – the hated tithe – to the dominant, minority Anglican Church.

The northern United Irishmen's first engagement with Government forces took place under the leadership of Henry Joy McCracken in Antrim town on 7 June 1798. McCracken had issued his orders to the 'Army of Ulster' on 6 June and Orr turned out in obedience, with the Broadisland/Islandmagee corps, hoping to make a reality of the 'year of liberty' his leader had proclaimed. Orr's 'A Prayer' (1798), demonstrates the inner conflict he suffered at the prospect of committing himself to violent action. In rhyme scheme and metre the work employs the verse form of the metrical Psalms, central to Presbyterian worship, and observes traditional decorum by addressing the Deity in a formal, standard English register. It follows the recognizable structure of a prayer, comprising adoration, confession of sins and supplication, while expressing faith in an essentially merciful God:

> How oft I've err'd! at pleasure's shrine
> How fondly bent my knee!
> But if I have not cruel been,
> Be clement, Lord!to me.[4] (ll. 5–8)

The strong rhymes, Biblical diction, and the occasional inversion of the syntax necessitated by the form employed, create the impression of relentless honesty, exercised while the speaker undertakes a logical, disciplined thought process. Frequent use of the imperative mood underlines the tone of urgent prayerfulness:

> Let not this frame, whose fleshless bones
> These summer suns may bleach,
> Lie writhing long; nor while it stands,
> The hand of pillage stretch. (ll. 21–4)

The first, intense and vivid image may recall the 'white banes' of the slain knight at the end of the bleak, gruesome popular ballad 'The Twa Corbies'. In addition, the speaker's employment of impersonal references to his self as 'it' (l. 22) and 'this frame' (l. 20), suggests he wishes to remain personally distanced from what he is about to do, and that he fears he may not behave in a manner consistent with his faith during the heat of battle. Occasionally a heartfelt exclamation or question within the text suggests that only the disciplined framework of the prayer is keeping under control emotions that would otherwise overwhelm the supplicant. Significantly, however, he appears to entertain no doubts that the call to arms must be obeyed: 'But, whilst as man I have to fight, / as man O may I feel!' (ll. 19–20).

The prayer reaches its climax in a tough self-interrogation, a series of questions in which the core issues are faced and the alternatives set out:

> Why dread to die? What griefs I've borne?
> What pains have pluck'd each nerve?
> Yet why not wish to grow more wise,
> And live my friends to serve? (ll. 29–32)

Presumably, a life lived out in service to one's friends represents a more attractive option than death in battle, but the speaker's acknowledgement of the pain and grief that inevitably accompany human experience assists him in accepting the prospect of death, as the penultimate stanza confirms in a strong declarative: 'Resigned I'll rest then' (l. 33). The final stanza repeats the first exactly:

> Almighty Lord of life and death!
> While men for strife prepare,
> Let but this heart thy favour feel,
> And peace will still be there. (ll. 37–40)

There is a distinct sense that the peace which was merely an aspiration at the start has now been achieved through a process of intense reasoning, informed by the supplicant's grasp of Christian principles, scriptural precepts and understanding of the character of God. Such a process was characteristic of Presbyterianism, particularly of the New Light variety which emphasized the right of private judgement.

Orr's voice in this instance expresses both passionate sincerity and practical faith. Circumstances could also imbue it with an edge of desperation as a further poem demonstrates. 'The Wanderer' takes its title from the name sometimes used of a pursued Covenanter, which sites the poem within Scottish and Ulster narratives of principled resistance to state authority.[5] It would have reminded Orr's readers that many of the Scots who had migrated to Ulster in the course of the seventeenth century had done so to escape persecution, and would, thus, have signalled Orr's belief in the justice of his cause, and the injustice of the government that opposed him (although Covenanting theology in itself did not attract him). It may be very directly based on Orr's own experiences when, following the defeat of the United Irishmen at the Battle of Antrim, he hid in the bleak district of the hill of Slemish with McCracken, Hope and others.[6] It is essentially a dramatically charged dialogue in Braid Scotch consisting of three stanzas, each made up of eight alternately rhyming iambic tetrameters in two quatrains – a meticulously constructed song, which he directed should be sung to the tune of the (then) popular 'Mary's Dream.'[7]

The subject is a mysterious and desperate stranger, who knocks at the window of a young woman's isolated cottage in the dead of night. In common with another popular genre, the ballad, in which the motif of the stranger who requests hospitality frequently occurs, little background detail is provided regarding the circumstances or the characters. The poem is deceptively simple, resting on oppositions such as light and darkness, and on the warmth and security inside the cottage where the 'lassie' is, contrasted with the cold and insecurity experienced by the wanderer outside. The desolate, eerie atmosphere is evoked through references to the hail, the 'piercin' night' (l. 14) and to the howling of the wind: 'the blast that brayed on Slimiss tap' (l. 3).[8] The man does not ask directly for shelter, but describes his experience of having been refused accommodation by a '*wight* ['individual'] / *Wham* aft I've help'd wi'*han*' an' purse'['whom', 'hand'] (l. 10).

The reader is likely to assume the wanderer and woman are strangers to each other until allusions to persons and issues outside the text suggest that a bond of understanding already exists between them. If there is a shepherd 'aboon [her] on the laft' (l. 8) as she warns, why is she keen that he should not be awakened by the wanderer's cries? The wanderer claims to be 'a frien'' (l. 5) and he uses her name, 'Leezie' (l. 13). His crimes, he says, are 'common' (l. 5), but she cannot understand this to imply robbery, murder or rape, or she would not let him in. In fact she becomes complicit with him, not only in offering a warm bed, but in deliberately ensuring that they do not attract the attention of 'the *picquet bauld*' ['bold patrolling officer'] (l. 21) with a fire. The text prompts the reader to construct a background narrative in which the picquet represents a System that polices a hostile population. The lassie and the wanderer, therefore, appear united as subversives. Within this community trust and relationships have in many instances broken down under the weight of imposed authority: a former friend lacks the courage to assist the wanderer, and the shepherd in the loft, perhaps, cannot be relied upon to keep the secret of his visit.

A brief analysis of the discourse between the woman and the wanderer demonstrates an interesting reversal of the usual male–female power relations. It is the young woman who challenges 'Wha's there?' (l. 1), instructs '*Mair lown*' ['more softly'] (l. 7), and acts decisively: 'I'm *gaun* to slip aside the bar' ['going'] (l. 16). The wanderer's speech is more pragmatic, a series of declaratives that play on her sympathy, flattering and invoking intimacy: 'He wadna let me stay a' nicht ... But Leezie's gentler – Hark that hail!' (l. 13). Once inside, he is permitted no speech at all. It is she who dominates, exclaiming, 'Waes me! How *wat* ye're' ['wet'] (l. 17), issuing instructions, 'dry your face wi' something- hae!' (l. 18), and taking decisions. Although she even allows him into her bed, she stresses her virtuous intentions: 'I'll sit up: my bed's no *cauld*, ['cold'] / *Gae* till't awee an' tak a nap' ['go'] (ll. 23–4). While this preserves the young woman's reputation, it could also be alleged that the speaker (or Orr the lifelong bachelor) is indulging himself with the fantasy of a mother figure who enters emotionally and uncritically into his experience while fussing over his physical needs. The text invites a variety of readings, and intrigues with hints of a longer narrative that remains undisclosed.

Several years after the publication of 'The Wanderer' the local historian Samuel McSkimin's account of a ramble in County Antrim was printed in the *Belfast Monthly Magazine*, to which Orr was then an occasional contributor. McSkimin referred to the Slemish district's poetic associations and links with the Rebellion:

> This country from being so wild and broken, was the chief refuge of many persons, who in 1798, were excluded from pardon by the government; and here that 'mountain nymph sweet liberty', held her revels in that inclement winter. A song composed

apropos, by one of those exiles, is still chaunted here; it compliments the inhabitants on their genuine hospitality but its political sentiments are violent, and enthusiastic in the extreme; which, however, is not strange, when we consider the situation of the author, and the season in which it was written.[9]

The song mentioned nudges the reader with memories of Orr's composition 'The Wanderer', although the printed version of this work does not include sentiments that could be called 'violent in the extreme'. One may conclude that a different song by another member of McCracken's routed force is being referred to, or perhaps even that a more extreme version of the piece existed before Orr, with necessary circumspection, produced the one that was eventually published. This would certainly explain the enigmatic, unfinished effect created by the printed work.

Orr developed the narrative of his rebel experiences in two poems which exploit one of the great Scots poetic genres: the *Christis Kirk* poem. Allan H. MacLaine's study of this genre as it developed from the Middle Scots period enabled him to pinpoint certain typical characteristics of these comic accounts of labouring-class behaviour on holidays or at fairs. Recurring features include a detached, satirical narrator; bawdy, brawling beggars; individual vignettes held together by 'a slender thread of narrative'; rapid pace and genial irony. MacLaine also rightly remarked that the stanza's demanding pattern of eight alternating iambic tetrameters and trimeters followed by a 'bobwheel', ensured that it was 'not a verse form for amateurs'.[10] Burns employed the *Christis Kirk* in the 1780s and extended its range to accommodate religious satire in poems such as 'The Ordination' (1786) and 'The Holy Fair' (1785), while earlier in the eighteenth century Fergusson's 'The Election' (1773) had demonstrated that it could carry political satire.

Several years before James Orr created a *Christis Kirk* poem, Samuel Thomson composed 'The Simmer Fair' and published it in the *Northern Star*, prefacing it with a note informing readers that it was 'in the manner of Burns'.[11] While Burns had employed the genre humorously to satirize licentiousness cloaked in religious devotion in 'The Holy Fair', and the emptiness or cant of a series of preachers in 'The Ordination', Thomson deploys the *Christis Kirk* conventions traditionally, while giving them a contemporary and, crucially, 'Norland', or north of Ireland, relevance. He portrays the convergence of the local populace on the fair in his home village of Templepatrick and records how violent brawling, drunkenness and illicit sexual encounters occur among raucous gangs of weavers and cobblers.

Thomson's narrative, though deft in its negotiation of broad comedy and of irony, is fairly unadventurous. He certainly does not attempt anything approaching the sophistication of Burns's religious satire. By contrast, James Orr exploits the possibilities of the *Christis Kirk* stanza and the traditions associated with it, in two works, and in a conspicuously original manner. 'The Passengers' is a dynamic account of an emigrant voyage to Newcastle on the Delaware.[12] The narrator, although here identified as one of the voyagers, for the most part takes a mocking, detached stance as he portrays a diverse group from the labouring classes enduring the rigours of the long Atlantic crossing. Orr must have drawn on his own experiences as a forced migrant, though he also cites the experiences of the Lockes, a family who, according to a note to his text, emigrated from Ballycarry in 1798. The poem races along with vignettes, alternately moving and comic, graphically recording the experience.

As the voyage progresses, the *Christis Kirk* motifs of brawling, debauchery and retching are given their place, though Orr adds a characteristic touch of greater delicacy by merely hinting at the latter two activities. Sex, for example, is suggested by the sly 'folk becam' obligin'' (l. 80), while chronic sea-sickness is rendered as:

> An' some, wi' *monie a twine an' throe*, ['many a contortion and spasm'
> Do something wad be nauceous
>   To name, this day.[13] (ll. 61–3)

The narrator also notes with relish how the Ulster 'blacks' on board, normally loud-mouthed arrogant young men, lie 'cheepin' like a chicken' while the ship pitches and rolls through a great storm.[14] In a discussion of this passage Julia M. Wright interprets 'blacks' literally as black slaves and explains their rueful memories of boxing 'in fairs wi' venom' as a reference to their forced participation in 'a slave sports economy' for the profit of their masters.[15] However, if one accepts that Orr's 'blacks' are tough young Presbyterian men – 'blackmouths', as discussed in Chapter 3 – it is clear that Orr is mocking their uncharacteristic loss of spirits as they suffer from seasickness. In all probability he is here making a knowing cross-reference to the belligerent cobblers and weavers Samuel Thomson had satirized in his earlier *Christis Kirk* poem, 'The Simmer Fair', which records a fight that broke out between rival groups of young men.

Unusually for a poem in this genre, Orr includes a passage of startling beauty as he recalls a calm night and the sheen of the moon on the water, confidently combining sibilance, Scots idiom and a hint of neoclassical poetic diction:

> To see at night the surface fine
>   That Cynthia made her path on;
> An' *snove, an' snore* thro' waves o' brine, ['moved speedily with a splashing sound'
>   That sparkle't like a heath on
>   A bleaze some day. (ll. 95–9)

Fleetingly, and without disturbing the balance of the mood, Orr weaves in melancholy, reflective moments to remind the reader that despite the general rambunctiousness, many of the passengers are in mourning for their lost homeland. As the journey progresses, 'Some frae the stern, wi' thoughts o' grief / *Leuk* back, their hearts to Airlan" ['look'] (ll. 56–7). Later, at the sight of new land ahead, 'The Exiles griev't' (the text dignifying them with an upper case 'E'), though Orr adds that all around them a kind of sacrilege is committed as 'the sharpers thiev't / While cronies *bous't* like fishes' ['boozed'] (ll. 106–7). Such passages demonstrate the confidence and expertise with which Orr assimilates the rollicking *Christis Kirk* genre into the literature of exile and loss. He is careful to allow the name of 'Airlan' to occur twice, thus underlining his purpose to explore and express Irish experience.

When the moment comes for the emigrants to disembark, Orr swiftly and without sentimentality effects the dispersal of this rich, varied, transient community to their various fates in the New World. A further touch of wry humour is added in the revelation that the appearance of the Ulster 'blacks', now fully restored to self-confidence, startles the gapers on the quayside into flight:

> *Gypes co'ert the wharf to gove*, an' stare, ['louts covered the wharf to gape'
> While out, in boats, we bustle:
> Creatures wha ne'er had seen a black,
> *Fu' scar't* took to their *shankies*; ['very frightened', 'legs'
> Sae, wi' our best *rags* on our back, ['clothes'
> We mixt amang the Yankies,
>   An' *skail't*, that day. (ll. 165–71) ['dispersed'

Julia M. Wright interprets this passage as if the people who saw the 'blacks' and ran off in fear were actually the Irish passengers, terrified at their first sight of black people. Because she has taken the poem's earlier reference to 'blacks' as referring to black slaves, she comments that this terror 'illogically implies that passengers on a small ship with an active communal culture never saw some of their shipmates', but she adds that 'in substance these lines also follow a common "myth" of Irish arrival in the United States in which Irish emigrants are terrified at seeing a black person for the first time'.[16] No doubt Orr was fully aware of this myth and here he is, in fact, ironically turning it on its head, for the lines make perfect sense if they are interpreted as humorously portraying the effect produced by the cocksure, aggressive Ulster Presbyterian men as they make their entrance to the New World. The lines actually depict the reactions of the 'gapers' on the quayside who are shown running off, terrified at their first sight of these redoubtable new arrivals. Thus Orr captures, and delights in mocking, the combative, confrontational demeanour of his co-religionists and fellow countrymen, while also making a clear point about their great resilience. The vitality and richness of this work would surely enhance and dignify any anthology of emigrant literature.

Christopher Whyte has explored the *Christis Kirk* genre in the light of Bakhtin's discussion of carnival, but appears to have believed that in the eighteenth century the genre appeared in Scotland only. His conclusions, nevertheless, bear some relevance to Orr's work, as 'The Passengers' certainly reveals. The poem's opening stanzas depict the 'living wake', whereby the emigrants and their friends and relatives perform a parting ceremony of ritualized grieving.[17] At the outset, then, the mood is heavy with a sense of loss that seems out of keeping with genre traditions. Once the passengers board, however, a transformation process begins in the ship's hold where families, individuals, young and old are forced into 'jostling, colliding, squeezing and rubbing against one another' in the manner of participants at a festive event such as a fair or carnival.[18] For Bakhtin

> Carnival was associated ... with a specific location in public space, most frequently the market place ... There the relations between different social and commercial groups and castes, normally mediated conceptually, through ideology and language, were replaced by a free bodily contact.[19]

In 'The Passengers' the confinement of the ship's hold is substituted for the crowded market place. Here different personalities and religious denominations who might normally avoid one another share an experience that temporarily binds them into a community while still permitting representative 'types' to emerge: a complaining wife, crying babies, aggressive young men, Catholics praying through the Rosary, and Old Light Presbyterians sermonizing and quoting Scripture. The stormy weather they endure is vividly recreated in the following passage which also shows how these diverse types are literally thrown and muddled together, with the drenching in sea water effecting a communal baptism, a rite of passage into life in the New World:

> But now a gale besets our bark,
>   Frae gulph to gulph we're tumble't;
> *Kists*, *kits*, an' fam'lies, i' the dark,   ['chests', 'luggage'
>   Wi' *ae* side-jerk are jumble't: ['one'
> Some *stauchrin'* thro' a pitch lays *laigh* –   ['staggering', 'low'
>   Some, *drouket*, *ban* the breaker;   ['soaked', 'curse'
> While surge, on surge, sae *skelps* her ... (ll. 100–6)   ['slaps'

Orr wrote two poems about the experience of emigration, one in Ulster Scots and one in English. A brief comparison of these two texts assists greater appreciation of his two very different poetic voices. 'Song, Composed on the Banks of Newfoundland' is melancholy and nostalgic, presenting the rigours of the voyage and the close proximity to other human beings with undisguised horror:

> How hideous the hold is! – Here, children are screaming,
> There dames faint, thro' thirst, with their babes on their knee;
> Here, down ev'ry hatch the big breakers are streaming,
> And, there, with a crash, half the fixtures break free:
> Some court – some contend – some sit dull stories telling –
> The mate's mad and drunk, and the tars task'd and yelling:

What sickness and sorrow, pervade my rude dwelling! –
A huge floating lazar-house, far, far at sea.[20] (ll. 17–24)

By turns the English poem voices maudlin self-pity or evokes hell on earth. It possesses none of the carnivalesque vigour that we find in the *Christis Kirk* version, where the stanza form, the vernacular idiom and the satirical voice combine to achieve a liberating effect. Here, disgorged from the teeming hold the exiles, now transformed to immigrants, 'skail' (l. 171), to begin new, independent lives. The message seems clear: Irish people, of whatever persuasion, are robust and unlikely to be cowed for long.

In describing Orr's next essay in the *Christis Kirk* form as 'a gnarled poem', John Hewitt captured something of the pithy, acerbic spirit present in 'Donegore Hill'.[21] However, he considered both it and 'The Passengers' as of 'limited aim' when, in fact, each of these texts is in its own right a complex and original work which significantly shapes the development of the genre.[22] 'Donegore Hill' addresses a recurring subject in both Irish and Scottish poetry – confrontation between insurgents and state forces. Eschewing the rollicking jollity of traditional *Christis Kirk* verse, the narrator opts for a brooding opening that unsettles with its references to trampled crops, untended fields and 'tortur'd' labourers. But if the purpose seems to be to prepare the reader for some heroic account of a grand-scale military encounter, the mood is speedily undercut in a series of images and details that reduce the narrative to the level of farce.

As Orr tells the story of how the Broadisland troop of United Irishmen gathered in Ballycarry village and marched to Donegore Hill to merge with McCracken's force he records that while many made vigorous preparations for battle, others cravenly sought to preserve themselves from danger:

> While close-leagu'd *crappies* rais'd the hoards ['croppies']
>   O' pikes, pike-shafts, forks, firelocks,
> Some melted lead – some saw'd deal boards –
>   Some *hade* like hens in *byre neuks*. (ll. 10–13) ['hid', 'cramped corners of byres']

The quoted passage illustrates a typical technique of the poet throughout, in which feminine rhymes are employed to underscore the satirical effect and reinforce the impression of weakness. The characteristically reductive Ulster Scots idiom is also in evidence when the speaker deplores the rebel force as 'An unco throuither squath'ry' ['an exceptionally mixed, untidy and awkward bunch'] (l. 8) or 'pale fac'd *randies*' ['ruffians'] (l. 71) who never intended to fight in the conflict for which they marched off. The lampooning effect is compounded further by the inclusion of vulgar, farcical *Christis Kirk* staples including references to bodily functions. Thus we learn that some tried to evade the engagement by squatting down behind a hedge and 'lettin' on their burn to mak', while later some 'took leg', scared into flight by the colours of bright 'rag weeds' in the distance which they took for the uniforms of Major-General Nugent's redcoat soldiers. The panic in the latter incident appears to have been caused by an individual whom the narrator designates a 'son o' shame' and who is identified in the text for readers 'in the know' by his name and surname of seven and five letters respectively, represented thus: ******* ***** (l. 68). The mini-narrative of individual cowardice and betrayal which is integrated within the text's broader account of the events of 7 June later depicts the same man returning to his domineering wife who, without irony, congratulates him on having had the wisdom 'to *rin or e'er* they saw ye' ['run before'] (l. 112). The narrator's tone in recounting such incidents is uncompromisingly withering, while the brusque dimeter tagline which concludes each stanza very graphically reinforces the idea of an enterprise that has gone off half-cocked:

> Tho' strong, untried, they swore in pride,
>   'Moilie wad *dunch* the yeomen', ['give a severe blow to'
>   Some *wiss'd-for* day. (ll. 79–81) ['wished for'

Liam McIlvanney has demonstrated how skilfully and with what originality Orr has woven traditional *Christis Kirk* features such as cowardice, brawling and vulgarity into a narrative about a military engagement in order to satirize the bragging but naive and spineless rebel forces who march in hopelessly ramshackle fashion to the mustering ground, only to fall back when they find themselves on the verge of something 'baleful and bloody'.[23] Strictly speaking, of course, the poem is not about a battle at all, since the full Broadisland corps never actually made it to Antrim to participate in McCracken's assault on the town. The fact that there was so little substance or outcome, despite years of preparation for revolt, makes the event a very appropriate target for satire. In its vigorous recounting of a military engagement of national significance which ended in confusion and disillusionment 'Donegore Hill' shows a degree of similarity to Burns's 'The Battle of Sherra-moor' (1790). The behaviour of those rebels who had no real stomach for the fight and who 'scar'd at blows / And hameward fast did flee, man' (ll. 49–50) certainly matches the actions of those members of Orr's troop whom he castigates.[24]

In a departure from *Christis Kirk* conventions the narrator does not remain sardonic and distanced from his material, but in several vignettes enters the narrative as a character, using direct speech or free indirect thought to express strong opinions or emotion. A passage where a review of troops is clearly taking place makes this evident, and, furthermore, suggests the speaker is closely identified with Orr himself – the troop commander and 'fifty pounder' who, following the debacle, had to go on the run. The same passage develops the heroic/cowardly opposition present from the outset by identifying two very different types of insurgent in the rebel forces:

> A brave man firmly *leain'* hame ['leaving'
> I ay was proud to think on;
> The wife-obeyin' son o'shame
> *Wi' kindling e'e I blink on*: (ll. 19–22) ['with a furious eye I blink at'

What follows is a vivid account of the march to Donegore which becomes ever more unruly, and culminates in the confusion and noise at the summit, the desertion of half the force, the cringing indecision of the remainder and the narrator's final, furious denunciation:

> 'Na, haste ye hame; ye *ken* ye'll 'scape, ['know'
>   'Cause martial worth ye're clear o';
> The nine-tail'd cat, or choakin' *rape*, ['rope'
>   Is *maistly* for some hero ...' (ll. 87–90) ['mostly'

That the speaker has a strong personal reason for his rage becomes evident in the penultimate stanza, the poem's climactic moment, when he makes clear he believes a deserting member of his troop, the same 'wife obeyin' son o' shame', has informed on him to the authorities in order to save his own skin:

> 'I'll *hae* to swear *** forc'd me out;[25] ['have'
>   Better he swing than I, on
>   Some hangin' day.' (ll. 115–17)

Stephen Dornan has argued against an interpretation of the poem which identifies the narrator too closely with Orr himself. While rightly pointing out the failure of commentators to acknowledge the sophistication of Orr's piece, Dornan traces this interpretation to an over-readiness to accept Orr's conventional apology for his rusticity in the preface to his 1804 volume. He asserts, in fact, that Orr's narrator is presented as a 'rustic' speaker, a persona assumed for the occasion. However, this view actually misses much of the speaker's, and the piece's, subtlety.[26] Dornan asserts, for example, that the speaker interprets the Rising in unambiguously local terms, citing the opening stanza which characterizes the rebels as 'chiels wha grudg'd to be sae tax'd / And tyth'd by rack-rent *blauth'ry*' [riff-raff] (ll. 5–6). He claims that 'There is no mention of the meta-narrative of a global and international struggle for liberty that Orr obviously believed he was engaging in'.[27] At no point, however, does the narrator of 'Donegore Hill' state that he shares the narrow aims of the rebels whose doings he chronicles. Rather he maintains distance throughout, excoriating their perfidy and cowardice. Nor is it likely that a skilful poet who wished to camouflage himself in the garb of a rustic would inadvertently let slip a learned reference to the Augustan master poet Alexander Pope, as the speaker does towards the conclusion.

In addition, far from failing to refer to 'the meta-narrative of a global and international struggle for liberty' the poem's lexis and references illustrate unambiguously that this is indeed the background against which the march to Donegore takes place. The allusions, however, are deftly made, expertly grafted into the text from the poem's wider context.

Such allusions include the ironic description of 'Repentant Painites at their pray'rs' (l. 39) – those who had professed atheism finding that cold fear has rekindled their faith – which recalls Paine's *The Rights of Man* and his atheistic *The Age of Reason*, both key texts in circulation among democrats and revolutionaries in Europe, America and Ireland. Orr also refers to the 'patriots' (l. 74), linking his poem to the struggle for freedom and democracy within Ireland as a whole, and he attacks the vicious state punishment system represented by 'The nine-tailed cat' and 'choakin' rape', meted out to 'some hero' (ll. 88–9). This serves as a reminder of the fates of leaders such as McCracken, Monroe and, eventually, Russell and Emmet, whose aspirations reached far beyond reform of the taxation system, which in itself was a major source of grievance throughout Ireland and was, therefore, a national issue.[28]

The narrator demonstrates particular skill in employing a characteristically deflating Ulster Scots turn of phrase with a 'rustic' or homely ring for satirical purposes, or as a means of cutting his subjects down to size. Thus, when Orr writes of those who would have '*bell'd the cat awee*, [successfully challenged the authorities] / Had they no been deserted' (ll. 120–1), he is understating what was actually a daring process of mounting a major challenge to the government. These few examples demonstrate that the poem is in reality exceptionally well-grounded 'in the meta-narrative of the national and global struggle for liberty in which Orr knew he was engaging'. It is the wry, frustrated, intelligent and thoughtful narrator, however, rather than his troop as he portrays them, who understands such issues.

The poem's deliberately understated conclusion effects an emotional anti-climax and allows a moment of reflection. Having exposed and excoriated the empty bravado of the 'loons' who had sworn brotherhood in their United Irish oath, boasted of how they would 'dunch the yeomen' but at the crisis thought only of saving their own skins, the speaker considers their behaviour more coolly, showing an understanding born of bitter experience. In finding the cowards and betrayers no worse than most people he signals his resignation but acknowledges the shattering of his own dream for a better Ireland:

> *Thae warks pat skill*, tho' in my *min'* ['these events put wisdom', 'mind'
> That ne'er was in't before, *mon*, ['man'
> In tryin' times, maist folk, you'll *fin'*, ['find'
> Will act like Donegore men
> On *ony* day. (ll. 122–6) ['any'

This is a moment of sad epiphany. McCracken's, and indeed United Irish hopes of establishing a democratic, just and inclusive Ireland by force were dead, from Orr's perspective killed by cowardice, disunity and treachery. Afterwards Orr's commitment to United Irish ideals may be traced in his Romantic and cultural nationalism, his commitment to emancipation and reform, and to acts of philanthropy. Though his concern for the poor and respect for all creeds never wavered, however, later works reveal him frequently grief-stricken and melancholic.

The four poems discussed above were published in the 1804 edition of Orr's poetry. Given that the Act of Union had been passed in 1801, and that Emmett and Russell had been recently hanged for their parts in the Rebellion of 1803 one admires Orr's nerve in including these and other poems in which radical experience and sympathies are so deeply embedded. By now it should be evident that he is to be admired also for his expertise as a poet working within the Scottish tradition not as an imitator but as an innovator, not confined by the tradition's structures but inspired to adapt them for his own context, and giving expression to the distinctive voice of a committed radical. That commitment was 'rewarded' with a period as a hunted fugitive in Ireland, followed by his brief, unhappy exile in America. Orr completed his narrative of rebel experience with the 'Epistle: To S. Thomson of Carngranny. A Brother Poet', addressed to his old friend Samuel Thomson who had encouraged him to write for the *Northern Star* in the 1790s. The poem is written in the third of the three great Scots stanza forms: the *Cherrie and the Slae* stanza, repopularized by Scots vernacular poets during the eighteenth century and chosen by Burns for a verse epistle to a friend.[29]

In a finely nuanced reading of the 'Epistle to Davie, a Brother Poet' (1785),[30] Fiona Stafford brought out the 'rich and complicated' make up of this work, showing how it was designed both to stimulate debate on the nature of true happiness and to provide some answers.[31] Within the poem, as Stafford explained, we find a confluence of the thoughts of Scottish and English poets. Ramsay's 'The Poet's Wish' (1721) is referenced explicitly in the quotation 'Mair spier na, nor fear na' (l. 25),[32] as Burns recalls that despite relative poverty he and Davie are 'hale and fier' (l. 24), but Burns also addresses a major issue raised by Alexander Montgomerie (*c.* 1555–97) in *The Cherrie and the Slae*: whether happiness is to be found through aspiration or in contentment.[33] In addition to these poets, traces of Pope are to be found in Burns's emphasis on the importance of self-knowledge, while Scottish Enlightenment thought is present in the poet's challenging of the assumption that wealth or position can bring happiness. Ultimately for Burns happiness lies in the true friendship he enjoys with Davie, and love, including sexual satisfaction, with Jean:

> Fate still has blest me with a friend,
>   In ev'ry care and ill;
> And oft a more endearing band,
>   A tye more tender still. (ll. 133–6)

If the poem's ending appears abrupt, even rather lame, this is surely deliberate, for in the concluding metaphor Burns indicates that his inspiration, his *'Pegasus'* (l. 147), is halting and needs some attention. It is as if he is awaiting a response from Davie that will further develop the debate he has started.

In the early 1790s, at the height of his enthusiasm for Burns, Samuel Thomson took up the issues Burns had raised, in his 'Epistle to Luke Mullan, A Brother Bard' (1791).[34] In the spirit of Burns, to whom he makes a direct reference, Thomson also considers what may be the nature of true happiness, and like Burns he addresses his 'Epistle' to a friend who is a fellow poet, but Thomson develops his own viewpoint on the issue and is careful to ensure that his poem incorporates many original features. Thus, while Burns sets his poem in the depths of winter when 'winds frae off BEN-LOMOND blaw, / And bar the doors wi' driving snaw, / And *hing us owre the ingle*' ['cause us to hang over the fireside'] (ll. 1–3), Thomson's work begins with a lament, in pastoral vein, for the 'flow'ry months o' joy' (l. 8) while he observes 'yellow Autumn' (l. 1) speedily stripping the trees of leaves and the 'lees' (l. 12) of flowers. Thomson's perspective on the theme does not arise at the cosy ingle-side, but develops as he surveys the outdoor landscape at the time of changing seasons when *'Boreas'* (l. 13) chills, warning of winter's approach. His starting point is the age-old theme of mutability, which he also foregrounds through the employment of a gloomy biblical reference, reminding himself and the reader/recipient that 'All flesh is like the grassy vest / That haps the *Simmer brae*' ['summer hillside'] (ll. 21–2).[35] These reflections, and the stress on the swift passage of time, add a degree of urgency to Thomson's melancholy mood. In common with Burns, Thomson recognizes that poverty is inevitably the lot of the 'rustic bard' (l. 44). He is more distressed, however, by a lack of congenial company. His dejection deepens as he begins to contemplate his life, imaged as a 'chrystal rill' (l. 57), flowing away to the sea of eternity.

Loneliness is a recurring theme in Thomson's poetry and letters but the companionship of a like-minded friend can relieve his melancholy. As he blows on his 'whistle' (l. 64) he vividly evokes the image of his fellow Burns enthusiast Luke Mullan,[36] and their love of reading and composing poetry together:

> With L—e whiles, a book *whiles*, ['for a while'
>   To pass a happy hour;
> I'm careless an' fearless
>   How faithless Fortune lour. (ll. 67–70)

This sudden turn in the mood arrives in the bobwheel of the stanza that had begun by depicting Thomson at his lowest ebb. The remaining two stanzas are imbued with joy and excitement as Thomson imagines himself and Mullan going into print together and achieving a kind of immortality while 'swains unborn of other days' appreciate their verse. Undoubtedly he views this partnership almost as a type of literary marriage, hinting that they may sleep together in death, 'Aneath some mossy stone' (l. 78) while waiting for the Day of Judgement. The concluding stanza positively brims with eagerness and a new, intensely optimistic urgency, as Thomson mentally exhorts Mullan to mount up and ride the short distance from his home at Craigarogan to Lyle Hill, designated *'Parnas' Hill'* (l. 90).

In a reversal of Burns's concluding image of his halting inspiration, Thomson opts for a strong ending, portraying Mullan, on horseback, vigorously thundering towards him. The pace quickens, and the strong stresses in the dimeters echo the beating of powerful hooves. Thomson's gloom has dissipated and he concludes with an ecstatic cry that anticipates fulfilment: 'Come haste an' let me hear!' (l. 98). In essence, then, Thomson's view of happiness comprises friendship allied to a creative partnership that appears to function for him as a substitute for the intensity of Burns's intimate and sexual alliance with Jean. Thomson's handling of the complexities of the difficult *Cherrie and the Slae* stanza form is assured and provides evidence of his skill in composition which attracted men such as Mullan and the even more skilful James Orr.

Orr's 'Epistle To S. Thomson of Carngranny, A Brother Poet' (1804), was written sometime after his return from America.[37] When he adopted the *Cherrie and the Slae* stanza he would have been aware, from his familiarity with the works of Burns and with Thomson's first volume, of its direct literary predecessors, and also of the stanza's history of use by Montgomerie and Ramsay. The themes of true happiness, friendship and the proper attitude to worldly wealth, all first raised by Burns and taken up by Thomson, are here addressed also by Orr, who clearly wishes to contribute to the debate. Ultimately, however, in this final entry in the narrative of his '98 related experiences, his purpose is to set out those radical principles on which there can be no compromise. He also communicates the first hint of wishing to establish himself as a bard of the nation. On his return to Ireland he found society no more democratic or inclusive than before; the poor were, of course, still in poverty and the Union was about to become an accomplished fact. In addition, friendships had splintered, and silence and distrust pertained where once there had been creativity and intimacy. In such circumstances, the issue of how happiness might be achieved took on national as well as personal significance.

It is to the social and intellectual stimulation of meetings in Thomson's home that Orr first alludes when he re-establishes contact, but his pleasant memories are immediately countered with a shocking opposite, and a signal to Thomson that Orr's experience of violent conflict has left him with a mighty abhorrence of it:

> ... the hag of strife,
> Wi' han's that reek't wi' *bluid* she'd shed, ['blood'
> *'Gan* wi' the hues o' black an' red, ['began'
> To strip my *wab* o' life. (ll. 3–6) ['web'

He emphasizes several times in the course of the poem his relief at being restored to his home, and his value for intelligent friendship. Just as Burns hung over the ingle to escape the winter cold, Orr is 'at [his] ain fire-side at last, / *Fu'* blythe' ['very'] (ll. 16–17), conscious and grateful that 'the han' o' heav'n' has saved him 'by lan', an' sea' (ll. 43–5). He gives the impression that he is attempting to woo Thomson back into a friendly relationship, with a nicely judged blend of respectful praise, familiarity and nostalgia: Thomson is honoured in the greeting 'Dear Thomson! Fav'rite o' the nine' (l. 1) and lauded as 'the minstrel, blythe an' bright' (l. 9); thus Orr takes up the idea of Lyle Hill as Mount Parnassus and acknowledges Thomson's expertise as a flautist. By the end of the first stanza he is more familiar: '*Ise sen' now, an' ken* now, ['I'll send now and find out'] / How things wi' SAMIE *gang*' ['are going'] (ll. 13–14).

He has sufficient *savoir-faire* to affect a casual demeanour, as if he fears appearing forward and gives the impression that he has written almost on the spur of the moment. He returns to this feigned detachment in the concluding stanza but only after pouring out his heart to his former friend and mentor, coaxing Thomson to reply:

> I hope your *muirlan* muse ye'll woo, ['moorland'
> To tell me how ye *wrastle thro*', ['struggle on'
> Some time when ye're *no thrang*. (ll. 88–90) ['not too busy'

The nonchalance projected is belied by other details. Orr has sat up writing in the dark and cold: 'The moon-beams gild [his] frost-wrought panes' (l. 86), and he is keen to set up an actual meeting. The conclusion strongly suggests that the two had become estranged through a quarrel, as Orr refers to 'bile' (l. 95), factiousness and fighting, and wishes peace may prevail between them:

> Meanwhile, sir, *sud* bile, sir, ['should'
> Mak' factious prose-men fight,
> May leisure, an' pleasure,
> An' peace be ours! – Good night. (ll. 95–8)

The increased pace and exhortatory tone create a good-humoured, no-nonsense effect, and the expression 'prose-men' recalls Thomson's 'Epistle to Luke Mullan' in which he characterizes the worldly money grubbers as 'sons o' tasteless prose' (l. 47). Leave faction and argument to them; we, the poets, are better than that, Orr seems to be urging.

Such is Orr's personal message to Thomson, eager and laconic by turns, but there is a further, deeper tale which he must have expected Thomson and, on publication, other knowing readers to have inferred from the very stanza form in which he chose to express himself. As Fiona Stafford has explained, eighteenth-century readers were 'quick to spot literary precedents'.[38] It is also the case that writers such as Orr were consciously engaging with the poetic tradition and expected their readers to be alert to the fact and to their signals.

Although often interpreted as a work recommending the sweetness of Catholicism (represented by the cherry) as against the bitterness of Protestantism (symbolized by the sloe), *The Cherrie and the Slae* achieved exceptional popularity among the Presbyterians of Ulster during the eighteenth century.[39] J. R. R. Adams discovered that there were Belfast editions of this poem in 1700 and again in 1771. He suggested that Protestant Ulster readers may have reinterpreted or reversed the symbolism so that the cherry was understood to represent Presbyterianism.[40] Presbyterians were habituated, of course, to the interpretation and application to their lives of scripture and of allegorical works such as *The Pilgrim's Progress*. Given the work's popularity, its allegorical nature, and Thomson's own close engagement with the Scottish poetic tradition, it is inconceivable that *The Cherrie and the Slae* had not been thoroughly discussed at the poetry 'seminars' in Thomson's home. Since Orr chose to remind Thomson of Montgomerie's poem by employing the stanza in an epistle that craves reconciliation and also refers to his relief at his liberation from 'the hag of strife' and his restoration to his home, we should ask how Orr may have understood the spiritual journey Montgomerie described, how it applied to himself, and what exactly he intended Thomson to infer.[41]

In its development, *The Cherrie and the Slae* can be seen to move through four broad phases: the episode involving the narrator and Cupid which culminates in his attempt to fly and to shoot; his subsequent despair and self-loathing; the debate between the narrator and various allegorical figures that occurs next; and the final decision to follow reason's guidance, which allows him to experience sweet contentment as a natural outcome. It is not difficult to see that these poetic episodes could represent phases in Orr's own life. First of all there was his 'young Turk' period of youthful enthusiasm for revolution, brought about if necessary by violent conflict. To Orr, reflecting on bitter experience, this period may well have appeared summated in the narrator's rueful lines describing his dangerous arrogance:

I sprang up with Cupido's wings,
Whose shots and shooting *geare* resignes, ['equipment'
To lend me for a day.
...
Wherewith I hurt my wanton heart
In hope to hurt another.
It hurt me, or burnt mee,

> While either end I handle;
> Come see now, in mee now,
> The butterflee and candle. (ll. 155-68)

To Thomson the hedge schoolmaster the following lines would have appeared a particularly pertinent admission of Orr's own rashness:

> Too late I went to schooles,
> Too late I heard the swallow preach,
> Too late Experience doth teach –
> The schoole-master of fooles. (ll. 183-8)

The shock of defeat, the fear of capture and execution, the unhappy experience of exile all must certainly have made the following passage particularly real for Orr:

> Sometime I sigh'd while I was sad,
> Sometime I musde, and most gone mad;
> I doubted what to doe.
> Sometime I rav'd halfe in a rage
> *As one into despare*, (ll. 242-6) ['like one in despair'

In such a frame of mind he landed in America. Lonely life there in enforced exile may have seemed well represented by Montgomerie's bitter sloe. The contentment of life in his beloved Broadisland must have appeared as tantalizing and unattainable as Montgomerie's sweet cherries.

At this point Montgomerie's debate with the allegorical figures may have seemed deeply relevant. Orr's only hope of achieving the restoration of personal peace and contentment lay in returning to Ireland, in facing again the horrors of a perilous sea voyage and a ravaged homeland where he had many enemies. This was clearly an enterprise fraught with danger. Montgomerie's narrator wavered before attempting to reach the cherry, on the grounds that he had nothing but Hope and Courage to spur him on. Orr may have come to feel that the United Irishmen's brief attempt at effecting revolution had been grounded on little else but those two qualities:

> That ever Courage keeps the keyes
> Of knowledge at his belt.
> Though he bid forward with the gunnes,
> Smal powder he provides; (ll. 411-14)

Even the imagery of certain lines must have recalled vividly for him the tense march to the summit of Donegore:

> Then Danger to declare began,
> How Hope and Courage tooke the man

> To leade him all their lanes;
> How they would have him up the hill ... (ll. 676-9)

In addition to fearing what welcome he might receive if he dared a second, homeward voyage, Orr may also have agonized over the impression that acceptance of the amnesty might give. Would it perhaps suggest that he had deserted his principles?

In the end Montgomerie's speaker, guided primarily by Reason, Skil ['discernment'] and Wit ['commonsense'], made a decision to attempt to reach the cherries he so deeply desired even though they hung from a tree that leaned over a perilous crag above a deep stream. To take some action seemed a reasonable alternative to wallowing in despair, so the attempt was made in a carefully planned journey, mapped out in advance by Wit. Once the decision to act was taken and the effort made, the narrator reached the base of the tree and, in a joyful climax, the cherries fell into his mouth, relieving his distress and leading him to an attitude of thankfulness. For Orr the return to friends, family and Ballycarry, though fraught with risks, offered him similar relief and contentment.

The above is offered as an elucidation of the subtext which may underlie Orr's 'Epistle to Thomson'. The chosen stanza form allows the addressee to infer Orr's development, which began with the youthful arrogance that demanded a 'quick fix' for Ireland's problems, then passed through despair, self-doubt and self-loathing, and concluded in balanced, calm rationality with the sweetness of home as the prize. Orr wished Thomson to understand that by the time he sent the 'Epistle' such a personal, spiritual journey had been made.

At surface text level Orr addresses the issues that concern him in the present and asks how it is possible to be happy in the Ireland to which he had returned, where none of the radical hopes for social justice have been achieved and where the Act of Union rather than independence is on the government agenda. As we have seen, the restoration of the friendship with Thomson appears to have been crucial to Orr's happiness and indeed it was soon achieved. Female companionship is also important to him but not because he is enticed by sexual allurements, or so Orr claims here. Instead he raises the interesting possibility of friendship between man and woman in the form of 'Sylvia', 'an engagin' frien'' (l. 51) who has attracted him with her fine conversation.

Also central to the purpose of the poem appears to be the wish to demonstrate that he has maintained his radical principles. For example, he rejects the idea that the wealthy have any right to sit in judgement on the behaviour of the poor:

> Lord! What this pridefu' heart has *thol'd* ['suffered']
> To hear a *cuif*, *whase* useless gold ['fellow', 'whose']
>   Ne'er made *ae* poor man happy, ['one']
> Expose some selfless son o' worth,
> Because *half-doil'd* wi' wine an' mirth, ['befuddled']
>   He *kent na* when to *stap* ay. (ll. 29-34) ['didn't know', 'stop']

He believes no good can come of accepting patronage from the rich and does not hesitate to warn Thomson against looking for any. Ultimately he concurs with the views of Burns and Thomson himself in recognizing that wealth alone can never bring contentment, therefore he is unequivocal in asserting the superior value of poetic 'Fancy an' taste' (l. 61) and of literary-intellectual life, 'rhyme or reason' (l. 28), over the humdrum world of money grubbing about 'dealin's an' *malins*' ['small farms'] (l. 25). In addition to these open and defiant messages, however, the poem is rich in allusions. Orr suggests that he and Thomson might meet at Roughfort, a townland with strongly radical associations. It was here that Jemmy Hope joined the Volunteers and was invited into the Society of United Irishmen. It was also the site of a reading society known as a meeting place for activists before 1798.[42] In addition, he asserts that he would 'rather drudge, an' do-blacks roast ... Than shine in ease' (ll. 35–7), on borrowed or donated cash. Since do-blacks are the particular strain of potato that he names as the food of the very poorest classes in 'To the Potatoe', he is indicating his intention to continue identifying with the poor, and speaking out on their behalf.

Equally, Orr is unequivocal in his identification with the nation of Ireland, represented by the landscape he eulogizes, and in his belief that his country's 'burns, an' bow'rs' (l. 81) belong to her people. His defiance of Ireland's foes: 'Deel tak' *her* faes an' *ours*' (l. 84) shows he is determined to remain his own man and not to acquiesce mentally in Ireland's absorption into the Union. Explicitly, he states his intention to be a poet of Ireland's landscape: to sing its praises with pride. Here we see him beginning to establish a bardic role, identified with the people, celebrating the land and defying the foes of both. But it should be noted that he is urging Thomson to share this role with him, as his use of the third person plural pronoun makes clear. It is '*We'se* sing the burns, an' bow'rs' ['we shall'] (l. 81). Orr would have recognized as a further literary precedent Ramsay's defiant nationalist work 'The Vision' which is also expressed in the *Cherrie and the Slae* stanza. In that work too the poet recognizes that he must resign himself to a political situation in Scotland which he finds very unsatisfactory, while maintaining an uncowed spirit.

The 'Epistle to Thomson' is without question one of Orr's most subtle, complex and important works. It contributes effectively to the dialogue on happiness established by Burns in his 'Epistle to Davie', but is also closely linked to earlier classic Scottish works. It presents a most apposite conclusion to Orr's poetic treatment of his period as an Irish radical activist. In this group of poems Orr enriches and complicates his portrayal of his experiences by drawing on his Scots heritage, and by significantly extending the range of what could be accommodated within traditional Scottish stanza forms. The series offers a powerful endorsement of the view that any perspective on Irish identity which denies or excludes Scottishness, or indeed Ulster Scottishness, is distorted and, ultimately, absurd.

8 THE ROBERT BURNS OF ULSTER?

The Ulster Scots poetic tradition was, as we have seen, characterized by a sturdy independence of the parent plant, even while its exponents were happy to acknowledge the relationship. The preceding chapters have argued that James Orr worked confidently and authoritatively within the Scottish poetic tradition, extending the range of its genres, and broadening it to accommodate Irish themes and tropes. The title 'The Burns of Ulster' with which his contemporaries were pleased to dignify him may be understood to have referred to his adept employment of Scots poetic forms and language and to his wide popularity.[1] Too often, however, it has been assumed to denote imitative or even derivative composition. Orr's plan, however much he admired the Scots bard's poetry, was certainly to draw a clear line between Burns and himself, even, or perhaps especially, in his vernacular works.

Orr's vernacular tribute to Burns, the 'Elegy, on the Death of Mr Robert Burns, the Ayrshire Poet', which he penned on hearing of Burns's demise in 1796, makes clear both his familiarity with the Scots bard's works and his admiration for them, as the following stanzas illustrate.[2] First he imbues the moment when he learns of the death with a sense of sublime significance, heralded by a thunderstorm, and by the appearance of a symbolic, sweet-singing lark, about to fall prey to a hawk:

> The *lift begud* a storm to brew, ['sky began'
> The cloudy sun was vext, an dark;
> A forket flash cam *sklentin'* thro' ['ripping/slanting'
> Before a hawk, that chas'd a lark;[3] (ll. 1–3)

The text is liberally sprinkled with repetition and exclamations that convey a sense of the momentous in a genuine, if rhetorically expressed, lament for what has been lost. Appropriately, the tribute incorporates a series of 'snapshots' that recall some of Burns's best loved pieces:

> Nae *mair* in kirk he *stan's* tip-tae, ['more', 'stands'
> To see the Rooks ordain the Raven;
> Nor hears the Cotter read an' pray,
> An' tell the weans the way to heav'n; (ll. 41–4)

If Orr's attitude is suitably respectful he is never awestruck; the preface to his 1804 volume, which contains most of his Scots poetry, suggests that he wishes to sing in a key of his own choosing. Of his own verses he writes: 'sorry would I be if they contained a single line that could foment party spirit, alarm the devout heart, or raise a blush on the angelic cheek of female virtue'.[4] If this suggests that a rather bland production is to follow, nothing could be further from the truth. A reading of 'Donegore Hill' quickly reveals Orr's sense of irony and his talent for the vivid, reductive verbal swipe that is characteristic of Scots speech.

A consideration of Orr's treatment of females and of relationships between the sexes speedily reveals his individuality of temperament and originality in tone. Resolutely he avoids the bawdy. Nor does he attempt anything approaching the intimacy of 'Lassie Lie Near Me' (1790).[5] An explanation for this may lie in Orr's relationship to his community. He writes as an 'insider' who may not have wished to risk acquiring a reputation as a sexual predator. Burns, while possessing and exploiting his insider's knowledge of local foibles, maintains a more detached position both in the official canon and elsewhere. That detached stance is performed in much of his love poetry, as becomes clear when we consider that very many of his amorous poems, however intense *in the moment*, deal with partings, casual encounters, travellers' one-night stands. That Burns's reputation affected his power to make a living is confirmed in a typically 'gossipy' passage included by Luke Mullan in his account of a meeting with Burns near Dumfries:

> he is not much respected in Dumfries on account of his infidelities to his wife – But as an officer of the Excise he is said to be very humane to poor people in short he is allowed to be a fine social companion and an honest man but too much inamour'd of the joys of *Venus* ... I believe he writes little now – he offers some to the Dumfries papers that is not accepted.[6]

In its obituary following the poet's death in 1796 the *Belfast News-letter* made a disapproving reference to Burns's 'frailties'.[7] If Orr was indeed known in his lifetime as 'the Burns of Ulster' he may have wished to reassure potential readers regarding the chaste and respectable nature of his verse creations.

Orr's individual approach may be inferred from any careful reading of his vernacular works. Take, for example, his presentation of folkloric material related to the supernatural. Burns in 'Address to the Deil' (1785–6), 'Tam o' Shanter' (1790) and 'Hallowe'en' (1785) exploits traditional beliefs to amuse and terrify his audience by turns, with an eye also to engaging the antiquarian intellectuals on whom he was to turn an ironic gaze in 'On the Late Captain Grose's Peregrinations' (1789).[8] By contrast, when Orr presents 'The Spae-Wife', about an old woman supposedly gifted with second sight, it is in order to pour a cold dose of Enlightenment rationalism on beliefs and practices he clearly regards as nonsensical. Here the speaker, to whom Orr gives the last word, is 'a *spunkie*' ['vigorous young man'] (l. 17), who first asserts that the Wife acquires her information about others through spying and gossip, then accuses her of damaging interference:

> 'Ye promise promotion, an' *sin', frae the mead* ['send from the meadow'
> 'The shepherd to sea, whare some shark soon he'll feed;
> 'The young thing, sae *bonie*, weds some *canker't clownie*, ['pretty', 'bad tempered boor'
> 'Because ye've presag'd that nae ither's decreed ... (ll. 25–8)

Orr includes nothing glamorous or intriguing here; he makes no attempt to encourage the reader's suspension of disbelief or to play, even for entertainment's sake, on the human love of the spine chiller that Burns exploits so effectively in his tale of Tam o' Shanter's brush with the devil and the young witch 'Cutty-sark' (l. 189) in Alloway Kirkyard. Doubtless Orr believed he was legitimately exposing and attacking an abuse that blighted the lives of individuals within his community. He shows little propensity or desire to emulate the teasing, ironic casing in which Burns nests his inspired, eerie pieces. He may even have disapproved of these works, for they are entirely absent from the series of poems he commends in his 'Elegy' in Burns's honour.

Orr's 'Ballycarry Fair' (1804), written to be sung to the tune 'Green Grow the Rashes', which Burns himself had employed,[9] is a rollicking, anarchic, carnivalesque celebration of a community holiday that utilizes *Christis Kirk*-style motifs of sport, brawling and drunkenness:

> Hartsome is the *claughin*, O, ['village'
> Hartsome is the claughin, O,
> Whare ev'ry hour I hae to spare
> Is past in mirth and laughin', O. (chorus).[10] (ll. 9–12)

The work as a whole certainly harmonizes with the spirit of much of Burns's work and must have pleased the village audience of whom Orr was beloved, but in a letter to Thomson of 4 January 1806 he expressed the heartfelt wish that 'Ballycarry Fair' had 'never been written'.[11] One can only speculate as to his reasons. Perhaps he felt it was overly frivolous, inconsistent with the gravitas he desired in his public persona. He may have feared appearing to condone the behaviours he chronicled. Or he may have wished to resist any accusation that he was 'doing' Burns.

'Address to Beer', a standard habbie poem printed in the *Belfast Commercial Chronicle* on 1 April 1809, seems less an attempted emulation of Burns and more of a direct and personalized counter-salvo. In 'Scotch Drink' (1785–6) Burns had claimed that relaxing together over a few beers enabled sparring neighbours to patch up their differences.[12] Orr, by way of contrast, cites 'Captain Whisky' as the *cause* of foolish disputes and of crime:

>   He *gied* the affront when frien's fell out,   ['gave'
>   Tho' *kin'* an' civil;   ['kind'
> ...
>   He forced the Transport to depart;
>   An' dragg'd the Convict to the Cart: (ll. 15–18)

Beer, however, he portrays as a friend of rationality and moderation:

>   Renown'd Reformer! Thou hast freed
>   Frae suff'rins tragic,
>   Unnumber'd fools, wha turn'd their head
>   Wi' Whiskey's magic. (ll. 9–12)

Scotch drink had been presented by Burns as the Scottish patriot's beverage of choice and, therefore, as a potent symbol of Scotland. Orr's retort proposes beer as Ireland's corresponding symbol but, crucially, he stresses it is 'poor Airlan's frothless frien', / In evil days' (ll. 3–4). 'Frothless' linked with 'frien' as it is here carries with it the suggestion of a person not given to making wordy promises and empty profusions. But Orr goes further still. While Burns believes that whisky 'Clears the head o' doited lear (l. 31) and causes his verses to come rattling out 'At ither's arses!' (l. 108), the Ulster poet asserts that 'the parts o' bright repute / He soon made drivel' (ll. 17–18). The phrase recalls, indeed partly echoes, a remark Orr makes in his 'Elegy on the Death of Mr Robert Burns' when he qualifies his eulogy by alluding, albeit sympathetically, to the Ayrshire poet's faults as 'the failin's o' a man o' parts' (l. 71).

Given the opposition of Ireland and Scotland deliberately postulated within his text, it is tempting to interpret the poem as arising from Orr's (and United Irish) disillusionment with Burns's supposed radicalism, and indeed with Scots radicalism. In the 1790s Ulster radicals in particular had cherished hopes for a rising of democrats throughout the three kingdoms, a rising that would have included the Scots.[13] These hopes Burns's radical verse had appeared to encourage, but they were dashed by his composition of the apparently loyalist 'The Dumfries Volunteers' (1795), which was read by many in Ulster as evidence that his former profusions had indeed been empty.[14] Liam McIlvanney has detailed the falling out that followed in his *Burns the Radical*, arguing that the Ulstermen missed a code within the text of 'The Dumfries Volunteers' that links it to the works of Joseph Addison and proves that it is 'completely consistent with the Real Whig ethos of British radicalism'.[15] John Gray, formerly of Belfast's Linen Hall Library, remains unconvinced, however, rejecting what he describes as McIlvanney's attempt '*in extremis*' to defend 'an immaculate radical' Burns two hundred years later.[16] But what did Orr believe? It seems strange that Orr should publish a poem expressing his resentment in 1809, many years after Burns's death and long after the Act of Union, but items among his still uncollected works reveal that until his death he continued to mourn bitterly what he referred to as 'my lov'd lost country' (l. 82).[17] That he felt the cold wind of isolation and neglect blowing on Ulster's little 'Scotch' community is crystal clear from the full text of 'The Irish Cottier's Death and Burial' (1817).[18] That poem he prefaces with a Burns quotation, taken from 'The Brigs of Ayr' (1786):

> ... nurst in the Peasant's lowly shed,
> To hardy Independence bravely bred,
> By early Poverty to hardship steel'd,
> And train'd to arms in stern Misfortune's field ... [19] (ll. 7–10)

Tellingly he ends the reference just short of the lines in which the poet asks 'Shall he be guilty of their hireling crimes, / The servile, mercenary Swiss of rhymes?' (ll. 11–12), but any Burns enthusiast will be conscious of the omitted passage. So what appears as Orr's tribute to the source of his inspiration may in fact be a further jibe – an aspersion cast on Burns's firmness of principle. Clearly, if Burns could send coded signals, he had his match in Orr.

High on the list of poems which Orr includes in his roll of honour is that most admired and often reviled work, 'The Cotter's Saturday Night' (1785–6).[20] The overt piety and endorsement of homely family values within this text jarred with the iconoclasticism of the later twentieth century and provoked a degree of 'cultural cringe' among Scots, but more recently scholars have drawn attention to the poem's skilful exploitation and development of genre conventions and, surprisingly, to its radicalism. Gerard Carruthers has argued that 'In both moral tone and form ... Burns has embarked on a thoroughly mainstream mode of Augustan didacticism', which, he explains, had been 'channelled through the eighteenth century by the English poets Matthew Prior and William Shenstone and by the 'Anglo-Scots' James Thomson and James Beattie'.[21] Furthermore, Nigel Leask has demonstrated that 'Burns unsettles the prescribed politics of late eighteenth century pastoral by shifting from a religious to a political sublime'. Burns, here, is truly radical in locating virtue and the spiritual grandeur of the nation with the peasantry rather than the nobility.[22]

Burns was, of course, building on territory that had been marked out by Robert Fergusson in 'The Farmer's Ingle' (1773). Both poets exploit the virtues of Scottish rural home life and employ the Spenserian stanza with great sophistication, thus adopting into a vernacular discourse this high cultural form, which James Beattie (1735–1803) had deemed suitable for his portrayal of the poetic life in *The Minstrel* (1771). A consideration of 'The Farmer's Ingle', to which Burns is certainly indebted, reveals that Fergusson has created a rich, atmospheric piece, at once elegiac and celebratory, which invests the rural peasantry with the status of archetypes.[23]

Fergusson records the return home of the 'gudeman' (l. 14) at evening, and his satisfaction that his 'housie looks sae *cosh* and clean' ['snug'] (l. 17), due to the industry of the 'gudewife' (l. 19) who is, in fact, the central figure in the poem, providing warmth, cleanliness, plenteous if simple provender, entertainment (storytelling and lore) and homespun clothing. The title foregrounds the welcoming fireside, and throughout the work the fire is frequently a reference point. At the gudeman's entrance it is 'bleezing' (l. 21); its fading signals the end of day and time to sleep. The gudeman operates as a director and guide to the young male labourers and the poem's title appears to accord him the presiding role in the home, but the living space flourishes under the direction of the gudewife, and it is here that the farmer himself is refreshed and renewed. The passage in which his instruction of the lads is reported by the narrator is capped by a parallel piece in which she directly instructs the young women:

> *Niest* the gudewife her hireling damsels bids ['next']
> *Glowr* thro' the byre, and see the *hawkies* bound, ['look thoroughly', 'cows']
> Take *tent* case Crummy tak her *wonted tids*, ['care', 'usual opportunity']
> And ca' the *leglin*'s treasure on the ground, ['milking pail']
> *Whilk* spills a *kebbuck* nice, or yellow pound. (ll. 95–9) ['which', 'cheese']

The omniscient, approving narrator cites particular, often sensuous details that enable the reader to appreciate the harmony, peace and generosity of the home:

> Wi' butter'd bannocks now the girdle reeks,
> I' the far nook the *bowie* briskly reams; ['big barrel']
> The readied *kail* stand by the chimley cheeks, ['greens',
> And had the *riggin het* wi' welcome steams, ['rafters hot']
> Whilk than the daintiest kitchen nicer seems. (ll. 23–7)

The use of the present tense lends immediacy but also the quality of an ongoing, nightly, dignified ritual to events. This is intensified by references to the natural rhythms of the seasons and to the passing of day and night with their set tasks and behaviours.

The central characters are left with features, mannerisms and other characteristics indeterminate. The children remain 'the bairnies' (l. 55) and 'the childer' (l. 57) but do not take on individuality. The telling of superstitious tales is defended as natural to both youth and old age, while religion is hardly allowed to intrude, except in the reference to 'the cutty-stool' and the clergyman's scolding endured by a girl who produced an illegitimate child. Within the framework of seasonal rhythms that Fergusson has evoked such practices and strictures seem unnatural intrusions.

The picture is not overly idealized. The family are clearly small farm tenants, not wealthy or even moderately well-off. They can be prey to the disasters caused by unpredictable weather. Although the figures retain their archetypal quality, there is a strong grain of realism which adds to their dignity and credibility, as Fergusson affirms the worth of honest toil and the virtues of the bucolic Scotsman and Scotswoman. References to food further endorse his patriotic-didactic purpose. Early in the text, when describing the homely fare available in the farmer's home the narrator has advised 'gentler gabs' (l. 28) that if they worked hard and followed such a diet: 'They'd *rax* fell strong upo' the simplest fare' ['grow'] (l. 30). But he goes further, attributing Scotland's historic victories against Danes and Romans to her traditional, home-grown produce.

The concluding stanza is a grateful prayer invoking a blessing on the husbandman and on the 'tribe' and nation whose representative he is. It weaves together the text's patriotic, moral, rhythmic, pastoral and realistic strands, bringing all to a satisfying, dignified conclusion:

> May Scotia's simmers ay look gay and green,
> Her yellow *har'sts* frae *scowry* blasts decreed; ['autumns/harvests', 'destroying'
> May a' her tenants sit fu' snug and *bien*, ['well'
> Frae the hard grip of *ails* and *poortith* freed, ['ailments', 'poverty'
> And a lang lasting train o' peaceful hours succeed. (ll. 113–17).

Fergusson's background was Episcopalian but, as we have seen, religion is hardly permitted to intrude into his timeless vision. In 'The Cotter's Saturday Night', Burns significantly develops Fergusson's scenario by rooting the family's virtues in their Presbyterianism, and giving central place to the Saturday night act of worship. In all matters, practical, moral and, crucially, spiritual, the Cotter himself is presented as a humane but authoritative director.[24] As Gerard Carruthers explains, 'Burns in his poem provides a measure of rehabilitation for the Presbyterian patriarch'.[25]

In Burns's poem the use of the vernacular is much less dense than in Fergusson's, which has the advantage of making it accessible to a wider audience, but he retains sufficient Scots to maintain a strong sense of authenticity. In the formal opening dedication and the passages dealing with worship Burns observes conventions of decorum by employing the standard register. Moreover, Burns writes with a patriotic intention: to present the people of rural Scotland with grace and dignity. Strong echoes of Fergusson can be detected in the second stanza with its references to the approach of winter, the conclusion of daily labour and the inevitable weariness. As the poem progresses there is a further similarity of emphasis on family unity, affection and on the virtues of simple fare, but in many respects Burns's depiction of rural life is greatly at variance with that of his predecessor. Fergusson was evoking a whole household but here the Cotter and his family are a much more self-contained unit.

The Cotter was a tenant labourer, socially lower on the scale than Fergusson's tenant farmer so there are no lads or hireling girls present, indeed the Cotter's eldest daughter is herself hired out as a servant on a neighbouring farm. The family's relative poverty may explain the greater frugality that characterizes the family's diet. Within this home the Cotter himself is a more authoritative figure than is the gudeman. His guidance is moral and spiritual/scriptural rather than simply practical, with his wife relegated to a supporting role. She mends clothes, brings forth the supper of '*healsome* Porritch' ['wholesome'] (l. 92); 'soupe' (l. 93) and '*weel-hain'd kebbuck*' [thriftily preserved cheese] (l. 96), but while Fergusson's gudewife entertains with her stories the Cotter's wife has little to contribute directly to the discourse. She observes her daughter Jenny's young man silently 'wi' a woman's wiles' (l. 70) but it is her husband who 'cracks' (l. 67) with him. Though he later describes her as 'garrulous', Burns limits her recorded speech to a banal remark about the cheese: "twas a *towmond* auld, sin' Lint was i' the *bell*' ['two months', 'bloom'] (ll. 98–9).

While the inspiration of Fergusson's model is evident, Burns has greatly strengthened the narrative elements and added interest through the development of his characters. The Cotter and his wife are defined individually as father and mother of a family. The arrival of their daughter Jenny with a new young man, and the interest and anxieties this raises, is a dramatic episode with potential for further development. Unfortunately, though, it leads only to the frequently lamented passage in which Burns indulges in a sentimental denunciation of 'A wretch! a villain!' (l. 83) who might 'Betray sweet *Jenny*'s unsuspecting youth' (l. 85). The notorious passage illustrates that Burns too maintains a strong authorial presence, signalling what the reader should notice, approve and disapprove. For much of the poem, however, it is the Cotter who holds centre stage, serving to foreground the scripture-based faith of the family.

The Cotter's evening has a clear programme. Food and gossip are mere sideshows, the prelude to the main event which is the worship of God in metrical Psalms, the exposition of the Scriptures, and prayer. Superstitious stories and self-indulgent entertainment are entirely absent from this Saturday night which prepares the family for the Kirk-centred observations of the Sabbath. While Burns does not overtly condemn such stories, his emphasis on the Scriptures suggests he wishes to demonstrate that in the homes of his virtuous Scots peasantry, faith and Biblical exposition are privileged over superstition. The atmosphere in the home is patriarchal in every sense, in that the stories explored are those of the Biblical patriarchs with whom the father, the centre of the home, is identified, while towards the conclusion he is designated 'The Saint, the Father and the Husband' (l. 137), whose earthly and spiritual roles are combined.

Burns is explicit in drawing a distinction between the showy 'Pageant' (l. 149) of organized, high, church-based religion and the real faith expressed in 'the language of the *Soul*' (l. 152). In the last glimpse Burns affords us of the Cotter and his wife they are once again disclosed in prayer, this time privately, after the children have retired to rest. Their earnest requests for wisdom, guidance and grace for their brood surely speak of life's uncertainties, in which God's protection may be the only defence and the only source of future hope. Nigel Leask has drawn attention to the research which 'identifies a process of lowland clearance every bit as drastic as the better known highland clearances', and argues that Burns's poetry 'is in some respects an elegy for the old rural way of life'.[26] In such circumstances, with the winds of change blowing chilly, Burns represents the loving, anxious concern of contemporary parents here, and his sentiments must strike a chord with parents in every generation who watch their children beginning to make their own way in the world.

While Fergusson cited Scottish victories over the Romans and Danes, Burns's reference is to Wallace, the victor of Bannockburn. The poem's patriotic message, however, is rooted in its presentation of thrifty, virtuous peasants who are inspired and comforted by Biblical teaching which they themselves can understand and apply without the mediation and instruction of a teacher or priest from the more formally educated classes. Its conservatism is underlined by the father's admonition to his children to obey: 'Their Master's and their Mistress's command' (l. 46), but even this has its roots in New Testament motifs of obedience and resignation, to which St Paul, for example, advised slaves to adhere.[27]

Burns's poem has been popularly beloved for the very didacticism and affirmation of conservative patriotic and family values for which it has often been critically derided.[28] It inspired much emulation, including 'The Cotter's Sabbath Day' by Samuel Walker (1803–85), which appeared in the *Belfast Penny Journal* in 1845. Walker, too, employed the difficult Spenserian stanza, but in workmanlike, rather than inspired fashion. The debt to Burns and respect for his genius are openly acknowledged, as is the poet's clear identification with the Scottish lowland culture in which Ulster Sabbath observance is rooted:

> O, for a spark of that poetic fire
>   That burned sae bright in Scotia's isle of yore,
> And caused the bard to tune his matchless lyre,
>   And sing that night the 'hallow'd day' before ...[29] (ll. 1–4)

On the face of it the frame of reference has shrunk: the nationalistic, patriotic element is not overtly expressed. The comfort of rural food is decidedly not available, for as the narrator primly reminds the reader: 'nae great dainties on the Sabbath day / Do Christian folk prepare, or yet desire' (l. 120). In addition, while this Cotter plays a crucial role in the instruction of his children, the family devotions are Kirk-centred. It is to the Kirk that Walker ascribes the chief role in communicating Biblical teaching to the peasantry. Here the minister's preaching comforts and excoriates by turns. He expounds a passage of the sacred Word and from it:

> ... Consolation does afford
>   To sin-sick souls, for such is found therein,

And a' the threats wherewith that book is stored,
   He thunders forth 'gainst them *wha* hellward *rin*, ['who', 'run'
And warns them o' their fate, if they persist in sin. (ll. 104–8)

In contrast to Burns's Cotter who exhibits intellectual mastery of the Scriptures, Walker's Cotter comprehends 'nearly a' that's said' (l. 114), and exercises a schoolmasterly, rather than a priestly role within his family, questioning them about the sermon and testing their proficiency in memorizing the answers to the 'question beuk' (l. 131), the Presbyterian Shorter Catechism.[30] In essence, Walker's poem illustrates the popularity of 'The Cotter's Saturday Night' and its power to spawn 'spin-off' works for political and didactic purposes some fifty years after Burns's death.

Orr contributed two poems to the 'Cotter tradition'. The first of these, 'The Penitent', included in his volume of 1804, will be discussed below. It is the second, 'The Irish Cottier's Death and Burial', the only vernacular work included in his posthumous volume, which has sometimes occasioned rather facile comparisons to be made between his composition and Burns's. In fact in setting, tone, mood and message it could hardly be more different. 'The Irish Cottier's Death and Burial' was certainly drawn with Broadisland as Orr's model and provides an intimate portrait of a northern Dissenter community.[31] The dying Irish Cottier is here both an individual and a symbolic figure. Orr depicts not simply an individual on his deathbed, but a whole community at the graveside, literally staring death in the face. Imaginatively he is postulating the whole Scotch community on the edge of the abyss.

The title is significant, in that it foregrounds the Irishness of the individual and of the society he is about to portray. By employing vernacular Scots he is, thus, affirming it as one of the languages of Ireland. The opening address, expressed in English according to the conventions established by Fergusson and Burns, is offered not to a person, but to 'Erin! my country! preciously adorn'd / with every beauty, and with every worth' (ll. 1–2), evincing patriotic pride and claiming ownership. The term 'Cottier' in itself varies from Burns's 'Cotter', and serves as a reminder of Arthur Young's description of the Irish 'Cottier System' in his *Tour of Ireland*.[32] Orr is not, therefore, primarily identifying with the region and customs depicted by Burns; he has relocated the discourse.

This poem has been admired by Lunney, Akenson and Crawford, and Hewitt, all of whom approved its secure, consistent employment of Scots and its revelation of the customs of a Presbyterian wake, though the sheer power and excellence of the poetry has never been given the attention it deserves. The opening address has attracted virtually no comment, but it is remarkable for the insight it affords into Orr's perception of the marginalized position of northern Scotch communities in post-Union Ireland:

> Erin! my country! preciously adorned
>   With every beauty, and with every worth,
> Thy grievances through time shall not be scorn'd,
>   For powerful friends to plead thy cause step forth:
>   But more unblest, oppression, want, and dearth,
> Did during life, distressfully attend
>   The poor neglected native of thy North,
> Whose fall I sing. He found no powerful friend,
> 'Till Death was sent by Heaven to bid his soul ascend. (ll. 1–9)

That raises several questions. First of all, whom may Orr have in mind when he cites Ireland's 'powerful friends' and what are the grievances they are addressing? Following the Union, there had been some hope of achieving Catholic Emancipation, a measure to which Orr gave unqualified support. While this, to the disappointment of many, was not granted immediately, Henry Grattan (1746–1820) argued passionately for Emancipation in the British House of Commons and thus must surely be understood as one of Ireland's 'powerful friends',[33] who, Orr hoped, would remove her people's grievances.[34] Orr clearly looks forward with approval to this event, but he is still distressed by the perceived marginalization of the 'native' of the north. Typically, he speaks of Ireland as a whole and of the north as a region within it, avoiding religious denominators and the appearance of sectarianism.

We should ask what reasons may Orr, whose stress in all the poetry so far examined has been on national unity, have had for imagining the northern natives 'more unblest' than natives of any other parts of rural Ireland, all of whom certainly suffered 'oppression, want and dearth'? In all likelihood, as this discussion will demonstrate, he believed them less blest, because they did not enjoy the same degree of acceptance or belonging in their own country as did the cottiers in other parts of the island. Orr would have been painfully, regretfully, aware that some important and increasingly influential figures within the force of cultural nationalism, which his work shows he had espoused, demonstrated little affection or fellow feeling for people whose culture was rooted in Scots traditions and language.

As we have seen, he greatly admired Sydney Owenson whose national tale *The Wild Irish Girl* ends in a symbolic marriage between Ascendancy and native Irish traditions. The attitude displayed in this text towards the Scotch communities of the north is contemptuous and exclusive.[35] Orr, writing as 'Censor' for the *Belfast Commercial Chronicle*, had stated his abhorrence of controversy, and he certainly did not indulge in it to denounce the offensive passages.[36] We have seen how he responded positively, stressing his own dissociation from 'bigot's blindness'. He must have been aware, however, that the cultural view of Ireland, as essentially a Gaelic or Milesian kingdom, which Owenson perpetuated, was taking hold as Owenson herself and the Romantic nationalist poet Thomas Moore (1779–1852) both became increasingly celebrated throughout the united kingdoms. Such exclusivity, accompanied as it was in Owenson's case by a jibe at Ulster's Dissenters, was raising a question mark over the perceived Irishness of Orr's own community.

Orr had openly celebrated and embraced Irish identity in his patriotic series of poems for the *Belfast Commercial Chronicle* during the years 1805–6. He and Moore both took up Gaelic themes and both, for example, composed songs in praise of Brian Borhu.[37] He even absorbed into his own work Irish grievances over horrific events such as the Massacre of Mullaghmast. But among the cultural nationalists whose work was attaining popularity at national level during the 1800s there was little evidence of any reciprocal embrace of plurality, as Owenson's *Patriotic Sketches of Ireland, Written in Connaught*, much of which Orr admired, makes clear.

On reading the *Sketches*, while welcoming Owenson's enthusiasm for the sublime Connaught scenery and endorsing her accounts of the appalling conditions suffered by the peasantry in that province, Orr must have noted certain other details in the text that certainly contributed to his sense of the 'neglect', or marginalization, of the *northern* Irish peasantry. It is not that she openly others them here as she had done in *The Wild Irish Girl*, but in generalizing passages about the traditions of the Irish labouring classes she simply writes difference out of the narrative. This is nowhere more evident than when she describes the Sabbath activities of 'the Irish peasant' which consist of attendance at Mass followed by participation in a hurling match or in dancing. Owenson was describing Connaught, certainly, but she uses the term Irish without qualification, has leisure to contrast the Irish peasant's Sunday activity with that of his English counterpart, who is portrayed reading a religious tract, and for good measure notes that 'The rigid principles of Calvinistical faith may condemn his festal mode of passing that day'.[38] Northern Irish cottiers in communities such as Ballycarry either conscientiously adhered to, or had to submit to, such 'rigid principles', but Owenson clearly regards these legalistic codes as non-Irish, while she perceives the Sabbath customs of Connaught as genuinely Irish. The careful reader notes the loss of Tone's vision of an Ireland that included Catholic, Protestant and Dissenter.

Such a diminution, in the post-Union era, of the tripartite United Irish vision clearly troubled an observer as acute, sensitive and inclined to the prophetic as Orr. 'The Irish Cottier's Death and Burial' (1817) is a clear response to what he sensed were forces that would condemn his community to exclusion.[39] In this work, perhaps his greatest, he lovingly, but in pessimistic spirit, leaves a vivid portrait of his own people, dignifying their traditions and insisting that they too are of Ireland. In the circumstances, his choice of the Braid Scotch tongue and the stanza form associated with Burns was both poignant and pointed.

Burns had demonstrated that pastoral poetry which evokes a conventionally idealized setting may prove a dynamic vehicle for the expression of regional and national identity. 'The Irish Cottier's Death and Burial' has a similar purpose, but is also quite deliberately a poem of social protest. Far from simply echoing

Burns's themes and tropes, Orr opposes them, articulating his northern community's experience of poverty, injustice and marginalization, even while he hopes that the grievances of Ireland as a whole may be addressed. Orr continues to extend the dimensions of the Cotter tradition here by further broadening the range of characters and including the whole community. While Burns had chosen to focus on a family's joyful, pious Saturday night ritual, Orr depicts humanity's most sombre rite of passage. He constructs four distinct episodes, presenting the Cottier's deathbed sufferings, his last words to his family, his wake and, finally, his burial in a rain and wind swept churchyard. This is no pastoral idyll, but a tragedy for which the Spenserian stanza's dignified pace and iambic rhythms are entirely appropriate.

If Burns's Cotter assumed the central position in home life, Orr too positions his Cottier centrally: he lies dying, surrounded by his family and helpless in the grip of delirium brought on by pleurisy, a disease aggravated by damp conditions. Infirmity and disempowerment are thus shown to be daily realities for people of his class. That the Irish Cottier is as conscientious a guide to his family as his Scottish counterpart is evident when he summons sufficient strength to deliver his last advice. While based on Scriptural precepts and offering the hope of heaven, the instructions reflect Orr's own radical outlook:

> Be honest an' obligin'; if ye thrive
>   Be meek; an' firm *whan* crosses come your road; ['when'
> Should rude men *wrang* ye, to forgie them strive; ['wrong'
> ...
>   Scorn nae poor man wha bears oppression's load,
> Nor meanly cringe for favours frae the proud; (ll. 55–60)

The Irish Cottier's desperate situation renders the devotion of his offspring particularly poignant:

> Ane to his lips the coolin' cordial *ha'ds*, ['holds'
> An' ane behin' supports his achin' head;
> Some *bin'* the arm that lately has been bled, ['bandage'
> An' some burn bricks his feet mair warm to mak;
>   If e'er he doze, how noiselessly they tread! (ll. 20–5)

The reader is drawn into the family's experience through Orr's unobtrusive and skilful employment of a range of effects as he relates the tale. These include mildly humorous, acutely observed cameos, such as the '*glaiket* wean' ['foolish'] (l. 31) who has to be entertained with a story. The mother's dilemma is expressed in a brief paradox which pays tribute to the husband–wife relationship as a self-sacrificial partnership. She '... ha'f pleas'd could see / Her partner eas'd by death, though for his life she'd die' (ll. 35–6). The Scottish Cotter's wife, by contrast, is relegated to stereotype, the butt of the narrator's patronizing masculine references to the 'frugal *Wifie*' (l. 98) with her 'woman's wiles' (l. 70).

While Burns portrays a family, Orr's project is more substantial: the performance of a whole community and its response to an event at once tragic and commonplace. He stresses that the community's identity is intimately bound up with its Scotch language and affectionately notes the failure of the rural folk's attempt to observe conventions of decorum by speaking, in the standard register when their minister arrives: 'To *quat* braid Scotch' ['leave off'] proves to be 'a task that foils their art' (l. 43). Here, and in the stanzas devoted to the wake, Orr permits some relief to the predominantly solemn mood by offering an insight into folk customs, thereby achieving an effect of exceptional richness. First, he enumerates the superstitions observed following the death, such as covering the mirror with a cloth, while noting that these would have earned the learned, rational Cottier's disapproval.[40] Then his eye roves over the attendant mourners, and with brief, acute observations he portrays the people as unpretentious, social and vibrant. The lines capture the individual personalities present, yet depict behaviours universally recognizable:

> Some argue Scripture – some play tricks – some greet;
> ...
> Or han' tradition down, an' ither fright,
>   Wi' dreadfu' tales o' witches, elves, an' *ghaists*. ['ghosts'
> The *soger* lad, wha on his pension rests, ['soldier'
> Tells how he fought, an' proudly bares his scaur;
>   While unfleg'd gulls, just looking *owre* their nests, ['over'
> Brag how they lately did their rivals *daur*, ['challenge'
> ...
> An' while some lass, though on their *cracks* intent, ['social chat'
>   Turns to the light and *sleely* seems to read ... (ll. 121–37) ['cunningly'

Later, the solemn context of bereavement underscores the piety expressed in the simple service led by 'an auld man' (l. 100), which consists of psalm singing and a Scripture reading 'That maks them sure the dead shall rise again' (l. 103). The construction chosen suggests the narrator is distancing himself from their certainty while communicating his affection for their trusting faith. As in 'The Cotter's Saturday Night' the sharing of a meal has a central place with hospitality a priority, but the family's greater poverty is evident in the reluctance of most present to partake of more than a few morsels of the 'Hard bread, an' cheese' (l. 111) and 'gills a piece o' rum' (l. 113).

The narrator draws attention to the crowds who attend: 'But see what crowds to wauk the Cottier come!' (l. 91). He observes also the natural courtesy with which they and the grieving family behave. Notable is the Ulster Presbyterian's eschewing of big, noisy displays of emotion: the wife is 'rack'd yet resign'd' (l. 69) and a son hands round the wake supper 'wi' becomin grace' (l. 109). Throughout the long night the cottage is constantly full of neighbours who have come to offer support. A passage in Owenson's *The Wild Irish Girl* includes the hero Horatio's observation of a Catholic peasant burial and Father John's description of a wake:

> The immediate relatives of the deceased sit near the body, devoted to the luxury of woe, which revives into the most piercing lamentations at the entrance of every stranger, while the friends, acquaintances, and guests give themselves up to a variety of amusements ... though in the midst of all their games should anyone pronounce an *Ave Maria* the merry group are in a moment on their knees.[41]

The details are striking in both their similarity to and difference from Orr's account of a Presbyterian wake. The support of friends and neighbours is common to both, as is the liveliness of community entertainment, but the incorporation of ritualized wailing and the communal change of posture and repetition of prayers learned by rote are replaced in the Presbyterian experience by Scripture readings and psalm singing. It is possible that Orr has been inspired by reading this passage in Owenson to portray a Presbyterian wake and burial, thus asserting the place of his community's rituals in Irish experience. Orr's drawing attention to the crowds who attend seems to echo Horatio's expressed 'surprise at the multitude which attended the funeral of a peasant'.[42]

In Orr's recreation of the abundant community, he brings together the disregarded and the undervalued in society, determined to record and honour their rites and individual personalities. Deliberately, he abandons narrative detachment and underlines his identification with the people by positioning his narrator in the cottage among the mourners where he makes a direct protest against the inequalities and callous attitudes which exacerbate already harsh conditions for bereaved families of this class:[43]

> Come hither, sons of Plenty! An' relieve
>   The bonny bairns, for labour yet *owre wee*, ['too small/young'
> ...
>   Had I your *walth*, I hame wad tak' wi' me ['wealth'
> The lamb that's lookin' in my tear-wat face;
>   An' that dejected dame should sit rent free
> In some snug cot ... (ll. 73–80)

By contrast, Burns's melodramatic railing against a hypothetical despoiler of 'sweet Jenny's unsuspecting youth' (l. 85) seems a calculated ploy to 'milk' the situation for maximum sentiment.

Abruptly, the mood grows utterly bleak as the burial follows upon the wake. In discussing the unrealistic cosiness of Burns's Cotter's home Peter Zenzinger remarks that 'the bad weather ... remains outside the cottage'.[44] Orr provides no such haven. The full potency of his refutation of idealized pastoral is unleashed as he exposes his characters, and the reader, to the desolate landscape and appalling weather:

> Warn'd to the Cottier's burial, rich an' poor
> Cam' at the hour, tho' win' an' rain beat *sair*; ['fiercely']
> An' *monie* met it at the distant moor, (ll. 145–7) ['monie']

Once more the observation of community customs is detailed, including the bier, '*shouther'd*' ['shouldered'] (l. 149) through the churchyard, and the two youths kneeling at the grave, personally laying in it 'their blest father' (l. 151).

Towards the end of 'The Cotter's Saturday Night' Burns includes a vision of the family united in heaven, 'While circling Time moves round in an eternal sphere' (l. 144). Orr's final images are earth-bound. It is the funeral crowd that circles in the disorientation of grief. They are unwilling to quit the 'church-yard drear' (l. 149) as they contemplate the disturbed earth that holds the 'dear dust' (l. 161) of previously-buried loved ones, and the headstones that 'only *tald* the inmates' years an' names' ['told'] (l. 159). The inadequacy of thus memorializing a human life is powerfully implicit.

Orr displays his grasp of the value of narrative restraint at this point. As community grief rises to a climax in a communal '*saut*, saut flood' ['salt'] (l. 160) shed for all the dead kinsfolk, he includes no didactic commentary but confronts the reader and his characters with the debris of the burial ground: 'empty sculls, an' jointless banes, / That, cast at random, lay like cloven wood' (ll. 156–7). No comforting resolution is, or can be, offered. Orr admired Thomas Gray's poetry, and within this poem echoes of the 'Elegy Written in a Country Churchyard' may be detected, but in contrast to the earlier poet, whose work communicates a sad tranquillity, Orr permits the desolate atmosphere and the imagery of disintegration to dominate and to appall. What he envisions here is the death of the whole community, symbolized by the Cottier himself. While these living northern Dissenters grieve for him and for their ancestors they are, implicitly, grieving for their own coming disintegration as individuals and as a people. Although often an outspoken didactic writer, Orr has the sophistication to allow the reader to draw the inference here.

In their conclusions both Orr and Burns discard the intimacy of the rural settings and focus attention on the nations represented by their protagonists. Once again the contrast is striking. Burns's Scotia is portrayed triumphant and secure. For her defence a 'wall of fire' is formed by her '*virtuous Populace*' around their 'much-loved ISLE' (ll. 179–80). Orr, located on the *other* isle, his 'Erin', imagines hosts of the nation's poor scraping only the most meagre living from the land. For them, patriotic heroism survives in a stubborn, desperate embrace:

> Full many a just man makes thy workshops ring;
> Full many a bright man strips thy meads to mow;

> Closer in thy distress to thee they cling;
> And though their fields scarce daily bread bestow,
> Feel thrice more peace of mind than those who crush them low. (ll. 169–71)

In his first essay in the Spenserian stanza, 'The Penitent', Orr had turned his attention away from the agricultural labouring class that often claimed his interest in order to explore the lives of his fellow handloom weavers. The poem is one of the few in Orr's first volume for which he included the date of composition: 1800, and follows Burns in that its opening stanza is a dedication, expressed in standard English. While Burns adopts a polite, refined tone when addressing Robert Aiken,[45] however, Orr's opening is ominous, even apocalyptic, appropriate to the state of Ireland in the post-Rebellion, pre-Union period while the Napoleonic conflict raged abroad. He seems to be signalling that a work of far greater gravitas is about to unfold:

> Earth feels the triple scourge wild warfare spreads,
>   Emaciate famine gnaws the husks and pines,
> And ev'ry friend, forsaking, inly dreads
>   The fated wretch, whom pestilence confines ...[46] (ll. 1–4)

His addressee is Rev. John Bankhead, his minister. The poem raises issues of the effectiveness of the Christian faith and the practices of another Dissenting denomination, the Methodists, which suggests that Orr is seeking to engage Bankhead in theological debate.

The poem modulates into a fairly dense vernacular register, and Orr employs the difficult Spenserian form with ease throughout its twenty-two stanzas. Much of the strength of Orr's narrative lies in its 'human interest' as it chronicles the sharp decline of the weaver Christy Blair who develops an addiction to alcohol. The tough lifestyle of the weaver community with its characteristic enjoyment of pastimes such as prizefighting and cockfighting is quickly sketched in, with Christy shown to be an enthusiastic participant:

> Rich rakes admir'd his *sprie*, sae weel he *kent* ['expertise', 'knew']
>   The way to *heel, an' han'* a guid game bird: ['train well, and handle']
> An' in the *pit he wadna twice be dar'd*, (ll. 30–2) ['in the boxing-arena he would
>   not be challenged twice'

Essentially, however, he is shown to be decent, generous, an indulgent father and a willing provider for his supportive family who participate with him in the weaving trade and supply an almost textbook picture of a cottage industry in operation:

> He weav'd himsel', an' *keepet twathree gaun*, ['kept two or three supplied'
>   Wha prais'd him ay for *hale* weel-handled yarn; ['good quality'
> His thrifty wife an' wise wee lasses *span*, ['spun'
>   While warps and queels employ'd anither bairn; (ll. 19–22)

Implicit in this realistic portrait is the recognition that Christy, a type of 'Everyman', would be incapable of providing the sort of authoritative Scriptural exposition for his family's guidance that Burns puts into the mouth of his pious Cotter. Christy is relaxed about the upbringing of his bairns, allowing them time off to run and play if they wish, while some of them attend classes on the Presbyterian catechism in a nearby barn.

Dramatic conflict arises in family life as a result of Christy's love of 'a gill' (l. 26). While Orr deals compassionately with his alcohol addiction, he is honest in depicting the personality changes and the physical 'qualms' associated with it and, in particular, the misery endured by the sufferer's family:

> *Belyve* he staid *hale* days an' nights frae hame, ['soon', 'whole']
> Tho' *ae* nights absence, *ance* he deem'd a curse; ['one', 'once']
> An' aft brought hame nought but an empty purse,
> O' a' the *hale wabs* price he took to sell; ['all the woven cloth from the loom']
> Then, sick *niest* day, poor Mary *boost* disburse ['next', 'must']
> Her pence, to get a glass his *qualms* to quell: ['delirium tremens']
> She grudg'd - he storm'd - the weans *grat* - hame grew hell. (ll. 39–45) ['cried']

As the downward spiral of the narrative progresses we may observe a further contrast with Burns's portrayal of family life. Orr ensures that Christy's wife's character is well realized, with his usual sensitivity to the marginalized position of women. Thus he points out the injustice of Christy's blaming his wife for the state of his home, to his drinking cronies, and when Mary in desperation comforts herself with 'a drap' (l. 66), which makes her the subject of gossip, the narrator observes ruefully that 'A drinkin' wife's ay deem'd for greater flaws' (l. 67). Furthermore, Orr pointedly demonstrates that a father's teachings could be the black antithesis of Burns's pious Cotter's:

> He learn'd the lasses *smut*, an' *gart* the boys ['cheek' or perhaps 'filth', 'made']
> Drink dreadfu' toasts, an' box for pence or praise;
> They'd ca' their mother *le'er*, an' curse her till her face. (ll. 61-3) ['liar']

While Christy makes several attempts to reform, he has lost the power to halt his self-destructive behaviour and it is at this point that Orr introduces a further, original trope by moving away from the strictly Presbyterian landscape not merely of Burns's poem, but of his own immediate community. He investigates the effect on Christy's life of Wesleyan Methodism, deeply influential throughout the British Isles since John Wesley's (1703–91) period of intense preaching in the mid-eighteenth century.[47] Orr explores the effects of what was to become a recurring phenomenon in Ulster, and indeed in Scottish community life, the evangelical revival, in which the emotional, experiential religion depicted is sharply at variance with the orderly instruction in Burns's Cotter's home, and with the Presbyterian rationalism of Bankhead, Orr's addressee, and of Orr himself.

Orr captures something of the flavour of the expressive early Methodist worship style when Christy, desperate and on 'the frightfu' edge / O' dreary ruin' (ll. 82–3), attends a service in a barn. Here 'Smyth, the methodie, harangu'd the folk: / They mourn'd, an' cried amen – he *fleech'd and fought*' ['harangued and challenged'] (ll. 87–8). The effect on Christy is powerful and immediate. He 'grew grave, an' thought he'd join the flock, / An' imitate their lives wham ance he us'd to mock' (ll. 89–90). The decision is no flash in the pan, but is evidenced in a changed life: Christy achieves freedom from his alcohol addiction, becomes once again industrious and enjoys a restoration of happy family life:

> sloth *leas* his hame; ['leaves']
> He has baith *kye* an' corn, an' sells some meal, ['cattle']
>   His frien's outbye add mister till his name;
> An' alter'd Mary's now a *douse* an' dainty dame. (ll. 114–17) ['neat']

Clearly, Orr has carefully researched the origins, popular literature and theology of Methodism to develop this work. Wesley had grasped the importance of engaging the heart as well as the mind if genuine change was to be effected, reporting that his personal commitment to Christ followed a meeting at which he felt his own heart 'strangely warmed'.[48] Christy's decline, fall and redemption demonstrate a strong similarity to experiences recounted in Methodist tracts which were designed to challenge the reader with a powerful personal testimony of sin and the effects of repentance. E. P. Thompson (1924–93) discusses such a text which describes the conversion of a sailor, Joshua Marsden, who leads a life of gaming, drunkenness and sexual indulgence until, following a brush with death, he accepts an invitation to a Methodist meeting at which he is convicted of his own sinfulness and, after a period of resistance, repents and is empowered to lead a changed life. Thompson emphasizes that according to the tract 'the new creation was manifested by new moral beauties'.[49]

The reformed Christy's overriding characteristic is a quiet humility, even as he fulfils his role as head of the family, for his transformation into a loving director of the home empowers all the members of his family to find their voices, and to contribute to an ongoing theological and literary conference. This is in marked contrast to the patriarchal discourse of 'The Cotter's Saturday Night'. Here males and females read and discuss the Scriptures together, but also enjoy classic authors:

> How nat'ral Joseph's Life was weel they kent;
> How Moses' muse her notes sublimely rais'd,
> ...
> How Young made night mair solemn wi' his plaint;
>   How Milton's Eve was fair, his Adam *fand*; ['foolish']
> How Gray was sad an' grave, an' Shakespeare wildly grand. (ll. 146–53)

Significantly, the family also read John Fletcher, the Methodist theologian whose teachings articulated Wesley's understanding of the nature of salvation, and his divergence from Calvinism. Essentially, Wesley and Fletcher taught that God's grace was available to all who repented. They favoured the view that human beings had free will to choose to follow Christ, rather than believing, as the Calvinists did, that only the 'elect', who had already been chosen by God, were predestined to salvation. Central to Wesleyan theology, however, was the conviction that salvation is conditional upon the penitent's continuing in a reformed life.[50]

Christy finds he has a new confidence in theological disputation, based on his common sense and learning. In demonstrating his transformation, Orr is clearly enlisting Methodist 'evidence' in his personal dispute with the Calvinists, who had mocked his own moral life, as he reveals in an 'Elegy', originally included in his collection of 1804:

> When calumny and care have clos'd this strife,
>   Around my bier the truthless sons of zeal
> Shall thwart my tenets – mock a moral life –
>   Affirm I'm lost – and boast the peace they feel.[51] (ll. 33–6)

Orr is careful to emphasize that while Christy and his family prosper due to hard work at the loom and on the land, they are exceptionally philanthropic, benefiting the community by sharing '*Wi'* frien's, wi' strangers, an' wi' a' in need' ['with'] (l. 164). It is in the sense of community life which Orr conveys that we can observe how he has further diverged from the territory ploughed by Fergusson and Burns. Throughout the narrative the reactions of the neighbours are briefly alluded to as the scenes shift. There is a strong consciousness of life lived in the eye of village scandalmongers from whom nothing can be hidden:

> *Gif* ye had pass'd his door, ye'd either heard ['if'
>   Him we his comrades madly makin' noise,
> Or squabblin' wi' the wife. (ll. 55–7)

However, neighbours are also quick to rally round to assist the family in practical ways as Christy's repentance becomes clear to all. Certainly everyone, both 'grave and gay' (l. 111), likes him the better for his Methodism. By the conclusion of the narrative Christy has achieved a significant role as a Class Leader, a layman's position which gave him responsibility for the discipline and pastoral care of a small number of fellow lay members within the local society of Methodists.

It is tempting to read into this poem a call for the healing of the Irish nation through evangelical religion, with Christy's story of repentance and faith a microcosm of what Ireland's story needs also to be. If that were the case, then Orr might appear, problematically, to have moved from political radicalism to apolitical, conservative religion.[52] However, this is highly unlikely. First of all,

Orr firmly sets Christy's story in the lost, unreachable past – the description of the ruined cottage in the second stanza makes that very clear: 'The beasts rub doon the cheeks o' *ilka* door; / Rank nettles hide the hearth on which he shav'd' ['every'] (ll. 15–16). Since the days when Wesley preached his message of salvation throughout the British archipelago an appalling, lengthy conflict has intervened to devastate the land's resources and to carry many of its young men off to serve and die in the armed forces. Roger Wells has argued, controversially, that many British people suffered appalling poverty and deprivation during the period 1793–1820, but the situation in Ireland was, in any case, most certainly further exacerbated by the effects and aftermath of the 1798 Rebellion.[53] Secondly, although the tale of Christy Blair demonstrates how renewal and restoration may have been effected in the Ireland of Wesley's generation, in the final stanza Orr returns to the current condition of the nation, with which he had opened, and offers a different, contemporary prescription for his country's ills. Though he links it to the same love of learning and reading which Methodism inspired in the Blair family, he does not relate his remedy to Methodism's specifically evangelical religious basis:

> May my wild brethren turn to wisdom's path
>   An' grace poor Erin, plagu'd with want and dearth!
> And banish from her shores religious wrath,
>   Desponding sloth, and dissipated mirth!
> May sun-like Science from the poor man's hearth
>   Chase Ignorance, the owl that haunts the stys!
> So patriots brave, when we lie low in earth,
>   'Harmless as doves, and yet as serpents wise,'
> Shall follow Truth and Right, and guard the land they prize. (ll. 172–80)

Akenson and Crawford characterized such sentiments as 'Nationalism through moralism',[54] but there is far more lurking in the subtext than appears in such a simple summation. First of all, whom does Orr mean by his 'wild brethren'? Could he be referring to those United Irishmen still at large in groups of banditti in the countryside, who are living evidence of Erin's desolate state?[55] That seems possible, since the United Irishmen were bound in a type of brotherhood by their oath. The idea of brotherhood also hints at a Masonic connection, however, especially in the light of the reference to Truth and Right in the final line. These are, of course, Christian virtues and, as such, relevant to the story of Christy that has just concluded, but they are also Masonic ideals, represented symbolically in Masonic ritual by the working mason's plumb line: 'the speculative freemason should be guided by the unerring principles of right and truth that are symbolized by the plumb, neither succumbing to the pressures of adversity nor yielding to the seductions of prosperity'.[56] Orr may be broadcasting signals for those who have ears to hear, that the brotherhood of Freemasonry offers a more legitimate way forward for the routed United Irishmen, dispersed, dispirited and dangerously at large.

More generally, he is certainly invoking tolerance and education; offering ideals that will unite and inspire; citing Scriptural precedent in Christ's admonition to his disciples to avoid conflict by being 'wise as serpents and harmless as doves'.[57] All these things will mark the true patriot and contribute to the healing and renewal of the land he loves. The subjunctive mood employed in several of the verbs imbues this final stanza with the character of a prayer, while the diction of the concluding lines has an upbeat tenor, showing faith in the possibility of progress. The poem was included in Orr's collection of 1804 just as he was about to move into his most active phase as a poet who had a message for the nation.

As the discussion of Orr's vernacular works has demonstrated, these Braid Scotch compositions cannot simply be dismissed as imitations of Burns, for they are too innovative and challenging for that. Nor are they simply Orr's attempts to excel Burns, though in several works he manages to do so. They are his most profound and compelling contribution to the stubborn embrace of Ireland he imagined at the conclusion of 'The Irish Cottier's Death and Burial'. They depict, celebrate, castigate and give a voice to the northern community he represented, and they provide a powerful endorsement for his implicit claim to be as 'native' in thought and in action, 'as any here'.[58]

9 ENLIGHTENED ROMANTIC

Major discussions of Romanticism since the 1960s have tended to be Anglocentric; they have reflected the political scene established within the British archipelago by the 1800s, when the Unions with Ireland, Scotland and Wales were all *faits accomplis*. That approach has undergone significant revision in recent years, however, and it is now conceded that among and within the four nations that made up the united kingdoms, the character of Romanticism varied, with cultural, or bardic, nationalism a significant feature of Romantic writing, particularly in Scotland, Wales and Ireland.[1]

Where does James Orr 'fit' within this model? As we have seen, he is an accomplished and original Scots vernacular poet who was patriotically devoted to Ireland. However, his teachers were the great literati of the Scottish Enlightenment, while the influence of the English philosopher Locke, and of eighteenth-century English poets, such as Gray and Pope, may be readily detected in his work. Orr and his generation of Ulster Scots poets worked on the cusp of the era when, traditionally, Romanticism has been portrayed as confronting and superseding the Age of Enlightenment. But as a recent study of Romanticism has shown, 'because of arguments that Romanticism makes a clear development out of rather than a radical break from Enlightenment ideas, we have begun to speak of a Romantic century that runs from 1750–1850'.[2] Perhaps because they have been so associated with Burns who died in 1796 and often, as in Orr's case, with the 1798 Rebellion, they have been regarded essentially as post-Augustan, late eighteenth-century poets. Thus, even though all Orr's extant, acknowledged published work dates from the 1800s, and allowing for the fact that he is often treated as part of a curious subset, such as 'rhyming weavers', folk poets or labouring-class writers, he is implicitly and sometimes explicitly regarded as exemplifying values, attitudes and literary styles typical of the previous century.[3] In this construction he appears a throwback to the Enlightenment in an Ulster of the Romantic era which has somehow missed the Romantic *Movement*. Scholarship, meanwhile, has appropriated Irish Romanticism for writers such as Moore, Owenson or Edgeworth.

The purpose of the present chapter is to demonstrate conclusively that Orr is an Irish Romantic poet by examining his work's engagement with trends and issues that characteristically feature on the spectrum of Romanticism. These include privileging of the imagination and personal feelings; a visionary or prophetic inclination; yearnings for lost times or distant places; an affinity with the spirits and atmospheres of landscapes; aspirations that are politically radical, even revolutionary; alienation, often evidenced in identification with outcasts and outsiders; fascination with the history, culture and language of individual nations or regions within nations; and resistance to the centralizing, imperializing political trend of the Union and post-Union eras.

Certainly within Orr's *oeuvre* Enlightenment values such as order and rationality are strongly evidenced, but the detachment and satirical wit of Augustan tradition are less marked in his writing than passionate feeling, originality in crafting his verse and an imaginative identification with his subjects, all of which reveal him as frequently in tune with the first generation of the 'Big Six' Romantic poets – a term now recognized as belonging to a narrow, 'elitist construction' of Romanticism.[4] Yet Orr's literary persona is still more complex, for a deconstruction of his work, and even of many individual poems within it, reveals that in addition to the Scottish influences discussed in the preceding chapters, he attuned himself to the Romantic nationalism of Anglophone Irish writers of the period, while remaining irrevocably committed to the Ulster Scots community he represented as bard. His best work, therefore, evinces the competing voices which fired his imagination.

This study has already considered how adeptly Orr conflated the roles of bard and prophet, informed by his knowledge of antiquarian researches into Irish Bardism, and by Presbyterian teaching on reading the signs of the times. Orr is, in fact, creatively incorporating Presbyterian tropes within poetry that may be seen as arising from the eighteenth- and early nineteenth-century revivalist movement discussed by Katie Trumpener as 'Bardic Nationalism', and which Trumpener demonstrates arose in England, Scotland and Wales 'as a patriotic resistance to English occupation'.[5] Trumpener's investigation does not include Orr, but she prefaces it with Evan Evans's 'Paraphrase of the 137th Psalm', which unequivocally 'envisions England as the site of Babylonian captivity' for the bards of Wales, and she argues that:

> Evans's adaptation of David's psalm becomes a manifesto for a new nationalist literature, as it links a latter-day cultural nationalism to a sanctified biblical precedent, to invest the Welsh with the Israelites' self-confidence as a chosen people and to raise cultural self-preservation to the status of a religious duty.[6]

There is a striking similarity in Evans's employment of Biblical material to the approach taken by Orr in his versifications of Biblical passages, particularly interesting since direct parallels have not, until now, been made between his poetry and that of Welsh poets working within a culturally nationalist tradition. Orr too can be observed linking 'cultural nationalism to a sanctified Biblical precedent', in his case to invest the *Irish* 'with the self-confidence of a chosen people':

> The youth, whose valour aw'd his foes,
> Grinds in a mill, and bears their blows;
> The weeping infant on the road,
> Sinks down beneath th'oppressive load.
>
> No more the elders in the gate,
> Give law and justice to the state;
> No more their sons attune the lyre
> To praise the virgins they admire:
> In domes where pleasure danc'd at eve,
> The sadden'd circles meet to grieve;
> Our wreaths are wither'd – woe to all
> The crimes that wrought our country's fall![7] (ll. 29–40)

The poem is replete with images of enslavement, desolation and of silenced music and song. There is a conspicuous similarity between this and Evans's 'Paraphrase of the 137th Psalm', which employs Old Testament tropes of captivity and hushed music to portray the plight of the Welsh Bards transported from their homeland by Edward I:

> What now avail our tuneful strains,
> Midst savage taunts and galling chains?
> Say, will the lark imprison'd sing
> So sweet, as when, on towering wing,
> He wakes the songsters of the sky,
> And tunes his notes to liberty?
> Ah no, the Cambrian lyre no more
> Shall sweetly sound on Avron's shore ...[8] (ll. 36–43)

There is no evidence that Orr had read Evans, or indeed any Welsh poetry, though his knowledge of history would have made him aware of the political status of Wales, conquered by England in 1284, and of the legend that Edward I had ordered that the Bards should be put to death in order to curb their potency as instigators of nationalist defiance. As an admirer of Thomas Gray, he would have been familiar with 'The Bard', a poem about the last Welsh poet-seer, who 'triumphs' over Edward in an act of self-martyrdom by choosing to plunge from a precipice to his death. Such literature contributed to the mystical, melancholy, patriotic construction of bardic identity that was clearly building in Orr's imagination.

Cathryn A. Charnell-White, writing about the Welsh poetic tradition, and the labouring-class poet Iolo Morganwg, has spoken of bardism as a 'composite construct ... which accommodates a variety of eclectic and seemingly disparate discourses. These include received notions of druidism, Jacobinism, Unitarian theology, orientalism, speculative Freemasonry and Arthuriana.'[9] With the exception of the latter, virtually all of these discourses can be traced in the work of James Orr. However, in his consciously bardic poems, Orr's incorporation of the discourse of Presbyterianism into his utterances at times causes his verse to evoke a different ethos from that prevailing in much generically similar contemporary literature. Dafydd Moore, in his investigation of *Ossian*, has discussed the 'romance of defeat' that is embedded within many bardic nationalist texts. He notes that

> From Macpherson's perspective, the failure of the redemptive model, the inability to believe in the perpetually deferred return, leads to a deformation or travestying of the world as it might be under the pressure of the world as it is[10]

Orr, on the other hand, highly Biblically literate, was fully aware of the oppositions inherent within Old Testament prophecy on which his bardic poetry frequently draws: these include exile and return, desolation and restoration, captivity and release. Frequently we see him expressing a faith in a Biblical 'redemptive model', which is absent from other bardic works. Evan Evans, for example, concludes his Psalmic paraphrase in unrelieved gloom, reiterating the bardic curse:

> And, where was erst Llewelyn's court,
> Ill-omened birds and wolves resort.
> There oft at midnight's silent hour,
> Near yon ivy-mantled tower,
> By the glow-worm's twinkling fire,
> Turning his romantic lyre,
> Gray's pale spectre seems to sing,
> 'Ruin seize thee, ruthless King'. (ll. 66–73)

Orr, however, in response to his own urgent questions, stresses that the remedy lies in the people's own hands: the practice of genuine Christian principles will bring about the longed-for restoration of the nation's 'eminence':

> When shall we rise? Will e'er thy pow'r
> Our ancient eminence restore?
> Oh! Turn our hearts to truth and Thee;
> Thy practiced truths would set us free. (ll. 49–52)

The Ulster historian A. T. Q. Stewart has pointed out the Romantic image projected by, or attributed to, many of the leaders of the '98 Rebellion:

> There is a fairly general perception that the United Irish movement, like the French Revolution itself, owed much to the rationalism of the eighteenth century, that its leaders were typical men of the Enlightenment. It has often occurred to me that, on

the contrary, they were more typical of the cultural movement that attacked and succeeded it ... the Romantic Movement. Wolfe Tone, Lord Edward Fitzgerald, Napper Tandy – these are Byronic figures seen against a stormy sky or on the field of battle, Dantons who would either save their country or go as martyrs to the guillotine.[11]

Orr too, in his persona of labouring-class revolutionary poet, man on the run and sometime exile, can certainly be said to cut a Romantic figure. In addition, the poets and philosophers with whom the English Romantic Wordsworth himself was familiar, not least Burns and Gray, Blair and Locke, would in many cases have been exactly those admired by Orr, so the influences on their thinking were in many respects similar. While one finds no specific references to Wordsworth or Coleridge in Orr's works, Coleridge was certainly known to him, for his 'Fears in Solitude' was printed in the *Microscope*, a periodical which Orr read.[12] It is safe to assume, then, that Orr was aware of the Romantic turn that was gaining strength in British writing. In politics his own development to an extent parallels that of Wordsworth and Coleridge: his initial enthusiasm for the French Revolution was followed by a growing horror of the violence that accompanied it and concluded with complete disillusionment concerning the perceived tyranny of Buonaparte.

While a powerful Romantic trend is manifest in Orr's poetry, his outlook was not Anglo-centric, rather he sought to address Ireland through the medium of poetry composed in English, the *lingua franca* of a diverse reading public. He had a model for this in the Presbyterian William Drennan, a prime mover in the Belfast Literary Society and founder/editor of the *Belfast Monthly Magazine*. Of Drennan, in relation to Tone, Russell and other United Irish national leaders, A. T. Q. Stewart ironically remarks: 'Drennan, being Presbyterian, had less of a flair for attitudes and personally no desire to be a martyr, but he was brimful of the Romantic ideal. His poetry is cluttered with the props of Romanticism – moonlight, ruins, ancient Druids ...'[13]

Norman Vance acknowledges the Romantic apparatus with which Drennan's poem 'Glendalloch' is ornamented, but insists that his vision is informed by 'Enlightenment values, a classical literary education and the formal disciplines of eighteenth-century English verse'.[14] For Vance, 'Glendalloch' is a memorial to 'the Enlightenment vision of light and liberty found and lost in the last decade of the Irish eighteenth century'.[15] In particular he cites Drennan's 'refusal to sentimentalize Ireland's harsh history' or to blame colonialism for her melancholy state after '98, which instead he lays at the door of the disunited Irish themselves:

> A land, by fav'ring Nature nurs'd,
> By human fraud and folly curs'd,
> Which never foreign friend shall know,
> While to herself the direst foe![16] (ll. 281–4)

It is Thomas Moore whom Vance believes must 'take some of the blame for perpetuating the melancholy mode and convincing a credulous public that this was the very soul of Ireland'. Vance, however, believes Moore 'at his best rises above marketable charm' and sentimentality. Significantly, he links the essential spirit of Moore's work with that of the English Romantics:

> Romantic rebellion and romantic emotion recollected in tranquillity impart depth, tension and seriousness to the best of the *Irish Melodies* ... Imaginatively, if not practically, he gradually came to identify himself with Ireland's struggle for national freedoms, a struggle already approximating to the Ossianic and Wordsworthian condition of 'Old unhappy far-off things / And battles long ago', though the most recent instalment, in 1798, was still a painful memory.[17]

Undoubtedly much of Orr's work, with the emphases we have observed on education, science and reason, reveals him to be an eighteenth-century rationalist in Drennan's mould but often, in Moore's idiom, he reaches back into the Celtic Twilight, picturing an Ireland heroically facing oppression and refusing to be cowed.

Both Orr and Moore composed pieces on Ireland's hero Brian Borhu, who is generally held to have broken Danish power in Ireland. A brief comparison of the two texts reveals some interesting contrasts. Moore's 'Remember the Glories of Brian the Brave' evokes Brian's memory; effectively employs stirring tropes of tyranny, slavery and martyrdom; and utilizes Anglicized forms of Gaelic place names as charms with which to conjure a sense of nostalgia and loss:

> Mononia! when Nature embellish'd the tint
>   Of thy fields, and thy mountains so fair,
> Did she ever intend that a tyrant should print
>   The footstep of slavery there?
> No! Freedom, whose smile we shall never resign,
>   Go, tell our invaders, the Danes,
> That 'tis sweeter to bleed for an age at thy shrine,
>   Than to sleep but a moment in chains.[18] (ll. 9–16)

The simple, concluding message is 'forget not the heroes of the past and ensure that their sacrifice was not in vain'. Murray Pittock recognizes the emotional 'feed' provided by material of this type and its ultimately rather cloying effect, designating it 'Moore's inflammatory saccharine'.[19]

Orr's 'Apostrophe of the Shade of Brian Boromhu, to his Harp', written for the *Belfast Monthly Magazine*, is altogether a more robust construction.[20] In this stirring nationalist piece, the ghost of the ancient Irish hero addresses his newly found harp, now mouldering and retained as a museum piece. He laments Erin's decline and submission to 'sloth, and to slavery too' and at his words the instrument itself awakens, striking up 'Erin Go Brah' [Ireland forever], a phrase chosen as a slogan by the United Irishmen, so its inclusion demonstrates some audacity on Orr's part. The work demonstrates that Ireland's spirit is preserved in her antiquities and may one day revive.

A poem which, in common with Drennan's 'Glendalloch' utilizes some of the typical paraphernalia of Celtic Romanticism but also reveals both Orr's yearning for a better world and his despair regarding humanity's likelihood of achieving it, is his 'Elegy, Composed in Islandmagee at the Tomb of an Ancient Chief'. This Romantic prospect piece is set on the tiny peninsula which lies opposite Orr's Ballycarry on the far shore of Larne Lough. It is bounded on the open sea side by spectacular cliffs known as the Gobbins, which in ancient times would have made it a natural setting for valiant, desperate attempts to repel Viking or other invaders. At the opening, as swirling mists descend to obscure his view of the busy port of Larne in the distance, Orr considers human experience throughout the ages, meditating on the transience of all man's endeavour and achievement:

> AS round pellucid Larne, yon misty cloud
>   Slow-stealing spreads, and all her beauty hides;
> O'er ev'ry honour that enshrines the proud,
>   Abhor'd Oblivion's gloomy chaos glides.[21] (ll. 1–4)

Inspired by the beauty of the setting, and by the landscape's associations with old, unhappy battles and massacres, he utters a prophetic excoriation of colonialism, bigotry and cruelty throughout the earth and in every age:

> Columbus found his world, and thither rush'd
>   The hordes of zeal, and ruin'd Montezume;
> The temple of the sun his priesthood crush'd,
>   The city's wrecks became the people's tomb. (ll. 45–8)

Archetypal Irish figures such as 'the Bard' (l. 28), 'the sage' (l. 27) and 'the pilgrim' (l. 87) are integrated into the narrator's denunciation of the religious and racial prejudices that are so destructive within Ireland and in the world at large. A pertinent local example is given in a reference to a massacre of Catholics who were driven over the edge of the cliff-top on Islandmagee itself during the period of the 1641 Rebellion:

> E'en this wrong'd Isle endur'd a deed, that Grief
>   Can ne'er forget, nor Shame permit to spread:
> The pilgrim mutely marks her hideous cliff
>   And moated hill, and sighs! and shakes his head. (ll. 85–8)

However, the phrase 'wrong'd Isle' may also encrypt Orr's view of Ireland's experiences both before and after the Union. When nearing his conclusion the grief and melancholy he continues to experience concerning the defeat of his youthful radical hopes is evident in the poignant phrase 'my lov'd lost country' (l. 82).

Stylistically the poem has many faults. While the general framework of the elegy, expressed in stanzas of alternately rhyming iambic pentameters, is appropriately dignified and well executed, it does not represent Orr at his most coherent or disciplined. At times his imagination and depth of feeling appear to soar beyond his power to express them. It has, nevertheless, some exceptionally striking and varied imagery and is remarkable in the breadth of its literary, contemporary and historical references. The era was dominated by the Napoleonic conflict and the poem was published in January 1809 at the start of yet another year of war. Four years after Nelson's famous victory at Trafalgar, the Peninsular campaign was still claiming lives among the Irish soldiery whom Orr had dignified through his patriotic series for the *Belfast Commercial Chronicle*.[22] His verse, while addressed to the nation, is motivated by supranational, humane convictions as his urgent question reveals:

> Why, for a few fields more, force out to die,
> Th'enveigled slaves, whose all ye grasp'd before;
> While Carnage grins, and Mercy with a sigh,
> Shrinks from your footsteps, trac'd in tears and gore? (ll. 33–6)

In the final stanza Orr recalls the Creation story in Genesis, and attempts to garner consolation by reflecting on the order brought out of chaos by the benign Deity:

> So, when no shore could bound the whelming deep,
> Nor sober beam impregn Earth's formless wild,
> The Eternal Spirit touch'd Confusion's heap,
> And Order, Peace and Beauty, rose, and smil'd. (ll. 73–6)

The comfort lacks conviction, however, overwhelmed by the images of cruelty and suffering that precede it.

A further, little-known work, 'The Massacre of Mullaghmast', develops the culturally nationalist strain in Orr's writing. It recalls an event which occurred during the Elizabethan colonization of Leinster, and reveals the capacity of this northern Irish Presbyterian to imagine and to identify with the pain of the Gael. The massacre, of as evil memory in Ireland as the massacre of Glencoe in Scotland, took place at the lonely Rath of Mullaghmast, County Kildare. Two English gentlemen, Sir Francis Cosby and Robert Hartpole, had been granted lands in the area by Elizabeth I. In an apparently friendly gesture towards the native Irish, Cosby summoned local chieftains to Mullaghmast for a banquet, but when the guests arrived they were murdered.[23] Orr's poem employs a lyric form and insistent trochaic meter which conveys the poet's anger at the act of treachery:

> Friend of Erin! When with strangers
> You rejoice in pleasure's ring,

> Think betimes what sudden dangers
>   From deceitfulness may spring:
> When with foes, false peace pretending,
>   You partake the rich repast,
> Think upon the bosom-rending
>   Massacre of Mullahmast [sic].[24] (ll. 1–8)

He contends that the patriot's mind will inevitably continue to mourn past 'sanguinary scenes' (l. 12), even when several ages intervene, thus parrying any accusation that he is dwelling on the past and needlessly creating martyrs. He then vividly recreates the surprise and violence of the massacre itself, and the legendary heroism with which the victims responded, his verse alive with the iconic Irish figures of the priest, the scholar and the warrior and the names of the families who were slaughtered:

> See the soldier, half omnific,
>   See the priest, his hallow'd guide,
> See the student scientific,
>   Blend their life-blood, side by side:
> See the great, whose Godlike honours
>   In rememb'rance still shall last,
> Moores and Dempsies, and O'Connors,
>   Sacrific'd in Mullahmast. (ll. 33–40)

At its conclusion the narrative discloses an image of the contemporary 'waste and wither'd' (l. 50) landscape of Mullaghmast, where he claims the national symbol, the 'green shamrock' (l. 51) will not grow. With cruel symbolism, nothing but 'orange vile ... worthless weeds' (ll. 52–3) thrive there above a mass grave. It is in spirit an unhappy, haunted, desolate place where 'Vengeful spirits' hover 'through time' (l. 55).

This angry, eerie, audacious composition bears little relation to Moore's 'saccharine', or indeed to Drennan's imaginative rationalism in 'Glendalloch'. In the first place, it evokes not a mythical event from the heroic past of the Celtic tribes but an era in early modern Irish history – the Plantations period from which the post-Union regime in Ireland was directly descended. Secondly, the opposing of the green shamrock with the uncompromising 'orange vile' brings the poem right up to date in addressing the contemporary antagonisms within Ireland, and in taking sides.[25] Despite the distaste for violence, which Orr characteristically expresses at the conclusion, this is a daring expression of Romantic nationalist sentiment, and it is hardly surprising that it is still virtually unknown among his works. Its existence strongly supports the view that during the post-Union era Orr was consciously attempting to write as a national bard, rather than simply representing his own community as a local folk poet.

In many respects Orr's poetry exemplifies the 'literary dialogue between national traditions' within the Romantic period which Murray Pittock has recently discussed, citing, for example, widespread regard for Moore, Edgeworth, Burns and Scott in popular and cultural *milieux* throughout the three kingdoms.[26] If, as Pittock argues, 'Language, literature, and to an extent music were the battlegrounds on which linguistic incorporation were resisted in Scotland and (later) in Ireland' then Orr, at least as much as Moore, is entitled to a place in the story.[27] Many of his standard register works demonstrate Homi Bhabha's idea of hybridity: 'a form of resistance to cultural authority that works by infusing the colonizer's language with local or "native" references'.[28] There is, of course, a further complicating factor within Orr's hybridity; while he identified himself uncompromisingly as an Irishman, he was viewed as a colonizer by the native Irish, yet to the Ascendancy he was a Scotch-speaking Dissenter of suspect loyalty. A Burns or a Moore did not have this additional conflict to resolve, and it informs some of Orr's best works, such as 'The Irish Cottier's Death and Burial'.[29]

There is a further, still broader, aspect of Romantic writing within which Orr's work sits comfortably. Duncan Wu remarks of those writers deemed Romantics:

> What really bound them together was the fact that they inhabited the same troubled world. The literature had its roots in an age of revolution ... The six canonical male writers believed that a better world was possible ... were one to point to what might be considered distinctive of the movement, it would be this: that unquenchable aspiration for universal betterment, the reclaiming of paradise.[30]

The same belief in the possibility of achieving a better world, and the emotional distress that followed the failure of his revolutionary aspirations, are among the most distinctive features of Orr's poetry during the post-Union era.

Since Orr was widely read in Augustan and neoclassical English and Anglo-Irish literature it is unsurprising to discover that his poetry, whether in Ulster Scots or in English, reflects the whole literary heritage of these islands in its forms and subject matter. One major, yet hardly known, work within his *oeuvre* is the long poem 'The Assizes' (1817). Executed in heroic couplets and articulating strong moral and didactic sentiments, this work appears characteristic of an eighteenth-century poetic tradition exemplified by Pope and Goldsmith. It is a meditation on the contemporary legal and penal systems and appears based on Orr's own observations at the regular assizes, most probably in Carrickfergus.[31] It is certainly as remarkable in its own way as the pastorals of Bloomfield or Duck, and as a sensitive labouring-class man's view of the justice system, it is a powerful, persuasive moral essay which indeed reflects some of the social concerns of those Romantic writers who sought a better world.

The narrator prays for inspiration, invoking the 'mighty Sire' (l. 7), whose hand 'inscrib'dst the rules of right' (l. 9) and who will one day judge the poet himself.[32] Thus, in Miltonic mode, he invests his message with a prophetic quality, expressing a sense of mission, but at the same time emphasizing his own humility. In a series of vivid episodes the narrative moves forward, first depicting the arrival of the prisoners to be tried, and among them both 'callous culprits' (l. 18), their hearts strengthened artificially with alcohol, and the 'unfleg'd felon' who 'trembles, prays, and kneels' (l. 17). Next follows the entrance of the judge, with suitable majesty, the crowd parting silently to let him pass. Human nature in all its hues is displayed. Called as witnesses there are the 'unabashed and proud' (l. 47), the 'clowns' (l. 47) who can barely speak coherently, the blushing, bashful young women, and 'some, self-taught in life's neglected vale' (l. 57), with whom Orr the autodidact must identify.

Undoubtedly Orr recognizes that the court makes powerful theatre, and he presents the many characters in a striking series of mini-narratives well calculated to entertain the reader. The trial allows Orr to exercise his satirical eye as he wryly demonstrates how opposing (and preening) lawyers can manipulate the responses of jury and spectators, employing the same evidence to reach entirely opposite conclusions:

> Now on the other side, with clouded brow,
> And 'with'ring look,' up starts the culprit's foe;
> When the same story is by him rehears'd,
> In judgment's eye the medal stands revers'd;
> He we wept o'er, seems now so much Hell's heir,
> We chide ourselves because we wish'd to spare,
> And scarce from smiting him restrain our hands; (ll. 107–13)

Later, after observing the misery of the confined prisoners, in a strongly rhetorical passage, the narrator petitions God himself on behalf of Ireland, which he characterizes as 'Erin wild, / For whom few care!' (ll. 173–4). As he moves to confess his country's faults, among them prejudice, intemperance, idleness and improvidence, he restrains his emotion. Augustan balance may be observed in the antithesis present in every couplet, but undoubtedly Orr is combining the personae of Old Testament prophet and national bard here, positioning himself as an intercessor who weeps over the nation while expressing his vision of restoration:

> May wisdom say, 'be still!' to passion's tide,
> And law and justice ne'er again divide,
> Till injur'd Erin on the pillars grand,
> Of elegance and order, honourably stand! (ll. 193–6)

In his seminal discussion of Romantic theory, M. H. Abrams demonstrated how in the course of the eighteenth century, mimetic poetry, which foregrounded the faithful imitation of nature, and what he terms 'pragmatic' poetry, designed to teach and delight the audience, was gradually displaced by a poetry in which the focus shifted to the poet himself, a poetry which was marked by the '*spontaneous overflow of feeling*'.[33] Orr's purpose in 'The Assizes' is clearly not only to depict the prison and legal systems in operation, and to set out a moral lesson, but to engage the emotions of his readers and to demonstrate his own, nowhere more clearly than in the passage where he bestows pity on young boys confined in the prison adjacent to the courthouse. He deplores the effects of their confinement, metaphorically presenting the gaol as a university of crime: a 'clos'd college, where professors old / To junior ruffians, guilt's dark arts unfold' (ll. 163–4), but his personal response to them is a spontaneous desire to alleviate their misery and to change their lives.

Orr displays an emotive, social reforming zeal, prefiguring Dickensian denunciations of abuses in Victorian England. He references Howard, the prison reformer, and has clearly drawn on his descriptions of the deplorable effects of prison life on the younger inmates: 'In some gaols you see (and who can see it without pain?) boys of twelve or fourteen eagerly listening to the stories told by practised and experienced criminals, of their adventures, successes, stratagems, and escapes'.[34] In attitude Orr is clearly in sympathy with the sentiments of Wordsworth's 'The Convict' (1796), which deplores the wretchedness of prison conditions, while expressing a sense of brotherhood with a prison inmate and a desire to see him rehabilitated.[35] Orr further adds to the persuasiveness of his essay by demonstrating that the system is often a blunt instrument, unable to discriminate between offences and offenders. When he demands 'If he who pick'd a pocket ought to bleed, / What's due to parricide?' (ll. 296–7), the question is essentially a demand for a sense of proportion. In its sober conclusion the poem looks ahead to the more precise justice that will be dispensed to judge, jury and spectators alike, at the Judgement Day.

Several factors make this a memorable work. First of all is Orr's mastery of his chosen form. His expertly executed rhyming couplets avoid the dreary sameness of unrelieved end-stopped lines through effective employment of enjambment and flexible use of the caesura. Original figures of speech embellish and enhance the work, as in the following passage which adeptly employs a local, topographical reference to convey that the judge's expression reveals he is about to utter a sentence of death before he has actually spoken the dreaded words:

> As when a sportsman from some thorny brake
> Fires at the fowl, on Larne's affrighted lake,
> The distant village marks the flash of light,
> Ere the slow sound has pierc'd the ear of night:
> So when the Judge looks down on the supreme
> Delinquent, waiting punishment extreme,

> His agitated eye th'award foreshows,
> Ere his loth tongue finds utt'rance to disclose. (ll. 274–81)

Orr's moral purpose is directed to the improvement of all his readers, but he is unashamedly on the side of the common man or woman as he records their experiences within the justice system. Technically, 'The Assizes' demonstrates his facility with the iambic pentameter, as do his occasional well-executed sonnets, which also show his mastery of a strict rhyme scheme.[36] As a whole his work is worthy of Hewitt's commendation, made in relation to the vernacular poems, of his 'craftsman's authority'.[37]

One particular genre permits Orr to demonstrate his capacity to employ a range of voices. Allan Ramsay, Pope, Swift and a host of less well-known and anonymous writers had all made essays in epistolary verse. Liam McIlvanney has pointed to the verse epistles of Robert Burns and his circle as evidence of a bardic fraternity in Ayrshire, where the poets exchanged real letters and the reading public was permitted to peer over the shoulders, so to speak, of writers and recipients.[38] While many authors of epistolary verse were of the middle and leisured classes, Burns confidently appropriated the genre for a class more habituated to manual work. Orr too, in the levelling, revolutionary spirit of Romanticism can be seen claiming the genre for himself and his own class of artisans, using it as a medium with which to address a variety of acquaintances.

His level of literacy and his self-education make possible not only his written addresses to his neighbours and friends but also his self-confident engagement with members of 'superior' classes. In addition to the friendly epistles, he wrote several Addresses which have something of the style of formal letters. These pieces often demonstrate great dignity and an independent spirit, none more so than the 'Address to Noah Dalway, of Bella-Hill Esq.',[39] printed in 'open letter' format in the *Belfast Commercial Chronicle* on 2 August 1806. Dalway and his wife both appear on the subscription list for Orr's 1804 volume and they had clearly communicated appreciation of the work to the poet himself. Orr's 'Address' is characteristically courteous and self-effacing but though the poem was composed at a time during which many of his contemporaries sought the sponsorship of wealthy patrons, it emphasizes Orr's personal determination to be beholden to no one.[40] Despite the regret he expresses elsewhere at the necessity of having to work at the loom when he would prefer to be writing poetry, here he insists that he 'toils his bread to gain, / But toils with pleasure' (ll. 1–2). While he expresses gratitude for Dalway's praise, he appears even more grateful for the autonomy his craft allows him; he can accept his labouring-class status as long as he has liberty to pursue excellence as a poet: 'Of independence proud, I'll work and sing, / Poor as a poet, happy as a king' (ll. 31–2).

Orr is so emphatic here, and throughout, that the reader suspects Dalway may have offered sponsorship of some kind which Orr is unequivocally rejecting. Publishing the work in the *Belfast Commercial Chronicle* makes his determined self-reliance very public; nowhere is there a clearer example of Orr, in William Dowling's words, employing the epistolary format as 'a mode of simultaneous address, a double register within which it is possible to speak to one audience directly while always addressing another by implication'. The verse epistle, therefore, while associated with the early and mid-eighteenth century 'epistolary moment' allowed Orr a vehicle for expressing the Romantic resolution and independence of a weaver and a true radical.[41]

Orr's 'Fragment of An Epistle to Mr W. H. D.', a standard habbie work in the vernacular, illustrates his affinity with Romantic preoccupations as he wrestles with his vision of himself as a creative artist. William Dowling contends that by the end of the eighteenth century the 'Augustan verse epistle … give[s] way to the lyric voice that a later age will agree to call Romantic'. He argues that 'mid-century poetry comes increasingly to dwell in [the] haunts of meditation', presenting the poet as a 'lonely wanderer in twilight groves whose surroundings belong at least as much to his own imagination as to any actual landscape'.[42] It is fascinating to observe that very process at work in the 'Fragment', in which Orr increasingly privileges the lyric voice as the epistle develops. The 'Fragment' was written to the Rev. W. H. Drummond, a Presbyterian minister who had been, in his teens, a supporter of the United Irishmen. This Ulster Scots poem depicts Orr's acute consciousness of himself as a poet, even while he laments what he deplores as his lack of skill. It evinces an introspective soul-searching, an unresolved frustration and a keen awareness of the power of the imagination at work within. He longs to bring the landscape and nature sensuously to life in his own style, agreeing implicitly with Wordsworth's view that the most powerful poetry overflows as a result of personal observation and from the recollection of vivid sensation:

> O Nature! Cud I set your stage,
> Wi' a its scenery on my page!
> My rainbows points the earth sud guage [*sic*],
>   My wild-fire wander;
> An', lakes an' rivers smile and rage,
>   Wi' grace an' grandeur.
>
> The purplin' morn, and pensive eve,
> Sud a their fine, fair tints receive;
> My cliff sud frown, my echo rave,
>   My shamrock smell,
> My night appear as gran'ly grave
>   As night hersel.[43] (ll. 7–18)

The repetitive use of the personal pronoun and the sensuousness accorded to the tiny shamrock, clearly as important to the writer as the sublime scenery and phenomena, signal a Romantic vision of nature that he is struggling to express. In the concluding stanzas, and in a more pensive mood, Orr evokes his own persona; he is the introspective, tortured artist, exhausted but still driven and intrigued by the uncanny, mysterious imperative of his calling as a poet:

> I needna strive. My want and woe
> Unnerves the energies, you know;
> Yet Nature prompts my muse ...
> ...
> Coy science spurn'd me frae her knee,
> An' fortune bad my shuttle flee;
> But, a' the while, smit strangely wi'
>   The love o' sang,
> I rudely rhyme the scenes I see,
>   Whare'er I gang. (ll. 37–48)

It is impossible to say definitively that Orr had read Wordsworth's poetry or the enlarged Preface of 1802 to the *Lyrical Ballads*. Whether he had or not, Wordsworth would surely have recognized in those final lines his own image of the wandering poet-seer, expressing his vision in 'the real language of men'.[44]

The poem is also linked with Romantic poetics due to its status as a 'Fragment', a genre frequently associated, as here, with the inadequacy of language to articulate the soaring sense of inspiration. The fragment or ruin motif appears in at least two further works among Orr's Scotch poems. The life of Christy Moore, the convert to Methodism in 'The Penitent', is reported to the narrator as an extended anecdote or flashback that is narrated by 'Brice, the auld herd on the moor' (l. 18).[45] This lends a legendary, distanced quality to the story, which is sited in a past several generations back, and employs a double narrator device. The nostalgia evoked for an era enlivened by an emotional engagement with religion, and the glimpses of persons long dead, subtly and powerfully draw the reader into an imaginative experience that is enhanced by the tantalizing depiction of Christy's ruined cottage, to which the poet devotes some poignant lines:

> Fu' aft I've pass'd the *wa'-stead* whare he leev'd; ['site'/'remains of the walls'
> An' auld ash tree stan's branchless now an' bare,
>   *Aboon* the spring, unnotic'd an unpreev'd: ['above'
> The side wa' co'ers the *causey* that he pav'd, ['cobbled path'
>   The beasts rub doon the cheeks o' *ilka* door; ['every'
> Rank nettles hide the hearth on which he shav'd ... (ll. 11–16)

A sense of loss and yearning is triggered by these disintegrating remains which progressively evoke once-vibrant lives. A similar mood develops in a contribution to the ruined cottage subgenre by Robert Southey (1774–1843):[46]

> I pass this ruin'd dwelling oftentimes
> And think of other days. It wakes in me
> A transient sadness ... (ll. 105–7)

Simon Bainbridge writes of William Wordsworth and Robert Southey:

> These writers made particular use of one of the sub-genres of war poetry of the period, the 'ruined cottage' poem which figures war's impact on the domestic sphere through the image of the increasingly dilapidated buildings ... Poets also used the 'ruined cottage form' to represent the more general social and economic crisis caused by conflict.[47]

In Orr's work, as the discussion in Chapter 6 has shown, the opening stanza of 'The Penitent' refers to the war and famine which are 'scourging' society in 1800, the year of the poem's composition. Since Christy the weaver and his family had achieved prosperity some generations earlier, their ruined cottage clearly serves as a symbol of the 'general social and economic crisis caused by the conflict' and shows Orr consciously employing a recognizable motif of the Romantic era.

A significant body of Orr's verse has precise locations in the Ulster countryside, specifically the east Antrim area, and employs the genres and tropes of pastoral verse, or of landscape poetry. Frequently, he suggests his own presence near to, but a little apart from, the scenes and characters he describes.[48] His is a reflective, meditative persona that seems inspired by Thomas Gray's 'Elegy Written in a Country Churchyard', but there are important, original differences of detail and of development which separate Orr's work from more typical eighteenth-century pastoral or landscape verse. 'The Glen', for example, the first entry in his *Poems on Various Subjects* of 1804, at first appears a conventional, bucolic piece. Orr imagines an idyllic existence with a young woman in Aldfrackyn Glen, adjacent to Ballycarry.[49] Closer examination, however, reveals an altogether more interesting subtext. While the diction appears at times consciously poetic, with 'cascade' (l. 9), 'gulph' (l. 29), 'ramparts' and 'thick shades' (l. 33), there is a freshness about the speaker's very physical exultation in the scenery, a mood underlined by the poem's fast pace and lilting anapaestic rhythm:

> The Oak from the bottom ascends,
>   And 'bove the steep cliff braves the blast:
> From the steep cliff that rudely impends,
>   I could step on his branches so vast.
>
> The Ivy ambitiously spreads
>   O'er heights, from whose summit we'd shrink; (ll. 24–30)

In some respects the poem has a strong subversive element. The glen of the title is, as Orr explains, on Richard Gervase Ker's estate. It was Ker who confiscated the weapons of his tenants on the eve of 7 June 1798, refused to intervene to save sixteen-year-old Willie Nelson from hanging, and declined to endorse Orr's attempt to join the yeomanry after his return from America.[50] While not a vicious oppressor of tenants, he was hardly a model of liberal tolerance or a friend of democracy, so it is surely with some audacity that Orr, artisan and returned rebel, imaginatively asserts ownership of the glen as a space in which he and his lass will live a life of unrestricted liberty.

Several works very precisely located in, or within walking distance, of the Broadisland and Islandmagee area demonstrate both his love of the landscape, and his determination to put his own stamp upon it. His upbeat prospect poem 'Fort-Hill', set on a hilltop in Broadisland, accommodates the motif of developing industrialization but presents it with a sinister aspect, just as Blake in 'Jerusalem' (1803–8) presents the 'Satanic mills' intruding into England's pastoral landscape:

> Observe yon proud city, how grand
> Her spire seems! How dreadful her tow'r!
> Grim-rising o'er both sea and land,
> Like the stern sprite on wild Patmos' shore.
> What smoke from yon found'ry aspires ...[51] (ll. 33–7)

The poet is distanced from the urban, industrial society he portrays, but through the inclusion of such images he clearly acknowledges the realities of the contemporary world. This is still, however, very much a poem that celebrates a self-sufficient, thriving community which defers to no one; he presents the villagers at work, at play, and enjoying the benefits of education in the community school. But the reader also detects a dash of Romantic *sehnsucht* as the speaker takes in the wider view, and incorporates the literary, linguistic, historical and mythic associations of the panorama into his vision:

> Immensity's self draws a veil
> On the skirts of the soul-raising scene:
> The heaths where, of yore, Ossian warr'd,
> The plains fam'd, poor Burns, by your quill,
> And the isle where the Manx tongue is heard,
> Conspicuous are all to Fort-Hill. (ll. 41–8)

Orr's 1804 and 1817 volumes were eclectic bodies of work 'on various subjects', the former paid for by subscription and, as he no doubt realized, perhaps the only opportunity for publication that would be afforded him as a working man. Nevertheless, a body of poetry within his *oeuvre* may be extrapolated that fulfils the very criterion Coleridge sets forth for a group of poems included in *Lyrical Ballads*:

For the second class, subjects were to be chosen from ordinary life; the characters and incidents were to be such as will be found in every village and its vicinity, where there is a meditative and feeling mind to seek after them, or to notice them, when they present themselves.[52]

The characterization of the poet as the man with the 'meditative and feeling mind' who is sensitive to the community and its vicinity is exactly the persona Orr adopts in many of his works. In addition, Orr presents very direct portraits or stories of individuals who are ordinary village dwellers, and whose feelings and affections are often violently agitated and disturbed by a variety of causes. The latter include natural disasters; the social displacement resulting from war; the effects of industrialization; and the injustice of laws which privilege the powerful and the rich. Orr chooses instead to privilege the experience of the poor and he makes an assertive, articulate spokesman for his own class. If Hazlitt deemed *Lyrical Ballads* to have been inspired by a 'levelling' Muse, and to have arisen from the revolutionary spirit of the age, then the same might be said of the 'local' poems and ballads in Orr's work.[53]

Frequently he foregrounds with compassion the misfortunes of unhappy individuals from the labouring classes. 'The Maniac's Petition' (1804) exemplifies a recurring minor theme: the man or woman driven from home because of parental disapproval of his or her romantic inclinations.[54] In this instance, the 'maniac' of the title further reveals that he is a returning soldier, wounded and scarred in the service of his country.[55] In simple, unaffected language and with great pathos he begs the inhabitants of his home village to relieve his suffering: 'Chill night comes on; be kind and let me in' (l. 29). The final image, however, discloses him buffeted by howling winds, his limbs bleeding from contact with rocks and brambles, while the sight of his lost love, hand in hand with her spouse, further compounds his misery.

Such poems fall naturally into the mini-genre of Romantic poetry that records the experiences of outcasts and wanderers, and in which, for example, Wordsworth's 'The Female Vagrant' (1794),[56] and Keats's 'Old Meg she was a Gypsey' (1818)[57] can be placed. In voicing the sufferings of the dispossessed and disempowered Orr gives dignity and importance to their lives. A further 'lyrical ballad' which fulfils this function is the pastoral narrative 'Edwin and Lucy,'[58] which tells of a rural disaster, the deaths of a young couple whose cottage roof caves in under a heavy weight of snow that kills them but spares their child. The opening of the work describes the male protagonist in bold imagery, evincing a strong flavour of the Irish and Scottish coastal seascapes:

> His looks were sweet, tho' strength was in his arm;
> In scenes of sport as wild as Morne's calm wave,
> In strife as wild as Orkney's in a storm. (ll. 2–4)

As their life together unfolds, an ominous note intrudes when the narrative allows the reader to infer that human activity and hopes appear fragile when set against the terrible, desolate beauty of nature in the dead season:

'Twas one wide waste where lately culture smil'd,
    The snow's deep strata glitter'd on the plain,
When Lucy's song the lonely hours beguil'd,
    And Edwin's pipe accompanied the strain. (ll. 21–4)

The influence of Thomson's *The Seasons* is clear in the awesome description of the land transformed into a vast snowscape, but the portrait of the couple innocently amusing themselves and their child in blissful ignorance of their impending fate engages the reader's human sympathy, thus the sublime, cruel unpredictability of nature which destroys the family seems doubly appalling:

No peasant knows how long the cottage stood,
    But when sharp sleet made mountains bare,
Sublimely dreadful roll'd the furious flood,
    Beside whose surge its wrecks were seen to stare.

The peasants dug them out ... (ll. 49–53)

One can easily imagine such a tale being handed on in anecdote in the neighbourhood, but the sad image of the couple's infant child, still alive beside the corpses of its parents and 'vainly tugging at the pulseless breast' of its dead mother raises it out of the ordinary and moves the reader to further meditation on what Wordsworth defined as the 'great and simple affections' of human nature.[59]

Chaplin and Faflak have argued that the 'abolitionist movement provides another significant context for the emergence and development of early Romanticism'.[60] Certainly, it comes as no surprise to learn that Orr shared the growing abhorrence of the Slave Trade and made several significant poetic contributions to the anti-slavery discourse of the age. Both Orr's and Wordsworth's imaginations were stimulated by the fate of Toussaint L'Ouverture, leader of the slaves' revolt in San Domingo who later died in the captivity of the French under Buonaparte. Wordsworth's poem 'To Toussaint L'Ouverture' (1802) appeared in the *Morning Post* on 2 February 1803. Whether or not Orr had read Wordsworth's work before completing his own, he tackles his subject in a very different style. Wordsworth offers a dignified sonnet, an address to Toussaint in his dungeon, comforting him with the assurance that his struggle has not gone unnoticed and that his life and example have inspired others to emulation:

... Thou hast left behind
Powers that will work for thee; air, earth, and skies;
There's not a breathing of the common wind
That will forget thee; thou hast great allies;

> Thy friends are exultations, agonies,
> And love, and man's unconquerable mind.[61] (ll. 9–14)

The language has an abstract quality, however, which lends the poem gravitas but also a vagueness that lessens its force.

Orr's 'Toussaint's Farewell to San Domingo', a rousing monologue, is an entry in his Napoleonic series for the *Belfast Commercial Chronicle*. In it, he voices the imagined thoughts of the former slave as he leaves his native land, 'A captive to pine in some dungeon of France' (l. 4). Once an exile himself, Orr incorporates grief at the loss of homeland into Toussaint's narrative, and employs horrific, graphic details, culled from his reading about the abuses of slavery:

> Proud Christians, who boast of their civilization,
>   Go far beyond Pagans in cruelty's art!
> A slave, in a cage, they hung days more than seven,
> Till the poor mangl'd flesh from his cheek-bones was riven,
> And his eyes were scoop'd out by the wild fowls of heaven,
>   While famine and thirst gnaw'd his sad sickly heart.[62] (ll. 19–24)

We may note how he aligns himself with many in the Abolitionist Movement by appealing to a universal, civilized Christian conscience which operates above and beyond national or commercial interest. Tim Matthewson has argued that the slave revolt was believed by most Americans to be 'anti-white and anti-plantation, leading to Negro massacre or domination of whites, the destruction of economy and industry, and a reversion to barbarism'.[63] Orr addresses any such fears that may have troubled his audience by putting into Toussaint's mouth an exhortation to the insurgent slaves to act humanely:

> Yet, since wrongs rouse the feelings, once more let me urge you,
>   To give unto all men, the treatment you'd gain;
> Though tyranny's satellites stab, shoot, and scourge you,
>   Make that no excuse to retaliate the pain. (ll. 33–6)

Typically, he (Orr) does not lose the opportunity to include a strong declaration of his own unequivocally egalitarian outlook and to emphasize that virtue and heroism are unrelated to racial origin: 'Whate'er clime or colour, the minds of the rabble / Are savage and rude; and of heroes, humane' (ll. 39–40).

The poem concludes with an intense lament that focuses on the brutalities meted out to slaves, and delivers an imaginative, empathetic rendition of Toussaint's despair:

> How long must thy sons feel the sharp thong of slav'ry,
> And their blood stain the stems of the sugar cane sav'ry!
> Oh! these plagues of the nations, ambition and knavery,
> They've thinn'd poor mankind, and brought ruin on me! (ll. 45–8)

The poem has additional popular appeal due to its relentless, insistent rhythm and repetitive rhyme scheme which give it the effect of a folk 'protest song', the stirring type of composition in which Orr's contemporary, James Campbell of Ballynure, excelled.

It is hoped that this exploration of Orr's work as it developed in the early nineteenth century will lend credence to the claim that he must be understood as a Romantic poet. After his return from America and until the end of his life he maintained an idealistic, radical, non-violent stance as a poet of, and for, the people. He was, as we have seen, demonstrably influenced by new trends in poetry and in prose fiction, particularly Romantic nationalism and Romanticism's foregrounding of the imagination, personal feelings and individual experience. He fully endorsed the era's revolutionary discourse of liberty, equality and brotherhood, contributing to it in many important poems and essays. As the above discussion shows, he moved well beyond the popular vogue for vernacular literature that had been stimulated by Burns's verse in the late eighteenth century.

The small imperfections and occasional stiffness apparent in some of Orr's English poetry should render it no less interesting to a literary historian. It confirms that Orr was not locked into the persona of the vernacular poet, or clinging to the easy popularity his Scotch poems brought him within his own community. He was a risk-taker with aspirations, eagerly embracing the contemporary scene and moving on.

CONCLUSION

James Orr's life ended on 24 April 1816. It was several years since he had published in any well-known newspaper, and twelve since the publication of his *Poems on Various Subjects*.[1] During that final, ostensibly silent period his personal reputation had suffered a decline. Orr himself had complained to Thomson as early as 1807 that the company he was often forced to keep lacked respectability, while McDowell, in his posthumous *Sketch* blamed what he euphemistically referred to as 'the errors of his later years' on Orr's bachelor state, and on bad companions who 'for pleasure's sake, become covetous of a superior man's company, while they steal from him his reason and his resolution'.[2] Since medical records are not available, the exact cause of Orr's death will probably never be determined, but the possibility that it was in some way alcohol-related certainly exists. McDowell was careful to stress, however, that Orr's posthumous works were at the poet's direction sold so that the profits might be 'distributed among the poor of the parish of Broad-Island' and that 'he retained to the last a manly and independent spirit'.[3]

The publication of the *Posthumous Works* and the successful appeal for funds to cover the cost of Orr's monument speak of the esteem in which he was held as 'Poet, Patriot and Philanthropist'. Nevertheless, the bare facts of Orr's decline permit us to infer a personal history marred by self-doubt, loss of direction and alienation. It is tempting to trace this anguish to the trauma he had suffered, specifically the failure of the 1798 Rebellion, the loss of many deeply admired friends from that period, the imposition of the Union and, following that, what he appears to have perceived as the loss in the country at large of the original, inclusive United Irish vision. Certainly, within his *oeuvre* as a whole one is conscious of two major oppositional forces: the melancholy of defeat that mourns a 'lov'd lost country', set against an enthusiastic embrace of contemporary Ireland for the purpose of asserting both the national identity and his own sense of belonging. It is probably accurate to conclude that in Orr's own psyche it was the former, the melancholy, that haunted him like a Doppelganger, while some of his apparently upbeat public pieces dating from the years 1805–13 carry the aura of what today would be recognized as denial.

Nevertheless, as the present study has demonstrated, Orr has left a substantial, major legacy in his extant *oeuvre*, the significance of which should now be properly appreciated. Until very recently, Orr was simply characterized as a local bard, folk poet, rhyming weaver, or vernacular writer. While each of these constructions evinces a measure of truth, all are far too limited to do justice to the range and quality of his output.

It is a testament to Orr's strength of character and sense of calling that he recovered sufficiently from defeat and exile in 1798 to carve out a place of some celebrity for himself as a regular contributor to a respected journal and to two Belfast newspapers.[4] This role he fulfilled with confidence, commentating most appositely on contemporary events such as the British anti-Napoleonic campaign. For an erstwhile United Irish rebel this was a course fraught with risks in a period when many newspaper poets throughout these islands competed to model an establishment-approved patriotism. In the Belfast press, as we have seen, this led some contributors to celebrate the British identity conferred by the Union. In such an atmosphere Orr's Napoleonic series for the *Belfast Commercial Chronicle*, discussed in Chapter 4, displays remarkable subtlety and astuteness in its rejection of what he perceived as Napoleonic tyranny, while at the same time keeping faith with his dedication to Ireland, and to the values of an Enlightenment republican. Thus his contribution to the poetry of the 'Age of War' is refreshingly original, running counter to conventionally 'scripted wartime identities'.[5] A text such as 'The Irishman', beloved and maligned in almost equal measure, when understood as an entry in this series, clearly balks convention and imperializing trends; its controversial commendation of the Irish national character represents an exhortation to Irish people to adhere to the ideals and example set by men such as Henry Joy McCracken, while its conclusion unequivocally privileges peace. This is not gung-ho jingoism. It is in marked contrast, for example, to Burns's 'The Dumfries Volunteers', written during an earlier invasion scare, which foregrounds the righting of 'British wrongs' (l. 16) and loyalty to the king.[6] By choosing to express himself in the standard register throughout the whole of this newspaper series, Orr enabled himself to reach a much wider demographic than would have been possible had he adhered to the vernacular. One might say that this choice was essential to the inclusive spirit of his patriotism.

Orr's newspaper verse, and much of the standard register work in his second, posthumous volume demonstrates that he understood his role as Bard of Ballycarry in a national, rather than a merely local sense. He was inspired and original in conflating the prophetic aspect of bardism with his Presbyterian concept of the Biblical prophet who acts as a watchman to denounce and correct the nation's faults in the hope of restoring and healing the condition of its people. It was an entirely appropriate persona for an Irish Dissenter patriot, but additionally allowed Orr consistently to endorse values such as truth, tolerance, justice and liberty that ultimately have universal rather than merely local or national application. Such values were also central to the poetry, essays and reports on international events that had once filled the columns of the *Northern Star* where Orr was first recognized as an extraordinarily gifted writer.

This study has sought to recover the reputation of Orr's standard register verse, for it is wholly inaccurate to interpret him as primarily a vernacular poet, even if the vernacular works are recognized as his most luminous, profound and complex creations. Neither John Hewitt, nor Akenson and Crawford felt much admiration for his English poems, evaluating them as stiff, and imitative of English models. This prejudiced dismissal of well over 80 per cent of Orr's *oeuvre* has influenced many within the academy with the result that, until now, the complexity and indeed the quality of Orr's standard English poetry has not received the scholarly attention it merits. Why, for example, has a major, expertly executed work such as 'The Assizes', a labouring-class writer's mature, vivid and radical appraisal of the contemporary justice system, never been anthologized? This and many other works which demonstrate Orr's mastery of form and poetic technique display a further aspect of the radicalism, which underpins his writing. In her discussion of the Welsh labouring-class poet Iolo Morganwg, Mary-Ann Constantine correctly argues:

> adherence to conventional models of verse and expressions of conventional sentiment are rather the rule than otherwise among self-taught writers of this period. Any expectation that a labouring-class writer should directly challenge social and literary norms is doubtless informed by our perception of exceptional (and more readily accessible) voices ... rather than by the evidence of the mass of writers as a whole. Most of these writers aimed to emulate their literary models, not to subvert them: the radicalism, if any, of their work lies in their mastery of an idiom denied them by birth and circumstance, and in their ability to participate in a literary culture at all.[7]

Unquestionably, Orr's is one of those 'exceptional voices'. He certainly challenges social norms throughout his *oeuvre*, and without doubt is strikingly innovative in his exploration of his chosen themes. In addition, however, his mastery of conventional forms such as the rhyming couplet or the sonnet, and the facility he demonstrates when working within literary and linguistic registers that are essentially alien, should also be interpreted as evidence of his radicalism, and of his poetic craftsmanship. He resists being shunted into a siding marked out for rustic, vernacular writers, and appropriates for his own class, and for non-standard speakers, the frameworks considered the birthright of the educated, British literary establishment.

Scholarly dismissal of Orr's English poetry has, in addition, distorted his image. He has been represented as dynamic in the vernacular, but unadventurous and constrained when writing in English. This study has revealed, however, that far from this he was negotiating space within *avant-garde* literary movements.

He was prepared to endorse the Gaelicism of a writer such as Owenson, but had the confidence, publicly, to administer a civilized but pointed corrective to the othering of his own community within her exceptionally popular text.[8] The Gaelic tropes and themes of Romantic nationalism are confidently employed in his *oeuvre*, in poems such as 'Brian Boromhu's Address to his Harp', or the 'Elegy, Composed in Islandmagee at the Tomb of an Unknown Chief'. The latter, as we have seen, despite some stylistic faults, resonates with an epic quality that effectively envisions the local and the national stories within a tragic and historic global narrative of colonialism and sectarian strife. In addition to providing a vehicle for his engagement with Irish national themes, the standard register works also demonstrate Orr's debt to the great literati of the Scottish Enlightenment, in particular to Blair, Robertson and Hume, whose rationalism underpins his often didactic message.[9]

Finally, it must now be recognized that Orr's standard register poems are highly significant because they provide compelling evidence that Orr was finely tuned in to the issues, attitudes and modes of Romanticism as it developed within the British archipelago. As the foregoing analysis has shown, works such as 'Elegy, Composed in Islandmagee' demonstrate Orr's imaginative engagement with the landscape and its associations; other pieces, for example 'The Glen', or 'Fort Hill' reveal him asserting popular ownership of the local environment, or over Ireland as a whole. Much of his poetry focuses on the experiences of the labouring-class man or woman and is frequently concerned with the very poor, the outcast and the mentally disturbed. Such pieces often combine strong narrative, individualized characters and lyrical imagery, while employing the metrical patterns and rhyme schemes found in ballads or folk and protest songs. Thus he joins his voice with those making that characteristic, levelling Romantic demand for a better world for all people.

Since it is for his vernacular works that Orr is best known, and because the quality of these pieces is uniformly outstanding, a significant proportion of this study, some three chapters, has been devoted to their analysis. Hewitt's conclusion that Orr was no more an imitator of Burns than Burns was of Fergusson or of Ramsay is not disputed. Nor has the present writer wished to contest Hewitt's view that 'in handling his native idiom Orr seemed unable to go wrong'. This study has, however, much more fully than Hewitt's, elucidated the originality and the extent of Orr's exploitation of traditional Scots stanza forms. It has also recovered the vigorous radical patriotism of works such as 'To the Potatoe', which Hewitt's regionalist approach tended to neglect.

The analysis of Orr's vernacular poetry undertaken in Chapters 6, 7 and 8 inevitably raised the question of what its significance may be to the literatures of Ireland and of Scotland; the analysis points also to the related question of where these poems should be sited from the point of view of critics and scholars. Are they to be understood as Irish literature or as Scottish literature, or may that issue legitimately be avoided by consigning them to the borderland of Irish-Scottish Studies? With regard to Scotland, Orr's vernacular poetry surely represents the best work produced within an independent branch of the Scottish poetic tradition. It is the literature of a Scots diaspora, settled for many generations in Ireland, but it demonstrates the extent to which the long and varied eighteenth-century vernacular tradition could still present opportunities for development to a dynamic and original writer. Far from imitating what Burns had achieved within established stanza forms Orr, as has been shown, confidently moved the discourse forward, broadening the subject matter, strengthening characterization and storyline, softening the tone or altering the focalization of the narrative. In addition, he is not shy of directly opposing Burns's consciously idealized vision of rural life, as when he confronts the reader with the very real physical hardships and threat of extinction facing his community in works such as 'The Irish Cottier's Death and Burial'.

When one turns to the literature of Ireland, Orr's native country, his description of the Irish Cottier as 'the poor neglected native of thy North' now appears prophetic, for it could so aptly in this context be applied to the poet himself. In Orr's vernacular poems, as we have seen, he demonstrates real genius by transforming Scottish generic forms in order to accommodate Irish experience, which he then articulates in Braid Scotch. In his northern voice, he has supplied Ireland with a poetic narrative that elucidates a seminal period in the national history. He portrays the rebel, the fugitive and the exile with a caustic realism that deromanticizes these figures and their experiences. His is also a voice that demands social justice for all Ireland's poor, and he links such demands to Ireland's distinctiveness and to the importance of her people as individuals and as a nation. The nation, the land and genuine religious faith are recurring, dominant motifs within Orr's *oeuvre*; the problem is simply that just as Orr feared, the Dissenter and the Scotch community which spawned him, for many years were most thoroughly othered, as the discussion of the anthologizing of Irish literature in Chapter 1 has demonstrated.

Some might argue that this community connived at its own othering within Ireland, particularly in the pre- and post-Partition periods and even into the present.[10] No one today, however, has any grounds for viewing Orr's most important contributions to the literature of Ireland through a post-Partition lens, simply because they are expressed in fairly dense Scots. Indeed, any critical approach which fails to take account of the historical context and the period, well in advance of twentieth-century partition, within which Orr's Ulster Scots poems were composed, should now be recognized as irrational, and as a failure of scholarship. Orr counselled Ireland's 'browbeat callans' to resist oppression; his stated commitment was to 'Airlan', our fair lan''; his tomb honours him as a patriot. He viewed himself as an Irish writer and that is unquestionably how he should be viewed today.

Orr and his Scotch poems have for far too long been left 'wintering out' in their native land.[11] They represent a northern school within Irish literature that is rooted in Scottish cultural, intellectual and religious traditions and which frequently expresses itself in its natural vernacular register. Only an outmoded essentialist construction of Irishness could fail to embrace the Scotch poetry produced in Ulster. Recently the argument has been advanced that the reason for the omission of Orr and his contemporaries from the national canons of both Ireland and Scotland has been due to the 'the tendency to organise the study of poetry along rigidly national lines'.[12] This may excuse Scottish critics; it does not excuse their Irish counterparts.

Much remains to be done if James Orr's place within Irish literature is to be established. First of all, research for the present study has disclosed two previously undocumented Orr poems within the editions of the *Belfast Commercial Chronicle* printed in 1805. It is more than likely, therefore, that further works, perhaps even further vernacular pieces, remain to be located, and this research should be a matter of priority. Secondly, Orr's *Collected Poems* of 1935, though it assisted in keeping his memory alive throughout the twentieth century, is clearly incomplete. It drew together and made available Orr's two published volumes but did not recover his numerous uncollected items, while Philip Robinson's recent anthology, although extremely significant in contributing to a revival of interest in Orr, provided no direct assistance with the interpretation of his vernacular poetry. The evidence of the present study surely suggests that it is time for the publication of a scholarly edition of Orr's complete works which would incorporate all his extant poetry and include a glossary and textual notes. Such a publication would permit the multiplicity of strands and influences in Orr's work to be grasped and its quality to be further and fully appreciated. A properly informed scholarly debate might then take place concerning Orr's significance to Irish literature and to Scottish Studies.

NOTES

Introduction

1. Quoted by A. McDowell in 'A Sketch of the Author's Life' (hereafter 'Sketch'), in J. Orr, *Collected Poems* (1935; Belfast: Mullan & Son, rpt. 1936), pp. 185–91, on p. 188. Attempts to trace the original article have proved unsuccessful.
2. J. Orr, *Poems on Various Subjects* (Belfast: Smyth and Lyons, 1804).
3. The *Belfast Commercial Chronicle*, the *Belfast News-letter* and the *Belfast Monthly Magazine*.
4. The local name for the district in which Ballycarry is situated. In Ulster Scots it is 'Braidislan'. The area is located in the parish of Templecorran.
5. J. Orr, *The Posthumous Works of James Orr of Ballycarry: With A Sketch of his Life* (Belfast: Francis D. Finlay, 1817; hereafter *Posthumous Works*).
6. McDowell, 'Sketch', in Orr, *Collected Poems*, p. 189.
7. 'Elegiac Stanzas', in Orr, *Collected Poems*, p. vi.
8. D. H. Akenson and W. H. Crawford, *Local Poets and Social History: James Orr, Bard of Ballycarry* (Belfast: Public Record Office of Northern Ireland [PRONI], 1977; hereafter *Local Poets and Social History*).
9. See Orr to Samuel Thomson, 4 January 1806, quoted in B. M. Walker, 'Country Letters: Some Correspondence of Ulster Poets of the Nineteenth Century', in J. Gray and W. McCann (eds), *An Uncommon Bookman: Essays in Memory of J. R. R. Adams* (Belfast: The Linen Hall Library, 1996; hereafter 'Country Letters'), pp. 119–39, on p. 128.
10. Orr's extant *oeuvre* consists of 140 poems in the standard register, both collected and uncollected, and 18 Braid Scotch poems.
11. J. Campbell, 'Dirge', in J. Campbell, *The Poems and Songs of James Campbell of Ballynure* (Ballyclare: Corry, 1870), pp. 39–41.
12. J. R. English, *Visits of the Muse, or A Leisure Hour* (Lanktree: Belfast, 1830), p. 106. English's appeal for funds was successful. Orr's monument is the most imposing in Templecorran churchyard.
13. Ibid., pp. 92, 106.
14. R. Huddleston, *Poems on Rural Subjects* (Belfast: Smyth and Lyons, 1844), p. xii.
15. See discussion of Orr's 'Epistle to S. Thomson' in Chapter 7.
16. 'Elegy, Composed in Island Magee', *Belfast Commercial Chronicle*, 7 January 1809, l. 82.

1 Critical Reception and Canonicity

1. C. A. Read and T. P. O'Connor (eds), *The Cabinet of Irish Literature: Selections from the Works of the Chief Poets, Orators and Prose Writers of Ireland*, 4 vols (London and New York: Blackie and Son, Samuel L. Hall, 1884; hereafter *Cabinet*), vol. 2, pp. 165–9. R. R. Madden (ed.), *Literary Remains of the United Irishmen: And Other Popular Lyrics of their Times, with an Essay on 'The Exile of Erin'* (Dublin: Duffy, 1887), pp. 63–8.
2. In this study the dates 1804 and 1817 indicate that the poem was first published in one of Orr's two volumes of verse, which appeared in 1804 and 1817 respectively.
3. Read (ed.), *Cabinet*, vol. 1, Preface, pp. v–vi, on p. v.
4. Read (ed.), *Cabinet*, vol. 2, p. 167.
5. D. J. O'Donoghue, 'Ulster Poets and Poetry', *Ulster Journal of Archaeology*, second series, 1:1 (1895), pp. 20–2, on p. 22.
6. D. Corkery, 'from: *Synge and Irish Literature* (1931)', in S. Deane (gen. ed.), *The Field Day Anthology of Irish Literature*, 5 vols (Derry: Field Day Publications, 1991–2002; hereafter *Field Day*), vol. 2, pp. 1008–13, on pp. 1011, 1010.
7. Deane (gen. ed.), *Field Day*, vol. 1, pp. 488–90.
8. D. O'Kane (ed.), *John MacCloskey's Statistical Reports of the Parishes of Ballinascreen, Kilcronaghan, Desertmartin, Banagher, Dungiven and Boveva in the County of Londonderry, 1821* (1983; Ballinascreen: Moyola Books and Braid Books, 1986), p. 83. Ivan Herbison asserts that in *Field Day* an act of 'cultural censorship' has been committed, and that the *Anthology's* exclusion of Ulster Scots 'is both studied and deliberate'. See I. Herbison, '"The Rest is Silence": Some Remarks on the Disappearance of Ulster-Scots Poetry', in J. Erskine and G. Lucy (eds), *Cultural Traditions in Northern Ireland: Varieties of Scottishness* (Belfast: Institute of Irish Studies, Queen's University Belfast, 1997; hereafter *Cultural Traditions*), pp. 129–45, on p. 141.
9. A. Carpenter (ed.), *Verse in English from Eighteenth-Century Ireland* (Cork: Cork University Press, 1998), pp. 482–9.
10. J. M. Wright (ed.), *Irish Literature 1750–1900* (Oxford: Blackwell Publishing, 2008), pp. 204–15.
11. Ibid., p. 204.
12. J. Orr, *Collected Poems* (1935; Belfast: Mullan & Son, repr. 1936). The 1936 reprint of the edition of 1935 is the primary source for quotations from Orr's poetry in this study.
13. Ibid., p. 6.
14. See also C. Baraniuk, 'Disagreeably Scottish?', *Drouth: Dialect*, 19 (Spring 2006), pp. 13–17. Some paragraphs from this article are here reproduced with the permission of the editors.
15. Hewitt offered his thesis for the degree of Master of Arts in the Faculty of Arts at Queen's University Belfast (QUB) in 1951.
16. J. Hewitt, *Rhyming Weavers and Other Country Poets of Antrim and Down* (1974; Belfast: Blackstaff Press, repr. 2004; hereafter *Rhyming Weavers*), p. 2.
17. J. C. Beckett to J. Hewitt, 17 October 1948, PRONI, The John Hewitt Papers, D 3838/3/18. With thanks to the Deputy Keeper of the Public Records, PRONI for permission to include this material.
18. Jeanne Foote to Hewitt, 3 November 1948, PRONI, The John Hewitt Papers, D 3838/3/18. With thanks to the Deputy Keeper of the Public Records, PRONI.
19. Since many of the poets were handloom weavers, Hewitt first published three articles in *Fibres, Fabrics, Cordage*, 15:7, 15:8 and 15:9 (1948), the magazine of Ulster's, then

thriving linen industry. These articles and the MA thesis of 1951 became the basis for *Rhyming Weavers*, published with an anthology of vernacular poetry in 1974 and reissued in paperback in 2004, with an introduction by Tom Paulin. Quotations are taken from the reprinted volume.
20. Hewitt, *Rhyming Weavers*, p. 94.
21. Ibid., pp. 156–61.
22. I. Herbison, 'Beyond the Rhyming Weavers', *Études Irlandaises*, 38:2 (2014), pp. 41–54, on p. 43.
23. Hewitt, *Rhyming Weavers*, p. 9.
24. A. Noble to the present author, 22 May 2013.
25. Hewitt, *Rhyming Weavers*, pp. 127, xiv, 126–7.
26. J. Hewitt, 'The Bitter Gourd', in T. Clyde (ed.), *Ancestral Voices: The Selected Prose of John Hewitt* (Belfast: Blackstaff Press, 1987), pp. 108–21, on pp. 111–12.
27. Ibid., p. 112.
28. Hewitt, *Rhyming Weavers*, p. 94.
29. Orr, *Collected Poems*, pp. 294–307.
30. Hewitt, *Rhyming Weavers*, p. 98.
31. D. H. Akenson and W. H. Crawford, *Local Poets and Social History*.
32. In the course of research for the present study two further uncollected works were located in the *Belfast Commercial Chronicle*. These will be discussed in Chapter 4.
33. Akenson and Crawford, *Local Poets and Social History*, p. 3.
34. Ibid., p. 3.
35. Ibid., p. 35.
36. J. Kerrigan, *Archipelagic English* (Oxford: Oxford University Press, 2008), p. 151.
37. Akenson and Crawford, *Local Poets and Social History*, p. 6.
38. Ibid., p. 10.
39. Ibid., p. 16.
40. Ibid., p. 33.
41. Ibid, pp. 30, 31.
42. Ibid., pp. 43–9. Newell informed on over two hundred United Irishmen. He was murdered and buried near Templepatrick in County Antrim.
43. See The Rebellion Papers, ms 620/54, fol. 111.
44. Lunney is a Royal Irish Academy linguist. She was also for a period a Board member of the Ulster Scots Agency, one of the cross-border language bodies created following the Belfast (Good Friday) Agreement of 1998.
45. Queen's University Belfast, 1981.
46. L. Lunney, 'Attitudes to Life and Death in the Poetry of James Orr, an Eighteenth-Century Ulster Weaver' (hereafter 'Attitudes to Life and Death'), *Ulster Folklife*, 31 (1985), pp. 1–12, on p. 1.
47. Ibid., p. 2.
48. The Rev. John Abernethy had preached a controversial sermon in Belfast on 9 December 1719 entitled 'Religious Obedience Founded upon Personal Persuasion', in which he stressed that the mind of God could be known only through rational enquiry and the operation of one's conscience, not through acceptance of the received opinions of others, even if those opinions had been laid down as church doctrine. See R. F. Holmes, 'The Reverend John Abernethy: The Challenge of New Light Theology to Traditional Irish Presbyterian Calvinism', in K. Herlihy (ed.), *The Religion of Irish Dissent 1650–1800* (Dublin: Four Courts Press, 1996), pp. 100–11. In 1829 Rev. William Glendy

established a non-subscribing (to all the doctrines of the Westminster Confession) congregation in Ballycarry village. Glendy is named on Orr's monument as having laid its foundation stone in Templecorran cemetery on 21 June 1831.
49. *Belfast Monthly Magazine*, 5:24 (1810), pp. 25–7. The essay is signed 'O., Ballycarry'. Lunney credits Orr as the author of further essays contributed to the *Magazine* which are signed 'O' or 'Censor'.
50. Orr wrote two poems entitled 'The Wanderer'. One appears in his 1804 volume, the other in his 1817 *Posthumous Works*.
51. Lunney, 'Attitudes to Life and Death', p. 6.
52. Ibid., p. 1.
53. L. Lunney, 'The Nature of the Ulster-Scots Language Community', in Erskine and Lucy (eds), *Cultural Traditions*, pp. 113–28, on pp. 120, 125, 121.
54. Lunney only very briefly references his poems 'The Ruin of Moscow' (1817), about the burning of the city in 1812, and 'The Dying African' (1806), about the heartbreak endured by those who suffered as a result of the slave trade. See Lunney, 'Attitudes to Life and Death', pp. 2, 3.
55. 'If you are lonely, I am equally so', Orr to Thomson, 4 January 1806. Quoted in Walker, 'Country Letters', p. 128.
56. R. Gregg, *The Scotch-Irish Dialect Boundaries in the Province of Ulster* (Ottawa: Canadian Federation for the Humanities, 1985).
57. L. Lunney, '"An' There Some Readin' to Themselves"?: Reading and Orality in Eighteenth-Century Ulster Poetry', in A. Smyth, M. Montgomery and P. Robinson (eds), *The Academic Study of Ulster-Scots: Essays for and by Robert J. Gregg* (Belfast: Ulster Folk and Transport Museum, 2006), pp. 51–9, on p. 52.
58. Orr, *Collected Poems*, pp. 122–5.
59. P. Robinson and J. R. R. Adams (eds), *The Country Rhymes of James Orr: The Bard of Ballycarry 1770–1816* (Bangor: Pretani Press, 1992, hereafter *The Country Rhymes of James Orr*).
60. Robinson published a respected study of the Ulster Plantation: *The Plantation of Ulster: British Settlement in an Irish Landscape, 1600–1670* (Dublin and New York: Gill and Macmillan, St Martin's Press, 1984). He also published *Ulster-Scots: A Grammar of the Traditional Written and Spoken Language* (1997; Belfast: Ullans Press, revised and extended 2007). He has produced original poetry and a trilogy of contemporary kailyard-style novels in Ulster Scots, beginning with *Wake the Tribe O' Dan* (Belfast: Ullans Press, 1998). His 2005 collection of poems, *Alang tha Shore* (Belfast: Ullans Press, 2005) employs Ulster Scots language and traditional Scots stanza forms.
61. Robinson and Adams (eds), *The Country Rhymes of James Orr*, p. vii.
62. Ibid., p. xii.
63. Ibid., p. xvii.
64. Ibid., p. x.
65. Edna Longley explains that Hewitt persuaded Douglas Young 'to include some Ulster Scots poetry in his anthology *Scottish Verse 1851–1951*' and that 'Tom Leonard has acknowledged the influence of Hewitt's *Rhyming Weavers* anthology on his *Radical Renfrew*'. See E. Longley, 'The Whereabouts of Literature', in G. Carruthers, D. Goldie and A. Renfrew (eds), *Beyond Scotland: New Contexts for Twentieth-Century Scottish Literature* (Amsterdam and New York: Rodopi, 2004), pp. 151–65, on pp. 159–60.
66. L. McIlvanney, *Burns the Radical: Poetry and Politics in Late Eighteenth-Century Scotland* (East Linton: Tuckwell Press, 2002; hereafter *Burns the Radical*), p. 224.

67. Ibid., p. 225.
68. Ibid., p. 223.
69. Ibid., p. 221.
70. Ibid., p. 226.
71. For Thomson's circle see *The Correspondence of Samuel Thomson (1766–1816)*, ed. J. Orr (Dublin: Four Courts Press, 2012).
72. F. J. Biggar, 'Thomas Beggs, an Antrim Poet: And the Four Towns Book Club', *Ulster Journal of Archaeology*, second series, 8 (1902), pp. 119–27, on p. 125. Biggar records that Mullan 'had spent much time as a purser aboard His Majesty's transports'.
73. McIlvanney, *Burns the Radical*, p. 227.
74. Ibid., p. 231.
75. Ibid., p. 236.
76. In his poem 'Elegy Written in the Church-Yard of Templecorran', Orr recalls his father's pride as he watched him march with other Broadisland men in 'self-raised ranks'. See Orr, *Collected Poems*, p. 131.
77. 'For ... Robert Burns ... the tradition of "Presbyterian radicalism" remained something of an academic pursuit' (McIlvanney, *Burns the Radical*, p. 239).
78. Hewitt, Akenson and Crawford, and Robinson had all to an extent drawn attention to the North-East Ulster Enlightenment.
79. McIlvanney, *Burns the Radical*, p. 228.
80. L. McIlvanney, 'Across the Narrow Sea: The Language, Literature and Politics of Ulster-Scots', in L. McIlvanney and R. Ryan (eds), *Ireland and Scotland: Culture and Society, 1700–2000* (Dublin: Four Courts Press, 2005; hereafter *Ireland and Scotland*), pp. 203–26, on pp. 214–15.
81. Ibid., p. 216.

2 Raising a Radical: Orr, Ballycarry and '98: James Orr (1770–98)

1. A. Day, P. McWilliams and N. Dobson (eds), *Ordnance Survey Memoirs of Ireland: Volume Twenty-Six, Parishes of Co. Antrim X, 1830–1, 1833–5, 1839–40* (Belfast: Queen's University of Belfast, The Institute of Irish Studies, 1994; hereafter *Memoirs*), p. 86.
2. Ibid., p. 96.
3. W. A. Montgomery, 'The First Presbyterian Congregation in Ireland', in A. Dowlin (ed.), *Ballycarry in Olden Days* (Belfast: Graham and Heslip, 1963), pp. 9–10, on p. 9.
4. Ibid., pp. 9–10. See also Rev. Dr John Nelson, 'Archaeology on our Doorstep', *Broadisland Journal* (1998), p. 9.
5. Day et al. (eds), *Memoirs*, pp. 106, 107, 103.
6. Ibid., p. 97.
7. English regiments such as the York Fencibles, and also the Monaghan Militia, raised in Co. Monaghan, were employed to quell the Rebellion in Antrim and Down.
8. The songs include 'Ballycarry Fair' (1804) in Orr, *Collected Poems*, pp. 158–9, to the tune of 'Green Grow the Rashes, O' and 'The Wanderer' (1804), p. 170, to the tune of the popular Scots song, 'Mary's Dream'.
9. J. Fullarton, quoted in W. M. Knox, *A Ballycarry Holiday* (Belfast: The Northern Whig, 1923), p. 16.
10. 'The end of all political associations is the preservation of the natural and imprescriptible rights of man; and these rights are liberty, property, security and resistance of oppression'.

T. Paine, *The Rights of Man; Being An Answer to Mr Burke's Attack on the French Revolution* (London: W. T. Sherwin, 1817), pp. 65–6.
11. McDowell, 'Sketch', in Orr, *Collected Poems*, p. 186.
12. 'Elegy Written in the Ruins of a Country School-House', in Orr, *Collected Poems*, pp. 281–4.
13. 'Elegy Written in the Church-yard of Templecorran', in Orr, *Collected Poems*, pp. 128–32.
14. W. H. Crawford, *The Handloom Weavers and the Ulster Linen Industry* (Belfast: Ulster Historical Foundation, 1994), pp. 24–35.
15. Orr, *Collected Poems*, pp. 173–80.
16. A. T. Q. Stewart describes Hope as 'a pioneer socialist before socialism had been articulated as a political creed'. *The Summer Soldiers: The 1798 Rebellion in Antrim and Down* (Belfast: Blackstaff Press, 1995), p. 61.
17. Orr, *Collected Poems*, pp. 223–5.
18. In the south they were known as the 'Whiteboys'.
19. D. H. Akenson, *Between Two Revolutions: Islandmagee, County Antrim 1798–1920* (Dublin: Meaney, 1979), pp. 12–13.
20. A. T. Q Stewart, '1798 and the Modesty of History', in *Presbyterians, the United Irishmen and 1798* (Belfast: Presbyterian Historical Society of Ireland, 2000), pp. 29–41, on p. 32.
21. The Ballycarry Presbyterian Church Session Book, PRONI, CR 3/31 fol. 2. Used with the permission of the Session of Ballycarry Old Presbyterian Church and of the Deputy Keeper of the Public Records, PRONI.
22. J. R. R. Adams, 'Reading Societies in Ulster', *Ulster Folk Life*, 26 (1980), pp. 54–65, on p. 56.
23. The paper's masthead motto: 'The public will our guide; the public good our end' proclaimed its democratic and reforming credentials.
24. G. O'Brien, 'Spirit, Impartiality and Independence: The *Northern Star* 1792–97', *Eighteenth-Century Ireland*, 13 (1998), pp. 7–23, on p. 17.
25. Orr, *Collected Poems*, pp. 27–46.
26. Dr. John Nelson, local historian and non-subscribing minister at Ballycarry, suggests a date in the 1820s while the *Memoirs* say 1831. See Day et al. (eds), *Memoirs*, p. 100.
27. Adams, 'Reading Societies in Ulster', pp. 56, 58.
28. F. J. Biggar, 'The Four Towns Book Club', *Ulster Journal of Archaeology*, 8 (1902), pp. 119–127, on p. 124.
29. S. Thomson, *Poems, on Different Subjects, Partly in the Scottish Dialect* (Belfast, 1793 [privately printed]), pp. 15, 16.
30. McDowell, 'Sketch', in Orr, *Collected Poems*, p. 187.
31. These include 'Address to Belfast' (1804); 'Ballycarry' (1806); 'To Miss Owenson' (1807), in Orr, *Collected Poems*, pp. 49–50, 223–5, 271–3.
32. Orr, *Collected Poems*, pp. 163–4, 173–80.
33. J. Hope, *The Memoirs of Jemmy Hope: An Autobiography of a Working-Class United Irishman* (Belfast: British and Irish Communist Organisation, 1972; hereafter *Memoirs of Jemmy Hope*), p. 10.
34. Volunteering originated during the American War of Independence when the government 'agreed to the creation of a citizen volunteer army, in theory independent and organized locally in companies and battalions ... it became a national pressure group for the reform of parliamentary representation'. See Stewart, *The Summer Soldiers*, pp. 9–10.
35. Hope, *Memoirs of Jemmy Hope*, pp. 14, 12.

36. Orr, *Collected Poems*, pp. 128–32.
37. Queen's University Belfast, Act of Union: Virtual Library, at http://www.actofunion.ac.uk/hansards.php?set=3, document no. 27, pp. 579–656, on pp. 579, 580 [accessed 26 February 2014].
38. Such links included seasonal transmigration of rural labourers at harvest time and the education of Ulster's Presbyterian ministers, mainly at the University of Glasgow.
39. E. W. McFarland, *Ireland and Scotland in the Age of Revolution: Planting the Green Bough* (Edinburgh: Edinburgh University Press, 1994; hereafter *Ireland and Scotland in the Age of Revolutions*), pp. 142–3.
40. *Northern Star*, 4 February 1792 and *Northern Star*, 26 June 1793.
41. Hope, *Memoirs of Jemmy Hope*, p. 13.
42. Madden, *Literary Remains*, p. 341.
43. D. Donaldson, *The Historical, Traditional and Descriptive Account of Islandmagee* (1927; Islandmagee: [n.p.], revised 1968; hereafter *Account of Islandmagee*), p. 56.
44. William Orr was alleged to have sworn members of the Monaghan Militia into the Society of United Irishmen. He was executed in 1797.
45. Knox, *A Ballycarry Holiday*, p. 12.
46. McDowell, 'Sketch', in Orr, *Collected Poems*, p. 188.
47. Donaldson, *Account of Islandmagee*, p. 60.
48. R. G. Ker to D. Ker, 16 June 1798, PRONI, The Ker Papers, D 2651/2 fol. 147. Used with the permission of the Deputy Keeper of the Public Records, PRONI.
49. Orr, *Collected Poems*, pp. 33–7.
50. Donaldson, *Account of Islandmagee*, p. 57.
51. Herdman was the innkeeper at Ballycarry.
52. Orr, *Collected Poems*, p. 34.
53. Donaldson, *Account of Islandmagee*, p. 57.
54. Orr, *Collected Poems*, p. 36.
55. Major-General Nugent was commander of the Crown forces in the north in June 1798.
56. This possibility was first suggested to the present author by Philip Robinson in a conversation of 2004.
57. McDowell, 'Sketch', in Orr, *Collected Poems*, p. 188.
58. Donaldson, *Account of Islandmagee*, p. 58.
59. R. M. Young, *Ulster in '98: Episodes and Anecdotes* (Belfast: Ward, 1893; hereafter *Ulster in '98*), p. 41.
60. Donaldson, *Account of Islandmagee*, p. 62.
61. Orr, *Collected Poems*, p. 170.
62. Quoted in Hewitt, *Rhyming Weavers*, p. 107.
63. J. Fullerton claimed in an article for the *Ulster Magazine* c. 1860, that during the winter of 1798–9 'the spirit of the Irish Government appears to have somewhat relaxed in severity, as Orr, and several others similarly implicated, in the course of the following spring, were permitted to emigrate to America at their own cost'. Quoted in J. Fullerton, 'James Orr', *Corran, Journal of the Larne and District Folklore Society*, 37 (Winter 1985–6), pp. 15–17, on p. 16.
64. Orr, *Collected Poems*, pp. 271–3.
65. The Defenders were an agrarian secret society formed partly for the protection of Catholics during the 1780s in the face of attacks by the Protestant Peep o' Day Boys. McCracken and Hope certainly cultivated links with the Defenders.
66. Young, *Ulster in '98*, p. 52.

3 The Construction of the Bard of Ballycarry: James Orr (1798–1804)

1. McDowell, 'Sketch', in Orr, *Collected Poems*, p. 188.
2. J. Tytler, *The Rising of the Sun in the West: Or the Origin and Progress of Liberty* (Salem, MA: Carleton, 1795).
3. Wolfe Tone to Thomas Russell, 7 August 1795. Quoted in D. A. Wilson, *United Irishmen, United States: Immigrant Radicals in the Early Republic* (Dublin: Four Courts Press, 1998; hereafter *United Irishmen, United States*), p. 36.
4. Orr, *Collected Poems*, pp. 135–41.
5. Ibid., pp. 167–8.
6. Samuel McCulloch, Heekenseek to his father, Carrickfergus, the *Belfast News-Letter*, Friday 29 April 1774, Centre for Irish Migration Studies Irish Emigration Database (hereafter CMSIED) 1200308.
7. The Press Ganging of 46 Passengers from the Susanna, the *Northern Star*, Friday 26 August 1796, CMSIED 9503259.
8. Extract from 'The Anecdotal Recollections of Morgan Jellett', PRONI D 2777/1, CMSIED 9406049.
9. Debates and proceedings of Congress, 1797. Quoted in Wilson, *United Irishmen, United States*, flyleaf.
10. Samuel Brown, Philadelphia to David Brown, Belfast, 23 December 1793, PRONI T 3525/1, CMSIED 9310019.
11. McDowell, 'Sketch', in Orr, *Collected Poems*, p. 188.
12. The Lockes, a family who left Ballycarry in 1798, are mentioned in 'The Passengers' (l. 30). Also see D. Hume, 'The Story of John Neilson c. 1770–1827', *Broadisland Journal*, 5 (1999), pp. 11–14.
13. M. Durey, *Transatlantic Radicals and the Early American Republic* (Lawrence, KS: Kansas University Press, 1997), pp. 248–51.
14. *Claypoole's American Daily Advertiser*, 10 October 1798, the British Library Board, M.misc.808.
15. *Philadelphia Gazette*, 10 October 1798, the British Library Board, M.misc.819. The returns for the representatives in Congress for Philadelphia and Delaware are recorded.
16. *Philadelphia Gazette*, 16 November 1798, the British Library Board, M.misc.819.
17. *Philadelphia Gazette*, 10 October 1798, the British Library Board, M.misc.819.
18. *Philadelphia Gazette*, 1 November 1798, the British Library Board, M.misc.819.
19. *Philadelphia Gazette*, 17 November 1798, the British Library Board, M.misc.819. For Orr's anti-slavery stance see, for example, 'The Persecuted Negro', the *Belfast Commercial Chronicle*, 20 May 1809.
20. Library of Congress Web Guides for researchers, at http://www.loc.gov/rr/program/bib/ourdocs/Alien.html [accessed 28 February 2014].
21. Wilson, *United Irishmen, United States*, p. 35.
22. Protest against the Alien and Sedition Laws, *Belfast News-letter*, Tuesday 21 April 1799, CMSIED 9606137.
23. McDowell, 'Sketch', in Orr, *Collected Poems*, p. 188.

24. Orr, 'Elegy', *Collected Poems*, pp. 90–1.
25. T. Moore, 'Epistle VI to Lord Viscount Forbes', *Epistles, Odes and Other Poems* (London: James Carpenter, 1806), pp. 172–82. See also 'Epistle VII to Thomas Hume Esq., M. D.', pp. 209–15, and 'Epistle VIII to the Hon. W. R. Spencer', pp. 265–71.
26. C. Teeling, *Sequel to Personal Narrative of the 'Irish Rebellion' of 1798* (Belfast: Hodgson, 1832), pp. 192–3.
27. T. Ghanem, 'When Forced Migrants Return "Home": The Psychosocial Difficulties Returnees Encounter in the Reintegration Process', Working Paper 16 (Oxford: Refugee Studies Centre, October 2003), p. 18.
28. P. Robinson and J. R. R. Adams (eds), *The Country Rhymes of Samuel Thomson, The Bard of Carngranny 1760–1816* (Bangor: Pretani Press, 1992; hereafter *The Country Rhymes of Samuel Thomson*), pp. 1–2.
29. See 'Epistle to S. Thomson', in Orr, *Collected Poems*, pp. 122–5.
30. Orr, *Poems on Various Subjects*.
31. I. McBride, 'Ulster Presbyterians and the Act of Union', in M. Brown, P. Geoghegan and J. Kelly (eds), *The Irish Act of Union, 1800: Bicentennial Essays* (Dublin: Irish Academic Press, 2003), pp. 68–83, on p. 71.
32. The Ker Papers, PRONI, D 2651/3, fol. 2. Used with the permission of the Deputy Keeper of the Public records, PRONI.
33. Akenson, *Between Two Revolutions*, p. 20. William McClelland of Islandmagee, also a 'fifty pounder', escaped to America, returned and was accepted into the Islandmagee yeomanry where he rose to the rank of lieutenant, so Orr's action was not peculiar to himself alone.
34. 'Soliloquy of Bonaparte', *Belfast Commercial Chronicle*, 14 October 1805.
35. Printed in Young, *Ulster in '98*, pp. 52–3.
36. Orr, *Collected Poems*, pp. 47–8.
37. S. Thomson, *New Poems* (Belfast: Doherty and Simms, 1799).
38. Orr, *Collected Poems*, pp. 122–5.
39. *Microscope*, 1:6 (1799), pp. 277–8, on p. 277.
40. *Microscope*, 1:4 (1799), pp. 182–4 and *Microscope*, 2:8 (1800), pp. 353–7.
41. Robinson and Adams (eds), *The Country Rhymes of Samuel Thomson*, p. 27.
42. Pieces such as Burns's 'Bruce's Address to his Troops at Bannockburn', in the *Northern Star*, 21 October 1794, had developed his perceived persona as a radical writer.
43. *Belfast News-letter*, 5 August 1800.
44. McIlvanney, *Burns the Radical*, p. 232.
45. *Belfast News-letter*, 22 August 1800.
46. *Belfast News-letter*, 6 January 1801. The poem is 'Keen Blaws the Wind o'er Donnocht Head' and it is anonymous. According to the editor of the *Newsletter* Burns is reported to have admired the poem very much, hence Currie included it in his edition.
47. For example 'I Burn, I Burn ... to Clarinda', on 25 June 1802.
48. Signed 'J. O.' and dated 'Ballycarry, September 13'.
49. H. Tynan, *Poems, by the Late Hugh Tynan of Donaghadee* (Belfast: Smyth and Lyons, 1803). John Hewitt recorded Tynan's detestation of 'the modern blasphemies' of Tom Paine. See Hewitt, *Rhyming Weavers*, pp. 83–4.
50. *Belfast News-letter*, 24 September 1802.
51. Orr, *Poems on Various Subjects*.

52. Another local gentleman, Noah Dalway Esq., and his wife subscribed. Rev. Bankhead took three volumes, but four of his daughters also took a volume each. See 'List of Subscribers', in Orr, *Collected Poems*, pp. 12–17.
53. Ibid., pp. 9–10.
54. R. Burns, *Poems, Chiefly in the Scottish Dialect* (Belfast: Magee, 1786).
55. Orr, *Collected Poems*, pp. 47–8.
56. Ibid., pp. 122–5.
57. J. Thomson, 'Winter', in *The Seasons and The Castle of Indolence*, ed. J. Sambrook (Oxford: Oxford University Press, 1972), pp. 130–62.
58. Orr, *Collected Poems*, pp. 163–4.
59. Ibid., 'Elegiac Verses to Maria of the Cottage', pp. 248–51. Orr makes a sympathetic reference to 'Desponding Wolstonecroft' (l. 56 – Orr's spelling). This suggests he had read *A Vindication of the Rights of Woman* (1792).
60. W. Wordsworth and S. T. Coleridge, Wordsworth's Enlarged Preface of 1802, in *Lyrical Ballads and Related Writings*, ed. W. Richey and D. Robinson (Boston, MA, and New York: Houghton Mifflin, 2002), pp. 390–416, on p. 404.
61. Orr, *Collected Poems*, pp. 67–9, 64–6, 165–6.
62. Ibid., pp. 78–81.
63. Ibid., pp. 160–1, 171–2.
64. Ibid., pp. 82–3, 71–3.
65. Ibid., 'Lambert, An Elegiac Ode', pp. 44–6.
66. Ibid., pp. 70, 133, 134.
67. Ibid., pp. 21–3, 24–6.
68. Ibid., pp. 92–3.
69. Ibid., pp. 142.
70. Ibid., pp. 90–1.
71. Ibid., pp. 153, 128–32.
72. Ibid.
73. Orr to Thomson, quoted in Walker, 'Country Letters', p. 128.

4 Bard in Residence: James Orr (1804–16)

1. Orr, *Collected Poems*, pp. 281–4.
2. Date of first publication.
3. 'The Deserted Village' would have been particularly interesting to Orr for the radicalism that some have found encoded within what at first appears conventional pastoral. As John Barrell explains, 'the lazy rustics of "The Deserted Village" who worked for no master, may have appeared in 1807 to have been republican', and 'by 1800 so apparently conventional a poem as "The Deserted Village" could seem to the literate poor an excitingly subversive one'. See J. Barrell, *The Dark Side of the Landscape: The Rural Poor in English Painting, 1730–1840* (Cambridge: Cambridge University Press, 1980), pp. 73, 87.
4. See D. Manson, *A New Pocket Dictionary; or English Expositor: With a Supplement ... Containing All the Uncommon Words ... To which are Prefixed, a Practical Grammar ... And a Plan for the Improvement of Children in Virtue and Learning, without the Use of the Rod. With the Present State and Practice of the Play-School in Belfast* (Belfast: Blow, 1762).
5. 'To the Public', *Belfast Monthly Magazine*, 1:1 (1808), pp. 1–6, on pp. 3–4.

6. 'Monthly Retrospect of Politics', *Belfast Monthly Magazine*, 1:4 (1808), pp. 382–95, on p. 393.
7. 'Biographical Sketch of Thomas Clarkson', *Belfast Monthly Magazine*, 8:43 (1812), pp. 114–22.
8. 'Biographical Sketch of Margaret Roper', *Belfast Monthly Magazine*, 8:47 (1812), pp. 463–7.
9. *Belfast Monthly Magazine*, 2:11 (1809), pp. 421–5.
10. Lunney, '"An' There Some Readin' to Themselves"?', p. 52.
11. *Belfast Monthly Magazine*, 4:23 (1810), pp. 444–5.
12. Holmes, 'The Reverend John Abernethy', p. 105.
13. Ibid., quoted p. 108.
14. These extended to allowing, in certain circumstances, armed resistance to an oppressive state. See McFarland, *Ireland and Scotland in the Age of Revolution*, pp. 14–6.
15. A. Holmes, *The Shaping of Ulster Presbyterian Belief and Practice 1770–1840* (Oxford: Oxford University Press, 2006; hereafter *Ulster Presbyterian Belief and Practice*), p. 109.
16. Ibid., p. 2 (quoted).
17. Ibid., p. 4.
18. Ibid., p. 5.
19. Ibid., p. 41.
20. Quoted in R. F. Holmes, 'The Reverend John Abernethy', p. 105.
21. Orr, *Collected Poems*, pp. 218–20.
22. See J. Locke, *A Letter Concerning Toleration* (Minneapolis, MN: Filiquarian Publishing LLC, 2007), p. 53. Also see J. Locke, *Two Treatises of Government*, ed. P. Laslett (1988; Cambridge: Cambridge University Press, repr. 2008), p. 357.
23. *Belfast Monthly Magazine*, 5:24 (1810), pp. 25–7.
24. Ibid., p. 26.
25. Ibid., p. 27.
26. S. Bainbridge, *British Poetry and the Revolutionary and Napoleonic Wars: Visions of Conflict* (Oxford: Oxford University Press, 2003; hereafter *British Poetry*), pp. 2–3.
27. At the wake described in 'The Irish Cottier's Death and Burial', one of the mourners is a 'soger lad' who has returned from active service. See Orr, *Collected Poems*, pp. 260–6, l. 131.
28. *Belfast Commercial Chronicle*, 1 July 1805; dated 26 June 1805. See Orr, *Collected Poems*, pp. 316–7.
29. Akenson and Crawford, *Local Poets and Social History*, p. 15.
30. Orr, *Collected Poems*, pp. 316–7.
31. Ibid., pp. 207–8.
32. *Belfast Commercial Chronicle*, 31 August 1805. See also Orr, *Collected Poems*, pp. 203–5.
33. On 11 November 1805, the *Belfast Commercial Chronicle* reported details of the 'Splendid Victory' over the French and Spanish fleets and the death of Lord Nelson, 'that noble ornament of his country'. Included was a copy of Admiral Collingwood's dispatch to the Admiralty Office, received on 6 November and sent from Cape Trafalgar on 22 October.
34. *Belfast Commercial Chronicle*, 18 November 1805.
35. M. Jay, *The Unfortunate Colonel Despard* (London: Bantam Press, 2004), pp. 238–9, pp. 294–7, 301–2.
36. *Belfast Commercial Chronicle*, 20 October 1806.
37. Holmes, *Ulster Presbyterian Belief and Practice 1770–1840*, pp. 35–6.

38. A. Peden, quoted in J. R. R. Adams, *The Printed Word and the Common Man: Popular Culture in Ulster 1700–1900* (Belfast: The Institute of Irish Studies, Queen's University Belfast, 1987), p. 88.
39. Ibid., pp. 88–9. Adams quotes extensively from S. McSkimin, *Annals of Ulster* (Belfast: [n.p.], 1849), pp. 49–50, 53–4.
40. Holmes, *Ulster Presbyterian Belief and Practice*, pp. 83, 83–4.
41. Orr, *Collected Poems*, pp. 285–7. This piece appears not to have been published in Orr's lifetime.
42. Ibid., pp. 241–3.
43. S. Owenson, *The Wild Irish Girl: A National Tale*, ed. K. Kirkpatrick (Oxford: Oxford University Press, 1999; hereafter *The Wild Irish Girl*), pp. 199–202.
44. J. C. Walker, *Historical Memoirs of the Irish Bards* (Dublin: Luke White, 1786), pp. 10, 11.
45. N. Rodgers, *Equiano and Anti-Slavery in Eighteenth-Century Belfast* (Belfast: Linen Hall Library in Association with the Ulster Historical Foundation, 2000), p. 9.
46. *Belfast Commercial Chronicle*, 12 July 1806.
47. *Belfast Commercial Chronicle*, 14 July 1806. Orr's response to the story of the huge loss of life among the slaves for sale in South Carolina was prompt indeed, appearing only two days after the original report.
48. He contributed two poems in appreciation of Owenson's work: 'To Miss Owenson', *Belfast Commercial Chronicle*, 2 May 1807, and 'The Recluse of Connaught', *Belfast Commercial Chronicle*, 20 April 1808.
49. Owenson, *The Wild Irish Girl*, pp. 197–8.
50. T. R. Robinson, *Juvenile Poems by Thomas Romney Robinson* (Belfast: Smyth and Lyons, 1806).
51. *Belfast Commercial Chronicle*, 7 September 1805.
52. Surely J. Geddis, Ballytresna, whose name appears on the subscription list to Orr's 1804 volume. See *Collected Poems*, p. 13.
53. *Belfast Commercial Chronicle*, 9 June 1806.
54. I am grateful to Dr J. Nelson, minister of the Old Presbyterian Church, Ballycarry, for this insight.
55. 'Song', in Orr, *Collected Poems*, pp. 160–1.
56. P. Mirala, *Freemasonry in Ulster 1733–1813* (Dublin: Four Courts Press, 2007), p. 247.
57. *Belfast Commercial Chronicle*, 26 March 1808.
58. 'St. John's Day', in Orr, *Collected Poems*, pp. 310–2.
59. Campbell, *Poems and Songs*, p. 41.
60. *Belfast Magazine*, 1 (1831), p. 265. Detail passed to me by Jennifer Orr.
61. Orr to Thomson, quoted in Walker, 'Country Letters', pp. 128–9. See Introduction, p. 3, n. 12.
62. Ibid., p. 129.
63. Orr to Thomson, 2 March 1804, the Thomson Correspondence, Trinity College Dublin, MS 7257, fol. 60. Used by permission of the Board of Trinity College Dublin.
64. J. Gray, 'Burns and his Visitors from Ulster: From Adulation to Disaccord' (hereafter 'Burns and his Visitors from Ulster'), *Studies in Scottish Literature*, 33:4 (2004), pp. 320–33, on p. 330.
65. 'Epistle to James Orr of Ballycarry, a Brother Poet', in J. Dickey, *Poems on Various Subjects* (Belfast: Berwick, 1818), pp. 83–8.

66. Dickey may be voicing the opinion that the Act of Union failed to deliver a better Ireland.
67. Orr, *Collected Poems*, pp. 193–5.
68. 'Resolution and Independence', in J. Butt (ed.), *Wordsworth: Selected Poetry and Prose* (Oxford: Oxford University Press, 1973), pp. 145–50, ll. 48–9.
69. K. R. Johnston, 'The Unromantic Lives of Others: The Lost Generation of the 1790s', *Wordsworth Circle*, 40:2–3 (2009), pp. 67–72, on pp. 68, 67.
70. *Belfast News-letter*, 13 August 1813. See Orr, *Collected Poems*, pp. 230–2.
71. Dickey, *Poems on Various Subjects*, pp. 90–2.

5 Rude Scotch Rhymer? Scottish Enlightenment Influences on James Orr

1. 'To subvert the tyranny of our execrable government, to break the connection with England ... and to assert the independence of my country – these were my objects. To unite the whole people of Ireland ... and to substitute the common name of Irishman in place of the denominations of Protestant, Catholic and Dissenter – these were my means'. Quoted in A. T. Q. Stewart, *A Deeper Silence: The Hidden Origins of the United Irish Movement* (London: Faber and Faber, 1993), p. 152.
2. McBride, 'Ulster Presbyterians and the Passing of the Act of Union', p. 82.
3. I. Herbison, *Language, Literature and Cultural Identity* (Ballymena: Dunclug Press, 1989), p. 6.
4. N. Vance, *Irish Literature: A Social History – Tradition, Identity and Difference* (Oxford: Basil Blackwell, 1990), p. 77.
5. *Burns the Radical*, pp. 229–30.
6. Orr had read Blair's lectures and must have noted Blair's reference to Hutcheson's *Inquiry into the Original of our Ideas of Beauty and Virtue* (F. Hutcheson, *An Inquiry into the Original of Our Ideas of Beauty and Virtue* (Glasgow: Foulis, 1772; hereafter *Inquiry*)). See H. Blair, *Lectures on Rhetoric and Belles Lettres*, 3 vols (London: Strahan and Cadell, 1798; hereafter *Lectures*), vol. 1:5, pp. 91–110, on p. 91 .
7. Hutcheson, *Inquiry*, p. 109.
8. Ibid., pp. 117–18.
9. Ibid., p. 161.
10. Ibid., pp. 170, 178.
11. Ibid., p. 168.
12. D. Hume, 'On Suicide', in D. Hume, *Essays on Suicide and the Immortality of the Soul* (Basil: [n.p.], 1799), pp. 3–7. Hume's views were so controversial that they were for a time suppressed, but an edition of his essay 'On Suicide' did appear in 1783. A new edition was printed in 1799.
13. Orr had certainly read Home's *Douglas* which had scandalized the conservative wing of the Kirk for, among other things, including a suicide. See 'The Vision – An Elegy' (1817), Orr, *Collected Poems*, p. 107.
14. Ibid., pp. 24–6.
15. Ibid., pp. 199–202.
16. *The Poems and Songs of Robert Burns*, ed. J. Kinsley, 3 vols (Oxford: Clarendon Press, 1968; hereafter *Poems and Songs*), vol. 1, pp. 116–19.

17. H. Blair, 'On the Influence of Religion upon Adversity', in *Sermons by Hugh Blair*, 7th edn (Dublin: Hallhead, 1779; hereafter *Sermons*), pp. 25–57, on pp. 29, 34.
18. Blair, 'On the Union of Piety and Morality', in *Sermons*, pp. 1–24, on p. 20.
19. Orr, *Collected Poems*, p. 114–15.
20. 'Elegy on the Death of Mr Robert Burns, the Ayrshire Poet', in Orr, *Collected Poems*, p. 29.
21. Blair, *Lectures*, vol. 1:3, pp. 41–64, on p. 43.
22. Ibid., vol. 2:18, pp. 1–28, on p. 3.
23. H. Blair, *A Critical Dissertation on the Poems of Ossian, the Son of Fingal* (London: Becket and De Hondt, 1763), p. 2.
24. Blair, *Lectures*, vol. 3:39, pp. 107–136, on p. 128.
25. L. McIlvanney, 'Burns, Blair and the Invention of Scottish Literature', *Eighteenth Century Life*, 29:2 (2005), pp. 25–46, on p. 26.
26. Ibid., p. 33.
27. P. Robinson, *Ulster-Scots: A Grammar of the Traditional Written and Spoken Language* (Belfast: Ullans Press, 2007), pp. 32–3.
28. F. Stafford, *Starting Lines in Scottish, English and Irish Poetry: From Burns to Heaney* (Oxford: Oxford University Press, 2000; hereafter *Starting Lines*), p. 53.
29. Ibid., p. 65. Also see p. 50.
30. N. Leask, 'Burns, Wordsworth and the Politics of Vernacular Poetry', in P. de Bolla, N. Leask and D. Simpson (eds), *Land, Nation and Culture: Thinking the Republic of Taste* (Basingstoke: Palgrave, 2005), pp. 202–22, on p. 204.
31. Orr, *Collected Poems*, pp. 234–6.
32. James Magee of Belfast printed the play in 1757, including the preface which recorded details of Kirk disapproval of the theatre, and of the Rev. Home for having written a play.
33. In his 'Elegy' (1804), in *Collected Poems*, pp. 90–1, Orr reflects that in the course of his life he has gained 'A little eminence, uprais'd by taste' (l. 21).
34. Blair, *A Critical Dissertation on the Poems of Ossian, the Son of Fingal* ,p . 2.
35. Blair, *Lectures*, vol. 2:18, pp. 1–28, on p. 25.
36. A reference to Blair's literary lectures.
37. Blair, 'Gentleness', in *Sermons*, pp. 145–72, on pp. 145, 147–8, 150.
38. See 'To the Potatoe' (1804), to be discussed in Chapter 6.
39. Orr, *Collected Poems*, pp. 107–10.
40. L. Lunney, 'Ulster Attitudes to Scottishness', in I. S. Wood (ed.), *Scotland and Ulster* (Edinburgh: Mercat Press, 1994), pp. 56–70, on pp. 59–60.
41. Burns, *Poems and Songs*, vol. 1, pp. 103–13.
42. *The Works of Allan Ramsay*, 6 vols (Edinburgh: Scottish Text Society, 1951–74), vol. 3, ed. A. M. Kinghorn and A. Law, pp. 80–95.
43. Orr, *Collected Poems*, pp. 107–10. Home's line reads 'And told the secrets of the world unknown', but Orr is signalling that he has a message concerning the future.
44. W. Robertson, *The History of Scotland during the Reigns of Queen Mary and of King James VI.*, 7th edn, 2 vols (Dublin: Printed for United Company of Booksellers, 1775), vol. 1:2, p. 77.
45. Ibid., vol. 2:7, p. 10.
46. Ibid., p. 35.
47. 'Elegy, Composed by Night Under the Gallows', *Belfast Commercial Chronicle*, 19 October 1805. This poem makes very clear Orr's abhorrence of extreme forms of state punishment.

48. R. D. S. Jack, 'Introduction', in C. Craig (ed.), *The History of Scottish Literature*, 4 vols (Aberdeen: Aberdeen University Press, 1988), vol. 1, p. 7.
49. Orr, 'Address to Mr A., Carrickfergus: Written After a Long Illness', *Collected Poems*, pp. 38–9.
50. 'The Cotter's Saturday Night' (1785–6), 'A *virtuous populace* may rise the while, / And stand a wall of fire, around their much-lov'd ISLE' (ll. 179–80), in Burns, *Poems and Songs*, vol. 1, pp. 145–52.
51. 'The public will our guide; the public good our end'.
52. Acts 1:7.
53. I. McBride, '"When Ulster Joined Ireland": Anti-Popery, Presbyterian Radicalism and Irish Republicanism in the 1790s', *Oxford Journals: Past and Present*, 157:1 (1997), pp. 53–93, on pp. 93, 86, 64–5.
54. Orr, *Collected Poems*, pp. 271–3.
55. G. Carruthers, 'The Return of Alexander Geddes', *Drouth: Bigotry*, 12 (Summer 2004), pp. 22–4, on p. 22.
56. A. Geddes, *Ode to the Honourable Thomas Pelham, Esq.* (London: [Printed for J. Johnston], 1795).
57. A. Geddes, *A Modest Apology for the Roman Catholics of Great Britain: Addressed to All Moderate Protestants; Particularly to the Members of Both Houses of Parliament* (London: [Sold by Faulder and Brooker], 1800), pp. 59–62.
58. Lunney, '"An' There Some Readin' to Themselves"?', p. 54.
59. 'Censor', 'On the Catholic Question', *Belfast Monthly Magazine*, 1:3 (1808), p. 189.
60. 'Criticus' to the editor, *Belfast Monthly Magazine*, 1:5 (1808), pp. 354–6.
61. 'Censor' to the editor, *Belfast Monthly Magazine*, 2:6 (1809), pp. 11–12.
62. A clear reference to Abernethy's controversial New Light sermon of 1719.
63. See 'An Account of the Life and Writings of the Late Dr Geddes', *Belfast Monthly Magazine*, 3:10 (1809), pp. 443–51.

6 Men of Independent Mind: Ulster Scots Poets and the Scottish Tradition

1. Craig (ed.), *The History of Scottish Literature*, vol. 2, Introduction, p. 5.
2. This chapter employs material from the following two essays: C. Baraniuk, 'Setting his own Standard: James Orr's Employment of a Traditional Stanza Form', *Journal of Irish and Scottish Studies*, 1:1 (2007), pp. 73–86, and C. Baraniuk, 'No Bardolatry Here: The Independence of the Ulster-Scots Poetic Tradition', in F. Ferguson and A. Holmes (eds), *Revising Robert Burns and Ulster: Literature, Religion and Politics c. 1770–1920* (Dublin: Four Courts Press, 2009), pp. 64–82. It also refers to ideas first briefly discussed in C. Baraniuk, 'The Leid, the Pratoe and the Buik: Northern Cultural Markers in the Works of James Orr', in J. P. Byrne et al. (eds), *Affecting Irishness: Negotiating Cultural Identity within and beyond the Nation* (Oxford: Peter Lang, 2009), pp. 103–20. All material has been reproduced with the permission of the respective editors and publishers.
3. McIlvanney, *Burns the Radical*, p. 223.
4. Ibid., p. 225.
5. J. Gamble, *A View of Society and Manners in the North of Ireland in the Summer and Autumn of 1812* (London: Craddock and Jay, 1813), p. 86.
6. Adams, *The Printed Word and the Common Man*, pp. 175–81.

7. Burns's *Poems, Chiefly in the Scottish Dialect* was very swiftly reprinted in Belfast by James Magee (1787), after its appearance in Scotland in 1786.
8. 'Tit for Tat; or The Rater Rated. A New Song, in Way of Dialogue, between a Laggen Farmer and his Wife', in F. Ferguson (ed.), *Ulster-Scots Writing: An Anthology* (Dublin: Four Courts Press, 2008), pp. 99–100.
9. M. Griffin and B. MacSuibhne, 'Da's Boat; or, Can the Submarine Speak? *A Voyage to O'Brazeel* (1752) and other glimpses of the Irish Atlantis', *Field Day Review*, 2 (2006), pp. 111–27, on p. 115.
10. Campbell, *Poems and Songs*, pp. 78–80.
11. Robert Fergusson's 'Caller Oysters' (1772) and Burns's 'To a Haggis' (1786) also sit within this tradition.
12. Campbell, *Poems and Songs*, pp. 61–6.
13. Mentioned as Arthur Young's 'celebrated *Tour in Ireland*' in the *Northern Star*, 11 February 1792.
14. C. Maxwell (ed.), *A Tour in Ireland by Arthur Young* (Belfast: Blackstaff Press, 1983), p. 185.
15. P. Robinson and J. R. R. Adams (eds), *The Country Rhymes of Hugh Porter, the Bard of Moneyslane c. 1780* (Bangor: Ullans Press), pp. ix–xiv.
16. 'The Strolling Piper', in F. Boyle, *Miscellaneous Poems* (Belfast: Lyons, 1811), pp. 32–7.
17. 'An Old Story', ibid., pp. 97–101.
18. Ibid., pp. 28–30.
19. McIlvanney, *Burns the Radical*, p. 226, n. 31.
20. *Northern Star*, 17 June 1793.
21. Mullan to Thomson, 20 May 1796, Trinity College Dublin, the Thomson Correspondence, MS 7257, fol. 2. Used by permission of the Board of Trinity College Dublin.
22. Mullan to Thomson, 29 September 1796, Trinity College Dublin, the Thomson Correspondence, MS 7257, fol. 4. Used by permission of the Board of Trinity College Dublin.
23. 'The Farmer Sowing', *Belfast Commercial Chronicle*, 8 March 1809.
24. Robinson and Adams (eds), *The Country Rhymes of Samuel Thomson*, pp. 62–3.
25. F. Ferguson, 'Irish on the Outside, Scottish Within: The Anthology of Ulster-Scots Literature', unpublished seminar paper, Institute of Irish Studies, Queen's University Belfast, 29 March 2006.
26. 'Epistle to S. Thomson of Carngranny, A Brother Poet', in Orr, *Collected Poems*, pp. 122–5.
27. R. D. S. Jack (ed.), *A Choice of Scottish Verse 1560–1660* (Edinburgh: Hodder and Stoughton, 1978), pp. 136–47.
28. A. M. Kinghorn and A. Law (eds), *Poems by Allan Ramsay and Robert Fergusson* (Edinburgh and London: Scottish Academic Press, 1974), pp. 3–6.
29. Ibid., pp. 121–3.
30. Burns, *Poems and Songs*, vol. 1, pp. 74–8.
31. Kinghorn and Law (eds), *Poems by Allan Ramsay and Robert Fergusson*, pp. 13–17.
32. D. Low, *Robert Burns* (Edinburgh: Scottish Academic Press, 1986), pp. 47, 51.
33. McIlvanney, *Burns the Radical*, p. 103.
34. Ibid., p. 102.
35. Burns, *Poems and Songs*, vol. 1, pp. 61–3.
36. Ibid., pp. 99–100.
37. Ibid., pp. 221–2.
38. 'Scotch Drink' (1785–6), ibid., pp. 173–6.

39. Ibid. pp. 103–13.
40. Lunney, 'The Nature of the Ulster-Scots Language Community', p. 120.
41. Orr, *Collected Poems*, pp. 60–3.
42. 'Epistle to Mr N. P., Oldmill' (1804), in Orr, *Collected Poems*, pp. 78–81.
43. Orr, *Collected Poems*, pp. 71–3.
44. Burns, *Poems and Songs*, vol. 1, pp. 127–8.
45. This is a theme to which he would return in 'The Irish Cottier's Death and Burial'. It is related to the issue of tenant rights in Ulster, where a widow and her family had the right to remain as tenants in an estate cottage as long as she could afford the rent.
46. G. Carruthers, *Robert Burns* (Tavistock: Northcote House Publishers, 2006), pp. 52–3.
47. Hewitt, *Rhyming Weavers*, pp. 155–6.
48. Orr, *Collected Poems*, pp. 56–9.
49. Orr contemptuously identifies the Anglican ruling class by linking them with 'prelates', or bishops.
50. Mashed potatoes with green vegetables, in this case 'kail' (cabbage) mixed in.
51. The following explanation was kindly provided by Anne Smyth, Ulster Folk and Transport Museum. 'The reference is to a *sowan-sieve*. Sowans is a particularly gruesome item of Ulster diet (its other name being *flummery*). It was made by pouring boiling water over the crushed husks of grain and steeping them in a tub for a week or so until they go sour, then boiling the strained mixture like porridge. It has a jelly-like consistency. The Orr reference is to the sieve through which this mixture was strained. I doubt if it was a sieve as we know it that was meant, but rather a riddle type of implement. I am assuming that there was a residual amount of this jelly in the husks which, mixed with the potato starch, produced a more durable product for use on clothes'. Email to the present writer of 25 March 2014.
52. S. Heaney, *Selected Poems 1965–75* (London: Faber and Faber, 1980), pp. 21–3.
53. The leaders of the United Irish movement had believed that 'Ireland's natural resources were greater than Britain's, and she would soon stand on her own feet'. See T. Pakenham, *The Year of Liberty: The Story of the Great Irish Rebellion of 1798* (London: Abacus, 2007), p. 290.
54. J. C. Pellicer, 'The Georgic', in C. Gerrard (ed.), *A Companion to Eighteenth-Century Poetry* (Oxford: Blackwell Publishing, 2006), pp. 403–16, on pp. 403, 404, 406, 414.
55. Orr, a friend of schoolmaster Samuel Thomson who knew Latin, would almost certainly have heard Thomson discuss Virgil's poetry. Since Orr was also exceptionally well-read in eighteenth-century poetry he was familiar with much British georgic or georgic-influenced verse, e.g. Pope's 'Windsor Forest' (1713), and Thomson's 'The Seasons' (1726–44).
56. Pellicer, 'The Georgic', p. 403.
57. McIlvanney, *Burns the Radical*, p. 227.
58. Burns, *Poems and Songs*, vol. 1, pp. 310–12.
59. Ibid., pp. 173–6.
60. 'Tam o' Shanter' (1790), Burns, *Poems and Songs*, vol. 2, pp. 557–64.
61. The full entry for 'claes' in the *Dictionary of the Scots Language* (*DSL*) cites a range of texts from the sixteenth and early seventeenth centuries in which the form 'clais' is employed. See http://www.dsl.ac.uk [accessed 21 June 2014]. Burns's glossary to his *Poems Chiefly in the Scottish Dialect* (1786), reprinted in Belfast in 1787 by James Magee, gives the forms 'claes' and 'claise'. The extended two-volume 1793 reprint of Burns's *Poems Chiefly in the Scottish Dialect*, also produced by Magee, includes 'Address to the Deil' (1785–6).

Orr renders the latter word 'deel' in his 'Letter to Mr A., Carrickfergus' (1804), *Collected Poems*, pp. 38–9, l. 29. Orr's texts clearly show that he was not imitating the spelling he had observed in Burns's works.
62. Burns, *Poems and Songs*, vol. 1, pp. 185–91.
63. C. Macafee (ed.), *A Concise Ulster Dictionary* (Oxford: Oxford University Press, 1996), p. 260. The forms 'praitie' and 'pratie' are given as Hiberno-English.
64. Ibid., p. 34.
65. *DSL*.
66. Ibid.
67. E. McFarland notes that 'in Ireland ... pedlars and packmen were ... employed directly to disseminate radical literature'. See *Ireland and Scotland in the Age of Revolution*, p. 143.
68. *DSL* cites 'wisp' employed figuratively. The phrase 'let out or louse the, or one's, wisp' means, 'divulge a secret, let the cat out of the bag, spill the beans'.
69. Robinson and Adams (eds), *The Country Rhymes of Samuel Thomson*, pp. 1–2.
70. I am grateful to Dr Philip Robinson, a native of the Ballycarry area where Orr lived and familiar with many traditions concerning him, for alerting me in the general sense to Orr's occasional employment of coded references to the Rebellion in his work. The particular interpretations discussed above, however, are my own.
71. A. Young, *A Tour in Ireland* (Belfast: Blackstaff Press, 1983), pp. 185–6.
72. Dickey, *Poems on Various Subjects*, pp. 93–100.
73. W. Cobbett, *Cottage Economy* (London: Peter Davis, 1926), pp. 49–52.
74. See, for example, 'The Enigma', in J. Killen (ed.), *The Famine Decade: Contemporary Accounts 1841–1851* (Belfast: Blackstaff Press, 1995), pp. 187–8.

7 The Rebel Experience

1. A substantial section of this chapter was first published as C. Baraniuk, 'James Orr: Ulster-Scot and Poet of the 1798 Rebellion', *Scottish Studies Review*, 6:1 (2005), pp. 22–32. The material is reproduced here with the permission of the editor of the journal, now the *Scottish Literary Review*.
2. As a narrative the poems fall into the following order: 'A Prayer': the prelude to battle'; 'Donegore Hill': rout and betrayal; 'The Wanderer': on the run in Ulster; 'The Passengers': exiled to America; 'Epistle to S. Thomson of Carngranny': restoration and response to the Union. To facilitate discussion of genre they will be considered in a slightly different order here.
3. E. Said, *Culture and Imperialism* (London: Vintage, 1994), p. xiii.
4. Orr, *Collected Poems*, pp. 47–8.
5. In his novel *Old Mortality*, a tale of the Covenanters, Walter Scott confirms that the title 'Wanderer' was often conferred on members of the Covenanting sect who had to go into hiding to escape state persecution. See W. Scott, *Old Mortality*, ed. A. Calder (1975; Harmondsworth: Penguin, 1985), p. 108.
6. The poet Thomas Beggs, Orr's relative, refers to Orr's period in hiding 'Where Slemish lifts his barren head', and confirms that 'Beneath the herdsman's hearth-less shed, / The smile of mercy met him there'. Quoted in Hewitt, *Rhyming Weavers*, p. 107.
7. Melody sourced in J. Johnson, *Scots Musical Museum* (Edinburgh: J. Johnson, 1787–1803), pp. 38–9. See Akenson and Crawford, *Local Poets and Social History*, p. 31.
8. Orr, *Collected Poems*, p. 170.
9. 'A Ramble Taken in 1810', *Belfast Monthly Magazine*, 8:45 (1812), pp. 263–6, on p. 265.

10. A. H. MacLaine (ed.), *The Christis Kirk Tradition: Scots Poems of Folk Festivity* (Glasgow: Association for Scottish Literary Studies, 1996), pp. v–vi.
11. *Northern Star*, 1 September 1792.
12. The discussion of Orr's 'The Passengers' and 'Song Composed on the Banks of Newfoundland' draws substantially on the essay by C. Baraniuk, 'Christ's Kirk on the Green Isle: Tragedy Commemorated in Comic Form', in M.-C. Considère-Charon et al. (eds), *The Irish Celebrating: Festive and Tragic Overtones* (Newcastle: Cambridge Scholars Publishing, 2008), pp. 118–32. Material from the essay has been reproduced here with permission.
13. Orr, *Collected Poems*, pp. 135–41.
14. See Chapter 3, pp. 43–4, for discussion of 'blacks'.
15. J. M. Wright, 'Atlantic Exile and the Stateless Citizen in Irish Romanticism', *Wordsworth Circle*, 40:4 (2009), pp. 36-44, on p. 40.
16. Ibid., p. 41.
17. This ritual was common in Dissenter and in Catholic communities. See, for example, L. O'Flaherty, 'Going into Exile', *Modern Irish Short Stories* (Oxford: Oxford University Press, 1977), pp. 133–46, on p. 145.
18. C. Whyte, 'Bakhtin at Christ's Kirk Part I: Carnival and the Scottish Renaissance', *Studies in Scottish Literature*, 28 (1993), pp. 178–203, on p. 179.
19. Ibid., quoted on p. 179.
20. The title, the first person narrator and Orr's note to the text indicating that it was written on the Banks of Newfoundland, suggest that Orr was among those 'Exiles' in 'The Passengers' who grieved at the first sight of the new land.
21. Hewitt, *Rhyming Weavers*, p. 90.
22. Ibid., p. 94.
23. 'Across the Narrow Sea', in McIlvanney and Ryan (eds), *Ireland and Scotland*, pp. 217–9.
24. Burns, *Poems and Songs*, pp. 425–7. I am grateful to Andrew Noble for drawing my attention to this poem.
25. 'Orr'. See discussion in Chapter 2, p. 39.
26. S. Dornan, 'Beyond the Milesian Pale: The Poetry of James Orr', *Eighteenth-Century Ireland*, 20 (2005), pp. 140–55, on p. 150.
27. Ibid.
28. Taxation is a potent subject, in any case. 'No taxation without representation' was the cry of the American revolutionaries, so the reference to taxation functions as a signifier of that international conflict with the British, not merely as a reminder of a local difficulty.
29. The *Cherrie and the Slae* stanza has a complex structure. Its fourteen lines fall into three sections – the first of six lines, followed by two sections of four lines each. The second of the four line sections, the bobwheel, consists of alternating dimeters and trimeters.
30. Burns, *Poems and Songs*, vol. 1, pp. 65–9.
31. F. Stafford, 'A Centre in the Breast: Robert Burns and Happiness', Centre for Robert Burns Studies, University of Glasgow, Inaugural Lecture, 21 July 2007.
32. The concluding lines of 'The Poet's Wish' offer the following advice: 'Mair speer na, and fear na, / But set thy Mind to rest, / Aspire ay still high'r ay, / And always hope the best' (ll. 53–6). *The Works of Allan Ramsay*, 6 vols (Edinburgh: The Scottish Text Society, 1951), vol. 1, ed. B. Martin and J. W. Oliver, pp. 243–4.
33. First printed 1597. See D. Gifford, S. Dunnigan and A. MacGillivray (eds), *Scottish Literature in English and Scots* (Edinburgh: Edinburgh University Press, 2002), p. 49.
34. Thomson, *Poems, on Different Subjects*, pp. 93–7.

35. 'A voice says, "Cry out." And I said, "What shall I cry? All men are like grass, and all their glory is like the flowers of the field."' Isaiah 40:6.
36. Thomson was a skilled flautist.
37. Orr, *Collected Poems*, pp. 122–6.
38. Stafford, 'A Centre in the Breast'.
39. Jack (ed.), *A Choice of Scottish Verse 1560–1600*, pp. 46–91.
40. Adams, *The Printed Word and the Common Man*, p. 72.
41. This is the only vernacular poem in Orr's extant *oeuvre* which employs this stanza, making the choice of it here all the more significant.
42. Adams, *The Printed Word and the Common Man*, p. 38. The Roughfort book club, founded in 1768, was one of four which amalgamated to become the Four Towns Book Club.

8 The Robert Burns of Ulster?

1. This chapter brings together material, in part revised and developed, from two essays: C. Baraniuk, 'An Antidote to the Burns Idyll: James Orr's "The Irish Cottier's Death and Burial"', *Burns Chronicle* (Spring 2006), pp. 6–11 and C. Baraniuk, 'Ulster's Burns? James Orr, the Bard of Ballycarry', *Review of Scottish Culture*, 19 (2007), pp. 54–62. Permission has been granted by the editors for the material to be reproduced here.
2. The piece was published in Orr's *Poems on Various Subjects* of 1804, but may have been composed close to the time of Burns's demise.
3. Orr, *Collected Poems*, pp. 29–32.
4. Ibid., pp. 9–10.
5. Burns, *Poems and Songs*, vol. 2, pp. 512–3.
6. Luke Mullan to Samuel Thomson, 20 May 1796, Trinity College Dublin, the Thomson Correspondence, MS 7257, fol. 2. Used by permission of the Board of Trinity College Dublin.
7. 1 August 1796, *Belfast News-letter*.
8. Burns, *Poems and Songs*, vol. 1, pp. 168–72; vol. 2, pp. 557–64; vol. 1, pp. 152–63, 494–8.
9. 'Green Grow the Rashes' (1784), in Burns, *Poems and Songs*, vol. 1, pp. 59–60.
10. Orr, *Collected Poems*, pp. 155–7.
11. Orr to Thomson, quoted in Walker, 'Country Letters', p. 128.
12. Burns, *Poems and Songs*, vol. 1, pp. 173–6.
13. Once Rebellion had begun, as E. McFarland has shown, 'Scots actively participated in the events of the summer of 1798, but rather than as radical brothers in arms, they served as members of His Majesty's forces charged with extinguishing all manifestations of rebellion'. *Ireland and Scotland in the Age of Revolution*, pp. 193–4.
14. Burns, *Poems and Songs*, vol. 2, pp. 764–6.
15. McIlvanney, *Burns the Radical*, p. 237.
16. Gray, 'Burns and his Visitors from Ulster', p. 329.
17. 'Elegy, Composed in Islandmagee, at the Tomb of an Ancient Chief', 7 January 1809, *Belfast Commercial Chronicle*.
18. Orr, *Collected Works*, pp. 260–6.
19. Burns, *Poems and Songs*, vol. 1, p. 281.
20. Ibid., pp. 145–52.
21. Carruthers, *Robert Burns*, p. 32.

22. N. Leask, 'The Cottage Leaves the Palace Far Behind', Paper for the Burns International Conference, Mitchell Library, Glasgow, 21 January 2006.
23. Kinghorn and Law (eds), *Poems by Allan Ramsay and Robert Fergusson*, pp. 161–4.
24. A cotter was a tenant cottager who also rented a small patch of land.
25. Carruthers, *Robert Burns*, p. 33.
26. Leask, 'The Cottage Leaves the Palace Far Behind'.
27. See, for example, Ephesians 6:5.
28. In discussing the 'ruined maid sequence', Andrew Noble suggests Burns may have realized 'that some of the poem was complicit with values he detested'. See A. Noble and P. Scott Hogg (eds), *The Canongate Burns* (Edinburgh: Canongate Books, 2003 [revised]), p. 93.
29. *Belfast Penny Journal*, 18 October 1845.
30. The Westminster Shorter Catechism, produced by Scottish and English theologians during the 1640s and designed to teach the fundamentals of Presbyterian doctrine.
31. Orr, *Collected Works*, pp. 260–6.
32. On 11 February 1792 the *Northern Star* referred thus to the text and its author: 'The celebrated Arthur Young whose *Tour in Ireland* was published c. twelve years ago'. Young supplied a detailed described of the Cottier system in Ireland. See Maxwell (ed.), *A Tour in Ireland*, pp. 183, 233.
33. In his maiden speech of 13 May 1805 Grattan put the case for emancipation and did so again in debates in the period 1808–12.
34. See also Orr's 'The Recluse of Connaught', 20 April 1808, the *Belfast Commercial Chronicle*. He addressed this to Sydney Owenson after reading her *Patriotic Sketches*. S. Owenson, *Patriotic Sketches of Ireland, Written in Connaught* (London: Richard Philips, 1807).
35. See discussion in Chapter 4, p. 74.
36. Orr's contemporary, the Larne-born novelist James McHenry, voiced his own anger concerning Owenson's characterization of the Ulster Scots in *The Wild Irish Girl*. See J. McHenry, *O' Halloran, or The Insurgent Chief: A Tale of the United Irishmen (Belfast: John Henderson, 1844), p. 13*.
37. J. Orr, 'Apostrophe of the Shade of Brian Boromhu, to his Harp', *Belfast Monthly Magazine*, 3:17 (1809), p. 468.
38. Owenson, *Patriotic Sketches, Written in Connaught*, pp. 98–9, 102–4.
39. Orr, *Collected Poems*, pp. 260–6.
40. Reflective surfaces were covered as it was feared these might cause the spirit of the departed to remain in the house.
41. Owenson, *The Wild Irish Girl*, p. 184.
42. Ibid., p. 182.
43. In Ulster, the widow and her family had the right to retain tenancy as long as the rent was paid. This was often impracticable.
44. P. Zenzinger, 'Low Life Primitivism and Honest Poverty: A Socio-Cultural Reading of Ramsay and Burns', *Studies in Scottish Literature*, 30 (1998), pp. 43–58, on p. 52.
45. 'Robert Aiken (1739–1807), eldest son of a sea-captain of Ayr and grandson of James Dalrymple of Orangefield; solicitor and surveyor of taxes in Ayr. He first met Burns c. 1783, and his early patronage is frequently acknowledged in the poet's letters.' See Burns, *Poems and Songs*, vol. 3, p. 1113, n. 1.
46. Orr, *Collected Poems*, pp. 173–80.

47. Wesley made several preaching tours in Ireland. His visits included Carrickfergus, near Ballycarry, where his preaching deeply affected many, 'rich as well as poor'. *The Journal of the Rev. John Wesley*, 4 vols (London: Everyman: 1938), vol. 3, p. 364.
48. Ibid., vol. 1, p. 102, point 14.
49. E. P. Thompson, *The Making of the English Working Class* (London: Gollancz, 1980), pp. 402–4.
50. Wesley's biographer Stephen Tomkins quotes Wesley as saying in August 1770, 'We have leaned too much toward Calvinism ... Whoever desires to find favour with God should "cease from evil, and learn to do well".' See S. Tomkins, *John Wesley: A Biography* (Oxford: Lion Publishing, 2003), p. 171.
51. Orr, *Collected Poems*, pp. 90–1.
52. Andrew Noble raised this issue in a communication with the present writer of 17 June 2013.
53. See, for example, R. Wells, 'English Society and Revolutionary Politics in the 1790s: The Case for Insurrection', in M. Philp (ed.), *The French Revolution and British Popular Politics* (Cambridge: Cambridge University Press, 2004), pp. 188–225.
54. Akenson and Crawford, *Local Poets and Social History*, p. 14.
55. These groups included the notorious Thomas Archer in the neighbourhood of Ballymena. As noted in Chapter 3, Richard G. Ker expressed concern about 'banditti' in the neighbourhood of Ballycarry in the early 1800s.
56. W. M. D. Falconer, 'The Working Tools of the Craft' (ch. 31), in W. M. D. Falconer, *The Square and Compasses: In Search of Freemasonry* (2002, revised), at http://www.freemasons-freemasonry.com/don5.html [accessed 18 February 2014].
57. Matthew 10:16.
58. So I because of all the buried men / in Ulster clay, because of rock and glen / and mist and cloud and quality of air / as native in my thought as any here ... (ll. 13–16). From J. Hewitt, 'Once Alien Here', in M. Longley and F. Ormsby (eds), *John Hewitt Selected Poems* (Belfast: Blackstaff Press, 2007), p. 8.

9 Enlightened Romantic

1. See, for example, M. Pittock, *Scottish and Irish Romanticism* (Oxford: Oxford University Press, 2008), p. 12; J. Kirk, A. Noble and M. Brown (eds), *United Islands? The Languages of Resistance* (London: Pickering & Chatto, 2012); J. Kirk, M. Brown and A. Noble (eds), *Cultures of Radicalism in Britain and Ireland* (London: Pickering & Chatto, 2013).
2. S. Chaplin and J. Faflak, 'Defining Romanticism', in S. Chaplin and J. Faflak (eds), *The Romanticism Handbook* (London: Continuum International Publishing, 2011), pp. xiii–xxxiii, on p. xiii.
3. Linde Lunney, for example, entitled a major article on Orr 'Attitudes to Life and Death in the Poetry of James Orr, an Eighteenth-Century Ulster Weaver'. In *Ulster Folklife*, 31 (1985), pp. 1–12.
4. Chaplin and Faflak, 'Defining Romanticism', p. xviii.
5. K. Trumpener, *Bardic Nationalism: The Romantic Novel and the British Empire* (Princeton, NJ: Princeton University Press, 1997; hereafter *Bardic Nationalism*), p. 5.
6. Ibid., p. 4.
7. Orr, *Collected Poems*, pp. 285–7.
8. See Trumpener, *Bardic Nationalism*, p. 2.

9. C. A. Charnell-White, *Bardic Circles: National, Regional and Personal Identity in the Bardic Vision of Iolo Morganwg* (Cardiff: University of Wales Press, 2007), p. 3.
10. D. Moore, *Enlightenment and Romance in James Macpherson's The Poems of Ossian: Myth, Genre and Cultural Change* (Aldershot: Ashgate, 2003), pp. 141, 146.
11. Stewart, '1798 and the Modesty of History', p. 36.
12. Orr to Thomson, 24 May 1807, quoted in Walker, 'Country Letters'.
13. Stewart, '1798 and the Modesty of History', p. 36.
14. Vance, *Irish Literature: A Social History*, p. 94.
15. Ibid., p. 96.
16. 'Glendalloch', *Belfast Monthly Magazine*, 6:33 (1811), pp. 308–12.
17. Vance, *Irish Literature: A Social History*, pp. 99, 104, 108.
18. Deane (gen. ed.), *Field Day*, vol. 1, pp. 1058–9.
19. Pittock, *Scottish and Irish Romanticism*, p. 17.
20. *Belfast Monthly Magazine*, 3:17 (1809), p. 468.
21. *Belfast Commercial Chronicle*, 7 January 1809.
22. See discussion in Chapter 4.
23. A. M. Sullivan, *The Story of Ireland* (Dublin: M. H. Gill and Son Ltd., 1867), pp. 236–42. This later nineteenth-century account has much in common with Orr's.
24. Orr, *Collected Poems*, pp. 279–81.
25. The Orange Order was formed in 1795 following the Battle of the Diamond between two agrarian secret societies, the Protestant Peep o' Day Boys, victors in the Battle, and the Catholic Defenders, who became allies of the United Irishmen. The Orange Order opposed the United Irishmen's radical plans for an independent Ireland and during the 1790s was accused of vicious persecution of Catholics. See J. Bardon, *A History of Ulster* (Belfast: Blackstaff Press, 2001), pp. 226–7. A sense of bitter enmity between defeated United Irish supporters and loyalist Orangemen continued in the post-Union era.
26. Pittock, *Scottish and Irish Romanticism*, p. 17.
27. Ibid., p. 22.
28. Ibid., quoted p. 24.
29. See Chapter 8.
30. D. Wu, 'Introduction', in D. Wu (ed.), *Romanticism: An Anthology*, 2nd edn (1998; Oxford: Blackwell, 2001), pp. xxxii–xxxv.
31. William Orr was tried and hanged here. Many of the Antrim participants in the 1798 Rebellion, including possibly Orr himself, were tried here following time 'on the run'.
32. Orr, *Collected Poems*, pp. 294–307.
33. Wordsworth and Coleridge, Wordsworth's Enlarged Preface of 1802, in *Lyrical Ballads*, quoted in M. H. Abrams, *The Mirror and the Lamp* (Oxford: Oxford University Press, 1971), p. 26. For Abrams's discussion of this shift in focus see pp. 8–26.
34. J. Howard, *The State of the Prisons in England and Wales, with Preliminary Observations, and an Account of Some Foreign Prisons* (Warrington: Eyres, 1777), p. 16.
35. Included in *Lyrical Ballads*.
36. See, for example, 'Humanity', Orr, *Collected Poems*, p. 134.
37. Hewitt, *Rhyming Weavers*, p. 94.
38. McIlvanney, *Burns the Radical*. See discussion on pp. 102–3.
39. Orr, *Collected Poems*, pp. 234–6. Bella-Hill is a townland adjacent to Ballycarry village.
40. Hugh Porter the County Down poet, for example, was patronized by Rev. Thomas Tighe, a member of the circle at Bishop Percy's home near Dromore. Orr's 'Epistle to S. Thomson' shows him attempting to discourage his friend from seeking wealthy sponsors.

41. W. Dowling, *The Epistolary Moment: The Poetics of the Eighteenth-Century Verse Epistle* (Princeton, NJ, and Oxford: Princeton University Press, c. 1991), p. 12.
42. Ibid., pp. 176, 168, 169.
43. Orr, *Collected Poems*, pp. 120–1.
44. Wordsworth and Coleridge, Wordsworth's Enlarged Preface of 1802, in *Lyrical Ballads and Related Writings*, pp. 390–416, on p. 408.
45. Orr, *Collected Poems*, pp. 173–80.
46. There is no direct reference to Southey in Orr, but Southey published this work in 1799 as 'English Eclogues 6: The Ruined Cottage' in his *Poems*, 2 vols (Bristol: Biggs and Cottle [for Longman and Rees, London], 1799), vol. 2, pp. 226–32.
47. Bainbridge, *British Poetry*, p. 40.
48. See, for example, 'The Vision – An Elegy', in Orr, *Collected Poems*, pp. 107–11, in which the speaker turns away from open air dancing in the centre of the village to reflect in the ruins of Templecorran church.
49. Ibid., pp. 21–3.
50. B. Wilsdon, *The Sites of the 1798 Rising in Antrim and Down* (Belfast: Blackstaff Press, 1997), pp. 87–8.
51. Orr, *Collected Poems*, pp. 64–6.
52. S. T. Coleridge, *From Biographia Literaria*, in *Lyrical Ballads and Related Writings*, pp. 416–22, on p. 416.
53. W. Hazlitt, 'Mr Wordsworth', in W. Hazlitt, *The Spirit of the Age* (2004; Grasmere: The Wordsworth Trust, 2007), pp. 201–12, on p. 204.
54. Orr, *Collected Poems*, pp. 86–7.
55. Bainbridge notes 'The returning soldier, often wounded or discharged, is a major figure in the war poetry of the period'. See Bainbridge, *British Poetry*, p. 41.
56. *Lyrical Ballads and Related Writings*, p. 51.
57. *The Poems of John Keats*, ed. J. Stillinger (London: Heinemann, 1978), pp. 266–7.
58. Orr, *Collected Poems*, pp. 147–9.
59. Wordsworth and Coleridge, Wordsworth's Enlarged Preface of 1802 in *Lyrical Ballads and Related Writings*, p. 394.
60. Chaplin and Faflak, 'Defining Romanticism', p. xv.
61. Butt (ed.), *Wordsworth: Selected Poetry and Prose*, p. 158.
62. 18 September 1805, *Belfast Commercial Chronicle*. Also see Orr, *Collected Poems*, pp. 205–27. Orr acknowledged J. H. St J. De Crevecoeur's *Letters from an American Farmer* as his source for this gruesome detail. See *Letters from an American Farmer*, ed. S. Manning (Oxford: Oxford University Press, 1997), pp. 163–4.
63. T. Matthewson, 'A. Bishop, "The Rights of Black Men", and the American Reaction to the Haitian Revolution', *Journal of Negro History*, 67:2 (Summer 1982), pp. 148–54, on p. 149.

Conclusion

1. His last known newspaper publication was 'Ode to a Butterfly' in the *Belfast News-letter*, 13 August 1813.
2. McDowell, 'Sketch', in Orr, *Collected Poems*, p. 189.
3. Ibid., pp. 190–1.
4. The *Belfast Monthly Magazine*, the *Belfast Commercial Chronicle* and the *Belfast News-letter*.

5. Bainbridge, *British Poetry*, pp. 2–3.
6. Burns, *Poems and Songs*, vol. 2, pp. 764–6.
7. M. A. Constantine, *The Truth against the World: Iolo Morganwg and Romantic Forgery* (Cardiff: University of Wales Press, 2007), p. 72.
8. See the discussion of Orr's newspaper verse in Chapter 4.
9. See, for example, 'Man was Made to Smile', or 'The Vision – An Elegy', in Orr, *Collected Poems*, pp. 107–110, 199–202.
10. As Frank Ferguson has observed, '"Ulster-Scots" has been implicated in the culture wars of Northern Ireland ... Ulster-Scots is viewed as part of the Unionist, Planter and Protestant set of belongings, in opposition to Nationalist, Republican, Catholic and Gaelic intellectual inheritance', in 'Introduction', in F. Ferguson (ed.), *Ulster-Scots Writing: An Anthology* (Dublin: Four Courts Press, 2008), pp. 1–22, on pp. 1–2.
11. S. Heaney, 'Servant Boy', in *Selected Poems*, p. 59.
12. McIlvanney, *Burns the Radical*, p. 228.

WORKS CITED

Primary Material

Manuscript Material
Centre for Irish Migration Studies
'The Anecdotal Recollections of Morgan Jellett', extract, PRONI D 2777/1, Centre for Irish Migration Studies Irish Emigration Database [hereafter CMSIED] 9406049.

'The Press Ganging of 46 Passengers from the Susanna', *Northern Star*, Friday 26 August 1796, CMSIED 9503259.

'Protest against the Alien and Sedition Laws', *Belfast Newsletter*, Tuesday 21 April 1799, CMSIED 9606137.

Samuel Brown, Philadelphia to David Brown, Belfast, 23 December 1793, PRONI T3525/1, CMSIED 9310019.

Samuel McCulloch, Heekenseek to his father, Carrickfergus, the *Belfast News-letter*, Friday 29 April 1774, CMSIED 1200308.

Public Record Office of Northern Ireland
The Ballycarry Presbyterian Church Session Book, PRONI, CR 3/31 fol. 2. Used with the permission of the Session of Ballycarry Old Presbyterian Church and of the Deputy Keeper of the Public Records, PRONI.

The John Hewitt Papers, D 3838/3/18. Used with the permission of the Deputy Keeper of the Public records, PRONI.

Richard G. Ker to David Ker, 20 December 1799, The Ker Papers, PRONI, D 2651/ 2 and D 2651/3. Used with the permission of the Deputy Keeper of the Public Records, PRONI.

Trinity College Dublin
The Thomson Correspondence, MS 7257 fol. 60. Used with the permission of the Board of Trinity College Dublin.

British Library Newspaper Archive Material

Philadelphia Burial Lists, *Claypoole's American Daily Advertiser*, 10 October 1798, the British Library Board, M.misc.808.

Election Returns for Philadelphia and Delaware, *Philadelphia Gazette*, 10 October 1798, the British Library Board, M.misc.819.

The French Occupation of Castlebar, *Philadelphia Gazette*, 10 October 1798, the British Library Board, M.misc.819.

Advertisements, *Philadelphia Gazette*, 1 November 1798, the British Library Board, M.misc.819.

Letters to the Editor, *Philadelphia Gazette*, 16 November 1798, the British Library Board, M.misc.819.

Philadelphia Gazette, 17 November 1798, the British Library Board, M.misc.819. All used with the permission of the British Library.

Printed Material

[Anon.], 'A Patriot', *Microscope*, 1:6 (1799), pp. 277–8.

[Anon.], 'To the Public', *Belfast Monthly Magazine*, 1:1 (1808), pp. 1–6.

[Anon.], 'Monthly Retrospect of Politics', *Belfast Monthly Magazine*, 1:4 (1808), pp. 382–95.

[Anon.], 'An Account of the Life and Writings of the Late Dr Geddes', *Belfast Monthly Magazine*, 3:10 (1809), pp. 443–51.

[Anon.], 'Biographical Sketch of Thomas Clarkson', *Belfast Monthly Magazine*, 8:43 (1812), pp. 31–41, 114–22.

[Anon.], 'Biographical Sketch of Margaret Roper', *Belfast Monthly Magazine*, 8:47 (1812), pp. 463–7.

Blair, H., *A Critical Dissertation on the Poems of Ossian, the Son of Fingal* (London: Becket and De Hondt, 1763).

—, *Sermons by Hugh Blair*, 7th edn (Dublin: Hallhead, 1779).

—, *Lectures on Rhetoric and Belles Lettres*, 3 vols (London: Strahan and Cadell; Edinburgh: Creech, 1798).

Bloomfield, R., *The Farmer's Boy; A Rural Poem*, 7th edn (Dublin: Wogan, 1803).

Boyle, F., *Miscellaneous Poems* (Belfast: Lyons, 1811).

Burns, R., *Poems, Chiefly in the Scottish Dialect* (Belfast: Magee, 1786).

—, *The Poems and Songs of Robert Burns*, ed. J. Kinsley, 3 vols (Oxford: Clarendon Press, 1968).

Butt, J. (ed.), *Wordsworth: Selected Poetry and Prose* (1964; Oxford: Oxford University Press, repr. 1973).

Campbell, J., *The Poems and Songs of James Campbell of Ballynure* (Ballyclare: Corry, 1870).

Carpenter, A. (ed.), *Verse in English from Eighteenth-Century Ireland* (Cork: Cork University Press, 1998).

'Censor', 'On the Catholic Question', *Belfast Monthly Magazine*, 1:3 (1808), p. 189.

— to the editor, *Belfast Monthly Magazine*, 2:6 (1809), pp. 11–12.

'Criticus' to the editor, *Belfast Monthly Magazine*, 1:5 (1808), pp. 354–6.

Deane, S. (gen. ed.), *The Field Day Anthology of Irish Literature*, 5 vols (Derry: Field Day Publications, 1991–2002).

Dickey, J., *Poems on Various Subjects* (Belfast: Berwick, 1818).

English, J. R., *Visits of the Muse, or A Leisure Hour* (Lanktree: Belfast, 1830).

Fenton, J. *The Hamely Tongue: A Personal Record of Ulster-Scots in County Antrim* (Belfast: Ullans Press, 2000).

Ferguson, F. (ed.), *Ulster-Scots Writing: An Anthology* (Dublin: Four Courts Press, 2008).

Geddes, A., *Ode to the Honourable Thomas Pelham, Esq.* (London: [Printed for J. Johnston], 1795).

—, *A Modest Apology for the Roman Catholics of Great Britain: Addressed to All Moderate Protestants; Particularly to the Members of Both Houses of Parliament* (London: [Sold by Faulder and Brooker], 1800).

Geddis, J., 'Stanzas Addressed to J.O.', *Belfast Commercial Chronicle*, 9 June 1806.

General Synod of the Church of Ireland, *The Book of Common Prayer* (Dublin: Association for Promoting Christian Knowledge, 1962).

Grant, D. (ed.), *Pope, Selected Poems* (Oxford: Oxford University Press, 1965).

Heaney, S., *Selected Poems 1965–75* (London: Faber and Faber, 1980).

Home, J., *Douglas: A Tragedy* (Belfast: Magee, 1758).

Howard, J., *The State of the Prisons in England and Wales, with Preliminary Observations, and an Account of Some Foreign Prisons* (Warrington: Eyres, 1777).

Huddleston, R., *Poems on Rural Subjects* (Belfast: Smyth and Lyons, 1844).

Hume, D., 'On Suicide', in D. Hume, *Essays on Suicide and the Immortality of the Soul* (Basil: [n.p.], 1799), pp. 3–7.

Hutcheson, F., *An Inquiry into the Original of our Ideas of Beauty and Virtue* (Glasgow: Foulis, 1772 [rpt of fourth edition]).

Jack, R. D. S. (ed.), *A Choice of Scottish Verse 1560–1660* (Edinburgh: Hodder and Stoughton, 1978).

Keats, J., *The Poems of John Keats*, ed. J. Stillinger (London: Heinemann, 1978).

Kinghorn, A. M. and A. Law (eds), *Poems by Allan Ramsay and Robert Fergusson* (Edinburgh and London: Scottish Academic Press, 1974).

Macafee, C. I. (ed.), A *Concise Ulster Dictionary* (Oxford: Oxford University Press, 1996).

McHenry, J., *O'Halloran, or The Insurgent Chief: A Tale of the United Irishmen* (Belfast: John Henderson, 1844).

Madden, R. R. (ed.), *Literary Remains of the United Irishmen: And Other Popular Lyrics of their Times, with an Essay on 'The Exile of Erin'* (Dublin: Duffy, 1887).

Manson, D., *A New Pocket Dictionary; or English Expositor: With a Supplement ... Containing all the Uncommon Words ... To which are Prefixed, a Practical Grammar ... And a Plan for the Improvement of Children in Virtue and Learning, without the Use of the Rod. With the Present State and Practice of the Play-School in Belfast* (Belfast: Blow, 1762).

Maxwell, C. (ed.), *A Tour in Ireland by Arthur Young* (Belfast: Blackstaff Press, 1983).

Moore, T., *Epistles, Odes and Other Poems* (London: James Carpenter, 1806).

Noble A. and P. Scott Hogg (eds), *The Canongate Burns* (Edinburgh: Canongate Books, 2003 [revised]).

'O', Ballycarry, 'On the Disasters and Deaths Occasioned by Accidents', *Belfast Monthly Magazine*, 5:24 (1810), pp. 25–7.

Orr, J., 'Address to Master Thomas Romney Robinson', *Belfast Commercial Chronicle*, 7 September 1805.

—, 'Lord Nelson's Song of Victory', *Belfast Commercial Chronicle*, 18 November 1805.

—, 'The Speech of John P. Palm', *Belfast Commercial Chronicle*, 20 October 1806.

—, 'Apostrophe of the Shade of Brian Boromhu, to his Harp', *Belfast Monthly Magazine*, 3:17 (1809), p. 468.

—, 'Stanzas on the Death of a Favourite Young Lady', *Belfast Monthly Magazine*, 4:23 (1810), pp. 444–5.

—, *Collected Poems* (1935; Belfast: Mullan & Son, repr. 1936).

—, *Poems on Various Subjects* (Belfast: Smyth and Lyons, 1804).

—, *The Posthumous Works of James Orr of Ballycarry: With A Sketch of his Life* (Belfast: Francis D. Finlay, 1817).

Owenson, S., *The Wild Irish Girl: A National Tale*, ed. K. Kirkpatrick (Oxford: Oxford University Press, 1999).

—, *Patriotic Sketches of Ireland, Written in Connaught* (London: Richard Philips, 1807).

Paine, T., *The Rights of Man; Being an Answer to Mr Burke's Attack on the French Revolution* (London: W. T. Sherwin, 1817).

Pierce, D. (ed.), *Irish Writing in the Twentieth Century: A Reader* (Cork: Cork University Press, 2000).

Ramsay, A., *The Works of Allan Ramsay*, 6 vols (Edinburgh: The Scottish Text Society third series, 1951–74), vol. 1, ed. B. Martin and J. W. Olivier; vol. 3, ed. A. M. Kinghorn and A. Law.

Read, C. A. and T. P. O'Connor (eds), *The Cabinet of Irish Literature: Selections from the Works of the Chief Poets, Orators and Prose Writers of Ireland*, 4 vols (London and New York: Blackie and Son, Samuel L. Hall, 1884).

Robertson, W., *The History of Scotland during the Reigns of Queen Mary and of King James VI.*, 7th edn, 2 vols (Dublin: Printed for United Company of Booksellers, 1775).

Robinson, P. and J. R. R. Adams (eds), *The Country Rhymes of James Orr: The Bard of Ballycarry 1770–1816* (Bangor: Pretani Press, 1992).

— (eds), *The Country Rhymes of Samuel Thomson: The Bard of Carngranny 1766–1816* (Bangor: Pretani Press, 1992).

Robinson, T. R., *Juvenile Poems by Thomas Romney Robinson* (Belfast: Smyth and Lyons, 1806).

Scott, W., *Old Mortality*, ed. A. Calder (1975; Harmondsworth: Penguin, repr. 1985).

Southey, R., *Poems*, 2 vols (Bristol: Biggs and Cottle [for Longman and Rees, London], 1799).

Thomson, J., *The Seasons and The Castle of Indolence*, ed. J. Sambrook (Oxford: Oxford University Press, 1972).

Thomson, S., *Poems on Different Subjects, Partly in the Scottish Dialect* (Belfast: Privately printed, 1793).

Tytler, J., *The Rising of the Sun in the West: Or the Origin and Progress of Liberty* (Salem, MA: William Carleton, 1795).

Tynan, H., *Poems by the Late Hugh Tynan of Donaghadee* (Belfast: Smyth and Lyons, 1803).

Walker, B. M., 'Country Letters: Some Correspondence of Ulster Poets of the Nineteenth Century', in J. Gray and W. McCann (eds), *An Uncommon Bookman: Essays in Memory of J. R. R. Adams* (Belfast: The Linen Hall Library, 1996), pp. 119–39.

Wordsworth, W. and S. T. Coleridge, *Lyrical Ballads and Related Writings*, ed. W. Richey and D. Robinson (Boston, MA, and New York: Houghton Mifflin, 2002).

Wright, J. M. (ed.), *Irish Literature 1750–1900* (Oxford: Blackwell Publishing, 2008).

Wu, D. (ed.), *Romanticism: An Anthology*, 2nd edn (1998; Oxford: Blackwell, repr. 2001).

'Report from the Committee of Secrecy to the House of Commons', made following the Rebellion in 1799. Queen's University Belfast, Act of Union: Virtual Library, at http://www.actofunion.ac.uk/hansards.php?set=3, document no. 27, pp. 579–656, on pp. 579, 580 [accessed 26 February 2014].

Secondary Material

Abrams, M. H., *The Mirror and the Lamp* (Oxford: Oxford University Press, 1971).

Adams, B. (ed.), *Ulster Dialects: An Introductory Symposium* (Belfast: Ulster Folk and Transport Museum, 1964).

Adams, J. R. R, 'Reading Societies in Ulster', *Ulster Folk Life*, 26 (1980), pp. 54–65.

—, *The Printed Word and the Common Man: Popular Culture in Ulster 1700–1900* (Belfast: The Institute of Irish Studies, Queen's University Belfast, 1987).

Akenson, D. H., *Between Two Revolutions: Islandmagee, County Antrim 1798–1920* (Dublin: Meaney, 1979).

— and W. H. Crawford, *Local Poets and Social History: James Orr, the Bard of Ballycarry* (Belfast: Public Record Office of Northern Ireland [PRONI], 1977).

[Anon.], 'Literary and Biographical Notices of Irish Authors: No. 12, James Orr', *Irish Shield and Monthly Milesian: A Historic Literary and Dramatic Journal*, 1:12 (1829), pp. 449–57.

Bainbridge, S., *British Poetry and the Revolutionary and Napoleonic Wars: Visions of Conflict* (Oxford: Oxford University Press, 2003).

Baraniuk, C., 'James Orr: Ulster-Scot and Poet of the 1798 Rebellion', *Scottish Studies Review*, 6:1 (2005), pp. 22–32.

—, 'An Antidote to the Burns Idyll: James Orr's "The Irish Cottier's Death and Burial"', *Burns Chronicle* (Spring 2006), pp. 6–11.

—, 'Disagreeably Scottish?', *Drouth: Dialect*, 19 (Spring 2006), pp. 13–17.

—, 'Setting his Own Standard: James Orr's Employment of a Traditional Stanza Form', *Journal of Irish and Scottish Studies*, 1:1 (2007), pp. 73–86.

—, 'Ulster's Burns? James Orr, the Bard of Ballycarry', *Review of Scottish Culture*, 19 (2007), pp. 54–62.

—, 'Christ's Kirk on the Green Isle: Tragedy Commemorated in Comic Form', in M.-C. Considère-Charon, P. Laplace and M. Savaric (eds), *The Irish Celebrating: Festive and Tragic Overtones* (Newcastle: Cambridge Scholars Publishing, 2008), pp. 118–32.

—, 'The Leid, the Pratoe and the Buik: Northern Cultural Markers in the Works of James Orr', in J. P. Byrne, P. Kirwan and M. O'Sullivan (eds), *Affecting Irishness: Negotiating Cultural Identity within and beyond the Nation* (Oxford: Peter Lang, 2009), pp. 103-20.

—, 'No Bardolatry Here: The Independence of the Ulster-Scots Poetic Tradition', in F. Ferguson and A. Holmes (eds), *Revising Robert Burns and Ulster: Literature, Religion and Politics c. 1770–1920* (Dublin: Four Courts Press, 2009), pp. 64–82.

—, 'James Orr, Napoleon and Lord Nelson', *Ullans: The Magazine for Ulster-Scots*, 11 (2010), pp. 107–8.

Bardon, J., *A History of Ulster* (Belfast: Blackstaff Press, 2001).

Barrell, J., *The Dark Side of the Landscape: The Rural Poor in English Painting, 1730–1840* (Cambridge: Cambridge University Press, 1980).

Biggar, F. J., 'Thomas Beggs, an Antrim Poet: And the Four Towns Book Club', *Ulster Journal of Archaeology*, second series, 8 (1902), pp. 119–27.

Carruthers, G., 'The Return of Alexander Geddes', *Drouth: Bigotry*, 12 (Summer 2004), pp. 22–4.

—, *Robert Burns* (Tavistock: Northcote House Publishers, 2006).

Chaplin, S. and J. Faflak (eds), *The Romanticism Handbook* (London: Continuum International Publishing, 2011).

Charnell-White, C. A., *Bardic Circles: National, Regional and Personal Identity in the Bardic Vision of Iolo Morganwg* (Cardiff: University of Wales Press, 2007).

Clyde, T. (ed.), *Ancestral Voices: The Selected Prose of John Hewitt* (Belfast: Blackstaff Press, 1987).

Cobbett, W., *Cottage Economy* (London: Peter Davis, 1926).

Constantine, M. A., *The Truth against the World: Iolo Morganwg and Romantic Forgery* (Cardiff: University of Wales Press, 2007).

Craig, C. (ed.), *The History of Scottish Literature*, 4 vols (Aberdeen: Aberdeen University Press, 1987–8).

Crawford, W. H., *The Handloom Weavers and the Ulster Linen Industry* (Belfast: Ulster Historical Foundation, 1994).

Day, A., P. McWilliams and N. Dobson (eds), *Ordnance Survey Memoirs of Ireland: Volume Twenty-Six, Parishes of Co. Antrim X 1830–1, 1833–5, 1839–40* (Belfast: Queen's University Belfast, The Institute of Irish Studies, 1994).

De Crevecoeur, J. H. St J., *Letters from an American Farmer*, ed. S. Manning (Oxford: Oxford University Press, 1997).

Donaldson, D., *The Historical, Traditional and Descriptive Account of Islandmagee* (1927; Islandmagee: [n.p.], revised 1968).

Dornan, S., 'Beyond the Milesian Pale: The Poetry of James Orr', *Eighteenth-Century Ireland*, 20 (2005), pp. 140–55.

Dowling, W., *The Epistolary Moment: The Poetics of the Eighteenth-Century Verse Epistle* (Princeton, NJ, and Oxford: Princeton University Press, c. 1991).

Durey, M., *Transatlantic Radicals and the Early American Republic* (Lawrence, KS: Kansas University Press, 1997).

Falconer, W. M. D., 'The Working Tools of the Craft' (ch. 31), in W. M. D. Falconer, *The Square and Compasses: In Search of Freemasonry* (2002, revised), at http://www.freemasons-freemasonry.com/don5.html [accessed 18 February 2014].

Ferguson, F., 'Irish on the Outside, Scottish Within: The Anthology of Ulster-Scots Literature', unpublished seminar paper, Institute of Irish Studies, Queen's University Belfast, 29 March 2006.

Fullerton, J., 'James Orr', *Corran, Journal of the Larne and District Folklore Society*, 37 (Winter 1985–6), pp. 15–17 (reprinted from the *Ulster Magazine c.* 1860).

Gamble, J., *A View of Society and Manners in the North of Ireland in the Summer and Autumn of 1812* (London: Craddock and Jay, 1813).

Ghanem, T., 'When Forced Migrants Return "Home": The Psychosocial Difficulties Returnees Encounter in the Reintegration Process', Working Paper 16 (Oxford: Refugee Studies Centre, October 2003).

Gifford, D., S. Dunnigan and A. MacGillivray (eds), *Scottish Literature in English and Scots* (Edinburgh: Edinburgh University Press, 2002).

Gray, J., 'Burns and his Visitors from Ulster: From Adulation to Disaccord', *Studies in Scottish Literature*, 33:4 (2004), pp. 320–33.

Gregg, R., *The Scotch-Irish Dialect Boundaries in the Province of Ulster* (Ottawa: Canadian Federation for the Humanities, 1985).

Hazlitt, W., 'Mr Wordsworth', in W. Hazlitt, *The Spirit of the Age* (2004; Grasmere: The Wordsworth Trust, 2007), pp. 201–12.

Herbison, I., *Language, Literature and Cultural Identity* (Ballymena: Dunclug Press, 1989).

—, '"The Rest is Silence": Some Remarks on the Disappearance of Ulster-Scots Poetry', in J. Erskine and G. Lucy (eds), *Cultural Traditions in Northern Ireland: Varieties of Scottishness* (Belfast: Institute of Irish Studies, Queen's University Belfast, 1997), pp. 129–45.

—, 'Beyond the Rhyming Weavers', *Études Irlandaises*, 38:2 (2014), pp. 41–54.

Hewitt, J., 'Weaver Poets', *Fibres, Fabrics, Cordage*, 5:7, 8, 9 (1948).

—, 'Ulster Poets 1800–70' (PhD dissertation: Queen's University Belfast, 1951).

—, *Rhyming Weavers and Other Country Poets of Antrim and Down* (1974; Belfast: Blackstaff Press, repr. 2004).

—, 'Once Alien Here', in M. Longley and F. Ormsby (eds), *John Hewitt Selected Poems* (Belfast: Blackstaff Press, 2007), p. 8.

Holmes, A., *The Shaping of Ulster Presbyterian Belief and Practice 1770–1840* (Oxford: Oxford University Press, 2006).

Holmes, R. F., 'The Reverend John Abernethy: The Challenge of New Light Theology to Traditional Irish Presbyterian Calvinism', in K. Herlihy (ed.), *The Religion of Irish Dissent 1650–1800* (Dublin: Four Courts Press, 1996), pp. 100–11.

Hope, J., *The Memoirs of Jemmy Hope: An Autobiography of a Working-Class United Irishman* (Belfast: British and Irish Communist Organisation, 1972).

Hume, D., 'The Story of John Neilson c. 1770–1827', *Broadisland Journal*, 5 (1999), pp. 11–14.

Jay, M., *The Unfortunate Colonel Despard* (London: Bantam Press, 2004).

Johnston, K. R., 'The Unromantic Lives of Others: The Lost Generation of the 1790s', in the *Wordsworth Circle*, 40:2–3 (2009), pp. 67–72.

Kerrigan, J., *Archipelagic English* (Oxford: Oxford University Press, 2008).

Killen, J. (ed.), *The Famine Decade: Contemporary Accounts 1841–1851* (Belfast: Blackstaff Press, 1995).

Knox, W. M., *A Ballycarry Holiday* (Belfast: The Northern Whig, 1923).

Leask, N., 'Burns, Wordsworth and the Politics of Vernacular Poetry', in P. de Bolla, N. Leask and D. Simpson (eds), *Land, Nation and Culture, 1740–1840: Thinking the Republic of Taste* (Basingstoke: Palgrave, 2005), pp. 202–22.

—, 'The Cottage Leaves the Palace Far Behind', Paper for the Burns International Conference, Mitchell Library, Glasgow, 21 January 2006.

Longley, E., 'The Whereabouts of Literature', in G. Carruthers, D. Goldie and A. Renfrew (eds), *Beyond Scotland: New Contexts for Twentieth-Century Scottish Literature* (Amsterdam and New York: Rodopi, 2004), pp. 151–65.

Locke, J., *A Letter Concerning Toleration* (Minneapolis, MN: Filiquarian Publishing, LLC, 2007).

—, *Two Treatises of Government*, ed. P. Laslett (1988; Cambridge: Cambridge University Press; 2008).

Low, D., *Robert Burns* (Edinburgh: Scottish Academic Press, 1986).

Lunney, L., 'Attitudes to Life and Death in the Poetry of James Orr, an Eighteenth-Century Ulster Weaver', *Ulster Folklife*, 31 (1985), pp. 1–12.

—, 'The Nature of the Ulster-Scots Language Community', in J. Erskine and G. Lucy (eds), *Cultural Traditions in Northern Ireland*, pp. 113–28.

—, '"An' There Some Readin' to Themselves"?: Reading and Orality in Eighteenth-Century Ulster Poetry', in A. Smyth, M. Montgomery and P. Robinson (eds), *The Academic Study of Ulster-Scots: Essays for and by Robert J. Gregg* (Belfast: Ulster Folk and Transport Museum, 2006), pp. 51–9.

Macafee, C. (ed.), *A Concise Ulster Dictionary* (Oxford: Oxford University Press, 1996).

McBride, I., *Scripture Politics: Ulster Presbyterians and Irish Radicalism in the Late Eighteenth Century* (Oxford: Oxford University Press, 1998).

—, 'Ulster Presbyterians and the Passing of the Act of Union', in M. Brown, P. Geoghegan and J. Kelly (eds), *The Irish Act of Union, 1800: Bicentennial Essays* (Dublin: Irish Academic Press, 2003), pp. 68–83.

—, '"When Ulster Joined Ireland": Anti-Popery, Presbyterian Radicalism and Irish Republicanism in the 1790s', *Oxford Journals: Past and Present*, 157:1 (1997), pp. 53–93.

McFarland, E., *Ireland and Scotland in the Age of Revolution: Planting the Green Bough* (Edinburgh: Edinburgh University Press, 1994).

McIlvanney, L., *Burns the Radical: Poetry and Politics in Late Eighteenth-Century Scotland* (East Linton: Tuckwell Press, 2002).

—, 'Across the Narrow Sea: The Language, Literature and Politics of Ulster Scots', in L. McIlvanney and R. Ryan (eds), *Ireland and Scotland: Culture and Society, 1700–2000* (Dublin: Four Courts Press, 2005), pp. 203–26.

—, 'Burns, Blair and the Invention of Scottish Literature', *Eighteenth-Century Life*, 29:2 (2005), pp. 25–46.

MacLaine, A. H. (ed.), *The Christis Kirk Tradition: Scots Poems of Folk Festivity* (Glasgow: Association for Scottish Literary Studies, 1996).

Matthewson, T., 'Abraham Bishop, "The Rights of Black Men", and the American Reaction to the Haitian Revolution', *Journal of Negro History*, 67: 2 (Summer 1982), pp. 148–54.

Mirala, P., *Freemasonry in Ulster 1733–1813* (Dublin: Four Courts Press, 2007).

Montgomery, W. A., 'The First Presbyterian Congregation in Ireland', in A. Dowlin (ed.), *Ballycarry in Olden Days* (Belfast: Graham and Heslip, 1963), pp. 9–10.

Moore, D., *Enlightenment and Romance in James Macpherson's The Poems of Ossian: Myth, Genre and Cultural Change* (Aldershot: Ashgate, 2003).

Nelson, J., 'Archaeology on our Doorstep', *Broadisland Journal* (1998), p. 9.

O'Brien, G., 'Spirit, Impartiality and Independence: The *Northern Star* 1792–7', *Eighteenth-Century Ireland*, 13 (1998), pp. 7–23.

O'Donoghue, D. J., 'Ulster Poets and Poetry', *Ulster Journal of Archaeology*, second series, 1:1 (1895), pp. 20–2.

O'Farrell, P., *The '98 Reader* (Dublin: The Lilliput Press, 1998).

O'Kane, D. (ed.), *John MacCloskey's Statistical Reports of the Parishes of Ballinascreen, Kilcronaghan, Desertmartin, Banagher, Dungiven and Boveva in the County of Londonderry, 1821* (1983; Ballinascreen: Moyola Books and Braid Books, 1986).

Pakenham, T., *The Year of Liberty: The Story of the Great Irish Rebellion of 1798* (London: Abacus, 2007).

Pellicer, J. C., 'The Georgic', in C. Gerrard (ed.), *A Companion to Eighteenth-Century Poetry* (Oxford: Blackwell Publishing, 2006), pp. 403–16.

Pittock, M., *Scottish and Irish Romanticism* (Oxford: Oxford University Press, 2008).

Robinson, P., *Ulster-Scots: A Grammar of the Traditional Written and Spoken Language* (Belfast: Ullans Press, 2007).

Rodgers, N., *Equiano and Anti-Slavery in Eighteenth-Century Belfast* (Belfast: Linen Hall Library in Association with the Ulster Historical Foundation, 2000).

Said, E., *Culture and Imperialism* (London: Vintage, 1994).

Stafford, F., *Starting Lines in Scottish, English and Irish Poetry: From Burns to Heaney* (Oxford: Oxford University Press, 2000).

—, 'A Centre in the Breast: Robert Burns and Happiness', Centre for Robert Burns Studies, Inaugural Lecture, 21 July 2007.

Stewart, A. T. Q., *The Narrow Ground: The Roots of Conflict in Ulster* (London: Faber and Faber, 1989).

—, *A Deeper Silence: The Hidden Origins of the United Irish Movement* (London: Faber and Faber, 1993).

—, *The Summer Soldiers: The 1798 Rebellion in Antrim and Down* (Belfast: Blackstaff Press, 1995).

—, *Presbyterians, the United Irishmen and 1798* (Belfast: Presbyterian Historical Society of Ireland, 2000).

Sullivan, A. M., *The Story of Ireland* (Dublin: M. H. Gill and Son Ltd., 1867).

Teeling, C., *Sequel to Personal Narrative of the 'Irish Rebellion' of 1798* (Belfast: Hodgson, 1832).

Thompson, E. P., *The Making of the English Working Class* (London: Gollancz, 1980).

Tomkins, S., *John Wesley: A Biography* (Oxford, Lion Publishing, 2003).

Trumpener, K., *Bardic Nationalism: The Romantic Novel and the British Empire* (Princeton, NJ: Princeton University Press, 1997).

Vance, N., *Irish Literature: A Social History – Tradition, Identity and Difference* (Oxford: Basil Blackwell, 1990).

Walker, J. C., *Historical Memoirs of the Irish Bards* (Dublin: Luke White, 1786).

Wesley, J., *The Journal of the Reverend John Wesley*, 4 vols (London: Everyman, 1938).

Whyte, C., 'Bakhtin at Christ's Kirk, Part I: Carnival and the Scottish Renaissance', in *Studies in Scottish Literature*, 28 (1993), pp. 178–203.

Wilsdon, B., *The Sites of the 1798 Rising in Antrim and Down* (Belfast: Blackstaff Press, 1997).

Wilson, D. A., *United Irishmen, United States: Immigrant Radicals in the Early Republic* (Dublin: Four Courts Press, 1998).

Wollstonecraft, M., *A Vindication of the Rights of Woman* (1792; London: Everyman, 1992).

Young, R. M., *Ulster in '98: Episodes and Anecdotes* (Belfast: Ward, 1893).

Zenzinger, P., 'Low Life Primitivism and Honest Poverty: A Socio-Cultural Reading of Ramsay and Burns', *Studies in Scottish Literature*, 30 (1998), pp. 43–58.

Web Resources

Dictionary of the Scots Language (DSL), at http://www.dsl.ac.uk [accessed 12 June 2014].

INDEX

Abernethy, Rev. John, 8, 16, 64–5
Abolitionist Movement
    and Romanticism, 183
    Orr and, 73–4, 183–5
Abrams, M. H., on Romantic theory, 175–6
Adams, J. R. R.
    and Robinson, *Folk Poets of Ulster* series, 19
    on Covenanters and Peden, 72
    on reading societies, 32
    on Scots literature in Ulster, 102
    on *The Cherrie and the Slae*, 139
Adams, John, US President, 46
Addison, Joseph, 86, 146
Aiken, Robert, 159
Akenside, Mark, 86
Akenson and Crawford
    on Orr, 13–16, 66, 70, 71, 152, 163, 189
    on 'The Irish Cottier ...', 152, 163
Akenson, Donald Harman
    and Crawford, *Local Poets and Social History: James Orr ...*, 13–15
    and Orr's undiscovered texts, 2
Aldfrackyn Glen, 180
America
    Alien and Sedition Acts, 46
    emigration to, 127–31
    Orr's exile in, 1, 8, 15, 19, 40–1, 43–7, 58, 115, 118, 135, 137
    slavery, 46, 47, 184–5
Amnesty Act 1798, 47
Anglo-Irish literature, anthologies, 8–19
Antrim, Battle of, 7 June 1798, 37–9, 55, 123–5, 131–5
Antrim Non-Subscribing Presbytery, 65
Ascendancy, 25–6, 31, 48, 74, 81, 87, 123, 153, 174
Augustan tradition, 6, 55, 88, 133, 147, 165, 166, 174–5

Bainbridge, Simon
    on verse in Napoleonic era, 68
    on Wordsworth/Southey, 180
Ballycarry (Broadisland), 1
    7 June 1798 Rising, 37–40
    conditions post-Rising, 45
    emigrants at Philadelphia, 45–7
    history, 25–7, 31
    Lunney on, 16
    Orr's return to, 48–9
    Presbyterian Church, *Session Book*, 32
    yeomanry, 41, 49
Bankhead, Rev. John, 31–2, 39, 49, 53
    Orr's 'The Penitent' addressed to, 159
bardic nationalism, 20, 87, 165, 166–8
bardism
    Irish, 6, 66, 72–3, 111–12, 142, 166–8, 188
    Scottish, 92, 110–11, 177
Barkley, J. M., on Ulster Synod, 65
Beattie, James, *The Minstrel*, 147
Beckett, J. C., on Ulster poets, 10
Beggs, Thomas, on hiding Volunteers, 40
Belfast Commercial Chronicle, 40, 49, 67–80, 87, 145, 153, 154, 172, 177, 178, 184, 188, 192
Belfast Literary Society, 169
Belfast Monthly Magazine, 16, 50, 87, 98, 99, 126, 169, 170
    'Monthly Retrospect of Politics', 62
    Orr and, 61–7
Belfast News-letter
    on Burns, 144
    Orr and, 61–3
    poetry column, 51–3
Belfast Penny Journal, 151
Beresford, John, on Dissenters, 31

Bhabha, Homi, 174
Bhurtpore, defence of, 69
blackmouths/blacks (Ulster Presbyterian men), 43–4, 128, 129
Blair, Hugh, 81, 82, 169, 190
　Lectures on Rhetoric and Belles Lettres, 85, 86
　on Burns, 87
　on 'Gentleness', 91
　works, Orr and, 85–91, 96
Blake, William, 'Jerusalem', 181
Bloomfield, Robert, 51, 54, 174
Boyle, Francis, 102, 105
　'Address to Robert Burns', 105
　and 1745 Rebellion aftermath, 105
Brian Borhu, 154, 170
Brice, Edward, 26
Broadisland, 1, 2, 181
　see also Ballycarry
Broadisland/Islandmagee corps, 124, 131–5
Burns, James 'The Old Croppy', on Orr, 37, 39–40, 49
Burns, Robert, 57, 102, 107, 169, 174, 190
　and *Christis Kirk* genre, 127
　and standard habbie, 108–10
　as radical, 20–2, 33
　Belfast News-letter and, 51–2
　Orr identified with, 2, 3, 5–6
　poems, Mullan on, 105–6
　popular enthusiasm for, 105–8, 121
　works
　　'A Poet's Welcome to his Love-Begotten Daughter', 109
　　'A Vision', 52
　　'Adam Armour's Prayer', 109–10
　　'Address to a Haggis', 114, 116
　　'Address to the Deil', 144
　　'Epistle to Davie ...', 135–6, 142
　　'Epistle to John Rankine', 109
　　'Hallowe'en', 144
　　'Holy Willie's Prayer', 108
　　Kilmarnock Preface, 54, 88
　　'Lassie Lie Near Me', 144
　　'Man was Made to Mourn', 84–5
　　'On the Late Captain Grose's Peregrinations', 144
　　'Scotch Drink', 21, 117, 145, 146
　　'Tam o' Shanter', 144, 145
　　'The Author's Earnest Cry and Prayer', 117
　　'The Battle of Sherra-moor', 132
　　'The Brigs of Ayr', 147
　　'The Cotter's Saturday Night', 147, 149–51, 152, 154–8, 160, 162
　　'The Dumfries Volunteers', 22, 146, 188
　　'The Holy Fair', 127
　　'The Ordination', 127
　　'The Vision', 92, 110
　　'To a Haggis', 21
　　'To a Mouse', 112, 113
　　verse epistles, 109

Calvinism, 65, 67, 162
Calwell, William, on Orr, 10
Campbell, James, of Ballynure, 10, 22
　anti-tithe poem, 103
　'Dirge', 77
　elegy on Orr, 2–3, 79
　'Epicure's Address to Bacon', 103–4
　'The Rejected Yeoman', 41
Carpenter, Andrew, *Verse in English from Eighteenth-Century Ireland*, 9
Carrickfergus, 25–6, 27, 31, 36, 39, 44, 53, 62, 76
　assizes, 174
Carruthers, Gerard
　on Burns, 113, 147, 149
　on Geddes, 97
Castlebar, French occupation, 46
Catholics
　as aliens in own country, 34
　emancipation, Orr and, 96–9, 153
'Censor', possible Orr pseudonym, 98–9, 153
Chaplin and Faflak, on Abolitionist Movement and Romanticism, 183
Charnell-White, Cathryn A., on Welsh bardism, 167
Cherrie and the Slae genre, 11, 18, 51, 135–42
Christis Kirk stanza, 11, 78, 127–32, 145
Clarkson, Thomas, biographical sketch, 62
Cobbett, William
　and potatoes, 120
　on Philadelphia United Irish, 45

Coleridge, Samuel Taylor
   'Fears in Solitude', 51, 169
   Lyrical Ballads, 6, 179, 181, 182
Connolly, Rosalind *see* Lunney, Linde
Constantine, Mary-Ann, on Iolo Morganwg, 189
Cooke, Edward, 15
Cooke, Rev. Henry, 65, 66
Corkery, Daniel, on Irish literature, 9
Cosby, Sir Francis, 172
Covenanters, 20, 65, 72, 95
Craigarogan, reading society, 33–4, 137
Crawford, William H.
   and Akenson on Orr, 13–16, 66, 70, 71, 152, 163, 189
   and Orr's undiscovered texts, 2
   on Ulster linen industry, 30–1
'Criticus', and 'Censor', 98–9
Currie, Dr, on Burns, 2, 52

Dalway family, 53
Dalway, John, 25
Dalway, Noah, 88, 177–8
de Courcy, John, 25
Deane, Seamus, *Field Day Anthology of Irish Writing*, 9
Defender movement, 40
Despard, Colonel Edward Marcus, treason trial, 70
Dickey, John, of Donegore
   on Cobbett and potatoes, 120–1
   on Orr and Thomson, 78
   'On the Death of James Orr, of Ballycarry', 2, 79–80
Dissenters, Ballycarry, 26, 29, 31–2
Doagh Reading Society, 32, 33
Donaldson, Dixon
   on Ballycarry Rising, 37–9
   on United Societies, 36
Donegore Hill, 7, 11, 53, 78, 131–3, 144
   desertions, 37–9, 41, 47, 49, 50, 55
   'SMS' on, 63
Dornan, Stephen, on 'Donegore Hill', 133
Dowling, William, on epistolary genre, 178
Draffen, Matthew, possible 'Tit for Tat' author, 103
Drennan, William, 120
   and Abolition, 74
   and *Belfast Monthly Magazine*, 62

   and *Microscope* ..., 50
   'Glendalloch', 169–71, 173
   'Irish Address', 61–2
   'The Wake of William Orr', 62
   Romantic nationalism, 169
Drummond, Rev. W. H., 53, 178
Dungannon, Viscount, 31

Edgeworth, Maria, 8
   Irish Romanticism, 165, 174
Edmonstone, William, 25–6
Edmonstones of Red Hall, 31
Elizabeth I Queen of England, 93
emigrant voyage, Orr on, 43–4
Emmet, Robert, 134, 135
   and Russell, rebellion attempt 1803, 55
English Ascendancy, 25–6, 31, 48, 74, 81, 87, 123, 153, 174
English, James Russell
   'The Late James Orr', 3
   and Orr's monument, 77
English lanuage, Orr and, 88–9
Enlightenment, Romanticism and, 165–85
Equiano, Olaudah, 73–4
'Erin Go Brah', 170–1
Evans, Evan, 'Paraphrase of the 137th Psalm', 166–8

Ferguson, Frank, on Thomson, 107
Fergusson, Robert, 18, 57, 88, 102, 106, 107, 114, 152, 162, 190
   'The Daft Days', 108
   'The Election', 127
   'The Farmer's Ingle', 147–51
Fletcher, John, 162
Fox, Charles James, 34, 74
France, changing attitudes to, 45–6
Freemasonry, 11, 17, 56, 76–7, 117, 163–4, 168
   and radical politics, 20, 22
French privateers, 44
Friends of the People (Scotland), 35, 62

Gamble, John, on Ulster Scots, 102
Geddes, Alexander, 97–8, 99
   Modest Apology for the Roman Catholics of Great Britain, 97–8
   'Ode to the Honourable Thomas Pelham', 97

Geddis, J., on Orr, 76, 78
Gibson, Covenanter, 72
Glendy, Rev. William, 66
Glenwherry, on the run at, 40
Goldsmith, Oliver, 13, 82, 106, 174
   'The Deserted Village', 61
Grattan, Henry, and Catholic Emancipation, 8, 77, 153
Gray, John, on Burns, 146
Gray, Thomas, 13, 57, 165, 167, 169
   'Elegy Written in a Country Churchyard', 61, 158, 180
Gregg, Robert, on linguistics, 18

Hartpole, Robert, 172
Hazlitt, William, on *Lyrical Ballads*, 182
Heaney, Seamus, 'At a Potato Digging', 115
Hearts of Steel, 31
Herbison, David, 10
Herbison, Ivan, on Hewitt, 11
Herdman, William, 53
Hewitt, John
   and vernacular poets, 102
   on Orr, 11–13, 14, 15, 19, 20, 54–5, 102, 114, 131, 152, 177, 189, 190
   on Orr's English poems, 189
   Rhyming Weavers and Other Country Poets of Antrim and Down, 10–13, 114
   Ulster Poets 1800–70, 7, 10–13
Highton Society of United Irishmen, 34
historians, local, and Orr, 5
Hogg, James, patronage, 3
Holmes, Andrew
   on Antrim Non-Subscribing Presbytery, 65
   on Millennarians, 72
Holmes, Finlay, on New Light theology, 64
Home, John, *Douglas*, 89, 92
Hook, Andrew, on vernacularity, 101
Hope, Jemmy (James), 1, 3, 5, 21, 22, 30, 142
   and Orr, 33, 40–1
   'McCracken's Ghost', 41, 49–50
   on United Irishmen, 34, 35–6
Howard, John, prison reformer, 176
Huddleston, Robert, on Orr, 3
Hume, David, 32, 81, 190
   works, Orr and, 84–5, 89

Hutcheson, Francis, 16, 64
   and Scottish Enlightenment, 81, 82
   Inquiry into the Original of our Ideas of Beauty and Virtue, 82–3

Iolo Morganwg, 167, 189
Irish bardism, 6, 66, 72–3, 111–12, 142, 166–8, 188
   prophetic role, 73
Irish culture, drive to promote, 61–3
Irish literature, anthologies, 8–19
Irish Literature 1750–1900, 9–10
Irish Romanticism, 165
Irish Shield and Monthly Milesian, on Orr, 7
Islandmagee, 31, 36, 53, 124, 171, 181, 190
   United men, 37

Jack, R. D. S., on attitudes to Mary Stuart, 94
Jackson, Tommy, 44
Jellett, Morgan, on French privateer attack, 44
Jeremiads, 72–3
Johnston, Kenneth R., on radical poets, 79

Keats, John, 'Old Meg she was a Gypsey', 182
Ker, Richard Gervase, Ballycarry landlord, 31, 37, 41, 181
   and Orr, 41, 49, 53, 181
   on post-Rising conditions, 48–9
Knox, John, 95
Knox, W. Mayne, on Ballycarry, 36

Larne, emigrants sail from, 43
Larne Lough, 171
Leask, Nigel
   on Burns, 147, 151
   on Scottish vernacular poets, 88
linguistics
   Gregg on, 18
   Lunney on, 15–18
Locke, John, 82, 165, 169
Locke family, 128
London Corresponding Society, 35
Low, Donald, on standard habbie, 108
Lowtown, reading society, 33
Lunney, Linde
   'Analysis of Some Linguistic Information ... Ulster Poetry', 16
   'Attitudes to Life and Death in the Poetry of James Orr ...', 16

on Orr, 15–19, 20, 63, 65, 98, 110, 152
'Censor', possible Orr pseudonym, 98–9
'The Irish Cottier's Death and Burial',
152

McBride, Ian
on millenarians and United Irish movement, 96
on post-Rising conditions, 48
on United Irish political thought, 81
MacCloskey, John, 9
McCracken, Henry Joy, 1, 3, 5, 21, 22, 25,
33, 35, 36, 40, 41, 49–50, 58, 127, 134,
135, 188
hiding at Slemish, 125
leads Antrim engagement, 123–4, 131–5
McDowell, Alexander (Sandy)
(ed.), *Posthumous Works of James Orr of Ballycarry*, 1–2, 61, 64, 67, 187
'Elegiac Stanzas on the Death of James Orr', 2, 78–9
on Orr, 58
and Rising, 37, 39
exile, 43, 45, 46–7
heavy drinking, 78–9
possible relationship, 79
Orr's instructions to, 91, 187
Sketch (of Orr's life), 33, 187
McFarland, Elaine
on Hutcheson, 64
on Ulster United Irishmen, 35
McIlvanney, Liam
Burns the Radical, 20–2, 146
on Blair, 87
on Burns, 177
'A Vision', 52
and Ulster poets, 102
verse epistles, 109
'On Irish Ground', 21–2
on Orr, 20–3
and *Christis Kirk* genre, 132
and Scottish Enlightenment, 82
MacLaine, Allan H., on *Christis Kirk* genre, 127
MacNeill, Hector, patronage, 3
Macpherson's *Ossian*, Blair on, Orr and, 86–7, 89, 169

McSkimin, Samuel ('SMS')
on Slemish, 126–7
'Sketch of a Ramble to Antrim, 10 July 1808', 62
Madden, R. R., *Literary Remains of the United Irishmen*, 7, 8
Mallusk, reading society, 33–4
Manson, David, educationist, 61
Mary Queen of Scots, 91, 93–7, 99
Matthewson, Tim, on Abolitionist Movement, 184
Methodism, 49
Microscope; or Minute Observer, 50, 51, 169
A Patriot's 'My Native Home', 51
Millennarian-prophetic stream, 72–3
Miltonic mode, 175
Mirala, Petri, on Irish freemasonry, 76
Monaghan Militia, 32
Monroe, Henry (United Irishman), 134
Montgomerie, Alexander, *The Cherrie and the Slae*, 102, 135, 137, 139–42
Moore, Dafydd, on *Ossian*, 168
Moore, Thomas, 8, 153, 154
'Remember the Glories of Brian the Brave', 170
Epistles ..., 47
Romantic nationalism, 165, 170, 174
Morganwg, Iolo, 167, 189
Morning Post, 183
Mullaghmast Massacre, 154, 172–3
Mullan, Luke, 21, 33, 136–8
letters, 105–6
on Burns, 144

Napoleon
and slavery, 183–4
Orr's Napoleonic series, 67–80, 95, 184, 188
tyranny, 46, 49, 188
Napoleonic invasion crisis, 41
nationalism, Romantic, 6, 14, 81, 135, 153, 166–85
Neilson, Samuel, 33, 73
Nelson, Admiral Horatio, and Despard, 70
Nelson, John, on Ulster liberals' theology, 65
Nelson, Willie, 181
New Light Presbyterians, 16, 19, 20, 29, 49, 64–73, 82

Newell, Edward John, 15
Noble, Andrew, 11
Non-Subscribing Presbyterians, 20, 64
Northern Star, 1, 21, 22, 45, 47, 53, 58, 73, 90, 95, 96, 104, 127, 135, 189
  activists and, 32–7
  on emigrant pressing, 44
  possible Orr essay, 34
Nugent, Major-General, redcoats, 39, 132

O'Connell, Daniel (poet), 8
O'Connor, T. P., preface to Read's *Cabinet*, 7–8
O'Donoghue, D. J., on Ulster vernacular verse, 8
Old Light Presbyterians, 20, 29, 64, 65, 130
Ordnance Survey Memoirs, 26, 27, 74
Orr, James
  life and death
    and alcohol, 5, 187
    and Ballycarry, 25, 27–41, 48–9
    background, 1
    boyhood/school, 29–30
    cottage, 29*f*2.2
    decline/death, 187
    elegies/odes for, 77–80
    instructions to McDowell, 91, 187
    monument, 3, 4*f*1.1, 7, 76, 77, 79, 187, 191–2
    possible relationship, McDowell on, 79
  political activity
    American exile, 1, 8, 15, 19, 40–1, 43–7, 58, 115, 118, 135, 137
    and radicalism, 25, 27–41, 146
    Antrim battle, 124–5, 131–5
    pre-Union period tensions, 48–9
    United Irishman, 1, 3, 5, 17, 19, 21, 22, 28, 31–41, 81–2, 87–9, 104–5, 117, 118
  religious/moral issues
    Abolitionist Movement, 73–4, 183–5
    and Owenson's works, 74, 153–4
    Catholic emancipation, 96–9, 153
    Dissenters, 29, 31–2
    Freemasonry, 56, 76–7, 117, 163
    New Light theology, 16, 19, 20, 29, 49, 64–73, 82
    patronage, 3, 51, 142
    rational conduct, 144–6
    superstition, 144–5
    Wesleyan Methodists, 160–3
    women, 144
  style
    and *Cherrie and the Slae* genre, 137–42
    and *Christis Kirk* genre, 127–35
    and georgic verse, 115–16
    and Scottish vernacular tradition, 4, 101–21
    and standard habbie, 110–15
    as 'Bard of Ballycarry', 1, 49–59
    as enlightened Romantic, 6, 55, 85–6, 113, 135, 165–85
    as Robert Burns of Ulster, 2, 3, 5–6, 87, 143–64
    Scots terms and covert imagery, 117–20
  works
    'A Prayer, Written on the Eve of the Unfortunate 7th June', 50, 55, 124–5
    'Address: Spoken in St Patrick's Lodge, Carrickfergus ...', 76–7
    'Address to Beer', 21, 145, 146
    'Address to Master Thomas Romney Robinson', 75–6
    'Address to Noah Dalway, of Bella-Hill, Esq.', 88, 177–8
    'Address to the Reverend William Glendy', 66
    and *Belfast News-letter*, 51–3
    and Hope, 'McCracken's Ghost', 41, 49–50
    'Apostrophe of the Shade of Brian Boromhu, to his Harp', 170–1
    'Ballycarry Fair', 31
    regretted, 145
    Biblical passages versifications, 166–8
    'Brian Boromhu's Address to his Harp', 190
    'Captain Whisky', 145–6
    'Censor' possible pseudonym, 98–9, 153
    Collected Poems, 70, 192
    'Come Let us Here my Brethren Dear', 56
    'Donegore Hill', 7, 11, 37–9, 41, 53, 55, 63, 131–5, 140–1, 144
    'Edwin and Lucy', 182–3

'Elegy', 47, 58
'Elegy, Composed in Islandmagee at the Tomb of an Ancient Chief', 171–2, 190
'Elegy on the Death of A. McCracken', 58
'Elegy on the Death of Hugh Blair, D. D.', 85–6, 87, 89–91
'Elegy on the Death of Hugh Tynan', 52
'Elegy on the Death of Mr Robert Burns ...', 10, 143–4, 145, 146
'Elegy Written in Templecorran Churchyard', 34, 59
'Elegy Written in the Ruins of a Country School-House', 61
'Epistle: To S. Thomson ...', 51, 135, 137–42
'Epitaph for the Author's Father', 59
'Fort Hill', 56, 181, 190
'Fragment of An Epistle to Mr W. H. D.', 178
'Gormal – An Elegy', 57–8, 84
'Humanity', 57
'Inscription, Proposed for the Monument of Locke', 66–7
'Lines Written under the Portrait of Newell', 15, 58
'Lord Nelson's Song of Victory', 70
'Man was Made to Smile', 84–5
Masonic poems, 76–7
Microscope probable pieces, 50–1, 169
Napoleonic series, 67–80, 184, 188
'Ode to a Butterfly on Wing in Winter', 79
'Ode to Danger', 8
'Ode to Henry Cooke', 66
'On the Disasters and Deaths Occasioned by Accidents', 16, 67, 98
'Part of the Tenth Chapter of the Apocalypse Versified', 73
Poems on Various Subjects, 1, 48, 53–4
'Preface' to, 53–4
Posthumous Works, 1–2, 61, 64, 67, 187
'Soliloquy of Bonaparte', 69
'Song, Composed in Spring', 56
'Song Composed on the Banks of Newfoundland', 8, 9, 44, 130–1
'Song, Written in Winter', 11, 34, 55–6, 82–3
'Stanzas on the Death of a Favourite Young Lady', 63–4
'Tea' comic monologue, 111
'The Assizes', 121, 174–7, 189
'The Banks of Larne', 56
'The Bull-Beat', 56
'The Dying African', 74
'The Dying Mason', 56
'The Glen', 57, 180–1, 190
'The Irish Cottier's Death and Burial', 8, 11, 17, 90, 121, 147, 152–3, 154–9, 174, 191
'The Irish Soldier', 69
'The Irishman', 8, 9, 68–9, 188
'The Maniac's Petition', 182
'The Massacre of Mullaghmast', 172–3
'The Passengers', 10, 11, 43–4, 127–31
'The Patriot's Complaint', 72–3
'The Penitent', 30, 49, 85, 152, 159–64, 179–80
'The Reading Society', 32
'The Spae-Wife', 144–5
'The Speech of John P. Palm', 71
'The Vision – An Elegy', 91–7
'The Wanderer', 40, 125–7
'To a Sparrow', 56, 112–13
'To Miss Owenson ...', 40, 74–5, 97
to 'N—P—, Oldmill', 56
to 'Thaunie', 112
'To the Potatoe', 11, 21, 114–21, 190
'Toussaint's Farewell to San Domingo', 183, 184–5
'Unanimity', 15
verse epistles, 111–12
Orr, James senior, 29–30, 58–9
Orr, William, 36, 62
Otis, Harrison Gray, on Irish migrants, 44–5
Owenson, Sydney
  Irish Romanticism, 165
  on Ulster Scots, 74, 153–4
  Patriotic Sketches ..., 154
  The Wild Irish Girl, 73, 74–5, 153, 154, 157

Paine, Thomas
  Rights of Man, 29, 50, 115, 134
  The Age of Reason, 134

Palm, John P., printer, *Germany in its Deep Humiliation*, 70–1
patronage, Orr on, 51
Peden, Alexander, 72
Pellicer, Juan Christian, on British georgic verse, 115–16
Peninsular campaign, 172
Percy, Bishop of Dromore, 104
Philadelphia, Orr probably at, 43, 45–7
Philadelphia Gazette
  on Ballycarry conditions, 45
  on French tyranny, 45–6
Philips, John, 'Cyder', 116
Pitt, William the Younger, 79
Pittock, Murray, 174
  on Romantic nationalism, 170
politics vs regionality
  Hewitt on, 11, 12
  Lunney on, 17–19
Pope, Alexander, 57, 86, 133, 135, 165, 174, 177
  Blair on, 89
Porter, Hugh, 19, 22, 104
  O'Donoghue on, 8
post-Augustan writers, 6
post-Union experience, 123, 135–42
pre-Union period tensions, 48–9
Presbyterian Dissenters, and Ulster vernacular verse, 81–2, 87–9
Presbyterianism, 11, 16, 17, 26, 29, 31–2, 64–6, 72, 94, 96, 99, 125, 139, 149, 168
prescopalian period, 26
Prior, Matthew, 147
prison, Orr on, 176

Ramsay, Allan, 57, 102, 104, 107, 177, 190
  'Elegy on Maggie Johnson', 107–8
  'Lucky Spence's Last Advice', 108
  The Gentle Shepherd, Blair on, 86, 88
  'The Poet's Wish', 135, 137
  'The Vision', 92, 142
Read, Charles, *Cabinet of Irish Literature (1879–80)*, 7–8
reading societies, 76
  Orr and, 32–3
rebel experience, 123–35
Rebellion 1641, 171
Rebellion 1745 aftermath, 105
Red Hall, Ballycarry, 37, 41

Redhall Masonic Lodge, Ballycarry, 76
Revelation, Book of, 72–3
Rising, Ballycarry, 7 June 1798, 37–40
Robertson, William, *History of Scotland*, 91, 93–7, 190
Robinson, Philip, 192
  and Adams, *Folk Poets of Ulster* series, 19
  Country Rhymes of James Orr ..., 19–20
  on Orr, 20, 87, 192
  on Ulster Scots, 87
Robinson, Thomas Romney, 75
Roman Catholics
  as aliens in own country, 34
  emancipation, Orr and, 96–9, 153
Romantic nationalism, 6, 14, 81, 135, 153, 166–85
Romanticism, 6, 14–15, 49, 55, 85–6, 113, 165–85
Roper, Margaret, biographical sketch, 62
Roughford
  reading society, 33
  Volunteers, 33, 34
Russell, Thomas, 36, 55, 134, 135, 169
Rutland, fourth Duke, Viceroy, on Dissenters, 31

Said, Edward, on stories, 123
school, Orr and, 29–30
Scots, and Ballycarry, 25–7
Scots Covenanters, persecution, 26
Scott, Walter, Romanticism, 174
Scottish bardism, 92, 110–11, 177
Scottish connection, Ulster United Irishmen, 35
Scottish Enlightenment, 5, 81–99, 165, 190
  Ulster Scots poets and, 7, 101–21
Semphill, Robert, of Beltrees, 'The Life and Death of Habbie Simson', 107, 108
Shenstone, William, 147
Sheridan, R. B., 8
slavery
  America, 46, 47
  Napoleon and, 183–4
  Orr on, 183–4
  see also Abolitionist Movement
Slemish
  hiding at, 40, 58, 102, 125
  McSkimin on, 126–7
Smart, Christopher, 'The Hop-Garden', 116
Smith, Adam, 81

Solemn League and Covenant, 95
Southey, Robert, 180
Spenserian stanza form, 147, 151, 155, 159
Stafford, Fiona, on Burns, 88, 135
standard habbie stanza, 11, 56, 104, 105, 107–11, 113–14, 145, 178
stanza forms, 11, 18, 51, 56, 78, 104, 105, 107–11, 113–14, 127–32, 135, 137, 139–42, 145, 147, 151, 155, 178
Steelboys, 31
Stewart, A. T. Q.
  on Presbyterians and '98 Rebellion, 31
  on Romantic nationalism, 168–9
Swift, Jonathan, 177

Teeling, Charles, on Amnesty Act 1798, 47
Templecorran Cemetery, 37
  and 'The Vision', 92, 94
  Orr's monument, 3, 4*f*1.1, 7, 34, 59, 76, 77, 79, 187, 191–2
Templepatrick, 33, 34, 36, 127
  Fair, 51
'The Twa Corbies' ballad, 124
Thompson, E. P., on Methodism, 161
Thomson, James, 13, 55, 57, 106, 147
  The Seasons, 55, 183
Thomson, Samuel, of Carngranny, 3, 9, 10, 12, 18–19, 21, 22, 33–4, 36, 47–8, 50–1, 53–4, 55, 59, 77, 78, 90, 102, 105–7, 119–21, 127–8, 135–42, 145, 187
  and *Microscope* ..., 50
  'Epistle to Luke Mullan ...', 136–7, 138
  'Lowrie Nettle' pseudonym, 78
  on *Poems on Various Subjects*, 59
  Orr and, 33, 50–1, 77–8
  'The Simmer Fair', 54, 127, 128
  'To a Hedgehog', 47–8, 119
  'To Captain M'Dougall ...', 106–7
  verse epistle to Burns, 21
Tighe, Rev. Thomas, 104
'Tit for Tat', early Ulster Scots poem, 102–3
tithes disputes, 28, 102–3
Tone, Wolfe, 8, 154, 169
  inclusive Irishness, 81, 82
  on Philadelphia, 43
Toussaint L'Ouverture, 183–5
Trafalgar, Battle of, 49, 68, 69–70, 172
Trail, Rev. Robert, 53

Trumpener, Katie, on bardic nationalism, 166–7
Tynan, Hugh, 52
Tytler, James 'Balloon', on Philadelphia, 43

Ulster, map, 28*f*2.1
Ulster Dissenter writers school, 5
Ulster Folklife, 17
Ulster liberals' theology, 64–5
Ulster linen industry, 30–1
Ulster Miscellany, 102–3
Ulster poets, Burns influence, 3, 5, 8, 9, 11, 19, 20–3
Ulster Scots poets
  and 1790s radicalism/United Irishmen, 104–5
  and Ballycarry, 25–7
  and Romanticism/Enlightenment, 165
  and Scottish tradition, 101–21
  early, 102–3
  vernacular verse, 7–23, 54–5, 56, 57, 101
    discounted, 8–9
  Presbyterian Dissenters, and, 81–2, 87–9
  Robinson on, 87
Ulster Synod, and New Light theology, 65
Unionism, challenges to, 61–3
United Irish society, Philadelphia, 45–7
United Irishman, 1, 3, 5, 17, 19, 21, 22, 28, 31–41, 81–2, 87–9, 104–5, 117, 118
  'Erin Go Brah', 170–1
  migrants, Philadelphia, 45–7
  movement, development, 28, 31–41
  political thought, 81, 87–9
  Rebellion 1798, 123–5, 131–5

Vance, Norman, on Romantic nationalism, 169–70
Volunteer companies, 22, 142, 146, 188
  Orr and, 34–41, 59

Walker, J. C., *Historical Memoirs of the Irish Bards*, 73
Walker, Samuel, 'The Cotter's Sabbath Day', 151–2
Wallace, William, 92, 151
Wells, Roger, on poverty, 163
Welsh bardic nationalism, 166–8
Wentworth, Lord Deputy, 26
Wesley, John, 160

Wesleyan Methodism, Orr on, 160–3
Whyte, Christopher, on *Christis Kirk* genre, 129–30
Wilberforce, William, 74
Wilson, David, on US Alien and Sedition Acts, 46
Wollstonecraft, Mary, *A Vindication of the Rights of Woman*, 35
Wordsworth, William, 169, 178, 179, 180, 183
   and Coleridge, *Lyrical Ballads*, 6, 179, 182
   on lives of poets, 79
   'The Convict', 176
   'The Female Vagrant', 182
   'To Toussaint L'Ouverture', 183–4
Wright, Julia M., 128, 129
Wu, Duncan, on Romantics, 174

Young, Arthur
   on Irish cottiers diet, 119
   Tour in Ireland, 104, 152
Young, Edward, 57
Young, R. M., *Ulster in '98* ..., 41

Zenzinger, Peter, on Burns, 157